Land and Buildings Transaction Tax 2024/25

Land and Buildings Transaction Tax 2024/25

Graeme Connell CA, CTA

Bloomsbury Professional
EDINBURGH • LONDON • DUBLIN • NEW YORK • NEW DELHI • SYDNEY

BLOOMSBURY PROFESSIONAL
Bloomsbury Publishing Plc
50 Bedford Square, London, WC1B 3DP, UK
1385 Broadway, New York, NY 10018, USA
29 Earlsfort Terrace, Dublin 2, Ireland

British Library Cataloguing-in-Publication Data

A catalogue record for this book is available from the British Library.

ISBN:	PB:	9781 52653 185 8
	ePDF:	9781 52653 187 2
	ePub:	9781 52653 186 5

Typeset by Evolution Design & Digital Ltd (Kent)

Preface

Land and Buildings Transaction Tax ('LBTT') replaced Stamp Duty Land Tax ('SDLT') as the tax which applies to transactions relating to the acquisition of land and buildings situated in Scotland, with effect from 1 April 2015.

LBTT was devolved to the Scottish Parliament by the Scotland Act 2012. The legislation governing LBTT can be found in the Land and Buildings Transaction Tax (Scotland) Act 2013 ('LBTT(S)A 2013'). Alongside LBTT(S)A 2013 sits the Revenue Scotland and Tax Powers Act 2014, a taxes management act, which *inter alia* establishes Revenue Scotland as a body corporate, makes provision about the functions and responsibilities of Revenue Scotland, establishes the Scottish Tax Tribunals, introduces a general anti-avoidance rule and deals with the collection and management of the devolved taxes, including LBTT.

LBTT(S)A 2013 was the first tax Act to be passed by the Scottish Parliament in over 300 years.

In addition to the primary legislation there is also subordinate legislation in the form of Scottish and UK Statutory Instruments and a list of the statutory instruments is set out in Appendix B.

Since the previous edition of 'Land and Buildings Transaction Tax' was published in 2018, there have been numerous developments in LBTT.

The most significant developments arguably relate to the Additional Dwelling Supplement ('ADS'). This has been increased from 3% to 4%, and then to 6% – a potentially significant cost to those acquiring additional residential properties. Various Tribunal cases (such as *Dr C Ewan H Crawford v Revenue Scotland*) brought to light how the existing legislation could create what would appear to be unfair results in certain circumstances. As a result, significant changes have been made to the ADS legislation from 1 April 2024. These should particularly benefit joint buyers, who were most likely to be impacted by the previous issues. Changes have also been made to extend the time for replacing a main residence from 18 months to 36 months, to disregard small shares in a jointly owned property, to disregard inherited dwellings (in specific circumstances) and to provide relief for separated spouses who retain an interest in the former family home.

However, whilst the new ADS position is undoubtedly improved, the ADS legislation has become extremely complex and ripe for simplification. The new changes effectively render some existing legislation obsolete, or provide multiple legislative routes to reach the same result. Worryingly, there are also still potential situations where unfair results could arise – sometimes even by chance.

Beyond the ADS, new reliefs have been introduced for purchases by local authorities and for qualifying land transactions within Scotland's two Green Freeports. Group relief is also no longer withdrawn where shares in a company are 'pledged' as security to a lender.

The tax rates and bands for non-residential transactions changed on 25 January 2019, although the residential rates and bands have remained the same throughout – with the exception of a temporary change in 2020/21, due to COVID-19.

There have been 45 decided First-Tier Tribunal cases relating to LBTT, at the date of writing. There are two clear strands of litigation – the ADS (23 cases) and tax administration, particularly penalties (20 cases). Success for the taxpayer has been few and far between – none of the ADS cases have been decided in favour of the taxpayer, though some cases appear to have been brought more in hope than expectation. However, of the three Upper Tribunal cases which have been brought by Revenue Scotland, all in relation to penalties, two of their appeals have been dismissed.

The book has been comprehensively updated for all of the changes above.

The aim of this book is to help the reader:

- understand the basic principles and concepts on which LBTT is based;
- deal confidently with matters which are not overly complex; and
- identify when specialist input is required.

Worked examples have been included where it is thought they may be helpful and there is extensive cross-reference to the legislation throughout the book.

It will be interesting to see how LBTT legislation and case law develops over the coming years, as the tax celebrates its 10-year anniversary in April 2025 and the UK Government continues to modify Stamp Duty Land Tax.

Graeme Connell
August 2024

Contents

Table of Cases

[*All references are to paragraph numbers and appendices*]

Table of Statutes

[*All references are to paragraph numbers and appendices*]

H

I

L

N

P

Table of Statutory Instruments

[*All references are to paragraph numbers and appendices*]

Table of Examples

[*All references are to paragraph numbers and appendices*]

Chapter 4 LBTT and Leases

Chapter 5 LBTT Exempt Transactions and Reliefs

Chapter 6 LBTT and Partnerships

Chapter 8 LBTT Administration and Compliance

Chapter 1

Introduction to Land and Buildings Transaction Tax

SIGNPOSTS

- Brief consideration of the origins of UK stamp duty and the reason for the move to stamp duty land tax in relation to transactions over land in the UK.
- Commentary on the Scotland Act 1998 which created the Scottish Parliament but gave that Parliament limited powers in relation to taxation.
- Coverage of the Scotland Act 2012 which, inter alia, devolved control of taxation on transfers of land situated in Scotland to the Scottish Parliament.
- Reference to the consultations by the Scottish Government on 'Taking forward a Scottish Land and Buildings Transaction Tax' and 'A Consultation on Tax Management' culminating, respectively, in the Land and Buildings Transaction Act 2013 (LBTT(S)A 2013) and the Revenue Scotland and Tax Powers Act 2014 (RSTPA 2014).
- Comments upon the establishment of Revenue Scotland.

HISTORY AND BACKGROUND TO UK STAMP TAXES

1.1 Stamp duty was introduced over 300 years ago, copying a Dutch tax. Like income tax, it was intended to be a temporary measure to finance a war. Unlike income tax, it did not require annual renewal. The tax was so successful it remains in place today but is now only chargeable on documents transferring shares and securities or interests in partnerships holding shares and securities.

1.2 Stamp duty has always been a tax on documents. As the name indicates, payment was, and still is in relation to documents transferring shares and securities, evidenced by fixing or embossing stamps on the relevant document; in general, if no document of transfer is created, there is no liability to stamp duty. During the latter half of the twentieth century, the scope of stamp duty was steadily reduced until it applied only to transactions in shares and securities, land and buildings, and intangible assets such as partnership interests, intellectual property and goodwill. Stamp duty reserve tax (SDRT) was introduced in 1986 in response to market developments which allowed transfer of beneficial ownership of securities without a document. There was at one stage a proposal to abolish stamp taxes on shares and securities. However, that proposal was abandoned and the new government of 1997 began to increase stamp duty rates on assets other than shares and securities. The yield to the Exchequer did not, however, increase as expected, because avoidance of the tax on larger value transactions became the norm. This reduced yield eventually led to stamp duty on property transactions being replaced by stamp duty land tax (SDLT) from 1 December 2003, and this is discussed further below.

1.3 In most cases there was no direct obligation to pay stamp duty or have a document stamped, but an unstamped document cannot be used for certain purposes. Where documents were executed outside the UK, it was the case for a long time that no interest and penalties accrued, provided the document was stamped within 30 days of first being brought into the UK. In the case of high value transactions, if there was no current need for the document to be stamped, it became standard practice to execute and retain it offshore (often in the Channel Islands or the Isle of Man) and many such unstamped documents remain there to this day. In an attempt to reduce the attractiveness of this practice, the rules were changed in 1999 to charge interest from 30 days after execution of the transfer document, no matter where this took place. Another common mitigation technique, in relation to land in England and Wales, was simply to avoid executing a conveyance (generally referred to as resting on, or in, contract). For example, legal title to the land might be held by a special purpose vehicle/company (SPV) for the benefit of the beneficial owner. The current beneficial owner would contract to sell the land to a purchaser. The purchaser would make payment, thus gaining beneficial ownership, and the owner would transfer the shares in the SPV to the purchaser. In the absence of a conveyance, no stamp duty arose. There were many disputes between taxpayers and the Stamp Office over whether other documents created in this process could be treated as conveyances, and therefore as chargeable to stamp duty. To discourage the practice, the rules were changed in 2002 to treat contracts for the transfer of land, for a consideration of more than £10 million, as conveyances.

1.4 Numerous other ingenious methods were devised to mitigate stamp duty, and the UK government began consultations on modernising the tax, concentrating on transactions over land. However, it quickly became clear that it would be very difficult to create a tax which was relatively simple and certain, yet dealt fairly with the wide range of modern land transactions. Consultations ended abruptly, and SDLT was introduced in the Finance Act 2003 (FA 2003), replacing stamp duty on transactions in UK land and buildings with effect from 1 December 2003. At the same time, the scope of stamp duty itself was restricted to transactions in stock and marketable securities (broadly shares and securities) and interests in certain partnerships which hold stock or marketable securities. The inadequacy of the consultation process was reflected in the complexity of SDLT, the uncertainty over its application to many transactions, and the amendments made to the legislation by regulations even before the tax came into effect and then in almost every subsequent Finance Act. Whilst the introduction of SDLT reduced the avoidance of tax on land transactions, as compared to the position under stamp duty, the tax planning industry continued to develop ever more artificial structures to try to avoid the tax. In particular a number of the mitigation techniques combined so called sub-sale relief, with another SDLT relief, to create a structure under which it was argued that no SDLT was payable. HMRC did have some success in the courts in litigating against these structures but, more than ten years after the introduction of SDLT, the Government still thought it necessary in 2013 to completely revamp the SDLT legislation dealing with sub-sales and, whilst the newer legislation may be robust against tax avoidance, it is also extremely complex, and that complexity can impinge on commercial transactions.

SDLT remains a complex tax, which can throw up anomalies when it is applied to the more complex commercial transactions. This then was the climate in which the Scottish Government introduced a new land transaction tax for properties situated in Scotland called Land and Buildings Transaction Tax (LBTT). The new tax applied from 1 April 2015. The LBTT legislation borrows heavily from the SDLT legislation, which means that a lot of the inherent complexities in the SDLT legislation of that time were carried over into the new LBTT legislation.

SCOTLAND ACT 1998

1.5 On 11 September 1997 Scotland went to the polls in a referendum which asked whether the Scottish people supported the creation of a Scottish Parliament with devolved powers and, if so, whether that Parliament should have tax varying powers. The answer given to both questions was 'yes' and this resulted in the Westminster Parliament passing the Scotland Act 1998 on 17 November 1998, with Royal Assent being granted on 19 November 1998. The Scotland Act provided for the creation of the Scottish Parliament, a Parliament which had the power to pass bills, in relation to matters which were not 'reserved matters',(ie matters over which the Scottish Parliament did not have legislative competence), and those bills become acts of the Scottish Parliament once they receive Royal Assent. The only mention in the Scotland Act 1998 relating to taxation was the provision that the Scottish Parliament may pass a resolution providing for the basic rate of income tax, payable by Scottish taxpayers, to be increased or reduced by not more than 3% from that determined by the Westminster Parliament, for any particular income tax year. Perhaps not surprisingly this is a power which the Scottish Parliament did not take advantage of in the 14 years during which it was available.

SCOTLAND ACT 2012

1.6 The Calman Commission was set up in 2007 by an opposition Labour Party motion to look at devolution ten years on from the creation of the Scottish Parliament. It made a number of recommendations including that the Scottish

Parliament should have the power to set a Scottish rate of income tax (within certain defined parameters) and that the power to raise tax on land transactions and disposal to landfill should be devolved to the Parliament. In response to that report the Scotland Bill 2012 was presented to the House of Commons on 30 November 2010, with the Scotland Act 2012 finally receiving Royal Assent on 1 May 2012. The Scotland Act 2012 amended the provisions of the Scotland Act 1998 in a number of areas. From a tax perspective the Act provided as follows:

- It repealed the power in the Scotland Act 1998 to vary the basic rate of income tax by 3% and gave the Scottish Parliament the power to set a Scottish rate of income tax (SRIT) for Scottish taxpayers. The basic rate, higher rate or additional rate of income tax, as determined by the Westminster Parliament for a particular tax year, were each reduced by 10%, after which the Scottish rate of income tax (if any) set by the Scottish Parliament was added to each of the tax rates. Thus the Scottish Parliament had the power to reduce income tax rates for each of the tax bands by up to 10%, and had an unlimited power to increase the tax rates for each of the tax bands. However, the SRIT had to be applied to each of the income tax rates. Therefore it was not possible, for example, for a SRIT of 10% to be added to the basic rate of tax but for a SRIT of 15% to be added to the higher rate, the SRIT added to both rates must be the same. This power first applied for the 2016/17 tax year, which commenced on 6 April 2016.
- Control of raising tax on transfers of property situated in Scotland, and on waste disposal taken to landfill in Scotland, were transferred to the Scottish Parliament.
- The Act also provided that additional taxes may be devolved to the Scottish Parliament by an Order in Council of the UK Government.

The UK Government reduces the annual grant it pays to the Scottish Government by an amount reflecting the expected income from the two devolved taxes and from the SRIT, with the objective that the total funds available to the Scottish Government should remain broadly as they would have been in the absence of the Scotland Act 2012 tax powers. It is then up to the Scottish Government as to whether it aims to raise more or less tax from its imposition of the devolved taxes and the SRIT. In the event the Scottish Parliament set a SRIT of 10% for 2016/17 such that the income tax rates for that year, in Scotland, were identical to those in the rest of the UK.

SCOTLAND ACT 2016

1.7 The Scotland Act 2016, which received Royal Assent on 23 March 2016, devolved wider powers over income tax to the Scottish Parliament giving it the power to set the rates of income tax, and the bands at which those rates apply, for non-savings and non-dividend income, of Scottish taxpayers. This power first applied for the 2017/18 tax year.

Scotland Act 2012 – Scottish tax on land transactions

1.8 The Scotland Act 2012, s 28 inserted a new Part 4A into the Scotland Act 1998 which provides that a tax charged on the acquisition of a 'chargeable interest' (see **2.12**) relating to land situated in Scotland is a devolved tax, that the tax may be chargeable irrespective of whether there is any document effecting the transaction and, if there is such a document, irrespective of where that document is executed. Finally, the residence of any party to the transaction is irrelevant in assessing liability.

The territorial limit on the Scottish tax on land transactions is set as it is provided that the tax cannot be imposed on land below the mean low water mark (see **2.1**)

Finally, it was provided that the Scottish tax on land transactions could not be charged until the Scotland Act 1998, s 29, which disapplied SDLT to Scottish land transactions, had effect in relation to land transactions. The Scotland Act 1998, s 29(4) provided that SDLT would not have effect in relation to Scottish land transactions with an 'effective date' (see **2.81**) on or after a date to be appointed by the UK Treasury. The UK statutory instrument entitled the Scotland Act 2012, Section 29 (Disapplication of UK Stamp Duty Land Tax) (Appointed Day) Order 2015 was made on 9 March 2015 and appointed 1 April 2015 as the day on which the Scotland Act 1998, s 29(4) had effect in relation to land transactions with an 'effective date' (see **2.81**) on or after that day. As a consequence, transactions over land situated in Scotland, with an 'effective date' on or after 1 April 2015, are chargeable to LBTT, and SDLT ceased to apply from that date. This is subject to the transitional provisions (see **2.85** et seq).

Section 29 of the Scotland Act 1998 amended the definition of a 'chargeable interest' for the purposes of SDLT so that it only relates to an interest in land situated in England and Wales or Northern Ireland and introduced the Scotland Act 2012, Sch 3 which made further amendments to the SDLT legislation as a consequence of the disapplication of SDLT to land situated in Scotland. The section also sets out the parameters for the transitional provisions covering the move from SDLT to LBTT and these are considered in detail at **2.85** et seq.

TAKING FORWARD A SCOTTISH LAND AND BUILDINGS TRANSACTION TAX

1.9 On 7 June 2012 the Scottish Government published a consultation document entitled 'Taking forward a Scottish Land and Buildings Transaction Tax' setting out its thinking on LBTT and requesting comments and suggestions.

In the Foreword to the consultation document John Swinney MSP (who was at that time the Cabinet Secretary for Finance, Employment and Sustainable Growth) stated 'We will establish a distinctly Scottish approach to the Land and Buildings Transaction Tax and the tax on disposals to landfill and will embed the legislation in Scots Law and practices'. It is open to debate how far this has been achieved given what is now included in LBTT(S)A 2013 and RSTPA 2014.

Chapter 3 of this book covers the key differences between SDLT and LBTT.

However, there was no attempt to align the taxation of partnerships and trusts with Scots law and practice as was proposed in the consultation document, with the complex SDLT provisions being imported wholesale into LBTT – see **Chapters 6** and **7**. The bulk of the targeted anti-avoidance legislation within the SDLT provisions also found its way into LBTT (see **9.14**), whilst at the same time RSTPA 2014 includes a general anti-avoidance rule which, although based on the UK General Anti-abuse Rule in the Finance Act 2013, is wider in scope and does not include the safeguards which support the UK rule – see **9.3** et seq.

Therefore, whilst some of the objectives set out in the consultation document have been achieved, much has not, and certainly LBTT can be as complex to apply in practice as SDLT.

A CONSULTATION ON TAX MANAGEMENT

1.10 A further consultation document entitled 'A Consultation on Tax Management' was published on 10 December 2012 to consider the establishment and powers of Revenue Scotland, the establishment of the Scottish Tax Tribunals, the introduction of a general anti-avoidance rule and the collection and management of the devolved taxes, currently consisting of LBTT and Landfill tax but, following the enactment of the Scotland Act 2016, which received Royal Assent on 23 March 2016, to include air passenger duty and aggregates levy.

Following this consultation the Revenue Scotland and Tax Powers Bill was introduced to Parliament on 12 December 2013, with the Finance Committee hearing evidence during February, March and April 2014 and Stage 2 of the Bill being considered on 11 June 2014. The Stage 3 proceedings were then held on 19 August 2014 and the Revenue Scotland and Tax Powers Act 2014 received Royal Assent on 24 September 2014.

REVENUE SCOTLAND

1.11 The RSTPA 2014 established Revenue Scotland as a body corporate which is a Non-Ministerial Department, meaning it is part of the Scottish Administration but is not part of the Scottish Government, so that it is accountable to the Scottish Parliament and not Scottish Ministers (RSTPA 2014, s 1). The function of Revenue Scotland is the collection and management of the devolved taxes however, in relation to LBTT, it can devolve any of its functions to Registers of Scotland although it must publish what functions have been delegated and the directions given to Registers of Scotland (RSTPA 2014, s 4). The Scottish Ministers must not give directions or in any way seek to control

Revenue Scotland in the exercise of its functions (RSTPA 2014, s 7). Whilst Revenue Scotland is not accountable to Scottish Ministers it must have regard to any guidance given to it by Scottish Ministers, and Scottish Ministers are required to publish guidance given to Revenue Scotland unless publication would prejudice the effective exercise by Revenue Scotland of its powers (RSTPA 2014, s 8). Revenue Scotland must prepare a Charter setting standards of behaviour which it will follow in dealing with taxpayers, and the standards it expects from taxpayers (RSTPA 2014, s 10), it must also prepare a Corporate Plan setting out its objectives, criteria for measuring success, and the activities it expects to undertake for the next three years (RSTPA 2014, s 11). Finally, it must prepare and publish an annual report on the exercise of its functions during each financial year being the year ending on 31 March (RSTPA 2014, s 12).

There are also provisions within RSTPA 2014 as to the purposes for which Revenue Scotland may use information it has obtained from the administration of the devolved taxes, the circumstances in which a Revenue Scotland official may disclose 'protected taxpayer information' and the penalties which can be imposed for the wrongful disclosure of 'protected taxpayer information' (RSTPA 2014, ss 13–19).

The Order under the Scotland Act 1998, s 104 establishing Revenue Scotland as a Non-Ministerial Department within the Scottish Administration, accountable to the Scottish Parliament, was made on 11 December 2014. The Order also provides for the sharing of taxpayer and other information between Revenue Scotland and HM Revenue & Customs.

A detailed consideration of the functions and powers of Revenue Scotland is beyond the scope of this book but further details can be found in *The Management of Taxes in Scotland* by Charlotte Barbour, MA,CA,CTA published by Bloomsbury as one of its Scottish Core Tax Annuals.

Chapter 2

LBTT – General Rules

SIGNPOSTS

- Provides an outline of the general scheme of LBTT and the meaning and importance of certain definitions used throughout the LBTT legislation.
- Explains what gives rise to a charge to LBTT and who is chargeable.
- Defines the meaning of 'chargeable consideration' and the special rules which have to be considered in measuring that consideration.
- Rates of LBTT for residential and non-residential property.
- Explains in detail the 'additional dwelling supplement' (6% added to each of the LBTT rates) which applies to the acquisition of most residential properties (dwellings) unless the buyer is an individual replacing his or her only or main residence.
- Brief consideration of Annual Tax on Enveloped Dwellings (ATED) which continues to apply in Scotland post 1 April 2015.
- When does LBTT have to be paid?
- Transitional provisions – which transactions are chargeable to LBTT and which are chargeable to SDLT.

2.1 Land and Buildings Transaction Tax (LBTT) replaced Stamp Duty Land Tax (SDLT) on transactions involving land and buildings in Scotland from 1 April 2015. The tax was introduced by the Land and Buildings Transaction Tax (Scotland) Act 2013 (LBTT(S)A 2013). LBTT is similar to SDLT in many respects and some of the legislation is a straightforward adoption of the corresponding SDLT law. However, there are some significant differences and these are highlighted in **Chapter 3** and also discussed throughout this book.

LBTT is a self-assessment tax, like SDLT, and is charged on the consideration given for a land transaction. The tax, or additional tax, is payable by the buyer, and it is generally payable within 30 days of the 'effective date' (see **2.81**) of the transaction but must be paid at the same time as the LBTT return, or a further LBTT return, is filed (LBTT(S)A 2013, s 40(2) and (3)). For these purposes the tax is treated as paid if '...arrangements satisfactory...' to Revenue Scotland are made for payment of the tax (LBTT(S)A 2013, s 40(4)).

Under these arrangements the buyer (or his agent) can make payment when filing the LBTT return online by direct debit (where payment is made by an agent using SETS), BACS, CHAPS, credit card or debit card. This is different from the position under SDLT where the return and tax can be paid at different times within the 14 day period from the 'effective date' of the transaction.

Under LBTT the buyer cannot have his title to the property registered unless a land transaction return has been filed and the tax paid ie 'arrangements satisfactory' to Revenue Scotland have been made for the payment of the tax. The rules to determine the occasions of charge, and the amount of consideration which is chargeable, closely parallel those for SDLT. As with SDLT, any VAT payable will be included in the measure of chargeable consideration, thus increasing the effective rate of tax for a business which is able to recover VAT as input tax (see **2.21**). Most SDLT reliefs are imported into the LBTT legislation, generally with similar conditions, however some have been omitted – see **Chapter 5**.

Throughout this book reference is made to 'LBTT obligations', meaning both the liability to pay tax and the obligation to notify a transaction or make a return. So wide ranging are these obligations, it is essential to consider the possible impact of LBTT on almost any change relating to the occupation of, or ownership of rights over, land and buildings in Scotland.

2.2 Almost all transactions in land and buildings in Scotland completed on or after 1 April 2015, even if commenced earlier, are within the scope of LBTT. Some 'old' transactions remain within the ambit of SDLT, or perhaps potentially fall within both regimes (see **2.85** et seq). For example, consider a situation where missives were concluded after 1 May 2012 (the date the Scotland Act 2012 received Royal Assent), the contract was 'substantially performed' (see **2.7**) before 1 April 2015, but settlement (completion) takes place after 31 March 2015. In these circumstances the substantial performance of the contract will be chargeable to SDLT but the settlement of the contract will be chargeable to LBTT. Credit is, however, given for any SDLT paid on 'substantial performance' in assessing what, if any, LBTT is payable on settlement (see **2.91**). LBTT is a true 'self-assessment' tax with the obligation to report liability and make payment falling on the buyer. The tax is triggered by entering into or performing 'land transactions' (as defined in the legislation), no matter how – or even whether – documented. There are enforcement powers and specific anti-avoidance rules similar to those that apply to other UK taxes, plus a general anti-avoidance rule included in the Revenue Scotland and Tax Powers Act 2014 (see **9.3**).

Focus

- LBTT obligations can continue after a land transaction has taken place, and subsequent events may have an impact on those obligations. Constant monitoring of potential liabilities is therefore required.

2.3 Obligations in relation to LBTT may extend beyond the time of the original transaction. In some circumstances, reliefs may be withdrawn or liabilities increased as a result of subsequent events as innocuous as the refinancing of a group company or a rent review. Special rules applying to leases require (in certain circumstances) three-yearly reviews, and a review on assignation or termination of the lease, to be carried out of the LBTT payable (see **4.21** and **4.26**). Constant monitoring of potential liabilities is therefore necessary. The tax applies irrespective of the country of establishment or residence of any of the parties to the transaction, and it is possible that a non-Scottish entity, unaware of the rules, may unknowingly trigger an LBTT charge. An example would be where land in Scotland is transferred in the course of a merger of overseas companies by operation of (overseas) law.

GENERAL SCHEME OF LBTT

Importance of definitions

2.4 The LBTT rules rely on a number of concepts and expressions which are defined in LBTT(S)A 2013. It is important to apply these definitions and not to rely on the general meaning of the relevant words. The table below details the statutory references for the definitions of key terms; there is also a useful list of statutory references in LBTT(S)A 2013, Sch 20. Some of the definitions are interdependent, so it is necessary to see the whole picture before it makes sense. The general interpretation of certain terms is dealt with in LBTT(S) A 2013, s 65. The following paragraphs give a general outline of the tax and the defined expressions are shown, in the next few paragraphs only, in ***bold italics***. Subsequent paragraphs and chapters examine the interpretation and application of the expressions in more detail.

Term	*LBTT(S)A 2013 Section/Schedule*
Acquisition and disposal	s 6
Buyer and Seller	s 7
Chargeable consideration	s 17, Sch 2
Chargeable interest	s 4
Chargeable transaction	s 15
Completion	s 64
Contract	s 65
Conveyance	s 65
Effective date	s 63
Exempt interest	s 5
Exempt transaction	s 16
Land transaction	s 3

Term	*LBTT(S)A 2013 Section/Schedule*
Land transaction return	s 65
Linked transaction	s 57
Major interest in land	s 60
Substantial amount of the consideration is paid or provided	s 14(3)
Substantial performance of a contract	s 14(1)

The charge

2.5 LBTT is charged on a ***land transaction***, whether effected by a document or not. Neither the place of residence of the parties, nor the place where any documents are executed, are relevant to the charge. The tax is under the control of the Tax Authority (LBTT(S)A 2013, s 1(3)) which is defined as Revenue Scotland (LBTT(S)A 2013, s 54), a Non-Ministerial Department with a legal personality separate to that of the Scottish Ministers (see **1.11**).

A ***land transaction*** for LBTT purposes means the ***acquisition*** of a ***chargeable interest*** (LBTT(S)A 2013, s 3). ***Acquisition*** may include not only a normal land sale and purchase, but also the creation, renunciation, release or variation of a ***chargeable interest***. The ***acquisition*** may occur by the actions of the parties, under the terms of a court order, by or under any enactment or by operation of law (LBTT(S)A 2013, s 6(5)). An indirect definition makes clear the intention that any party whose interest in land benefits under the transaction is to be regarded as the ***buyer*** (LBTT(S)A 2013, s 6(3)(b) and (c)). However, a person will only be treated as a ***buyer*** if he has either given consideration for, or is a party to, the transaction (LBTT(S)A 2013, s 7(2)).

A **chargeable interest** is an interest (of any kind) in or over 'land in Scotland' or the benefit of an obligation, restriction or condition affecting the value of such a right or interest. The territorial limit to the charge to LBTT is the land border with England and the mean low water mark around the coast of Scotland. Thus any land beyond the mean low water mark around the Scottish coast (ie the seabed) does not constitute 'land in Scotland' for the purposes of LBTT (LBTT(S)A 2013, s 4(3)), and any transaction relating to such land is not chargeable to LBTT. Revenue Scotland state in their LBTT legislation guidance that they consider that jetties and similar structures attached to land in Scotland, are within the charge to LBTT (LBTT1002). The charge also includes land under water above the low water mark, such as lochs and rivers.

Timing

2.6 In general, LBTT obligations must be satisfied within the 30-day period after the ***effective date*** (see **2.81**) of the transaction (LBTT(S)A 2013, s 29(3) and s 40(2)). At the latest, the ***effective date*** is the date of ***completion***. The term ***completion*** is defined in relation to a lease as the time when the lease is executed by the parties (see **2.81**) and in relation to any other transaction as the time when 'settlement' of the transaction takes place (LBTT(S)A 2013, s 64). The term 'settlement' is not defined in the legislation and, therefore, bears its normal legal meaning, broadly summarised as completion of the transaction when the price is paid by the buyer to the seller in return for the land being acquired. However, in some cases, the ***effective date*** is triggered by ***substantial performance*** (see **2.7**) of an agreement to enter into a ***land transaction*** before completion has taken place (LBTT(S)A 2013, s 10(2)).

Substantial performance

2.7

> **Focus**
>
> - LBTT obligations can arise, before completion (settlement), on a contract to enter into a land transaction, which is to be completed by a conveyance, if the buyer takes possession (which is widely defined) of the whole or substantially the whole of the property, or pays a substantial amount of the consideration or there is an assignation, sub-sale or other transaction as a result of which a person other than the original buyer becomes entitled to call for a conveyance of the land.

Substantial performance is defined using a combination of terms such as 'possession', (see **2.82**), which are themselves not exhaustively defined, together with measurement of the proportion of any consideration actually paid. In any dispute as to whether an agreement has been ***substantially performed***, expert legal advice may be required as to the meaning of the terms. However, in general, a contract is ***substantially performed*** where either:

(a) the buyer, or a person connected with the buyer, takes possession of the whole or substantially the whole of the property passing under the contract;

(b) a ***substantial amount*** of the consideration is paid or provided; or

(c) there is an assignation, sub-sale or other transaction as a result of which a person other than the original buyer becomes entitled to call for a ***conveyance*** to that other person (LBTT(S)A 2013, s 14(1)).

The legislation provides that for these purposes a substantial amount of the consideration is paid or provided, if none of the consideration is rent, where the whole or substantially the whole of the consideration is paid or provided (LBTT(S)A 2013, s 14(3)).

In relation to SDLT, HMRC have indicated that they will regard 90% or more as a ***substantial amount*** of the consideration (ie as substantially the whole of the consideration) but that they may not consider themselves tied to this figure if they detect an attempt to exploit it for avoidance. In LBTT Technical Bulletin 1 (para 6.2), published on 14 October 2016, Revenue Scotland make it clear that what constitutes a ***substantial amount*** of the consideration paid or provided for LBTT purposes will be considered on a case-by-case basis. They specifically state that the Scottish Parliament did not set a specific amount, that an amount less than 90% might be substantial in this context, and that the words must take their plain English meaning. This has also been reflected in Revenue Scotland's LBTT guidance (LBTT1005). Consequently, if there is doubt as to whether the quantum of the 'chargeable consideration' (see **2.17**) given for a transaction, in advance of completion, might cause a contract to be 'substantially performed', it is suggested that an opinion (see **8.49**) be sought from Revenue Scotland. Any payment of rent under the terms of a lease will be regarded as ***substantial performance*** (LBTT(S)A 2013, s 14(3)(b) and (c)(ii)) of the agreement for lease (or missives of let not constituting a lease), as will the buyer becoming entitled to the receipt of rent (LBTT(S)A 2013, s 14(2)).

Under LBTT there is an additional event which will trigger substantial performance, (compared to the position under SDLT), and that is any assignation, sub-sale or other transaction as a result of which a person other than the original buyer becomes entitled to call for a conveyance under a contract to acquire land, or an agreement for lease (including missives of let not constituting a lease) (LBTT(S)A 2013, s 14(1)(c)). Such an event will therefore give rise to LBTT obligations for the original buyer. This is the case even though the original buyer has not taken possession of the property, or paid a substantial amount of the consideration (see **2.83** and **2.84**). This may cause commercial issues as the original buyer may not have the funds to pay the LBTT at that stage since the second buyer may not have paid any consideration for the assignation, sub-sale or other transaction.

Formal completion

2.8 If a contract for a ***land transaction*** is entered into and is completed by a formal '***conveyance***' (which includes any instrument – see **2.9**) not later than the time of ***substantial performance***, the contract and formal ***conveyance*** are treated as a single ***land transaction***, taking effect at the date of completion (LBTT(S)A 2013, s 9). Assuming that the transaction is notifiable (see **8.2**), submission of a land transaction return and payment of the tax will be due within the 30-day period after that date. Where, however, the contract is entered into and ***substantially performed*** before completion, the contract itself is treated as a ***land transaction***, the effective date of the transaction being the date of ***substantial performance*** (LBTT(S)A 2013, s 10(1) and (2)). The return and tax payment are due within the 30-day period after that date. If such a contract is later completed by a formal ***conveyance***, that formal ***conveyance*** will be a separate ***land transaction***, but LBTT will only be payable to the extent that the tax payable on the ***conveyance*** is greater than the tax paid on ***substantial performance*** of the contract – consequently there should be no overall 'double charge' to tax (LBTT(S)A 2013, s 10(3)(b)). However, care is needed where reduced or zero LBTT is paid at the time of ***substantial performance*** because of a relief or exemption – in some circumstances, the later ***completion*** can trigger further liability because conditions for the relief or exemption are not satisfied at that later time. The circumstances in which two or more returns may be required for the same transaction are explored in more detail at **8.15** et seq.

Where a contract which is to be completed by a ***conveyance*** is ***substantially performed*** without being ***completed*** and, some time later, the contract is to any extent rescinded or annulled, or is for any reason not carried into effect, any tax paid on ***substantial performance*** is to that extent to be repaid by Revenue Scotland (LBTT(S)A 2013, s 10(4)). The repayment must be claimed by amending the land transaction return filed on ***substantial performance*** (LBTT(S)A 2013, s 10(5)). Consequently, if the contract is rescinded or annulled more than 12 months after the date by which the land transaction return for the substantial performance of the contract had to be filed, it is not clear that it will be possible to reclaim any of the tax paid. This is because a land transaction return must be amended within 12 months of the date by which the return had to be filed (RSTPA 2014, s 83(2)).

What is chargeable?

2.9

> **Focus**
>
> - In addition to transactions in or over real rights under Scots property law, LBTT obligations can also arise in respect of a transaction in relation to options in land, rights of pre-emption in relation to land, statutory rights such as community interests in land, etc.

The term ***conveyance*** is defined as including any instrument (LBTT(S)A 2013, s 65). Accordingly, it covers the grant of a lease as well as a transfer of land. A ***land transaction*** is chargeable unless it is an ***exempt transaction*** or a relief applies so that it is otherwise exempt from charge (LBTT(S)A 2013, s 15). The ***exempt transactions*** are detailed in LBTT(S)A 2013, Sch 1 (see **5.6**), and LBTT(S)A 2013, s 27 lists the schedules providing for the various reliefs from the tax in LBTT(S)A 2013 (see **Chapter 5**). Those reliefs in certain cases provide for a 100% relief from tax, and, where they apply, ***land transactions*** are referred to in the act as being 'exempt from charge'. The difference between an ***exempt transaction*** and a relief is that the former applies without the requirement to make a claim, whereas the latter will have to be claimed in a ***land transaction return***. For example the grant, assignation or renunciation of a lease of residential property which is not a 'qualifying lease' (see **4.4**), or of a licence to occupy land, are ***exempt transactions***. ***Chargeable interests*** comprise real rights (ie a right which is enforceable against everyone and not just a particular person) or other interests in or over land in Scotland, as well as the benefit of any obligation, restriction or other condition that would affect the value of any such right or interest (LBTT(S)A 2013, s 4(2)). The main real right is ownership of the land and the person holding that right is known as the owner or proprietor. There are also subordinate real rights which are real rights in something, and are held by a person other than the owner. The types of subordinate rights which are recognised under Scots property include the following:

- servitude (allows a land owner to enter or make limited use of neighbouring land);
- negative real burden (an obligation in relation to land which requires that something should not be done);
- proper life rent (the right to use someone else's property for life);
- right in security (a right held by a creditor for the purpose of ensuring payment of his debt – for LBTT purposes this is an exempt interest (see **2.14**)); and
- a tenant's interest in land subject to a lease.

The definition of chargeable interest is therefore very broad and, as well as the real rights under Scots property law outlined above, it also includes options in land or a right of pre-emption in relation to land (LBTT(S)A 2013, s 12) and statutory rights such as community interests in land. However, standard securities (mortgages) and similar security interests are excluded as they are ***exempt interests*** (LBTT(S)A 2013, s 5). The extension of the definition of ***chargeable interests*** to include the benefit of obligations and restrictions affecting the value of land will mean, for example, that a payment to the owner of a neighbouring plot of land for a use restriction preventing a nuisance, may give rise to LBTT obligations. For some purposes, it matters whether an interest is a ***major interest in land*** (LBTT(S)A 2013, s 60). For example, if one of the land interests involved in an exchange (see **2.31**) is a ***major interest in land*** then the chargeable consideration for both transactions in the exchange is the greater of market value and the actual consideration (LBTT(S)A 2013, Sch 2, para 5(3) and (4)). If none of the interests in land involved in the exchange are ***major interests in land*** the chargeable consideration for both transactions is restricted to the amount or value of any other consideration given, and the value of the land interests involved in the exchange is ignored (LBTT(S)A 2013, Sch 2, para 5(5)). The term ***major interest in land*** covers both land which is owned outright and a tenant's interest in land subject to a lease.

A ***chargeable interest*** will include items which in law have become part of the land, but will not include moveable property. In the context of a house purchase fitted kitchen units, cupboards and sinks, fitted bathroom sanitary ware, intruder alarms, central heating systems etc are likely to be part of the land so that consideration apportioned to such items will be chargeable to LBTT. In contrast, items such as curtains and blinds, carpets, free standing furniture, kitchen white goods etc should be treated as moveables, which are not chargeable to LBTT.

2.10 The grant of an option to acquire an interest in land is specifically identified as a ***land transaction*** (LBTT(S)A 2013, s 12). The transfer or exercise of an option is a separate ***land transaction*** from the grant, but the two may be ***linked transactions*** (see **2.79**) for determining the amount of tax due. This is intended to counter attempts to take advantage of lower rates of LBTT by splitting an acquisition into two steps. An option is not, itself, a ***major interest in land***, although this fact is of little practical significance unless it is a component in an exchange (see **2.31**). It does, however, mean that the grant of an option will not be notifiable to Revenue Scotland unless LBTT is payable on the transaction, or it would have been payable but for the availability of a relief (LBTT(S)A 2013, s 30(1)(c)). This analysis applies equally to rights of pre-emption in relation to land.

2.11 If interests in land are exchanged, each transfer is separately chargeable and the basis for calculating the chargeable consideration is different depending upon whether one of the interests is a ***major interest in land*** – see **2.31**.

OCCASIONS OF CHARGE

Chargeable transactions

2.12 LBTT is charged on a chargeable land transaction – that is, any acquisition of a chargeable interest unless the transaction is an exempt transaction (see **5.6**) or a relief applies so that the transaction is exempt from charge (see **Chapter 5**). Any interest in land and buildings in Scotland is a chargeable interest unless it is specifically identified as exempt (see **2.14**). Examples of chargeable interests include ownership of land, leases of residential property (however transactions in relation to most leases of residential property are exempt transactions – see **5.6**) and non-residential property (including missives of let constituting a lease), options in land, licences to occupy land (however see **4.7** et seq) and statutory rights such as community interests in land – but this list is not exhaustive (see **2.9** for examples of subordinate real rights which are chargeable interests). The following give rise to the acquisition of a chargeable interest:

- acquisition of all or part of the ownership of land in Scotland (LBTT(S) A 2013, s 3 and 4(2)(a));
- grant of a lease out of owned land, or out of a tenant's interest in land under a superior lease, where the lease is over land in Scotland (LBTT(S) A 2013, s 6(3)(a));
- renunciation of a lease over land in Scotland to the landlord (LBTT(S) A 2013, s 6(1)(b) and (3)(b);
- assignation of a lease over land in Scotland to a new tenant (LBTT(S) A 2013, s 3 and 4(2)(a));
- variation of a lease over land in Scotland so as to reduce the rent payable under the lease or to reduce the term of the lease (LBTT(S)A 2013, Sch 19, para 29(1) and (3));
- any other variation of a lease over land in Scotland where any consideration in money or money's worth (other than an increase in rent) is given by the tenant for the variation (LBTT(S)A 2013, Sch 19, para 29(2)). Where

the rent payable under a lease is increased, and the grant of the lease was notifiable (see **8.2**), or became notifiable, any additional tax liability should be brought into account for LBTT purposes by the three-yearly review process or the review on assignation or termination (see **4.21** and **4.26**). However, where a lease is varied such that its term is extended, or the rent increased, and the effect of that variation is that the grant of the lease would have been notifiable had the lease originally been for the extended term and/or the increased rent the buyer must file a land transaction return (see **4.45**);

- the grant, transfer, variation or renunciation of an interest in property in Scotland other than an ownership of land or the tenant's right in land subject to a lease – for example licences to occupy property, a servitude, sporting or mineral rights, community interests in land etc (LBTT(S)A 2013, ss 3 and 4(2)(b)).

2.13 What in law is the assignation of a lease may, in certain circumstances, be treated as the grant of a new lease for LBTT purposes (see **4.35**). The LBTT liability on the grant of a new lease may be greater than that on an assignation of an existing lease, particularly if the rent payable under the existing lease is a market rate, as the lease may have little capital value.

Exempt interests

2.14 A 'security interest' is regarded as an exempt interest, so that no LBTT liability or notification obligation arises on its creation, assignment, variation or renunciation (LBTT(S)A 2013, s 5). All other interests in land are chargeable interests. A security interest is a real right or other interest in or over land in Scotland held for the purpose of securing the payment of money or the performance of other obligations, for example, a standard security (mortgage). This definition is expanded to include the interest held by a financial institution as a result of an 'alternative property finance' transaction (LBTT(S)A 2013, Sch 7, paras 21 to 24 – see **5.31**).

Exempt transactions

2.15 Even if the land interest itself is not exempt, the transaction may be exempt – see **5.6** for details (LBTT(S)A 2013, Sch 1).

THE BUYER IS CHARGEABLE

2.16

Focus

- The buyer, who is the person liable to pay the LBTT and file a land transaction return, may not be obvious in less straightforward transactions.

LBTT obligations fall on the buyer, identified in the legislation as the person who acquires the chargeable interest, or whose existing interest is enlarged or enhanced, or who benefits from the variation of the interest. The identity of the buyer is obvious in straightforward transfers of land and grants of leases, but less obvious in some other cases. In particular:

- if a chargeable interest is transferred or granted to the trustees of a 'settlement' (see **7.3** for the meaning of 'settlement'), the trustees are buyers of the whole of the interest acquired (including the beneficial interest) (LBTT(S)A 2013, Sch 18, para 10);
- if an existing chargeable interest is transferred to bare trustees or nominees ('T') (see **7.3** for the meaning of 'bare trustees'), the buyer is the person for whom T is trustee or nominee ie the beneficiary (LBTT(S) A 2013, Sch 18, para 5);
- if a lease is granted to bare trustees, those trustees are (jointly, if more than one) buyers of the whole of the interest acquired (LBTT(S)A 2013, Sch 18, para 8);
- if a lease is renounced or the term shortened, the landlord is the buyer (LBTT(S)A 2013, s 6(3)(b) and Sch 19, para 29(3));
- if the rent under a lease is reduced, the tenant is the buyer (LBTT(S) A 2013, Sch 19, para 29(1)); and
- if any chargeable interest other than a lease is varied, whoever benefits is the buyer (LBTT(S)A 2013, s 6(3)(c)). This is a puzzling definition, since it is normally the essence of a commercial transaction that both parties benefit, but it should probably be read as the person whose interest in land is enhanced.

However, a person cannot be a buyer unless he gives consideration or is a party to the transaction (LBTT(S)A 2013, s 7(2)).

Example 2.1 – Identifying the buyer

Peter has a 50-year lease (with 35 years' of the term remaining) of property F, and Rachel owns property G which abuts property F.

Peter pays his landlord £100,000 for the removal of a negative real burden (an obligation in relation to land which requires that something should not be done) within the terms of the lease. This is a land transaction and Peter is the buyer (LBTT(S)A 2013, Sch 19, para 29(2)).

Rachel agrees to pay Peter £500 per annum for the right to bring maintenance vehicles through the car park of Peter's property F to service the rear of Rachel's building on her property G. This is a land transaction and Rachel is the buyer (LBTT(S)A 2013, s 3 and s 4(1) and (2)(b)).

Peter and Rachel agree to exchange small parts of their respective properties to create better shaped plots, allowing construction of better buildings on both.

Peter is the buyer in respect of the parcel of land he gains, and Rachel is the buyer in respect of the parcel she gains – that is, there are two chargeable transactions, even though no money changes hands (LBTT(S)A 2013, s 3 and s 4(1) and (2)(a)). Furthermore this is an exchange: see **2.31**.

CONSIDERATION

Measuring consideration – valuation

2.17

> **Focus**
>
> - The full face value of consideration is chargeable to LBTT even though its payment may be postponed or it may be contingent or unascertained. However, in certain circumstances, it may be possible to defer the payment of LBTT where the consideration is subject to a contingency or is unascertained.

The basic definition of chargeable consideration is 'any consideration in money or money's worth given for the subject-matter of the transaction, directly or indirectly, by the buyer or a person connected with the buyer' (LBTT(S)A 2013, Sch 2, para 1). The full face value of consideration must be taken into account – no discount is given for the fact that the consideration may be postponed, payable in instalments etc (LBTT(S)A 2013, Sch 2, para 3). However, where payment of consideration is postponed because it is contingent or the amount is uncertain, it is sometimes possible to apply for postponement ('deferment' in the legislation) of the corresponding LBTT (see **8.26**). In some circumstances where instalments are payable over many years, the consideration is taken to be the amount payable over 12 years (LBTT(S)A 2013, s 21 – see **2.27**). Non-sterling consideration is valued at the London closing exchange rate for the effective date of the transaction, unless the parties have used a different rate for the purposes of the transaction (LBTT(S)A 2013, Sch 2, para 10(2)); consideration which is not in the form of money or debt must be valued at its market value at the effective date (LBTT(S)A 2013, Sch 2, para 7). However, some forms of consideration are ignored in some transactions (see **2.25**, **2.32** and **5.42**) and in some cases, actual consideration is replaced or supplemented by deemed consideration (see **2.28**). When a lease at rent is in point, there are specific computational rules (see **4.56–4.64**).

Contingency and uncertainty

2.18 If payment of any part of the consideration is contingent on some future event, it is assumed that the outcome of the contingency is that the amount will be payable (or that the amount does not cease to be payable) and LBTT must be paid accordingly (LBTT(S)A 2013, s 18).

If the amount of the consideration is uncertain or has not been finally ascertained by the time payment and submission of the LBTT return are due, a reasonable estimate must be used (LBTT(S)A 2013, s 19).

In the case of contingent consideration, once the contingency occurs or it becomes clear it will not occur, and in the case of uncertain or unascertained consideration, once all or part of the consideration becomes ascertained, the buyer must file a land transaction return if the effect of any of these events occurring is as follows (LBTT(S)A 2013, s 31):

- the transaction becomes notifiable;
- additional tax is payable in respect of the transaction; or
- tax is payable where none was payable before.

The land transaction return must be filed within the 30 day period commencing on the day after the event occurred (ie the contingency occurred or it became clear it would not occur, or the consideration, or any instalment of consideration, became ascertained), it must include an assessment of the tax payable, and any LBTT payable must be paid at the same time (LBTT(S)A 2013, s 31(4) and s 40(2)(b)). The tax payable is calculated by reference to the tax rates and tax bands in force at the effective date (see **2.81**) of the original transaction (LBTT(S)A 2013, s 31(5)). If the final figures show that too much LBTT has been paid, the LBTT overpaid may be reclaimed either by amending the original return within the 12 month time period allowed for such an amendment (see **8.17**) or, if that time period has expired, by making a claim to Revenue Scotland – see **8.54** (LBTT(S)A 2013, s 32).

The requirement to amend the LBTT return once the contingency is settled or the consideration has been ascertained does not apply to consideration consisting of rent since, if the grant of the lease was notifiable, the lease will then be subject to the three year periodic review of the tax chargeable (see **4.21**) and a review if the lease is assigned or terminated (see **4.26**). Those reviews should therefore take account of any increase or decrease in the rent as a result of the contingency ceasing or the amount of the rent becoming ascertained. The exception to this rule is where the contingency ceasing, or the amount of the rent being ascertained, causes the grant of the lease to become notifiable, in circumstances where it was not previously notifiable. In such circumstances a return must be made including an assessment of, and payment of, the tax due (LBTT(S)A 2013, s 31(6)). The buyer (assuming he has not assigned the lease and the lease has not been terminated) will then have an obligation to carry out a review of the LBTT chargeable on the lease on the third anniversary of the date on which the contingency ceased or the consideration, or any instalment of consideration, became ascertained (LBTT(S)A 2013, Sch 19, para 10(1)(b)(i) and 10(7)(b)) – see **4.21**.

As noted at **2.17**, where contingent and/or uncertain consideration may not be payable until sometime after the effective date of the transaction, it may be possible to apply to postpone payment of the corresponding LBTT (LBTT(S)

A 2013, s 41(1)). However, as explained in **8.29**, there are tight deadlines for applying for this postponement, so prompt application is essential. It is not possible however to postpone the payment of LBTT in relation to rent (LBTT(S)A 2013, s 41(5)).

Example 2.2 – Measuring consideration

Ewan agrees to transfer a plot of land M to Norman. In return, Norman agrees to pay Ewan £150,000 cash, payable in ten annual instalments of £15,000, commencing immediately, and to have his family company Quickbuild Ltd build Ewan a new house on a different plot of land P, which Ewan also owns. Norman is subject to LBTT on the acquisition of M, and the consideration chargeable to LBTT is £150,000 plus the market value of the building work to be undertaken by Quickbuild Ltd. As the building work is not to be carried out on the land (M) acquired by Norman under the transaction, the value of that work will count as consideration chargeable to LBTT (see **2.25**). Ewan gets a new house out of the arrangement, this is built on land he already owns, so he has no LBTT obligations.

Assuming that the market value of the building work to be undertaken by Quickbuild Ltd can be ascertained at the effective date of the transaction, no part of the consideration will be contingent or uncertain, and therefore Norman will not be able to defer payment of the LBTT.

Attribution of consideration

2.19 When two or more related transactions are entered into, or there is a composite transaction for the acquisition of various assets, the overall consideration must be apportioned between the assets on a just and reasonable basis (LBTT(S)A 2013, Sch 2, para 4(1)). Under SDLT, apportionment between chargeable and non-chargeable assets often gave rise to difficulties. Where the amount apportioned to chargeable interests was close to the upper limit for a lower SDLT rate, it was likely that HMRC would take a close interest in whether the apportionment was justified. In the Tax Tribunal (First-tier) case of *Orsman v CIR* [2012] UKFTT 227 (TC), released on 28 March 2012 (see www.financeandtaxtribunals.gov.uk/judgementfiles/j6342/tc01921.pdf), the taxpayer attributed £250,000 to the fabric of a house and £8,000 to non-liable chattels. On this basis SDLT was due at 1%, £2,500. However, HMRC investigated and concluded that some of the 'chattels' were, in fact, fixtures forming part of the house. The Tribunal agreed that a further £800 should be attributed to the house. This took the consideration into the 3% SDLT band, increasing the SDLT due to £7,524. Under LBTT (and SDLT on or after 4 December 2014 in relation to residential property and on or after 17 March 2016 in relation to non-residential property) the benefit of allocating consideration to moveable property will be less given the progressive nature of the tax. The fact that it is only that part of the consideration falling within the higher rate tax band that will be chargeable to the higher rate of LBTT, means that there should be much less incentive to allocate consideration to moveable property. The case does however contain interesting comments on the general basis for attributing consideration between assets and is worth reading where such attribution is required.

Inherent goodwill

2.20

> **Focus**
>
> - The distinction between goodwill which attaches to the property and the general goodwill of a business can be difficult to make and specialist advice may be required if the amount of the LBTT at stake warrants it.

The purchase and sale of a business often involves consideration attributed to 'goodwill'. Where the assets transferred include interests in land situated in Scotland, the question may arise as to whether any of that goodwill should be regarded as inherent in or attached to the interests in land, such that it should be subject to LBTT. As regards SDLT, HMRC have set out their view on the point at https://www.gov.uk/government/publications/practice-note-apportioning-the-price-paid-for-a-business-transferred-as-a-going-concern. It would seem likely that Revenue Scotland will adopt a similar approach, although this should be confirmed with Revenue Scotland if it is relevant to a particular land transaction. In general terms, if the 'goodwill' element of the consideration can be shown to relate to matters such as contracts with customers and suppliers, the specific customer base or a trade name/reputation, it may be accepted that this is true goodwill, separable from the property. However, if the goodwill arises from the location of the property or the fact that the property is constructed or adapted in a way which particularly suits the business, Revenue Scotland may argue that the whole or part of the amount attributed to goodwill should be added to the amount paid for the property. Many disputes have arisen in this area in relation to SDLT and specialist expert help may be required if the amounts of LBTT at stake warrant it.

VAT

2.21 If the consideration is subject to VAT, this must be included in the amount on which LBTT is charged. If the buyer is able to recover the VAT suffered as input tax, this means that LBTT is charged on a greater amount than the cost. At current VAT rates, the effective rates of LBTT on non-residential property are 0%, 1.2% and 6% rather than the stated rates of 0%, 1% and 5%. If the land is not subject to VAT at the effective date (see **2.81**) of the transaction, but may become so through exercise of the 'option to tax', VAT is not taken into account, provided the option to tax is not exercised until after the effective date of the transaction (LBTT(S)A 2013, Sch 2, para 2).

Example 2.3 – LBTT on VAT

Thomson Sharpshooters Ltd (T) buys a plot of land from MacGowan Packages Ltd (M) for £600,000 (plus VAT if chargeable), intending to build a new factory. M has exercised the VAT 'option to tax' the land and charges VAT, but T is able to recover this fully through its own VAT returns. T also negotiates to pay the VAT to M on the same day it recovers it from HMRC. So, commercially, the real cost of the land is simply £600,000. LBTT is chargeable on the VAT inclusive price of £720,000 as follows:

Purchase Price	*Rate*	*LBTT*
£	%	£
150,000	0	NIL
100,000	1	1,000
470,000	5	23,500
720,000	3.403	24,500

The overall effective rate of LBTT on the true cost of the land is therefore 4.083% (£24,500/£600,000), rather than the stated effective rate of 3.403%.

Debt as consideration

2.22 If land is transferred in satisfaction (or in return for the release) of a debt due to the buyer or owed by the seller, or in return for the buyer assuming responsibility for a debt, the amount of the debt (including any interest due but unpaid) which was satisfied, released or assumed counts as consideration (LBTT(S)A 2013, Sch 2, para 8(1)). However, if the amount of the debt which was satisfied, released or assumed exceeds the market value of the land, the chargeable consideration is limited to that market value (LBTT(S)A 2013, Sch 2, para 8(4)). For these purposes 'debt' means 'an obligation, whether certain or contingent, to pay a sum of money either immediately or at a future date' (LBTT(S)A 2013, Sch 2, para 8(5)).

2.23 The position may be less clear where there is a debt secured on the property before the transfer, which remains in place after the transfer. In principle, it may be possible for the property to be transferred without the buyer taking on responsibility for payment of the debt, in which case the debt should not be taken into account as consideration for the transfer.

Example 2.4 – Debt as consideration?

Parent has purchased a house with the aid of a loan secured on the house. The house is occupied by a Student. Parent transfers the house to the Student for no consideration and retains full and sole responsibility for the loan. The amount of the loan should not be taken into account as consideration for LBTT purposes.

2.24 With a view to the prevention of avoidance, it is provided that the amount of debt secured on the property immediately before and immediately after the transaction *will* be taken into account as chargeable consideration if the rights or liabilities of any party to the transaction in relation to the debt, are changed in connection with the transaction (LBTT(S)A 2013, Sch 2, para 8(2)). In **Example 2.4** above, arrangements between the Parent and the lender would require very careful drafting to ensure that the Parent's rights and obligations in relation to the loan remain unchanged when the property is transferred – and it may prove difficult to persuade a lender to accept the necessary drafting.

Where the chargeable consideration for a land transaction includes the assumption of debt which is secured on the property being transferred and, immediately before the transaction there were two or more persons each holding an undivided share of the property transferred, the amount of the secured debt which has been assumed is to be calculated as if the debt was owed by each person holding the undivided share of the property, in proportion to their undivided share in the property at the time of the transfer (LBTT(S) A 2013, Sch 2, para 8(3)).

Example 2.5 – Debt secured on property – two or more persons with an undivided share in the property

S and B own an undivided share in a property in the proportion 80:20. The property is transferred to B subject to a pre-existing debt secured on the property with S being released from having any liability in relation to the secured debt. B is treated as assuming debt equal to 80% of the amount owing, on the basis that B is treated as owing 20% of the debt before the transfer and 100% after the transfer.

Focus

- If the consideration for a land transaction includes the carrying out of construction, improvement or repair works to a building, or other works to enhance the value of land, the value of those works will be chargeable to LBTT unless certain conditions are satisfied.

Carrying out works on land (LBTT(S)A 2013, Sch 2, para 11)

2.25 Under SDLT this is a widely misunderstood and, in practice, fairly limited exclusion from chargeable consideration. As the wording is similar under the equivalent LBTT provision, although it is even narrower in scope, it is likely that this confusion will continue.

The point of confusion arises as this provision is supposed to prevent the value of construction works given as consideration by the buyer, from being charged to LBTT, in certain limited circumstances. However, the third condition to be satisfied if the provision is to apply is that it is not a condition of the transaction that the works are carried out by the *seller.* This makes no sense where it is the buyer which is giving consideration, and effectively makes the third condition otiose. It is unfortunate that this wording has been carried over into the LBTT legislation.

If the consideration given for a chargeable transaction includes works of construction, improvement or repair of a building, or other works to enhance the value of land, the value of those works is excluded from chargeable consideration if the following conditions are met (LBTT(S)A 2013, Sch 2, para 11(1)(a) and (2)):

(a) the works are carried out after the effective date (see **2.81**) of the transaction;

(b) the works are carried out on the land acquired or to be acquired under the transaction; and

(c) it is not a condition of the transaction that the works are carried out by the seller or someone connected with the seller.

Where a contract or agreement for lease has been substantially performed (see **2.7**) before it was completed or a lease granted, so that there are two notifiable land transactions, then condition (a) above is treated as satisfied in relation to the completion/grant of lease transaction, if it was satisfied when substantial performance took place (LBTT(S)A 2013, Sch 2, para 11(3)).

If any of these conditions are not satisfied then the value (the amount which a third party would have to be paid to carry out the works) of the works is chargeable to LBTT (LBTT(S)A 2013, Sch 2, para 11(1)(b)).

The exclusion from chargeable consideration is actually narrower under LBTT than it is under SDLT, as the provision within the SDLT legislation allows the work to be carried out not only on land acquired by the buyer as part of the transaction, but also on other land held by the buyer or a person connected with him. Thus under LBTT, even if the first and third conditions are satisfied, if the works are carried out on land held by the buyer (or someone connected with the buyer), other than the land acquired under the transaction, then those works will be chargeable to LBTT. In contrast, under the SDLT regime, the value of the works would not be treated as chargeable consideration. It is not clear why LBTT should be payable if the works of construction etc are carried out on other land owned by the buyer, rather than the land acquired under the transaction.

However, an important point to remember is that to be chargeable to LBTT in the first instance the works must be consideration for the land transaction, given by the buyer or a person connected with the buyer. If the works are not consideration for the land transaction there is no need to consider the availability of this exclusion from chargeable consideration, as the value of the works will simply not be chargeable to LBTT.

If the value of works of construction, improvement or repair is excluded from being chargeable consideration by virtue of the LBTT(S)A 2013, Sch 2, para 17(4)(b) (Arrangement involving public or education bodies – see **5.40**), then the provisions of the LBTT(S)A 2013, Sch 2, para 11 do not apply (LBTT(S)A 2013, Sch 2, para 11(5)) and there is therefore no need to consider whether conditions (a) to (c) above are satisfied.

Example 2.6 – Works which do not count as consideration chargeable to LBTT

Newton Co Ltd (N) agrees to sell land to Goodwin Builders Ltd (G). The land is contaminated and N is under an obligation to carry out decontamination works within one year. In consideration for the transfer, G pays £500,000 and agrees to engage an unrelated company to carry out the required decontamination works at an expected cost of £1 million. The works do not commence until after the settlement of the transaction. The value of the decontamination works does not count as consideration for the transfer of the land, and G pays LBTT only on the £500,000 cash consideration. This is on the basis that the requirements of the LBTT(S)A 2013, Sch 2, para 11(1)(a) are satisfied as the works are carried out after the effective date of the transaction, the work is carried out on the land acquired under the transaction, and the works are not to be carried out by the seller.

Example 2.7 – Works which are consideration chargeable to LBTT

Amanda (A) agrees to buy a plot of land from Landbank Ltd (L) for £200,000 (its true market value) and, on the same day, engages McLean Builders Ltd (M) to construct a house on the plot at a cost of £300,000. L and M are connected with each other but unconnected with A. The provision excluding the carrying out of works from the consideration chargeable to LBTT has no application in this scenario. The £300,000 is being paid for the construction of the house and is not consideration for the transfer of the plot of land ie it is not the buyer which is providing the construction services. Instead, it is necessary to consider the case of Prudential Assurance Co Ltd v IRC [1992] STC 863. Whilst this was a UK stamp duty case Revenue Scotland accept that the same principles apply to LBTT, as they do for UK stamp duty. In LBTT2004, Revenue Scotland state: 'We will consider whether or not a contract for the sale of land and a contract for building services properly constitutes the sale of land with completed buildings such that the chargeable consideration for the transaction will be the aggregate consideration for the contracts. Generally, unless the purchase and development contracts are so inter-related that default of one will prevent completion of the other or would otherwise render one invalid, LBTT should be charged only on the consideration attributable to the land transferred (where necessary, apportioned on a just and reasonable basis).' Consequently, provided the land purchase and building services contracts are genuinely independent of each other, LBTT should only be charged on the price paid for the land. In the present example, unless it can be shown that the two contracts are not inter-related, and that default on one contract will not prevent completion of the other contract, it may be difficult to convince Revenue Scotland that this is anything other than a single transaction, with LBTT due on £500,000.

Services as consideration

2.26 Where services (other than the carrying out of works on land referred to in **2.25** above) are provided as consideration, they are valued at the amount which would have been paid in the open market for such services. In general, this is likely to be more than the cost to the buyer of providing the services, since an open market provider would expect to make a profit (LBTT(S)A 2013, Sch 2, para 12). If the value of the services is excluded from being chargeable consideration by virtue of the LBTT(S)A 2013, Sch 2, para 17(4)(c) (Arrangement involving public or education bodies – see **5.40**) then the provisions of the LBTT(S)A 2013, Sch 2, para 12(1) do not apply (LBTT(S)A 2013, Sch 2, para 12(2)).

Payment in instalments

2.27 If consideration is payable in instalments, the effective date (see **2.81**) of the transaction may be triggered by something other than payment of consideration (for example, occupying the property or even formal completion). Once the effective date arrives, LBTT is payable on the whole consideration, no matter when that consideration is payable (LBTT(S)A 2013, Sch 2, para 3). In certain circumstances, it is possible to apply to defer payment of some of the LBTT, as mentioned at **2.17** (see **8.26** for details).

However, where the consideration comprises or includes an annuity capable of lasting for at least 12 years, the consideration is taken to be 12 years' instalments (LBTT(S)A 2013, s 21(2)). For these purposes, any consideration (other than rent) payable periodically is an annuity (LBTT(S)A 2013, s 21(7)). If the yearly amounts vary, the highest 12 separate years are taken into account, although increases in line with the Retail Prices Index, the Consumer Prices Index or any other similar index are ignored (LBTT(S)A 2013, s 21(3) and (4)). If any of the payments is subject to a contingency, then the amount of the payment is determined on the assumption that the outcome of the contingency is that the consideration is payable or does not cease to be payable (LBTT(S)A 2013, s 21(6)). Similarly, if the payment is uncertain or unascertained then the payment is to be determined based on a reasonable estimate (LBTT(S)

A 2013, s 21(6)). If this treatment applies (ie annuity treatment), it is not possible to apply for deferment of any of the LBTT, and there is no adjustment to reflect actual consideration if the total payable proves to be more or less than the 12 years' payments initially assessed (LBTT(S)A 2013, s 21(9)).

Example 2.8 – Annuities

On 1 July 2024, April sells her house to ER plc in return for:

(1) a lump sum of £100,000; plus

(2) a rent-free occupation of the house for life (valued at £40,000); plus

(3) an annuity for life, initially at £15,000 pa, increasing to £20,000 pa after four years and increasing in line with RPI thereafter.

The consideration on which ER plc must pay LBTT is the sum of (1) and (2) plus 12 times the £20,000 annuity – £380,000 in total. For these purposes, since the annuity is for life, it is assumed April will live at least until 30 June 2033, so that at least 12 instalments at £20,000 will be payable, but the subsequent RPI increases are ignored. The LBTT is due by 31 July 2024, with no facility to defer and no adjustment if April dies before 30 June 2036.

Focus

- If a company is the buyer in relation to a land transaction, and is connected with the seller, LBTT is chargeable on an amount not less than the market value of the land/property which is the subject of the transaction. There are exceptions to this general rule.

Substitution of market value

2.28 LBTT is generally chargeable by reference to the value of the actual consideration given for the transaction, but in some circumstances this is substituted by the market value of the property acquired. One example is where property is transferred in payment of a debt exceeding the value of the property (see **2.22**); another is where properties are exchanged (see **2.31**) and the actual consideration, including any VAT, is less than the market value of the property acquired.

In addition, where a land transaction is entered into by reason of the buyer's employment, or by reason of the employment of a person connected with the buyer, LBTT is charged on the greater of: (a) the market value of the land/property acquired as at the effective date (see **2.81**) of the transaction, and (b) the actual consideration given for the land/property acquired (LBTT(S)A 2013, Sch 2, para 13).

Transfer to connected company

2.29 Perhaps the main relevance of market value is when a company is the buyer under a chargeable land transaction and the company is connected with the seller. When this happens, the chargeable consideration is to be taken as not less than the market value of the interest transferred (plus any actual rent payable where the transaction is the grant of a lease) (LBTT(S)A 2013, s 22(1) and (2)). For these purposes, 'connected' is as defined in the Corporation Tax Act 2010 (CTA 2010), s 1122 (LBTT(S)A 2013, s 58(b)). If the actual consideration (including any VAT payable) is greater than market value, LBTT is chargeable by reference to the actual consideration, unless the transaction is exempt from charge due to the availability of a relief (see **Chapter 5**), for example, group relief.

However, the exemption for transactions where no chargeable consideration is given (see **5.6**) does not apply (LBTT(S)A 2013, s 22(4)). Consequently, a gift of a property to a connected company will be charged to LBTT based on the market value of the property. Any other exemption (see **5.6**) or relief (see **Chapter 5**) will, however apply including, for example, group relief (see **5.10** et seq.) if the requisite conditions for the relief to apply are satisfied.

The same 'market value rule' applies where the buyer is a company and some or all of the consideration for the transaction consists of the issue or transfer of shares in a company (the company issuing the shares will not be the buyer otherwise LBTT(S)A 2013, s 22(1)(a) would apply) with which the seller is 'connected' (LBTT(S)A 2013, s 22(1)(b)). In this context 'shares' includes securities issued by a company, for example, if the relevant company issued loan notes (LBTT(S)A 2013, s 22(3)).

For the purposes of this rule 'market value' is the price that the interest in land might reasonably be expected to fetch on a sale in the open market and this definition comes from the Taxation of Chargeable Gains Act 1992, s 272(1) (LBTT(S)A 2013, s 62). Market value does not include VAT, even if VAT is chargeable on the actual transaction. This is because 'market value' is determined based on a hypothetical transaction between a willing seller and a willing buyer, and is not based on the actual transaction. If the 'market value' of the interest in land is not clear it may be necessary to obtain a valuation from a professionally qualified valuer.

Exceptions from the market value rule

2.30 The market value rule described above does not apply in the case of some transfers to corporate trustees (LBTT(S)A 2013, s 23(3) and (4)). Nor does it apply where the seller is a company and the transfer is, or is a part of, a distribution of the assets of that company whether or not in connection with its winding up. However, an anti-avoidance rule re-applies the market value rule to a distribution of the assets of a company if group relief has been claimed on the property (or on a superior interest, if the property is a lease) by the seller within the previous three years (LBTT(S)A 2013, s 23(5)). If any of these exceptions apply the chargeable consideration for the transaction will be the actual consideration given in money or money's worth, including any VAT (LBTT(S)A 2013, Sch 2, paras 1 and 2).

There are two noteworthy points which may cause confusion. First, there is no general relief available where the transfer to a connected company occurs in the course of incorporation of a business by a sole trader or a partnership. Reliefs for other taxes are available to ease the process of incorporation but, where the business has substantial property assets, the LBTT cost may act as a significant disincentive. There is a very specific relief on transfer from an unincorporated partnership to a limited liability partnership; see **5.45**. Additionally, application of the special partnership rules may reduce the LBTT on transfers between partners, partnerships and other connected persons, including companies in some cases. For detail on this see **Chapter 6** and in particular **Example 6.8.**

Secondly, where a lease at rent is granted to a connected company, there is no requirement to substitute a market rent. Rather, if the rent is less than a market rate, the lease itself will have a capital value (ie at arm's length, a lease at that rent would also attract a premium). LBTT is chargeable on the actual rent plus the capital value as if paid as a premium.

Focus

- Where owned land or a lease is the subject of an exchange, LBTT is chargeable on the greater of: (a) the market value of the property or lease acquired (plus the actual rent payable if it is the grant of a lease), and (b) the value of the property given in exchange plus any other consideration given in money or money's worth.

Exchanges and partitions

2.31 Where major interests in land (ie owned land and the tenant's interest in land subject to a lease – LBTT(S)A 2013, s 60) are exchanged (sometimes referred to as 'excambions'), this is treated as two land transactions. Assuming at least one of the interests transferred is a major interest (see **2.9**), the chargeable consideration for each acquisition is the greater of: (a) the market value of the property or lease acquired and, if the transaction is the grant of a lease, the actual rent payable, and (b) the value of the property given in consideration together with any other consideration given, for example, any 'equality money' paid (LBTT(S)A 2013, s 13 and Sch 2, para 5). Given that taxpayers may assume that LBTT is simply chargeable on the market value of the property acquired, this rule may cause some uncertainty and administration for commercial transactions where there is no attempt to avoid LBTT.

Example 2.9 – Exchanges

Eileen agrees to transfer a plot of land, X, to Lesley, in exchange for Lesley transferring plot of land Z to Eileen. It is agreed that the open market value of X is £200,000 and that of Z is £180,000. The parties agree to ignore the difference in value for commercial reasons. Eileen will pay LBTT on the acquisition of Z, based on £200,000, being the greater of the market value of Z (£180,000), and the value given in consideration (ie in this case the value of plot of land X given as consideration which is £200,000). Lesley will pay LBTT on the acquisition of X, based on £200,000, again being the greater of the market value of X (£200,000) and the value of the property given in consideration (£180,000). The overall LBTT bill would have been lower if each had sold to the other for cash equivalent to the respective market value of each property – but there may have been more pressing commercial reasons for proceeding by way of exchange.

In a subsequent transaction, Lesley transfers plot of land W, valued at £1.2 million, to Eileen. In return, Eileen transfers plot of land Z back to Lesley, and agrees to make cash payments to Lesley based on a formula which takes account of the eventual sales proceeds of houses which Eileen will construct on plot of land W. Eileen will have to pay LBTT based on the greater of: (a) the market value of plot of land W (£1.2 million), and (b) the total consideration which will actually be given by Eileen ie the market value of plot of land Z (£180,000) plus the cash payments based on the agreed formula, and taking account of the eventual sales proceeds of the houses. Initially a reasonable estimate will have to be made of the sales proceeds which will be generated from the houses to be constructed on plot of land W. Once that total consideration is finally determined – presumably after all of the houses have been constructed and sold – Eileen will have to consider whether a further return and payment of LBTT are due (for example if the total consideration exceeds both the original estimate and the original market value of plot of land W).

Lesley will pay LBTT on the market value of plot of land Z namely £180,000. This is on the basis that it is considered that the actual consideration given by Lesley to Eileen should be allocated as follows:

	£
Purchase of plot of land Z	180,000
Purchase of right to receive future payments based on sale proceeds of houses constructed on plot of land W	1,020,000
	1,200,000

2.32 If none of the interests exchanged is a major interest in land (see **2.9**) (that is, the interests are limited to options or matters such as sporting rights, mineral rights etc.), the chargeable consideration for each acquisition is simply the amount of any further consideration given apart from the interest in land itself (LBTT(S)A 2013, Sch 2, para 5(5)).

Example 2.10 – Exchanges, not major interests

Rowan Ltd owns fishing rights over a stretch of Minnow River. Unrelated company Gorse Ltd owns shooting rights over Sparrow Glen. The companies agree to exchange their rights, with Rowan paying Gorse £300,000 cash, being the agreed difference in values. Rowan will pay LBTT based on consideration of £300,000. Gorse will not pay LBTT, as the deemed chargeable consideration for its acquisition of the fishing rights will be nil.

The LBTT exchange provisions (LBTT(S)A 2013, s 13 and Sch 2, para 5) do not apply if the arrangement between the parties falls within the provisions of the LBTT(S)A 2013, Sch 2, para 17 (Arrangements involving public or educational bodies) – see **5.40**.

Joint ownership

2.33 Where two or more persons are jointly entitled to a property, they are treated for LBTT purposes as owning separate and distinct (but undefined) parts of the property. A property held in this way may be partitioned, so that each person takes a specific part. If this happens, the interest which each gives up is not treated as consideration for the part of which he becomes sole owner. The only consideration for LBTT purposes will be any payment or other consideration in money's worth which one may give to the other, perhaps to compensate for differing values of the parts taken by each (LBTT(S)A 2013, Sch 2, para 6).

Example 2.11 – Partition of property to which there is joint entitlement

Brothers Brian and Allan own a plot of land worth £1 million, divided into two paddocks, to which they are jointly entitled. They agree to partition it so that Brian owns paddock A and Allan owns paddock B. They agree that paddock A is worth £100,000 more than paddock B, but Brian is short of cash and they agree he will give Allan only £20,000 in compensation for his loss of value. For LBTT purposes, Brian is treated as giving consideration of £20,000 (and, since this is below the relevant threshold, Brian has no LBTT liability or notification obligations); Allan is treated as giving no consideration. Neither the market value of the overall plot nor the difference in values of the divided plots is relevant.

Market values could be relevant where one of the owners is a company which is connected to one or more of the other owners (see **2.29**).

Sundry liabilities not treated as consideration

2.34 The following liabilities and obligations taken on by a buyer do not count as chargeable consideration:

- an indemnity given by the buyer to the seller in respect of a liability to a third party arising from a breach of an obligation owed by the seller relating to the land transferred (LBTT(S)A 2013, Sch 2, para 14);

- an agreement by the buyer to bear any inheritance tax liability arising from the transfer (LBTT(S)A 2013, Sch 2, para 15);
- an agreement by the buyer to bear any capital gains tax liability arising from the transfer if it is not (or is treated as not being) a bargain at arm's length (LBTT(S)A 2013, Sch 2, para 16(1)). However, this provision does not apply if the buyer gives chargeable consideration for the transaction other than the agreement to bear the capital gains tax liability (LBTT(S) A 2013, Sch 2, para 16(2)).

RATES OF LBTT

2.35 The rate at which LBTT is charged on chargeable consideration other than rent depends on the amount of the chargeable consideration, and whether the transaction is a residential property transaction or a non-residential property transaction. In relation to residential property it also depends upon whether or not the 'additional dwellings supplement' (see **2.37** et seq) applies to the transaction. The rates of LBTT are progressive (like personal income tax); so that it is only that part of the consideration falling within a particular tax band which is taxed at the rate for that tax band. An order must be made by the Scottish Parliament to set the tax rates and bands which are to apply to both residential and non-residential property (LBTT(S)A 2013, s 24). On 17 March 2015, the Land and Buildings Transaction Tax (Tax Rates and Tax Bands) (Scotland) Order 2015, SSI 2015/126 was made, setting the tax rates and bands for residential property, non-residential property and rent which applied from 1 April 2015. In the case of the residential rates and bands, these have never changed (with the exception of a temporary change due to COVID-19). The Land and Buildings Transaction Tax (Tax Rates and Tax Bands etc) (Scotland) Amendment Order 2018, SSI 2018/372 changed both the non-residential rates and bands with effect from 25 January 2019.

The current rates for residential and non-residential property are set out in the table below. The Scottish Government have confirmed that the rates and bands will stay at their current level until 2026.

On the grant (or deemed grant) of a lease at rent, special rules apply for the calculation of the LBTT on the rent and any premium paid (see **4.13** et seq and **4.60–4.64**) and the tax rates and tax bands applicable to chargeable consideration consisting of rent are set in accordance with the LBTT(S)A 2013, Sch 19, para 3. The rates and bands were set by the Land and Buildings Transaction Tax (Tax Rates and Tax Bands) (Scotland) Order 2015, SSI 2015/126 and modified (in the case of rent with a NPV in excess of £2,000,000) by the Land and Buildings Transaction Tax (Tax Rates and Tax Bands) (Scotland) Amendment Order 2020, SSI 2020/24.

The Land and Buildings Transaction Tax (Amendment) (Scotland) Act 2016, which received Royal Assent on 24 March 2016, initially set the ADS (see **2.37** et seq) at an amount equal to 3% of the 'relevant consideration' (see **2.57**). This was increased to 4% by The Land and Buildings Transaction Tax (Tax

Rates and Tax Bands etc) (Scotland) Amendment Order 2018 (SSI 2018/372) and to 6% by the Land and Buildings Transaction Tax (Additional Amount: Transactions Relating to Second Homes etc) (Scotland) Amendment Order 2022 (SSI 2022/375), which took effect on 16 December 2022. The resultant aggregate rates are set out in the table below.

The 'additional dwellings supplement' (see **2.37** et seq) can be payable even where the transaction (or transactions) is a non-residential property transaction (see **2.68**).

A transaction is a residential property transaction if the chargeable interest acquired under the transaction consists entirely of an interest in residential property or, if the transaction is one of a number of linked transactions (see **2.79**), the chargeable interests acquired under each linked transaction consist entirely of residential property (LBTT(S)A 2013, s 24(3)).

A transaction is a non-residential property transaction if the chargeable interest acquired under the transaction either consists of, or includes, an interest in land that is not residential property. If the transaction is one of a number of linked transactions (see **2.79**), it will be a non-residential property transaction if the chargeable interest acquired under any of the linked transactions consists of, or includes, an interest in non-residential property (LBTT(S)A 2013, s 24(4)).

Thus the rates for residential property will only be applicable if the transaction(s) consist(s) entirely of residential property.

For the meaning of residential and non-residential property see **2.36**.

There have been numerous SDLT cases in relation to whether houses with land (eg paddocks or woodland), country houses, landed estates etc. could be considered to comprise any element of non-residential property. The trend of Tribunal decisions has been generally in favour of HMRC (who view the properties as wholly residential), but there have been some recent taxpayer victories where this may not have been expected to be the case, therefore making it a difficult area to analyse. To date, there has only been one LBTT case in relation to mixed-use property (*Sloss & Anor* [2021] FTSTC 1), which was decided in favour of the taxpayer.

Consideration (£)	*Residential property*[1, 2] *(Additional Dwellings supplement does not apply)*	*Residential property*[1] *(Additional Dwellings supplement applies)*
Up to £145,000	0%	6%
Over £145,000 up to £250,000	2%	8%
Over £250,000 up to £325,000	5%	11%
Over £325,000 up to £750,000	10%	16%
Above £750,000	12%	18%
	Non-residential[1] *or mixed property*	
Up to £150,000	0%[3]	

Over £150,000 up to £250,000	1%
Above £250,000	5%

1 See next paragraph.

2 The 0% threshold is increased from £145,000 to £175,000 for first-time buyers provided certain conditions are satisfied (see **5.31A** et seq).

3 1% in the case of a premium on the grant of a lease of non-residential or mixed property with a yearly rent of £1,000 or more attributable to the non-residential part (see **4.59**).

Residential property and non-residential or 'mixed' property

2.36 Residential property means property used or suitable for use as a dwelling (or in the process of being constructed or adapted for such use) and includes associated gardens, grounds, outbuildings and other rights which subsist for the benefit of the property – for example, access rights across adjacent property (LBTT(S)A 2013, s 59(1)). The use of the property at the effective date (see **2.81**) of the transaction is determinate, and trumps any previous or intended future use. The status of a house or flat is usually obvious. The legislation provides a list of other categories of building which are treated as residential property (LBTT(S) A 2013, s 59(3)), but then removes many examples from the list (LBTT(S) A 2013, s 59(4)), as set out below. The distinction is important as higher rates of LBTT apply for the acquisition of residential properties compared to non-residential property. In many instances the additional dwellings supplement (see **2.37** et seq) will also apply to a residential property transaction.

Non-residential property is any property which is not residential property (LBTT(S)A 2013, s 59(2)). For example, undeveloped land will be non-residential property unless, at the 'effective date' (see **2.6**) of the transaction, a residential property is being built on the land (LBTT4012).

Where conditional planning permission has been granted in relation to a residential property for a change of use to commercial premises, the property remains residential property for LBTT purposes until a completion notice is granted for planning consent and a completion certificate is given for any work requiring building warrants (LBTT4010).

A hotel, inn or similar establishment is specifically stated to be non-residential property (LBTT(S)A 2013, s 59(4)(f)) and the Revenue Scotland LBTT legislation guidance states that a bed and breakfast or guest house which has bathing facilities, telephone lines etc installed in each bedroom, and is available all year round, would normally be treated as non-residential property (LBTT4012). Holiday homes and lets, including those that cannot be used all year round, are considered to be residential property (LBTT4010).

The 'additional dwellings supplement' (see **2.37** et seq) can be payable even where the transaction (or transactions) is a non-residential property transaction (see **2.68**).

Where six or more separate dwellings are the subject of a single transaction, involving the transfer of the ownership of the dwellings, or the transfer of the tenant's interest in the dwellings, or the grant of a lease over the dwellings, they are treated as non-residential property (LBTT(S)A 2013, s 59 (8)), which limits the highest rate of LBTT to 5% at consideration over £250,000. However, the availability of multiple dwellings relief should also be considered (see **5.25**).

Where six or more separate dwellings are the subject of a single transaction it is possible to claim exemption from the additional dwellings supplement (LBTT(S)A 2013, Sch 2A, paras 9 and 10) (see **2.68**), although the availability of multiple dwellings relief (see **5.25**) should again be considered.

The legislation does not define what is meant by 'a single transaction' but it is the author's view that it means one contract between the same seller and buyer (and not including parties connected with the seller and buyer) for the acquisition of the agreed number of properties. The term 'a single transaction' would not cover, for example, a situation where there are multiple independent contracts between the same seller and buyer, since in such a situation there would be a number of transactions, although they would be 'linked' (see **2.79**) for the purposes of LBTT(S)A 2013, s 57. The treatment of the purchase of six or more dwellings as the acquisition of non-residential property now has even greater importance given that the additional dwelling supplement may apply to the purchase of dwellings (see **2.37** et seq**).** Care will therefore need to be taken to ensure that where six or more dwellings are being acquired the deal is structured as a single transaction, and not a number of separate transactions, if a claim is to be made for exemption from the additional dwelling supplement.

Residential	*Non-residential*
Residential accommodation for school pupils	Home or other institution providing residential accommodation for children
Residential accommodation for Students	Halls of residence for students in further or higher education
Residential accommodation for members of the armed forces	–
An institution which is the sole or main residence for at least 90% of its residents	Home or other institution providing residential accommodation with personal care to those in need of such care by reason of age, disability, drug/alcohol dependence or mental disorder
–	Hospital, hospice, prison or similar establishment, hotel/inn or similar establishment

Additional dwellings supplement – background

2.37 At the Autumn Statement 2015, the UK Chancellor of the Exchequer announced that on or after 1 April 2016 higher rates of SDLT would apply to purchases of additional residential properties, such as second homes and buy-to-let properties. In fact the SDLT legislation is much wider than the policy description and, for example, applies to first and subsequent purchases of residential properties by companies and certain trusts. In response to the Chancellor's announcement, and ostensibly to avoid distortions in the property market between Scotland and the rest of the UK, the Scottish Government announced that it would also introduce a higher rate of LBTT (referred to throughout the rest of this chapter as the additional dwellings supplement (ADS)) for purchases of additional residential properties but, like its SDLT equivalent, it is also much wider than the policy description and it applies to first and subsequent purchases of residential properties by companies, individuals acquiring a dwelling as part of a business of investing or dealing in land (either conducting the business as a sole trader or as a partner in a partnership) and certain trusts. There are however some important differences between the two regimes (see **3.4**). If the ADS is applicable the LBTT rates are as shown at **2.35**.

Date from which the ADS applies

2.38 If the relevant conditions are satisfied (see below) the ADS applies to a 'chargeable transaction' (see **2.12**) where the missives for the transaction were concluded on or after 28 January 2016 (the date upon which the Bill for the Land and Buildings Transaction Tax (Amendment) (Scotland) Act 2016 (LBTT(A)(S) Act 2016) was published) if the 'effective date'(see **2.81**) of the acquisition of the dwelling is on or after 1 April 2016 (LBTT(A)(S) Act 2016, s 3).

Meaning of dwelling

2.39 For the purposes of the ADS 'dwelling' means a building or part of a building used or suitable for use as a single dwelling or in the process of being constructed or adapted for such use, together with any garden or other grounds to be enjoyed with it (LBTT(S)A 2013, Sch 2A, para 20(2) and Sch 5, paras 24 to 27).

The ADS may also apply to an 'off plan' purchase of a dwelling or dwellings. Thus where a buyer enters into a contract to acquire a building, or part of a building, which is to be constructed or adapted for use as a dwelling, and that contract is 'substantially performed' (see **2.7**) before construction of the building, or part of the building, has commenced, and before the settlement (completion) of the contract has taken place (so that the 'effective date' (see **2.81**) of the transaction is the date of 'substantial performance') then the subject matter of the contract is taken to be an interest in a dwelling to which the ADS can apply (LBTT(S)A 2013, Sch 2A, para 20(2) and Sch 5, paras 28 and 29).

In determining what is and what is not a dwelling, LBTT(S)A 2013, s 59(3)–(6) applies so that the list of categories of buildings set out in s 59(3) are dwellings for the purposes of the ADS, subject to those categories of buildings taken out of the meaning of a dwelling by s 59(4): see **2.36** (LBTT(S)A 2013, Sch 2A, para 20(2) and Sch 5, para 30).

Holiday homes and lets, including those that cannot be used all year round, are considered by Revenue Scotland to be dwellings (LBTT10018). This view may be debateable if, for example, restrictions are placed on when the property can be used as a holiday let. The level of services provided as part of the holiday let may also be important as there may be an argument that the holiday let is an establishment similar to a hotel which is specifically treated as non-residential property (LBTT(S)A 2013, Sch 2A, para 20(2), Sch 5 para 30 and s 59(4)(f)).

Caravans, mobile homes or houseboats will not normally be considered as dwellings on the basis that they are moveable. However, in LBTT10018 Revenue Scotland do caution that '… if a moveable asset such as this becomes sufficiently fixed to the land that it becomes part of the land then we would no longer consider it to be a caravan, mobile home or houseboat. In such cases, the resulting building or structure may be a dwelling if it meets the normal definition.' This means that, for example, a static caravan may be a dwelling for the purposes of the ADS dependent upon the degree to which the caravan is attached to the land.

Intention behind the legislation

2.40 The broad thrust of the legislation is that where an individual or a couple replace their main residence (see **2.44**) the ADS does not apply and LBTT is paid at the normal rates as set out at **2.35**. However, in most (but not all) other circumstances where a dwelling is acquired the ADS is likely to apply and 6% is added to each of the normal LBTT rates in calculating the tax payable (see **2.35**).

Outline of the legislation

2.41 The legislation covering the ADS can be found in LBTT(S)A 2013, Sch 2A introduced by LBTT(A)(S) Act 2016. The legislation is divided into six sections as follows:

- Part 2 – identifies the transactions to which the ADS applies;
- Part 3 – details the additional amount of tax chargeable;
- Part 4 – sets out how the ADS applies in relation to certain types of buyer;
- Part 5 – includes provisions for repayment of and relief from the ADS in certain circumstances;
- Part 6 – details special rules for determining the ownership of dwellings for the purposes of the ADS;
- Part 7 – sets out the powers Scottish Ministers have to modify the ADS legislation;

The nature of the buyer can impact whether the ADS is payable

2.42 The conditions which have to be satisfied if the ADS is to apply to the acquisition of a dwelling are different depending upon whether the buyer is:

(a) an individual (but is not acquiring the dwelling in the course of a property investment or dealing business carried on by that individual either as a sole trader or as a partner in a partnership) (LBTTS(A) 2013, Sch 2A, para 2); or

(b) is not an individual, or is an individual but is either acquiring the dwelling;

  (i) in the course of a property investment or dealing business carried on by that individual either as a sole trader or as a partner in a partnership; or

  (ii) as trustee of a settlement (see **7.3**) and under the terms of that settlement no beneficiary is entitled to occupy the dwelling acquired for life nor are they entitled to income (whether net or gross) in respect of the dwelling (NB: this type of settlement is referred to below as an 'opaque settlement' for ease of reference only) (LBTTS(A) 2013, Sch 2A, para 3).

Buyer is a sole individual

2.43 The ADS will apply to a land transaction in relation to which the buyer is an individual (but is not acquiring the dwelling in the course of a property investment or dealing business carried on by that individual either as a sole trader or as a partner in a partnership) if the following four conditions are satisfied (LBTT(S)A 2013, Sch 2A, para 2(1)):

- the transaction consists of or includes the acquisition of ownership (see **2.48**) of a dwelling;
- the 'relevant consideration' (see **2.57**) for the transaction is £40,000 or more;
- at the end of the day that is the effective date (see **2.81**) of the transaction the buyer owns (see **2.49**), or is deemed to own (see **2.50** to **2.56**), more than one dwelling; and
- either (a) the buyer is not replacing his or her only or main residence, or (b) the buyer is replacing his or her only or main residence but the transaction also includes the acquisition of ownership of one or more other dwellings in addition to the dwelling which the buyer intends to use as his or her only or main residence.

Example 2.12 – Acquisition of a second home

Rory owns a property (which is worth £40,000 or more) situated in England and which he uses as his main residence. On 25 August 2024 Rory decides to purchase a holiday home in Aviemore, in Scotland, for a purchase consideration of £280,000. Settlement of the acquisition of the holiday home takes place on 25 November 2024 without any intervening event, which would have triggered 'substantial performance' (see **2.7**) of the contract and therefore the 'effective date' (see **2.81**) of the transaction is 25 November 2024.

The additional dwelling supplement applies to the transaction as the requisite conditions are satisfied as follows:

- Under the transaction Rory is acquiring ownership of the property in Aviemore.
- The 'relevant consideration' (see **2.57**), which in this case is simply the 'chargeable consideration' (see **2.17**), is £40,000 or more.
- At the end of the day which is the 'effective date' (see **2.81**) of the acquisition of the Aviemore property (ie 25 November 2024) Rory owns more than one dwelling (he owns his main residence situated in England); and
- Rory is not replacing his main residence as he intends to use the Aviemore property as a holiday home.

The LBTT payable is calculated as follows:

Purchase Price (£)	*Rate (%)*	*LBTT (£)*
145,000	6	8,700
105,000	8	8,400
30,000	11	3,300
280,000		20,400

Rory must therefore file a land transaction return by 25 December 2024 and pay the LBTT due of £20,400.

When is a buyer replacing their only or main residence?

2.44 A buyer is replacing their only or main residence if each of the following conditions are satisfied (LBTT(S)A 2013, Sch 2A, para 2(2)):

- during the period of 36 (18 prior to 1 April 2024) months ending with the effective date (see **2.81**) of the acquisition of the dwelling which is being purchased the buyer has disposed of the ownership of a dwelling;
- the dwelling which was disposed of was the buyer's only or main residence at any time during that period of 36 (18 prior to 1 April 2024) months; and
- on the effective date (see **2.81**) of the transaction the buyer intends to occupy the dwelling which is being purchased as his or her only or main residence.

The term 'only or main residence' is not defined in the legislation; however, commentary on this point is given at LBTT10020 of the Revenue Scotland legislation guidance. The guidance states that an individual can only have one main residence at any one time and, in most cases, it will be clear which dwelling is an individual's main residence. There is no ability for an individual to elect as to which of the dwellings owned is their main residence and Revenue Scotland state that they will use the same factual test as that applied in deciding where a person lives within the UK for the purposes of determining whether the Scottish Rate of Income Tax (SRIT) will apply. If HMRC has already made a determination as to where a person lives for the purposes of the SRIT Revenue Scotland will accept that position for the purposes of the ADS. The guidance goes on to state that an individual's main residence will usually be where they live and spend most of their time. It does not matter whether the individual owns or rents their main residence or lives in it free of charge.

However an individual's main residence may be where they spend less time if that is where:

- most of the individual's possessions are;
- where their family lives if they are married or in a civil partnership;
- where they are registered with their bank, GP, insurance company, etc; or
- where they are a member of clubs or societies.

In this context an individual may spend less time at their main residence if they live away from home because of work commitments.

Which dwelling is an individual's main residence will be a question of fact, and other factors that Revenue Scotland will take into account are as follows:

- if the individual has children where do they go to school;
- where the individual is registered to vote; and
- where the individual works.

The straightforward example given in the guidance is of a married couple who own two dwellings, one of which is convenient for work and their children's school, and where they spend most of their time, and the other a holiday home which they visit occasionally. The first of these is stated to be the couple's main residence for the purposes of the ADS. However, not all cases will be as straightforward as this and it will be necessary to consider the factors set out above in more complex situations.

If an individual rents the property that he or she uses as their only or main residence, moving from that rented accommodation to a dwelling that they own will not constitute a replacement of their main residence for the purposes of the ADS. For example, if an individual owns a dwelling, for example a buy-to-let property, and they then acquire ownership of a property which they intend to use as their only or main residence, moving out of rented accommodation, the ADS will apply to the acquisition of the ownership of the only or main residence as they will not be replacing their main residence.

If the buyer is acting as the trustee of a settlement' (see **7.3**) under which the beneficiary is entitled to occupy the dwelling for life or is entitled to the income (whether net or gross) in respect of the dwelling, the question of whether the buyer is replacing his or her only or main residence is tested by reference to the beneficiary rather than the trustee (ie the buyer) (LBTT(S)A 2013, Sch 2A, para 7(1) and (2)). In such circumstances the question as to whether the dwelling was the buyer's only or main residence at any time during the 36 months ending with the 'effective date' (see **2.81**) of the acquisition of the new main residence, and whether the buyer intends to occupy the dwelling as their only or main residence, is tested by reference to the beneficiary and not the trustee (LBTT(S)A 2013, Sch 2A, para 7(1) and (2)).

ADS exemption for sole individual buyers

2.44A LBTT(S)A 2013, Sch 2A, para 8(1) always provided an exemption from payment of the ADS.

In the case of a sole individual buyer, exemption from payment of the ADS under para 8(1) is available where:

- within the period of 36 months beginning with or ending with the effective date of the transaction, the buyer … disposes of the ownership of a dwelling (other than one that was or formed part of the subject-matter of the chargeable transaction),
- that dwelling was the buyer's … only or main residence at any time during the period of 36 months ending with the effective date of the transaction, [and]
- the dwelling that was or formed part of the subject-matter of the transaction has been occupied as the buyer's … only or main residence[.]

If these conditions can be met before the land transaction return is due to be filed (see **8.8**), no ADS will be payable. This will normally be the case where the former main residence is disposed of within the 30 days following the effective date of the acquisition of the new dwelling.

2.44B Changes to LBTT(S)A 2013, Sch 2A, para 8(1) were introduced by The Land and Buildings Transaction Tax (Miscellaneous Amendments) (Scotland) Order 2024, SSI 2024/104, which took effect on 1 April 2024. These extended the exemption from payment of the ADS buyers replacing their only or main residence, through the extension of the first condition to 36 months prior to the acquisition of the new dwelling. However, the circumstances in which this extended exemption will apply where para 2(2) does not already apply are very narrow

For the purposes of initial payment of the ADS, the first two conditions now essentially mirror those of para 2(2) and therefore the only difference arises in the third condition. For para 2(2) to apply there must be an intention, on the effective date, that the buyer will occupy the dwelling as their only or main residence. If there is no such intention, the ADS would be payable (assuming the other conditions are satisfied). However, if there is actual occupation of the dwelling as the buyer's only or main residence prior to the land transaction return being submitted, then para 8(1) will now apply to exempt the transaction from being subject to the ADS. A potentially useful exemption from payment of the ADS where the buyer's plans change in the 30 days following the effective date, but unlikely to arise frequently.

2.44C For completeness, para 2(2) is not now redundant in the case of a sole individual buyer, for the opposite of the reason above. Assuming all other conditions are met, if there is an intention, at the effective date, for the buyer to occupy the dwelling as their only or main residence, para 2(2) provides relief from payment of the ADS. However, in order for para 8(1) to apply to exempt the transaction from payment of the ADS, there would have to be actual occupation as the buyer's only or main residence before the land transaction return was due to be filed. This may not always be the case, although the intention to do so may remain.

2.44D LBTT(S)A 2013, Sch 2A, para 6 has also been updated to include the new para 6(1A).

For the purposes of the exemption from the ADS under para 8(1) (see **2.44A**), a dwelling which is disposed of by the buyer's spouse, civil partner, or cohabitant is treated as being disposed of by the buyer.

Similarly, a dwelling which is disposed of by a person under the age of 16 who is a child of the buyer, the buyer's spouse, the buyer's civil partner, or the buyer's cohabitant, is to be treated, for the purposes of the ADS, as being disposed of by the buyer.

A dwelling disposed of by the buyer's spouse or civil partner, or the spouse or civil partner's child under the age of 16, does not count if they no longer live together and do not intend to live together again (LBTT(S)A 2013, Sch 2A, para 6(2) and (3)).

For these purposes a person is the buyer's cohabitant if the two of them live together as though married to one another (LBTT(S)A 2013, Sch 2A, para 6(4)).

These provisions extend the 'single economic unit' rules, such that the potential exemption from ADS is widened in cases where ownership (and therefore disposal) of the previous main residence is not by the buyer. However, the extension only assists in considering whether a previous main residence has been disposed of. The other conditions in para 8(1) (see **2.44A**), namely, the previous occupation of the former main residence and the actual occupation of the new main residence must be met by the buyer themselves – the "single economic unit" extension does not apply for these purposes.

Joint buyers

2.45 If there are two or more buyers who will be 'jointly entitled' (see **2.54**) to the dwelling being acquired, and at the end of the day that is the 'effective date' (see **2.81**) of the transaction one or more of those joint buyers owns one or more other dwellings, para 2 will apply unless each of the joint buyers is replacing his or her only or main residence (see **2.44**) (LBTT(S)A 2013, Sch 2A, paras 2, 5 and 17).

Where one of the joint buyers is a non-natural person, for example a company or an 'opaque settlement' (see **2.42**), the ADS will apply, as the non-natural person is deemed to be the owner of the newly purchased dwelling and as the ADS applies to all acquisitions of dwellings by non-natural persons (assuming the relevant consideration is £40,000 or more) the question as to whether each of the joint buyers is replacing their main residence will be irrelevant (LBTT(S) A 2013, Sch 2A, para 17(2)).

2.46 The rule in **2.45** above (LBTT(S)A 2013, Sch 2A, para 5) meant that where spouses, civil partners or cohabitants jointly acquired a dwelling as their only or main residence and, prior to that acquisition a dwelling was sold, and the dwelling which was sold, whilst it was the main residence of both individuals, was owned by only one of them, and at the 'effective date' of the acquisition of the new dwelling either individual owned another dwelling, then the ADS would have applied as both individuals were not replacing their only or main residence. This was considered iniquitous and a relief from the ADS was introduced, but only in relation to contracts entered into on or after 20 May 2017 and where the 'effective date' (see **2.81**) of the transaction is on or after 30 June 2017 (The Land and Buildings Transaction Tax (Additional Amount-Second Homes Main Residence Relief) (Scotland) Order 2017). This was subsequently given retrospective effect to 1 April 2016 by Land and Buildings Transaction Tax (Relief from Additional Amount) (Scotland) Act 2018. The relief from the ADS is available provided each of the following conditions are satisfied (LBTT(S)A 2013, Sch 2A, para 9A):

(1) There must only be two buyers of the dwelling being acquired.

(2) The buyers must either be spouses, civil partners or cohabitants and must be jointly entitled to ownership of the dwelling being acquired.

(3) During the period of 36 months ending with the 'effective date' (see **2.6**) of the transaction under which the dwelling is acquired either of the two buyers must have disposed of a dwelling.

(4) The dwelling disposed of must have been the only or main residence of both buyers at any time during the 36-month period ending on the effective date of the transaction.

(5) Finally, on the 'effective date' of the transaction under which the dwelling is acquired both buyers must intend to occupy the dwelling being acquired as their only or main residence.

For the purposes of this relief two buyers are cohabitants if they live together as though married to one another (LBTT(S)A 2013, Sch 2A, para 9A(2)).

The relief from the ADS must be claimed in the land transaction return to be filed within 30 days of the 'effective date' (see **2.81**) of the acquisition of the dwelling or in an amendment to that return (see LBTT10040).

2.46A Following the changes introduced by The Land and Buildings Transaction Tax (Miscellaneous Amendments) (Scotland) Order 2024, SSI 2024/104, with effect from 1 April 2024, an additional exemption from payment of the ADS is now available under LBTT(S)A 2013, Sch 2A, para 8(1).

The additional exemption provided by para 8(1) may apply where para 9A (see **2.46**) does not already, if:

- there are more than two joint buyers;
- the joint buyers are not spouses, civil partners or cohabitants;
- the existing dwelling is not disposed of within the 36 months prior to the effective date;
- one of the joint buyers did not meet the residence condition; or
- there was no intention, at the effective date, for one or more of the joint buyers to occupy the new dwelling as their only or main residence.

The exemption from the ADS is available, in the case of joint buyers, provided each of the following conditions are satisfied:

(1) Within the period of 36 months beginning with or ending with the effective date of the transaction, … one of the buyers disposes of the ownership of a dwelling (other than one that was or formed part of the subject-matter of the chargeable transaction),

(2) That dwelling was one of the buyers' only or main residence at any time during the period of 36 months ending with the effective date of the transaction,

(3) The dwelling that was or formed part of the subject-matter of the transaction has been occupied as all of the buyers' only or main residence, and

(4) Where there are two or more buyers who are or will be jointly entitled to the interest acquired, each of whom own a dwelling or dwellings other than the subject-matter of the transaction, all of the buyers must meet the above conditions.

If these conditions can be met before the land transaction return is due to be filed (see **8.8**), no ADS will be payable. This will normally be the case where the former main residence is disposed of within the 30 days following the effective date of the acquisition of the new dwelling.

Para 8(1) also provides some flexibility to the exemption under para 2(2) as, where not all of the buyers own additional dwellings, only one of the joint buyers needs to dispose of a dwelling and only one of the buyers needs to have occupied that dwelling as their only or main residence.

Where all of the buyers own additional property, all of the buyers must meet all of the conditions, which puts them in essentially the same position as under para 2(2) (see **2.44** and **2.45**), although see **2.46C** below.

2.46B The new legislation produces some anomalies. Where there are, say, three joint buyers, only two of whom own additional dwellings, the final condition in **2.46A** will not be met and therefore a disposal of a former main residence could be made by only one of the buyers in order to meet conditions 1 and 2. This is unexpected, as two of the joint buyers own additional property at the effective date.

It is also not clear from the legislation at which point the conditions must be met. It is assumed that, in order to avoid payment of the ADS, the conditions must be met prior to the land transaction return becoming due (see **8.8**).

2.46C As discussed in **2.44B**, the change made to para 8(1) to extend the first condition to 36 months prior to the effective date of the acquisition of the new dwelling also provides a narrow extension to the exemption provided by para 2(2) where one or more of the joint buyers does not intend to occupy the new dwelling as their only or main residence at the effective date of acquisition, but there is actual occupation by all of the joint buyers prior to the land transaction return being required to be submitted.

2.46D The extension to the 'single economic unit' provisions (see **2.44D**) only extend to the disposal of dwellings by other members of the single economic unit, which is relevant only for condition 1 in **2.46A**. They extension does not apply to any of the other conditions and therefore these conditions (occupation and ownership) will be assessed by reference to each joint buyer alone.

2.46E The only situation the author can envisage where an exemption may be available under para 9A, but not under the extended para 8(1) is where only one of the spouses or civil partners is disposing of the former main residence and (as in **2.44C**), there is an intention, at the effective date, for the spouses or civil partners to occupy the new dwelling as their only or main residence but, at the date of the land transaction return, there has been no actual occupation as such. This is likely to be a particularly niche situation.

2.46F The third and final possible exemption from payment of the ADS is offered by LBTT(S)A 2013, Sch 2A, para 8A. This relief was introduced at the same time, and for the same reasons, as para 9A (see **2.46**). The relief from the ADS is available provided each of the following conditions are satisfied (LBTT(S)A 2013, Sch 2A, para 8A):

(1) There must only be two buyers of the dwelling being acquired.

(2) The buyers must either be spouses, civil partners or cohabitants and must be jointly entitled to ownership of the dwelling being acquired.

(3) During the period of 36 months beginning with or ending with the 'effective date' (see 2.6) of the transaction under which the dwelling is acquired either of the two buyers must have disposed of a dwelling.

(4) The dwelling disposed of must have been the only or main residence of both buyers any time during the 36-month period ending on the effective date of the transaction.

(5) Finally, both buyers must have occupied the dwelling acquired as their only or main residence.

2.46G The modifications to para 8(1) made by para 8A do not sit neatly with the redrafted para 8(1), applicable from 1 April 2024.

The effect of para 8A is to modify the definition of the 'buyer' in para 8(1), where there are joint buyers who are spouses (as set out in (3), (4) and (5) above). However, following the changes to para 8 made by The Land and Buildings Transaction Tax (Miscellaneous Amendments) (Scotland) Order 2024 (SSI 2024/104), para 8 now already caters (in a more beneficial way than as provided for by para 8A) for joint buyers. It seems unlikely that the intention of the legislation would be to treat joint buyers who are spouses more harshly than other joint purchasers. The difference between the two is that, under para 8(1)(b), the dwelling must have been the former main residence of one of the joint buyers in the 36 months prior to the effective date of the transaction. Under the modifications made by para 8A(2)(b), both of the spouses or civil partners must have occupied the dwelling as their main residence during that same period.

As such, the author cannot envisage a situation where para 8A would provide for an exemption from payment of the ADS which would not also be provided for by the redrafted para 8.

2.46H There is now a substantial amount of overlap between paras 2, 8, 8A and 9A. Revenue Scotland should take the opportunity to review the legislation and clarify the above areas of uncertainty.

2.47 If there are joint buyers and one of those buyers is acting as the trustee of a settlement' (see **7.3**) under which the beneficiary is entitled to occupy the dwelling for life or is entitled to the income (whether net or gross) in respect of the dwelling, the test is by reference to the beneficiary of that trust rather than the joint buyer (LBTT(S)A 2013, Sch 2A, para 7(1) and (2)).

Example 2.13 – Individual replacing his main residence

James has ownership of two properties situated in Scotland one of which he uses as his main residence and the other is let out to third parties. On 1 August 2024, James agrees to sell his main residence and acquire a new property, which is also situated in Scotland, and which he intends to use as his main residence, for a purchase price of £300,000. The settlement of the transactions to sell his previous main residence, and acquire his new main residence, both take place on 30 September 2024, with no intervening event to 'substantially perform' (see **2.7**) the contracts, so that the 'effective date' of both transactions is 30 September 2024. The ADS does not apply to the acquisition of the new main residence as James is replacing his main residence (see **2.44**).

Example 2.14 – One spouse owns main residence which is sold with joint purchase of new main residence

Pamela and Cameron are married and live in a dwelling that is solely owned by Pamela. Cameron owns a flat, which he rents out to students. Pamela and

Cameron decide to sell Pamela's property and jointly purchase a replacement main residence.

Cameron will own, and Pamela will be treated as owning (LBTT(S)A 2013, Sch 2A, para 6(1)), two dwellings (the flat owned by Cameron and the replacement main residence owned jointly), at the 'effective date' (see **2.81**) of the acquisition of the replacement main residence; however, only Pamela will have sold her main residence within the 36-month period prior to the acquisition of the replacement main residence. The contract to acquire the replacement main residence was entered into on 11 June 2024, and the 'effective date' (see **2.6**) of the acquisition of the replacement main residence was 14 August 2024. On this basis Pamela and Cameron can claim relief from the ADS under LBTT(S)A 2013, Sch 2A, para 8 or 9A, despite the fact that only Pamela has disposed of a dwelling in the 36 months prior to 14 August 2024. The relief from the ADS should be claimed in the LBTT return which must be filed by 13 September 2024 (LBTT10040).

Why is ownership of a dwelling important for the purposes of the ADS?

2.48 Ownership of the dwelling is important for two reasons. First, the ADS can only apply if the transaction involves the acquisition of the ownership of the dwelling, and secondly, one of the conditions which must be satisfied for the ADS to apply is that the buyer must be the owner of more than one dwelling at the end of the day which is the effective date (See **2.81**) of the transaction under which the dwelling in question is acquired (see **2.43**). Consequently, LBTT(S)A 2013, Sch 2A, paras 11–18 deal with what constitutes ownership for the purposes of the ADS and, in some cases, deem certain persons to be the owner of the dwelling for the purposes of the ADS (see **2.50** to **2.56**).

The Land Registration (Scotland) Act 2002 provides that 'Registration of a valid disposition transfers ownership; An unregistered disposition does not transfer ownership.' Consequently, under Scots law, a buyer does not own a property until the disposition is registered in the Land Register. However, for the purposes of the ADS, the buyer is treated as being the owner of the dwelling, and the seller is treated as ceasing to be the owner of the dwelling, as from the end of the day that is the 'effective date' (see **2.81**) of the transaction, and not the date the disposition is registered in the Land Register (LBTT(S)A 2013, Sch 2A, para 12(2) and (3)). For properties in England and Wales or Northern Ireland, when determining ownership of a dwelling, 'effective date' and 'land transaction' have the meanings which they have in Pt 4 of the Finance Act 2003 (SDLT) (LBTT(S)A 2013, Sch 2A, para 12(4)). For properties located outside of the UK the term 'effective date' means any date which is equivalent under the relevant overseas law to 'settlement' or 'completion' of the land transaction and 'land transaction' means any transaction for the transfer of ownership of the dwelling (LBTT(S)A 2013, Sch 2A, para 12(5)).

What counts as a dwelling owned by a person at the end of the day which is the 'effective date' of the transaction?

2.49 In determining whether a buyer owns more than one dwelling at the end of the day that is the effective date (see **2.81**) of the transaction (see **2.43**) the following rules apply:

- Ownership of a dwelling situated outside of Scotland (as well as within Scotland) is counted. This means that a buyer's ownership of dwellings throughout the world, and not only those in Scotland, are taken into account in determining whether the ADS applies to the transaction (LBTT(S)A 2013, Sch 2A, para 11(2)).
- If the acquisition of a dwelling has been subject to the ADS because, for example, it was acquired for the purposes of a property investment or dealing business carried on by the individual (either as a sole trader or as a partner in a partnership) (see **2.66**), or the individual made the acquisition as trustee of an 'opaque settlement' (see **2.42**), then that dwelling is not to be counted in determining whether the buyer owns more than one dwelling at the end of the day that is the 'effective date' (see **2.81**) of the transaction. Equally, if the dwelling is situated outside of Scotland and the ADS would have applied to its acquisition for the reasons outlined in this paragraph, but for the fact that the dwelling is situated outside of Scotland, then that dwelling is not to be counted in determining whether the buyer owns more than one dwelling at the end of the day that is the 'effective date' (see **2.81**) of the transaction (LBTT(S)A 2013, Sch 2A, para 11 (3)).

Example 2.15 – Partner in a property dealing partnership acquiring first property in own name

Cara rents the property that she uses as her main residence and owns no property in her own right. She is however a partner in a partnership whose sole or main activity is dealing in residential property situated in Scotland. The ADS has been charged on the acquisition of each of the properties acquired by the partnership. Cara acquires ownership of a property situated in Scotland, which she intends to let out to third party tenants. Despite the fact that LBTT(S) A 2013, Sch 17, para 3(1)(a) treats Cara as having an interest in each of the properties held by the partnership, the ADS does not apply to Cara's acquisition of the buy to let property as LBTT(S)A 2013, Sch 2A, para 11(3)(a) provides that Cara's ownership of an interest in the properties held by the partnership is not to be counted in determining whether Cara owns another property at the end of the day which is the 'effective date' (see **2.81**) of the day on which the buy-to-let property is acquired. As Cara owns no other property the ADS does not apply to the acquisition of the buy-to-let property.

- Ownership of a dwelling with a market value of less than £40,000 is not taken into account in determining whether the ADS applies to the transaction. The market value of the dwelling includes the market value of any subordinate real rights pertaining to the ownership interest (LBTT(S)A 2013, Sch 2A, para 11(4) and (5)).

- If there are two or more buyers who will be 'jointly entitled' (see **2.54**) to the dwelling being acquired the condition that the buyer must own more than one dwelling at the end of the day that is the effective date (see **2.81**) of the transaction is satisfied if it is satisfied in relation to any one of the buyers (LBTT(S)A 2013, Sch 2A, para 5).

- For the purposes of determining whether a person owns a dwelling at the end of the day that is the effective date (see **2.81**) of the transaction under which a dwelling is acquired, a dwelling which is owned by the buyer's spouse, civil partner, or cohabitant is treated, for the purposes of the ADS, as owned by the buyer.

  Similarly, a dwelling which is owned by a person under the age of 16 who is a child of the buyer, the buyer's spouse, the buyer's civil partner, or the buyer's cohabitant, is to be treated, for the purposes of the ADS, as being owned by the buyer (LBTT(S)A 2013, Sch 2A, para 6(1)).

  A dwelling owned by the buyer's spouse or civil partner does not count if they no longer live together and do not intend to live together again (LBTT(S)A 2013, Sch 2A, para 6(2) and (3)).

  For these purposes a person is the buyer's cohabitant if the two of them live together as though married to one another (LBTT(S)A 2013, Sch 2A, para 6(4)).

- If the buyer is acting as the trustee of a settlement (see **7.3**) under which the beneficiary is entitled to occupy the dwelling for life or is entitled to the income (whether net or gross) in respect of the dwelling, the condition that the buyer must own more than one dwelling at the end of the day that is the effective date (see **2.81**) of the transaction is tested by reference to the beneficiary rather than the buyer (LBTT(S)A 2013, Sch 2A, para 7(1) and (2)). In such circumstances, any dwelling owned by the spouse, civil partner, cohabitant or person under the age of 16 (as described above) of the beneficiary will count in determining whether the beneficiary owns more than one dwelling at the end of the day that is the effective date (see **2.81**) of the transaction (LBTT(S)A 2013, Sch 2A, para 7(1) and (2)).

Beneficiaries of bare trusts and trusts where the beneficiary has a relevant interest

2.50 Where a dwelling is acquired by the trustees of a 'bare trust' (see **7.3**) or a 'settlement' (see **7.3**) under which the beneficiary has a 'relevant interest', which means that the beneficiary is entitled to occupy the dwelling for life or is entitled to the income (whether net or gross) in respect of the dwelling, the beneficiary of the trust is treated as the owner of the dwelling for the purposes of the ADS (LBTT(S)A 2013, Sch 2A, para 15). A 'liferent trust' in Scotland is an example of a settlement under which the beneficiary has a 'relevant interest'. Liferent trusts create 'improper (or beneficial) liferents' under which the liferenter enjoys the benefit of property by way of trust. This contrasts with 'proper liferents' under which an interest in the property is vested directly to the liferenter (see **2.53**).

Trustees and personal representatives of another person

2.51 Where a person owns a dwelling as a trustee or a personal representative of another person, that person is treated as not being the owner of the dwelling for the purposes of the ADS. This provision does not prevent the trustee or personal representative being treated as the owner of the dwelling for the purposes of the ADS in some other capacity, for example if the person is a beneficiary of a bare trust (LBTT(S)A 2013, Sch 2A, para 14).

Dwellings subject to a long lease

2.52 Where a dwelling is subject to a lease granted for a term of more than 20 years it is the tenant under the lease who is treated, for the purposes of the ADS, as being the owner of the land and not the landlord (LBTT(S) A 2013, Sch 2A, para 15). In Scotland it will be rare for a lease of more than 20 years to be held over residential property. The Land Tenure Reform (Scotland) Act 1974 (the 1974 Act) effectively prevents leases with a term of more than 20 years being granted over residential property in Scotland. In addition 'qualifying leases' (see **4.4**) granted before the commencement of the 1974 Act were converted to ownership on 28 November 2015 under the Long Leases (Scotland) Act 2012. However, if the buyer of a dwelling does hold a lease over residential property which was granted for a term of more than 20 years before the commencement of the 1974 Act, and it did not meet the conditions for conversion to ownership on 28 November 2015, then the tenant's interest in that lease will be counted as a dwelling owned by that buyer for the purposes of the ADS.

Leases granted for a term of more than 20 years are common in both England and Wales and non-UK jurisdictions with a similar legal system, and again the tenant's interest in such a lease will be counted, for the purposes of the ADS, as a dwelling owned by a buyer of a dwelling in Scotland.

Where a buyer acquires a 'qualifying lease' (see **4.4**) the interest acquired is an ownership interest and not a tenant's interest, as such leases converted to ownership on 28 November 2015, and therefore the ADS could potentially apply to that land transaction. However, if the buyer acquires a lease over a dwelling, which was granted for a term of more than 20 years but did not convert to ownership on 28 November 2015, the transaction will be exempt from LBTT (see **4.4** et seq) but will count as ownership of a dwelling if other additional dwellings are being acquired.

Person holds a liferent over a dwelling under a proper liferent

2.53 Where a person holds a liferent over a dwelling under a proper liferent (the liferenter has a direct interest in the land and has the right to occupy the property for life) the liferenter is treated as the owner of the dwelling for the purposes of the ADS and neither the granter of the liferent nor the fiar (the person who gains possession of the dwelling once the liferent terminates) are treated as being the owner of the dwelling (LBTT(S)A 2013, Sch 2A, para 16).

Joint and common owners

2.54 Where two or more persons are jointly entitled (ie entitled as joint owners or common owners: LBTT(S)A 2013, s 65) to the ownership of a dwelling each of those persons is generally treated as the owner of the dwelling for the purposes of the ADS. However, following changes made by The Land and Buildings Transaction Tax (Miscellaneous Amendments) (Scotland) Order 2024, SSI 2024/104, if the market value of the share in the ownership interest of the dwelling of any of the persons is less than £40,000, that share is not to be counted for the purposes of determining whether the ADS applies (LBTT(S)A 2013, Sch 2A, para 17(2)).

In relation to a dwelling situated in England and Wales, when determining whether a buyer owns more than one dwelling 'jointly entitled' means entitled as joint tenants or tenants in common. In Northern Ireland it means entitled as joint tenants, tenants in common or coparceners. In relation to a dwelling situated outside of the UK 'jointly entitled' means having an interest equivalent to the meaning of that term as described above for the different parts of the UK (LBTT(S)A 2013, Sch 2A, para 17).

The ADS will not apply to a transaction where a joint owner of a dwelling is acquiring a further part of the dwelling that they already jointly own. However, the transaction may still be notifiable and chargeable at the normal residential property rates of LBTT (without ADS) if any 'chargeable consideration' (see **2.17** et seq) is paid or provided for the additional interest in the property (see LBTT10061).

Inherited dwellings

2.55 Revenue Scotland consider (LBTT10066) that an inherited dwelling is to be counted as being owned by a beneficiary from the earlier of:

- the date that the period of administration of the estate ends – Revenue Scotland indicate that this would generally be the date the residue of the estate has been ascertained, rather than when the executor has carried out all work in relation to the estate;
- the date the dwelling is transferred to the beneficiary – that is the date the executor grants a disposition or a docket transfer in favour of the beneficiary (whether or not registration of title is at a later date);
- under the law in another country, when the deceased's interest passes to the beneficiary as an heir to the estate;
- the date when the interest is actually transferred from the personal representative to the beneficiary in satisfaction of a bequest of that particular dwelling; and

- the date when the interest is actually transferred from the personal representative to the beneficiary in satisfaction of a pecuniary legacy or an interest in residue, following agreement with the beneficiary to accept the interest.

From 1 April 2024, the inherited dwelling can be excluded from the number of dwellings owned for ADS purposes, but only when:

- the buyer (or, where there are two or more buyers who are or will be jointly entitled to the interest acquired, one of the buyers) owns two dwellings on the effective date;
- the buyer has inherited a dwelling through transfer or conveyance from executors; and
- the date on which they acquire the inherited dwelling is after they enter into a contract to purchase a dwelling, but before the date of completion of this transaction (LBTT(S)A 2013, Sch 2A, para 9B).

For these purposes, the date on which the buyer acquired ownership of a dwelling by virtue of a conveyance or transfer in their favour by the executor of a deceased person is the date on which the conveyance or transfer was delivered by the executor to the buyer.

Separated or divorced spouses and civil partners

2.55A From 1 April 2024, where the conditions below are met, in the case of separated or divorced spouses and civil partners, the former family home is not counted for the purposes of the ADS where the buyer retains an interest in the family home, without living there.

The conditions are:

- at the end of the day that is the effective date of the transaction, the buyer is the owner of two dwellings;
- the first of the two dwellings was at any time before the effective date of the transaction the only or main residence of the buyer and the buyer's spouse, civil partner, former spouse or former civil partner;
- the first of the two dwellings is the only or main residence of the buyer's spouse, civil partner, former spouse or former civil partner;
- the buyer and the buyer's spouse, civil partner, former spouse or former civil partner do not intend to live together again; and
- the buyer retains an ownership interest in the first of the two dwellings in pursuance of an order of a court or agreement of the parties made in contemplation or otherwise in connection with the dissolution or annulment of the marriage/civil partnership, their judicial separation or the making of a separation order in respect of them (LBTT(S)A 2013, Sch 2A, para 9C).

There is no relief provided for separated cohabitants.

Dwellings outside of Scotland: what counts as ownership?

2.56 A person owns a dwelling situated outside of the UK if that person has an interest in the dwelling that is equivalent to ownership in Scotland.

Relevant consideration

2.57 For the ADS to apply, the 'relevant consideration' must be £40,000 or more. If the transaction is a residential property transaction, ie it consists entirely of the acquisition of one or more residential properties, the 'relevant consideration' is simply the 'chargeable consideration' (see **2.17** et seq) for the transaction (LBTT(S)A 2013, Sch 2A, para 4(3)(a)).

Alternatively, if the transaction is a non-residential property transaction, ie it includes the acquisition of non-residential property as well as residential property, the 'relevant consideration' comprises so much of the 'chargeable consideration' (see **2.17** et seq) as is attributable, on a just and reasonable apportionment, to the acquisition of ownership of the dwelling(s) acquired as part of the transaction (LBTT(S)A 2013, Sch 2A, para 4(3)(b)).

As discussed at **2.35** a transaction is a non-residential property transaction if the 'chargeable interest' (see **2.9**) acquired under the transaction, or any 'linked transaction' (see **2.79**), either consists of or includes non-residential property. The LBTT rates for non-residential property apply to a transaction which is a non-residential property transaction, and that continues to be the case following the introduction of the ADS. The effect of LBTT(S)A 2013, Sch 2A, para 4(3)(b) is therefore that the chargeable consideration must be allocated to the dwelling or dwellings acquired as part of the transaction, or 'linked transactions', on a just and reasonable apportionment basis, and then an additional 6% ADS is payable on the apportioned consideration, whilst the total chargeable consideration is charged to tax using the non-residential property LBTT rates. This is an entirely new concept within the LBTT regime and means that part of the consideration for a transaction, or a number of linked transactions, is charged at the non-residential rates with a further charge arising at the 6% ADS rate (see **Example 2.20**).

In circumstances where the buyer is replacing his or her only or main residence (see **2.44**), but the transaction also includes the acquisition of ownership of one or more other dwellings, in addition to the dwelling which the buyer intends to use as his or her only or main residence, the ADS does not apply to the acquisition of the replacement main residence. As a result, in these circumstances, the 'relevant consideration' excludes so much of the 'chargeable consideration' (see **2.17** et seq) for the transaction as is attributable, on a just and reasonable apportionment, to the acquisition of ownership of the dwelling that the buyer intends to use as his or her only or main residence (LBTT(S)A 2013, Sch 2A, para 4(4)).

Example 2.16 – Individual replacing main residence but also acquiring a buy-to-let property

Richard owns a property that he uses as his main residence and decides to sell that property and acquire a new main residence, which comprises a main house with a separate holiday cottage. Settlement of both transactions takes place on the same day. At the end of the day that is the 'effective date' (see **2.81**) of the transaction, Richard will have ownership of two properties being the main house and the holiday cottage. The ADS will not apply to the acquisition of the main house as Richard is replacing his main residence (see **2.43**). However, it will apply to the acquisition of the holiday cottage. The ADS payable will be based on the 'relevant consideration' (see **2.57**) apportioned to the holiday cottage based on a just and reasonable apportionment. It is assumed that the 'relevant consideration' (see **2.57**) apportioned to the holiday cottage is £40,000 or more since, if it were not, the ADS would not apply.

Repayment of the ADS (from 1 April 2024)

2.58 If ADS has been paid on the acquisition of a dwelling then, in certain circumstances, a claim may be made to have it repaid (LBTT(S)A 2013, Sch 2A, para 8).

The detailed conditions which must be satisfied if the ADS is to be repayable are as follows (April 2024 changes in bold):

- within the period of **36** months starting **or ending** on the 'effective date' (see **2.81**) of the acquisition of the new dwelling the buyer **or, where there are two or more buyers who are or will be jointly entitled to the interest acquired, one of the buyers** must dispose of the ownership of a dwelling;
- the dwelling disposed of must have been the buyer's, **or, where there are two or more buyers who are or will be jointly entitled to the interest acquired, one of the buyers'** only or main residence at some time during the **36** months ending with the 'effective date' (see **2.81**) of the acquisition of the new dwelling;
- the new dwelling must have been occupied as the buyer's **or, where there are two or more buyers who are or will be jointly entitled to the interest acquired, all of the buyers'** only or main residence (see **2.43**); and
- **where there are two or more buyers who are or will be jointly entitled to the interest acquired, each of whom own a dwelling or dwellings other than the new dwelling acquired, then all of the buyers must meet the conditions above.**

The changes introduced by The Land and Buildings Transaction Tax (Miscellaneous Amendments) (Scotland) Order 2024, SSI 2024/104, which took effect from 1 April 2024, are highlighted in bold above. These significantly widen the possibility of a repayment of the ADS under para 8, particularly where there are joint buyers. For more on repayments to joint buyers, see **2.60** et seq.

2.58A The above timescales were 18 months prior to 1 April 2024 (with the exception of 24 September 2018 to 24 March 2020, when a temporary extension was given due to Covid-19). No transitional rules have been provided in The Land and Buildings Transaction Tax (Miscellaneous Amendments) (Scotland) Order 2024, SSI 2024/104 for the change to 36 months. However, LBTT(S) A 2013, para 8(1) and LBTT10070 appear to make it clear that the relevant date (in terms of the legislation applicable to the repayment conditions) is the effective date of the disposal which gives rise to the ADS ie the disposal of the former main residence must be on or after 1 April 2024 for the 36-month period to apply.

2.58B Prior to 1 April 2024, the first condition above only referred to the period following the effective date of the acquisition. As such, a buyer who had paid the ADS could only obtain a repayment in the situation that their former main residence was not disposed of by the effective date, but at some point in the following 36 months (and the other two repayment conditions were met).

The changes made by The Land and Buildings Transaction Tax (Miscellaneous Amendments) (Scotland) Order 2024, SSI 2024/104, with effect from 1 April 2024, appear to widen the scope of these repayment provisions.

Prior to 1 April 2024, a buyer who disposed of their former main residence in the 36 months ending on the effective date of the transaction but, at the effective date, had no intention to occupy the new dwelling as their only or main residence, would be liable to pay the ADS without any possibility of repayment (as they could not meet the first repayment condition at that time, as described above). However, from 1 April 2024, it should be possible to obtain a repayment of the ADS if the new dwelling subsequently becomes the buyer's only or main residence. In this case, the repayment conditions should all be able to be met as (1) the former main residence, occupied as such, would have been disposed of within 36 months ending on the effective date of acquisition of the new dwelling and (2) the new dwelling would now be occupied as the only or main residence.

The above potentially applies for up to 5 years and 30 days from the effective date of the transaction (being the deadline for overpayment claims to be made under RSTPA 2014, s 107).

Example 2.17 – Delayed replacement of main residence

Cameron decides to acquire ownership of a property, on 30 June 2024, that he will use as his main residence. However, the property is in a poor state of repair and will therefore require a considerable amount of work to be done before he can move in. He will not therefore be selling his existing main residence until some months after he acquires the new property. At the end of the day that is the 'effective date' (see **2.81**) of the acquisition of the new main residence Cameron will own two dwellings and will not have replaced his main residence. As a consequence the ADS will be payable on the acquisition of the new main residence.

However, Cameron will be able to reclaim the ADS paid, with interest, if he sells his previous main residence within the 36-month period beginning with the day after the 'effective date' (see **2.81**) of the acquisition of the new main residence.

If the repayment claim is made within 12 months of the date by which Cameron was required to file the land transaction return notifying the acquisition of the new main residence, the claim is made by amending that return accordingly (LBTT(S)A 2013, Sch 2A, para 8(3)(a): see **8.18**).

Alternatively, if the claim is made after that 12-month period has elapsed it should be made by way of a claim to Revenue Scotland for a repayment of the ADS under RSTPA 2014, s 107 (LBTT(S)A 2013, Sch 2A, para 8(3)(b)) (see **8.54**).

2.58C As explained in **2.44D**, LBTT(S)A 2013, Sch 2A, para 6 has also been updated to include the new para 6(1A).

For the purposes of repayment of the ADS under para 8(1), a dwelling which is disposed of by the buyer's spouse, civil partner, or cohabitant is treated as being disposed of by the buyer.

Similarly, a dwelling which is disposed of by a person under the age of 16 who is a child of the buyer, the buyer's spouse, the buyer's civil partner, or the buyer's cohabitant, is to be treated, for the purposes of the ADS, as being disposed of by the buyer.

A dwelling disposed of by the buyer's spouse or civil partner, or the spouse or civil partner's child under the age of 16, does not count if they no longer live together and do not intend to live together again (LBTT(S)A 2013, Sch 2A, para 6(2) and (3)).

For these purposes a person is the buyer's cohabitant if the two of them live together as though married to one another (LBTT(S)A 2013, Sch 2A, para 6(4)).

These provisions extend the 'single economic unit' rules, such that the potential for repayment of the ADS is widened in cases where ownership (and therefore disposal) of the previous main residence is not by the buyer. However, the extension only assists in considering whether a previous main residence has been disposed of. The other conditions in para 8(1), namely, the previous occupation of the former main residence and the actual occupation of the new main residence must be met by the buyer themselves – the 'single economic unit' extension does not apply for these purposes.

2.59 If the buyer is acting as the trustee of a settlement (see **7.3**) under which the beneficiary is entitled to occupy the dwelling for life or is entitled to the income (whether net or gross) in respect of the dwelling, the question of whether the conditions outlined in **2.58** are satisfied is tested by reference to the beneficiary rather than the buyer (LBTT(S)A 2013, Sch 2A, para 7(1) and (2)).

2.60 Where there are joint buyers of a dwelling, ADS may have been payable at the time of the transaction (see **2.45** et seq).

Prior to 1 April 2024, the ADS payable on the acquisition of the new dwelling only became repayable, under para 8, if:

- both of the joint buyers disposed of the ownership of a dwelling within 18 months starting on the day after the 'effective date' (see **2.81**) of the acquisition of the new dwelling;
- the dwellings disposed of by each of the joint buyers were the only or main residence of each joint buyer at some time during the 18 months ending with the 'effective date' (see **2.81**) of the acquisition of the new dwelling; and
- the new dwelling has been occupied by each of the joint buyers as their only or main residence.

2.60A The issue of joint buyers and their inability to reclaim payment of the ADS due to their particular circumstances has been the subject of a number of LBTT first-tier tribunal cases:

- *Dr C Goudie & Dr A Sheldon v Revenue Scotland* [2018] FTSTC 3;
- *John Frank Cameron Walter v Revenue Scotland* [2019] FTSTC 9;
- *William Ross v Revenue Scotland* [2019] FTSTC 5;
- *John William Wallace and Laura Anne Avril Hogg v Revenue Scotland* [2019] FTSTC 13;
- *Neil Doherty v Revenue Scotland* [2019] FTSTC 14;
- *Lachlan and Catherine Joan Macdonald v Revenue Scotland* [2020] FTSTC 4; and
- *C Ewan H Crawford v Revenue Scotland* [2022] FTSTC 3.

Some of these cases produced results which seemed particularly unfair for the taxpayer, but the Tribunal was bound by the legislation as it existed at the time.

As a result of the above cases, and as explained in **2.58** above, the scope of para 8(1) has been significantly widened in the case of joint buyers. Para 8(1) now sets out conditions which must be met for a repayment claim to be made by joint buyers.

(1) Within the period of 36 months beginning with or ending with the effective date of the transaction, … one of the buyers disposes of the ownership of a dwelling (other than one that was or formed part of the subject-matter of the chargeable transaction),

(2) That dwelling was one of the buyers' only or main residence at any time during the period of 36 months ending with the effective date of the transaction,

(3) The dwelling that was or formed part of the subject-matter of the transaction has been occupied as all of the buyers' only or main residence, and

(4) Where there are two or more buyers who are or will be jointly entitled to the interest acquired, each of whom own a dwelling or dwellings other than the subject-matter of the transaction, all of the buyers must meet the above conditions.

2.60B The effect of the changes described in **2.60A** and **2.58C**, for joint buyers, are that:

- All of the buyers previously had to dispose of a dwelling, within 18 months following the effective date of the transaction. Unless all of the joint buyers own additional dwellings, this condition now only requires one buyer to make a disposal, within the 36 months before or after the effective date of the transaction. Where all of the joint buyers own additional dwellings, all buyers must make a disposal, but now have 36 months before or after the effective date of the transaction to do so. In either case, this condition can be met by any member of the "single economic unit" (see **2.58C**) making a disposal.
- All of the buyers had to be disposing of a dwelling which was their only or main residence in the 36 months ending with the effective date of the transaction. Unless all of the joint buyers own additional dwellings, that condition can now be met by any of the joint buyers in respect of the dwelling disposed of. The author assumes that the intention was that the buyer disposing of the dwelling should also have been the one who occupied it as their main residence, but that is not what the legislation says.
- Where all of the joint buyers own additional dwellings, all of the buyers now have 36 months, rather than 18 months, to meet the conditions. The "single economic unit" concept (see **2.58C**) does not apply to ownership of dwellings for the purposes of para 8.

Revenue Scotland and the Scottish Government should be commended for attempting to remedy some of the problems caused by the original drafting of para 8. However, there are still certain fact patterns which could lead to the ADS being payable and not being able to be recovered where, on the face of it, both buyers have replaced their only or main residence. If advising in this area, particularly where couples do not live together before purchasing a joint property, the fact pattern should be considered very carefully before arriving at a conclusion.

2.61 As described in **2.46** above, where spouses, civil partners or cohabitants jointly acquired a dwelling as their only or main residence and, after the 'effective date' (see **2.81**) of that transaction, but within 36 months of it, the individuals sold their previous main residence, and that previous main residence was owned by only one of them, then the ADS would have been payable on the acquisition of the replacement dwelling, and it would not become repayable because both individuals were not replacing their main residence. However the law was changed in relation to contracts entered into on or after 20 May 2017 and where the 'effective date' (see **2.81**) of the transaction for the acquisition of the replacement dwelling is on or after 30 June 2017

(The Land and Buildings Transaction Tax (Additional Amount-Second Homes Main Residence Relief) (Scotland) Order 2017). The Scottish Government subsequently introduced the Land and Buildings Transaction Tax (Relief from Additional Amount) (Scotland) Act 2018, which gave retrospective effect to the relief from the ADS introduced by The Land and Buildings Transaction Tax (Additional Amount-Second Homes Main Residence Relief) (Scotland) Order 2017, meaning that taxpayers in this situation were able to reclaim the ADS on relevant transactions which took place from 1 April 2016.

As a result of the change in law, the ADS will be repayable in the circumstances described above provided each of the following conditions are satisfied (LBTT(S)A 2013, Sch 2A, para 8A):

(1) There must only be two buyers of the new main residence which has been acquired.

(2) The buyers must either be spouses, civil partners or cohabitants and must be jointly entitled to ownership of the new main residence acquired.

(3) During the period of 36 months beginning with the 'effective date' (see **2.6**) of the transaction under which the new main residence was acquired either of the two buyers must dispose of a dwelling.

(4) The dwelling disposed of must have been the only or main residence of both buyers at any time during the 36-month period ending with the 'effective date' (see **2.6**) of the transaction under which the new main residence was acquired.

(50 Finally, both buyers must have occupied the new dwelling as their only or main residence.

For the purposes of this relief two buyers are cohabitants if they live together as though married to one another (LBTT(S)A 2013, Sch 2A, para 8A(3).

2.61A However, the modifications to para 8(1) made by para 8A do not sit neatly with the redrafted para 8(1), applicable from 1 April 2024.

The effect of para 8A is to modify the definition of the "buyer" in para 8(1), where there are joint buyers who are spouses (as set out in (3), (4) and (5) above). However, following the changes to para 8 made by The Land and Buildings Transaction Tax (Miscellaneous Amendments) (Scotland) Order 2024, SSI 2024/104, para 8 now already caters (in a more beneficial way than as provided for by para 8A) for joint buyers. It seems unlikely that the intention of the legislation would be to treat joint buyers who are spouses more harshly than other joint purchasers. The difference between the two is that, under para 8(1)(b), the dwelling must have been the former main residence of one of the joint buyers in the 36 months prior to the effective date of the transaction. Under the modifications made by para 8A(2)(b), both of the spouses or civil partners must have occupied the dwelling as their main residence during that same period.

As such, the author cannot envisage a situation where para 8A would provide for repayment of the ADS which would not also be provided for by the redrafted para 8.

2.62 As outlined in **Example 2.17**, the claim for the repayment of the ADS can be made in one of two ways as follows (LBTT(S)A 2013, Sch 2A, para 8(3)(a) and (b)):

- If the claim is made within 12 months of the date by which the land transaction return notifying the acquisition of the new only or main residence had to be filed, it is made by amending that return accordingly (LBTT(S)A 2013, Sch 2A, para 8(3)(a)) (see **8.18**).
- If the claim is made out-with that 12-month period it should be made by way of a claim to Revenue Scotland for a repayment of the ADS under RSTPA 2014, s 107 (LBTT(S)A 2013, Sch 2A, para 8(3)(b)). Such a claim must be made within five years of the filing date of the original LBTT return (see **8.54**).

2.63 Where the buyer has been able to sell his or her former main residence in the period between the 'effective date' (see **2.81**) and the date of filing the land transaction return in relation to the acquisition of the new main residence it is not necessary to pay the ADS and then claim a repayment, the return can be filed on the basis that the ADS does not apply.

2.64 If the transaction involved the purchase of more than one dwelling, and the buyer intended to use one of the dwellings acquired as their main residence, the ADS will have been paid on the whole of the 'chargeable consideration' (see **2.17** et seq) given for the transaction. If the buyer then meets the conditions for repayment (see **2.58**), the repayment will be based on a just and reasonable apportionment of the 'relevant consideration' (see **2.57**) to the acquisition of ownership of the dwelling which is the new only or main residence (LBTT(S)A 2013, Sch 2A, para 8(5)).

Buyer is not an individual or is an individual but is acting in a particular capacity

2.65 The ADS will apply to a land transaction if the following conditions are satisfied (LBTT(S)A 2013, Sch 2A, para 3(1)):

- the transaction consists of or includes the acquisition of ownership (see **2.48**) of a dwelling;
- the relevant consideration (see **2.57**) for the transaction is £40,000 or more; and
- the buyer is (a) not an individual, or (b) is an individual, but is either acquiring the dwelling (i) in the course of a property investment or dealing business carried on by that individual (either as a sole trader or as a partner in a partnership), or (ii) as a trustee under an 'opaque settlement' (see **2.42**).

The property investment or dealing business carried on by the individual can comprise properties situated outside of Scotland as well as properties situated in Scotland (LBTT(S)A 2013, Sch 2A, para 3(3)). In addition the reference to a property investment and dealing business being carried on by the individual is also a reference to such a business being carried on by a partnership of which the individual is a partner (LBTT(S)A 2013, Sch 2A, para 3(4)).

2.66 The effect of LBTT(S)A 2013, Sch 2A, para 3 is therefore that the ADS will, for example, apply in the following circumstances, assuming that the 'relevant consideration' (see **2.57**) is £40,000 or more:

- the first and subsequent purchase of a dwelling by a company;
- the first and subsequent purchase of a dwelling by an individual for the purposes of a property investment or property dealing business carried on, or to be carried on, by that individual either as a sole trader or in partnership. The Explanatory Notes to LBTT(A)(S) Act 2016 state, at paras 23 and 24:

  > 'When an individual buys a dwelling with the intention of renting it out, it will not necessarily be the case that this transaction is considered to be undertaken in the course of a business, the sole or main activity of which is buying or investing in property. If an individual works away from home, for example in the armed forces, and buys their first residential home to rent out, at least initially, then the purchase made by that individual will not be within paragraph 3, unless there are other characteristics of the transaction, for example business accounts drawn up, or a business plan, that bring it within it. The transaction will therefore be relevant to paragraph 2, and if the individual does not own an existing dwelling, the supplement will not be payable.
  >
  > However, if an individual does not own an existing dwelling and buys a dwelling through a business they run and the sole or main activity of the business is dealing or investing in property, then the purchase will be relevant to paragraph 3 and so the supplement will be payable. For example, the individual's business could already own a number of non-residential properties and when that business purchases its first dwelling, the supplement will be payable on the purchase price.'

  Consequently, where the buyer is an individual a crucial point will be whether that individual acquires the dwelling for the purposes of a property investment or dealing business that they are carrying on and, if they do, the ADS will apply irrespective of whether that individual owns another dwelling at the relevant time.

  If the individual is a partner in a partnership, and the partnership's sole or main business is dealing or investing in property, then the ADS will apply to the acquisition of a dwelling (located in Scotland) by the partnership.
- the first and subsequent acquisitions of a dwelling by the trustees of an 'opaque settlement' (see **2.42**) (LBTT(S)A 2013, Sch 2A, para 3(1)(c) and (5)).

Example 2.18 – First purchase of a dwelling by an individual carrying on a property investment business

Ewan carries on a property investment business as a sole trader and, to date, the business has only invested in non-residential property. However, Ewan decides to acquire a residential property as part of his property investment business. He currently lives in rented accommodation and does not own any other property. Despite the fact that the acquisition of the residential property will be the first dwelling which Ewan will own the ADS will apply to the transaction as the dwelling has been acquired in the course of a property investment business (LBTT(S)A 2013, Sch 2A, para 3(1)(c)(ii) and (2)).

If the acquisition of the residential property had been the first property Ewan had invested in, the ADS would have applied if that acquisition had been made in the course of a property investment (or property dealing) business. In practice the difficulty is likely to be determining whether a business is being carried on or whether the residential property is simply being let out otherwise than as part of a commercial business. The term 'business' is not defined in the legislation but is wider than 'trade' and is generally taken to mean an activity undertaken on a commercial basis with sufficient degree of organisation and continuity (see **2.66** and the commentary included in that section from the Explanatory Notes to LBTT(A)(S) Act 2016).

Example 2.19 – First purchase of a dwelling by a company

Arable Farms Ltd, which operates out of rented premises, trades as a retailer of farm plant and equipment but decides to use surplus cash of £300,000 to invest in a residential property which it will let out to third parties to generate rental income. At the end of the day that is the 'effective date' (see **2.81**) of the transaction under which the residential property is acquired, the company will own only one dwelling. However, as every purchase, including the first purchase, of a dwelling by a company is subject to the ADS, the ADS will apply to Arable Farm Ltd's purchase of the residential property (LBTT(S)A 2013, Sch 2A, para 3).

ADS does not apply if a relief is available

2.67 Irrespective of whether the buyer is an individual or non-individual the ADS only applies to a 'chargeable transaction' (see **2.12**) and therefore, if the transaction is exempt from charge because a relief applies (for example group relief, charities relief, certain acquisitions by registered social landlords etc: see **Chapter 5**), the ADS is not chargeable.

The ADS can apply to a non-residential property transaction

2.68 There are two scenarios where a transaction involves the acquisition of one or more dwellings but the transaction is taxed as a non-residential property transaction and, in only one of those scenarios, should the ADS apply in addition to an LBTT charge based on the non-residential LBTT rates. The two scenarios are as follows:

- A transaction is a non-residential property transaction (see **2.35**) if either it consists entirely of the acquisition of non-residential property (in which case the ADS would have no application), or it includes the acquisition of both residential and non-residential property. A common example of the latter type of transaction would be the acquisition of a shop with a residential flat above the shop. As both LBTT(S)A 2013, Sch 2A, paras 2(1)(a) and 3(1)(a) refer to the subject-matter of the transaction consisting of or including the acquisition of ownership of a dwelling, the ADS can apply where the transaction involves the acquisition of both residential and non-residential property. It can also apply where the transaction is one of a number of 'linked transactions' (see **2.79**) and both residential and non-residential properties are acquired under those linked transactions. Where the ADS does apply to a non-residential property transaction the 6% additional charge will be applied to that part of the 'relevant consideration' (see **2.57**) attributable, on a just and reasonable apportionment, to the dwelling or dwellings acquired.

- Where ownership of six or more separate dwellings are acquired as part of a single transaction (ie a single contract between the same buyer and seller), then for LBTT purposes those dwellings are treated as non-residential property (LBTT(S)A 2013, s 59(7)). In such a scenario, provided a claim for relief is made, the transaction is exempt from the ADS (LBTT(S) A 2013, Sch 2A, paras 9 and 10). The claim for the relief must be made in the first land transaction return filed in relation to the transaction, or in an amendment to that return (LBTT(S)A 2013, Sch 2A, para 10(1)). The period allowed for the amendment of a land transaction return is 12 months from the date by which the original return had to be filed (see **8.18**).

Example 2.20 – ADS applies to non-residential property transaction

Craig owns a property situated in Scotland, which he uses as his main residence. On 11 March 2024 Craig agrees to acquire ownership of a shop with a flat above for a consideration of £380,000. Settlement of the transaction takes place on 31 March 2024 without any intervening event triggering substantial performance of the contract so that the 'effective date' (see **2.81**) of the transaction is 31 March 2024. The 'relevant consideration' (see **2.57**) is £180,000, ie this is the proportion of the 'chargeable consideration' (see **2.17**) which is attributable, on a just and reasonable apportionment, to the acquisition of the flat.

As the transaction consists of the acquisition of both non-residential property (the shop) and residential property (the flat) it is a non-residential property transaction for LBTT purposes (see **2.35**) and the LBTT payable is calculated, using the non-residential property LBTT rates as follows:

Purchase Price (£)	*Rate (%)*	*LBTT (£)*
150,000	0	Nil
100,000	1	1,000
130,000	5	6,500
380,000		7,500

However, as Craig already owns another property at the end of the day which is the 'effective date' (see **2.81**) of the acquisition of the new property (ie 31 March 2024), the 'relevant consideration' (see **2.57**) apportioned to the flat is £40,000 or more, and Craig is not replacing his main residence, the ADS applies to the acquisition of the flat. The amount of the ADS payable is calculated as follows:

Purchase Price (£)	*Rate (%)*	*LBTT (£)*
145,000	6	8,700
35,000	6	2,100
180,000		10,800

The total LBTT payable is therefore as follows:

	£
LBTT at non-residential rates	7,500
Additional Dwellings Supplement	10,800
	18,300

Interaction of the ADS with multiple dwellings relief

2.69 Multiple dwellings relief is available where two or more dwellings are acquired as part of a single transaction, or as part of a number of linked transactions (see **2.79**) and, if a claim for the relief is made, it may reduce the LBTT payable. The relief is considered in detail at **5.25** et seq.

If the ADS applies to some but not all of the dwellings acquired, the basis upon which the LBTT payable is calculated, if a claim for multiple dwellings relief is made, is slightly different. The tax due in relation to a dwelling ('DT': see Step 3 at **5.25**) is calculated in exactly the same manner, however the calculation must be done separately for each dwelling acquired, with the ADS being applied to the acquisition of those dwellings which fall within the provisions of LBTT(S)A 2013, Sch 2A, paras 2 or 3, and the normal rates of LBTT being applied to any dwelling which, for example, is replacing an individual's main residence so that the ADS does not apply. Once the 'DT' (tax due in relation to a dwelling) has been calculated for each dwelling they must be added together to determine the LBTT chargeable in relation to the chargeable consideration given for dwellings. For transactions where the ADS does not apply, once the DT (tax due in relation to a dwelling) has been calculated it is multiplied by the number of dwellings acquired to arrive at the LBTT payable.

Where six or more separate dwellings are acquired as part of a single transaction (ie a single contract between the same buyer and seller), and a claim is made to exempt the transaction from the ADS (LBTT(S)A 2013, Sch 2A, paras 9 and 10 – see **2.68**), the calculation of DT (tax due in relation to a dwelling) in respect of the transaction is done on the basis that the ADS does not apply, and therefore the normal residential rates of LBTT are used in the calculation.

Example 2.21 – Multiple dwellings relief – no additional dwelling supplement payable

On 30 September 2024, as part of a single transaction, Reid and Wright Ltd agree to purchase six flats, together with four shop units on the ground floor, for £1,600,000, from an unrelated seller. Settlement of the contract takes place on 30 November 2024, without any prior event triggering substantial performance, so that the 'effective date' (see **2.81**) of the transaction is 30 November 2024. The 'chargeable consideration' (see **2.17**) attributable to the shops, allocated on a just and reasonable basis, is £400,000.

As the transaction involves the acquisition of six or more separate dwellings, Reid and Wright Ltd can make a claim in the land transaction return to exempt the transaction from the ADS (LBTT(S)A 2013, Sch 2A, paras 9 and 10).

Multiple Dwellings Relief Claim

Average purchase price per dwelling £1,200,000 ÷ 6 = £200,000.

Purchase Price (£)	*Rate (%)*	*LBTT (£)*
145,000	0	Nil
55,000	2	1,100
200,000		1,100

Six dwellings × £1,100 per dwelling = £6,600

However, the LBTT payable cannot be less than the minimum prescribed amount (the Land and Buildings Transaction Tax (Prescribed Proportions) (Scotland) Order 2014, SI 2014/350, art 2: see **5.25**).

If multiple dwellings relief had not been claimed, the non-residential rates of LBTT would have applied to the transaction, as the transaction involves the acquisition of both residential and non-residential property (see **2.35**), and the LBTT chargeable would have been calculated as follows:

Purchase Price (£)	*Rate (%)*	*LBTT (£)*
150,000	0	Nil
100,000	1	1,000
1,350,000	5	67,500
1,600,000		68,500

The LBTT liability is allocated as follows:

		£
Remaining property	£400,000/£1,600,000 × £68,500	17,125
Dwellings	£1,200,000/£1,600,000 × £68,500	51,375
		68,500

The minimum prescribed amount is therefore £12,843 (25% × £51,375) and, as this amount exceeds the tax due in respect of dwellings, the LBTT payable in relation to dwellings is £12,843.

The total LBTT payable is therefore as follows:

	£
Minimum prescribed amount	12,843
Non-residential property	17,125
	29,968

Reid and Wright Ltd must therefore file a land transaction return by 30 December 2024 and pay the LBTT liability of £29,968.

ANNUAL TAX ON ENVELOPED DWELLINGS (ATED)

2.70 The Finance Act 2013, Pt 3 (ss 94–174 and Schs 33–35) introduced a new UK tax known as annual tax on enveloped dwellings, or ATED. A brief account of this tax is included here because:

- the tax was introduced partly in response to the alleged avoidance of SDLT by transferring shares of companies which held residential property;
- the rules for the administration of the tax appear to have been derived from those relating to SDLT;
- administration of the tax has become the responsibility of the section of HMRC which also deals with SDLT; and
- ATED continued to apply to dwellings in Scotland after the introduction of LBTT with effect from 1 April 2015. We therefore have the faintly ridiculous position that ATED continues to apply to properties in Scotland even though it is seen as an extension of the 15% SDLT charge on the acquisition of high value residential property by 'non-natural persons' (for example a company) which does not apply to land in Scotland from 1 April 2015 onwards.

The following description is no more than an outline, primarily to allow readers to determine whether there is a risk that the tax may apply to a particular situation. A more detailed, in-depth explanation may be found in *Property Taxes* (Bloomsbury Professional). Section and schedule references in this part are to the Finance Act 2013 unless otherwise indicated.

2.71 The key attributes of ATED are as follows:

- the tax applies when an interest in a single dwelling, with a value of more than £500,000, is held by a company, partnership or collective investment scheme at any time in the 'chargeable period'. It applies to a partnership only if the partners include one or more companies.;

- the tax applies to 'chargeable periods', being years from 1 April to 31 March. The first chargeable period for properties with a value of more than £2 million was that commencing 1 April 2013. The first chargeable period for lower valued properties commenced on 1 April 2015 in relation to properties with a value of more than £1 million but not more than £2 million and from 1 April 2016 in relation to properties with a value of more than £500,000 but not more than £1 million;
- the amount of tax payable for each chargeable period depends on the value of the interest in the dwelling; and whether the interest is held for the whole chargeable period;
- it is a self-assessment tax;
- there are reliefs for properties held by certain entities;
- there are anti-avoidance provisions;
- interest, penalty and enforcement rules apply and are similar to those applying to SDLT.

Single dwelling

2.72 There is a detailed definition of 'single dwelling interest' (s 108), designed to prevent mitigation of the tax. If more than one dwelling is held, each must be evaluated separately. Specific rules attempt to deal with single or linked buildings which may be regarded as a single dwelling or more than one dwelling (ss 112, 116, 117). There is no provision equivalent to SDLT/LBTT multiple dwellings relief (see **5.25**) to average the values of the properties.

Amount of tax

2.73 The tax is based on the market value of the interest held, initially on 1 April 2012 or on the first day on which the tax applies to the company etc, if later. The market value must then be reappraised every fifth anniversary of 1 April 2012, although the reappraised valuation does not apply in determining the tax payable for the chargeable period beginning with that five-yearly valuation date (FA 2003, s 102(2A), inserted by FA 2015, s 71). This is to ensure that there is sufficient time to obtain the five-yearly valuation before the ATED return has to be filed, and applies for chargeable periods beginning on or after 1 April 2015. This means that the market value of dwellings within the ATED regime must be reappraised on 1 April 2022 with the updated valuation applying for the chargeable period 1 April 2024 to 31 March 2025 (being the second year of the current five year period). However, if there is an acquisition or part-disposal with consideration of £40,000 or more this also gives rise to the need to reappraise the market value (ss 102, 103).

Value	*Tax*
More than £500,000	£4,400
More than £1 million but not more than £2 million	£9,000
More than £2 million but not more than £5 million	£30,550
More than £5 million but not more than £10 million	£71,500
More than £10 million but not more than £20 million	£143,550
More than £20 million	£287,500

The amounts of tax shown above are those which apply for the year commencing 1 April 2024 (s 99). For subsequent years the tax payable will be increased in line with increases in the Consumer Prices Index to the previous September, rounded down to the next £50 (s 101).

Where the tax applies for only part of the chargeable period, for example because the property is acquired or disposed of part way through the year, the amount payable is pro-rated on a daily basis. Tax is initially payable on the assumption that the property will be held from the start of the year or later date of acquisition until the end of the year.

If the property is disposed of before the end of the year (or if its value falls so as to reduce the tax, or if a relief begins to apply), it is possible to apply for repayment of the tax overpaid. That application may be made during, or up to one year after the end of, the chargeable period by amending the original return. This means there is effectively a one-year time limit on making such a claim (s 100).

Self-assessment

2.74 An obligation to submit a return and pay tax generally arises within 30 days of the start of the chargeable period. If the tax begins to apply to a company, partnership or collective investment scheme part way through a chargeable period (for example because a property is acquired), the return and payment obligations generally arise 30 days after the date of the event which causes the tax to apply (ss 159, 163).

Where a company, partnership or collective investment scheme is claiming a relief (see **2.75**) from ATED, it must do so by submitting a return (FA 2013, s 100). It is possible to file a simplified return called a 'relief declaration return' which must specify the type of relief being claimed but does not need to contain information identifying the particular property (or properties) in relation to which the relief is being claimed or their valuation (FA 2013, s 159A inserted by FA 2015, s 73(3)). A 'relief declaration return' can be made in respect of more than one property but can only be in relation to one particular relief, ie separate returns must be filed if different reliefs are being claimed for different properties. The return will be treated as made in respect of any property held by the company, partnership or collective investment scheme which is within the charge to ATED, is relievable from the charge to ATED by virtue of the relief specified in the return and there is no day in the chargeable period, prior to the submission of the 'relief declaration return', in relation to which the property is not relieved from the charge to ATED.

Reliefs

2.75 Reliefs are provided for:

- dwellings held by property traders and developers or property rental businesses (ss 133, 134, 138, 139 and 141);
- those opened to the public in the course of a trading activity (s 137);
- financial institutions, provided the dwelling was acquired in the course of a lending activity and is to be disposed of without undue delay (s 143);
- a dwelling held by an 'authorised plan provider' who has entered into a regulated home-reversion plan relating to the single-dwelling interest and on which the 'occupation condition' is satisfied. This is a plan under which an individual sells all or part of their home to the plan provider in return for an annuity or lump sum and a life tenancy. The 'occupation condition', if no 'qualifying termination event' (Regulated Activities Order, Art 63B) has occurred, is that the person who was originally entitled to occupy the dwelling under the regulated home reversion plan is still entitled to do so. If a 'qualifying termination event' (Regulated Activities Order, Art 63B) has occurred the 'occupation condition' is that the single dwelling interest is being held with the intention that it will be sold without delay and no non-qualifying individual is permitted to occupy the dwelling. This relief applies for chargeable periods beginning on or after 1 April 2016 (s 144A).
- a dwelling, which is a flat, is held by a company ('the management company') for the purposes of caretaker accommodation, the flat is contained in premises which also contains two or more other flats, the tenants of at least two of the flats in the premises are members of the management company, the management company owns the freehold of the premises and the management company is not carrying on a trade or property rental business. This relief applies for chargeable periods beginning on or after 1 April 2016 (s 147A).
- providers of social housing (s 150);
- charities (s 151);
- properties occupied by certain employees or partners working in a trade or property rental business (see FA 2016, s 135(3) – the amendment to include qualifying property rental businesses applies for chargeable periods beginning on or after 1 April 2016) carried on by the property owner (or a group company), provided the employee/partner has a less than 10% interest in the business (s 145); and
- farmhouses occupied by someone working on the farm (or a former long-serving farm worker) (s 148).

Anti-avoidance provisions

2.76 The rules have been carefully framed throughout in an attempt to provide certainty and to prevent avoidance. This accounts for a high proportion of the 80 pages of legislation. In addition to the general attempt to define closely how and when the tax applies, there are specific provisions to prevent reduction of the value of a dwelling by fragmenting ownership between different people (ss 109, 110) or by physically dividing the dwelling into separate parts (s 115).

The tax is within the DOTAS (Disclosure of Tax Avoidance Schemes) rules and its application to the tax is set out in the Annual Tax on Enveloped Dwellings Avoidance Schemes (Prescribed Descriptions of Arrangements) Regulations 2013, SI 2013/2571.

The main effect of the regulations is to add ATED to the taxes covered by the DOTAS regulations. As a result the general requirements for promoters and users to provide information to HMRC, often within very short time limits, apply to arrangements expected to provide an advantage in relation to ATED. There is a very wide description of the kind of arrangement that is caught, being an arrangement under which:

- a company, partnership or collective investment scheme ceases to meet the ownership condition (see below for the meaning of this term) with respect to the chargeable interest;
- the taxable value of the chargeable interest is reduced to £500,000 (from 1 April 2016) or less; or
- the taxable value of the chargeable interest is reduced with the consequence that the chargeable interest falls within a lower ATED tax band than it otherwise would.

For these purposes the ownership condition is met where the dwelling is held by a company, a partnership with a company member or a collective investment scheme.

Certain arrangements are then excluded from the obligation to disclose, including an arrangement under which the transfer constitutes a 'settlement'. It is not clear why such arrangements should be excluded, unless HMRC believe that avoidance arrangements involving such transfers are already blocked.

A separate version of form AAG4 (AAG4 (ATED)) is provided for notification of the use of a scheme (see www.hmrc.gov.uk/aiu/form-aag4-kana.htm).

The tax is also subject to the UK general anti-abuse rule in the FA 2013, ss 206–215.

Administration and compliance

2.77 As with other taxes, there are requirements for the taxpayer to keep records (Sch 33, Part 2), interest is charged on late paid tax and penalties are chargeable if returns are late or incorrect (Sch 34, Part 2). HMRC have the power to carry out enquiries (Sch 33, Part 3), correct errors in returns and to make determinations of tax payable or assessments as necessary (Sch 33, Parts 4 and 5). The provisions governing enquiries into returns and settlement of disputes are similar to those for SDLT. Routine assessments cannot normally be made more than four years after the end of the chargeable period, or six years if to recover tax lost as a result of carelessness. However, this is extended to 20 years in cases attributable to the deliberate action of the taxpayer, or where there has been a failure to make a return or provide information required under the DOTAS rules (Sch 33, para 25(3)).

The SDLT rules on collection and recovery of the tax (FA 2003, Sch 12) are directly applied to this tax. HMRC provided some guidance on the administrative aspects of ATED in Stamp Tax Bulletin 1/2014, available at webarchive.nationalarchives.gov.uk/20140109143644/http://www.hmrc.gov.uk/so/bulletin01-2014.pdf.

The tax is charged because the property is located in the UK. The location of the company etc which owns the property is irrelevant. In the case of SDLT and LBTT there is a practical need to deal with any liability because it should not be possible to register ownership of the property at the land registries until this has been done. There is no equivalent requirement attached to the payment of ATED. There must therefore be some risk that non-UK companies, with no UK presence other than ownership of a dwelling, will fail to comply with their ATED obligations.

De-enveloping a dwelling

2.78 A decision may be taken to transfer a property situated in Scotland out of a company to prevent a future liability to ATED arising. Care is needed if this is to be done without creating a liability to LBTT. Provided the company is debt-free the property can be transferred as a distribution in the winding-up of the company and no LBTT charge will normally arise. However, if the company has debt – typically in the form of a mortgage secured on the property – a transfer in return for the shareholder taking on the debt will be a transfer for consideration and liable to LBTT.

In relation to SDLT, HMRC have confirmed that where the debt is owed to the shareholder, so that it simply disappears when the company is wound-up and the property transferred to the shareholder, this will not be regarded as giving consideration. However if there is a third party debt and the shareholder provides funds for it to be paid off (whether by loan, gift or by subscription for further shares) HMRC will consider whether FA 2003, s 75A applies (SDLT general anti-avoidance provision). If they consider that the provision of the funds to pay off third party debt is 'involved in connection with the disposal' of the property to the shareholder, they will seek to apply s 75A and charge SDLT as if the third party debt had been assumed by the shareholder. See SDLTM04042 for details of HMRC's views on this matter.

It is not known what approach Revenue Scotland will take if:

- the debt is due to the shareholder and the property is distributed to the shareholder subject to the debt; or
- the debt is due to a third party but the shareholder provides funds to the company to pay off the debt.

In the author's view a shareholder taking steps to repay debt prior to the distribution of a property out of a company ought not to be an 'arrangement' to which Revenue Scotland would look to apply the general anti-avoidance rule (see **9.3**). Whilst there may be a 'tax avoidance arrangement', it would not seem to be 'artificial' (see **9.4**) and therefore it is considered that the general anti-avoidance rule should not apply. If that view is correct, and given that there is no equivalent of FA 2003, s 75A within the LBTT legislation, the analysis should be that no LBTT would be payable in these circumstances. However given that no specific guidance has been issued by Revenue Scotland on the matter it is suggested that a formal opinion (see **8.49**) be sought from Revenue Scotland in circumstances where a property is to be extracted from a company and there is debt involved.

LINKED TRANSACTIONS

2.79

> **Focus**
>
> - If two or more transactions are linked the chargeable consideration is aggregated to determine the rates at which LBTT will be charged. This is an anti-avoidance provision to prevent what is, essentially, one transaction being split into a number of transactions, with the aim of reducing the rates at which LBTT is charged on the transaction.

If two or more transactions are linked, the chargeable consideration for all of the linked transactions is aggregated to determine the rates of LBTT (LBTT(S) A 2013, s 26(1) and (2)). Transactions are linked if they form part of a single scheme, arrangement or series of transactions between the same seller and buyer or, in either case, persons connected with them (LBTT(S)A 2013, s 57). Connected persons are as defined in CTA 2010, s 1122 (LBTT(S)A 2013, s 58(d)). Whether transactions are linked is a question of fact, but transactions between the same seller and buyer, which occur around the same time, are likely to be presumed by Revenue Scotland to be linked unless there is evidence to the contrary. In the UK stamp duty case of *Attorney General v Cohen* [1936] 2 KB 246, [1936] 1 All ER 583, several purchases of properties by the same purchaser, from the same vendor at auction, were held not to be part of a series of transactions, because each property was the subject of a separate bidding process.

In the case of linked acquisitions of residential properties the rates of LBTT charged on the transactions may then be reduced if multiple dwellings relief is claimed, see **5.25**.

Entering into separate contracts will not prevent the transaction from being treated as linked if, in reality, they are part of a single deal.

The buyer in an earlier transaction must file a land transaction return, or further return, where the effect of a later transaction, which is linked to that earlier transaction, is any of the following (LBTT(S)A 2013, s 34(1) and (2)):

- the earlier transaction becomes notifiable;
- additional tax becomes payable in respect of the earlier transaction; or
- tax is payable in respect of the earlier transaction where none was payable before.

The return, or further return, must be filed within the 30 day period beginning with the day after the effective date (see **2.81**) of the later transaction (LBTT(S) A 2013, s 34(3)). The return must include an assessment of any tax payable on the earlier transaction, as a result of the later linked transaction and any tax so chargeable is calculated by reference to the tax rates and tax bands in force at the effective date of the earlier transaction (LBTT(S)A 2013, s 34(4) and (5)).

The requirement to file the land transaction return, or further return, in relation to the earlier transaction, does not affect any obligation to file a land transaction return in relation to the later transaction (LBTT(S)A 2013, s 34(6)).

Example 2.22 – Linked transactions

Pamela agrees to buy two houses, located in different towns in Scotland, from Andrew – the first for £160,000, and the second for £400,000. Pamela plans to let the two houses to third party tenants and she already owns a property which she uses as her main residence. The additional dwellings supplement (see **2.37** et seq) will therefore apply to the transactions. Different solicitors are engaged to deal with the two purchases. The first is completed on 10 September 2024 without prior substantial performance, but the second is delayed, while the title to the property is investigated, and does not complete (again, without prior substantial performance) until 15 January 2025.

By 10 October 2024 Pamela must file a land transaction return in relation to the acquisition of the first house and pay LBTT of £9,900 (£145,000 × 6% + £15,000 × 8%).

However, the two transactions are linked, because they were agreed in principle between the same people as part of an overall deal. Once the second house is purchased, the consideration for both houses must be aggregated giving £560,000, which falls in the 6%, 8%, 11% and 16% LBTT bands, so that LBTT of £13,186 is now due on the first purchase and £32,964 on the second. The LBTT liabilities are calculated as follows:

Purchase Price	*Rate*	*LBTT*
£	%	£
145,000	6	8,700
105,000	8	8,400
75,000	11	8,250
235,000	16	37,600
560,000		62,950
First purchase	£160,000/£560,000 × £62,950	17,986
Second purchase	£400,000/£560,000 × £62,950	44,964
		62,950

Pamela must therefore file a further land transaction return by 14 February 2025 in relation to the first house purchase and pay the additional LBTT due of £8,086 (£17,986 – £9,900). She must also file a land transaction return in relation to the second house purchase by that same date, and pay the LBTT due of £44,964. Separate returns are required for each of the house purchases as the linked transaction have different effective dates (LBTT(S)A 2013, s 57(2)).

However, if Pamela claims multiple dwellings relief (see **5.25**) the LBTT is reduced to £6,857 on the first house and £17,143 on the second house.

Multiple Dwellings Relief Claim

Average purchase price per dwelling – £560,000 ÷ 2 = £280,000.

Purchase Price	*Rate*	*LBTT*
£	%	£
145,000	6	8,700
105,000	8	8,400
30,000	11	3,300
280,000		20,400

2 dwellings × £20,400 per dwelling = £40,800

However, the minimum amount of LBTT (the Land and Buildings Transaction Tax (Prescribed Proportions) (Scotland) Order 2014, SI 2014/350, art 2) is:

25% × £62,950 = £15,737

As the minimum prescribed amount of £15,737 is less than the LBTT liability on dwellings of £40,800, the LBTT liability is £40,800.

The LBTT liability is allocated to the two purchases as follows:

		£
First purchase	£160,000/£560,000 × £40,800	11,657
Second purchase	£400,000/£560,000 × £40,800	29,143
		40,800

On the making of a claim for multiple dwellings relief the further land transaction return in relation to the first house purchase would show an additional LBTT liability of £1,757 (£11,657 – £9,900) and the land transaction return in relation to the second house purchase would show a liability of £29,143.

Example 2.23 – Transactions not linked

Andrew attends an auction where he successfully bids for two houses in the same street, which are sold as separate lots. Andrew already owns a property, which he uses as his main residence. Andrew pays £110,000 for one and £145,000 for the other. After the auction, he discovers the seller is the same for both houses. The transactions are not linked, because each purchase was agreed totally independently of the other; the LBTT payable on the first house is £6,600 (£110,000 × 6%) and on the second house is £8,700 (£145,000 × 6%). It is not possible to make a claim for multiple dwellings relief as the properties are acquired under separate transactions which are not linked.

TIMING OF OBLIGATIONS

2.80 In general, payment of any LBTT must be made at the same time as the land transaction return is submitted and the land transaction return must be submitted within 30 days of the effective date (see **2.81**) of the transaction (LBTT(S)A 2013, s 29(3) and s 40(2)). The processes for making a return and payment, together with details of the circumstances in which further returns may be needed, are set out in **Chapter 8**.

The effective date

2.81 There is more than one statutory definition of the effective date, covering separate specific circumstances, but they each seek to achieve the same overall result (LBTT(S)A 2013, s 63). In essence, the effective date for a transaction is the earlier of:

- the date of completion – that is, the date of settlement of the transaction, or the date upon which a lease is executed, giving the transaction final legal effect (LBTT(S)A 2013, s 64). In Scotland the date upon which a lease is granted is the date of the last execution of the lease. It is common for both parties to sign the same final lease document. Consequently, unless both parties are present at the same meeting, which would be unusual, one party to the lease will often sign the lease after the other party has signed it. In these circumstances the lease is granted when it has been signed by the last party to sign it. Where a lease is to be constituted by missives of let, and is not to be followed by the grant of a formal lease, the date of conclusion of the missives is the date upon which the lease is granted; and

- the date on which an agreement to enter into a land transaction, under which the transaction is to be completed by a conveyance (see **2.9**), is 'substantially performed' (LBTT(S)A 2013, s 14). This date depends on the nature of the transaction and is the earlier of the following:
  - the date on which the buyer, or a person connected with the buyer, takes possession of the whole or substantially the whole of the property. 'Possession' is not comprehensively defined, but is considered further at **2.82** (LBTT(S)A 2013, s 14(1)(a));
  - the date on which a substantial amount of any consideration is paid or provided (LBTT(S)A 2013, s 14(1)(b)). If the consideration includes payment of rent, this is the earlier of the date on which the first payment of rent is made and the date on which a substantial amount of any other consideration is paid (LBTT(S)A 2013, s 14(3)). For consideration other than rent, a 'substantial amount' means the whole or substantially the whole. Although not set out in the statute, HMRC, in relation to SDLT, consider that 90% or more is substantially the whole, but they reserve the right to argue for a smaller proportion if they believe avoidance of SDLT is involved. In LBTT1005, Revenue Scotland make it clear that what constitutes a 'substantial amount' of the consideration paid or provided for LBTT purposes will be considered on a case-by-case basis. They specifically state that it is not defined by a percentage figure and that an amount less than 90% might be substantial in this context. Consequently, if there is doubt as to whether the quantum of the 'chargeable consideration' (see **2.17**) given for a transaction, in advance of completion, might cause a contract to be 'substantially performed', it is suggested that an opinion (see **8.49**) be sought from Revenue Scotland; or
  - the date on which there is an assignation, sub-sale or other transaction (relating to the whole or part of the property which is the subject of the original contract) as a result of which a person other than the original buyer becomes entitled to call for the property to be transferred, or the lease granted, to him (LBTT(S)A 2013, s14(1)(c)). Such an event does not trigger substantial performance under the equivalent SDLT provisions and is discussed further at **2.83**.

Possession

2.82 The term 'possession' is not comprehensively defined within the legislation. The following explanation sets out the view which HMRC are understood to take in relation to SDLT. HMRC's view is that the purchaser takes possession of the property when he first occupies or uses it, or becomes entitled to occupy or use it. This is not restricted to the time when the purchaser finally moves in, but may include, for example, having the right to enter the property for the purpose of fitting out. In addition, a person also has possession if he receives rents or other profits from the land, or has the right to receive them. It does not matter whether any of these occurs under the terms of the contract governing the transaction, or under a licence (LBTT(S)A 2013, s 14(2)). However, if the buyer already has possession of the property under one interest, before entering into an agreement to acquire a different interest in the same property, the prior possession should not itself cause the agreement to be substantially performed.

In LBTT6002, Revenue Scotland make it clear that what constitutes possession of 'substantially the whole' of the subject-matter of the contract for LBTT purposes will be considered on a case-by-case basis. They specifically state that it is not defined by a percentage figure. Consequently, if there is doubt as to whether a contract has been substantially performed as a result of the buyer taking possession of the property, it is suggested that an opinion (see **8.49**) be sought from Revenue Scotland.

Example 2.24 – Occupation under previous interest

John occupies an office building under a lease which has 25 years to run. The current rent is £100,000 per year, payable quarterly in advance. His landlord is Caroline, who owns the property. John agrees to buy the property from Caroline for £750,000, subject to satisfactory structural survey etc. The agreement provides that John will pay £375,000 within ten days of delivery of the structural survey, and the balance of £375,000 on the date of settlement. The agreement also provides that the final instalment will be reduced by any rent which John pays, and which relates to the period after delivery of the structural survey. John occupies and therefore has possession of the property immediately after the agreement is signed. However, he occupies under the terms of the existing lease and not as a result of entering into the agreement to buy the property. Therefore, the agreement should not be regarded as substantially performed by reason of John's occupation. 50% of the purchase price is paid prior to settlement, or possibly slightly more because of the adjustment of the final instalment to allow for rent paid; however, in the author's view payment of slightly more than 50% of the purchase price should not represent payment of substantially the whole of the purchase price and therefore the agreement should not be regarded as substantially performed until the remaining 50% is paid, on settlement.

Example 2.25 – Receipt of rents as substantial performance

The same fact pattern applies as in **Example 2.24**, except that John's property-holding company Reid and Wright Ltd, rather than John himself, agrees to buy the property from Caroline. As part of the agreement, Reid and Wright Ltd is entitled to receive all rent payable on the property from the date the structural survey is delivered and the £375,000 is paid. The agreement will be regarded as substantially performed on the date that Reid and Wright Ltd becomes entitled to receive the rents which should be the date upon which the structural survey is delivered and payment of the £375,000 is made.

Assignation, sub-sale or other transaction triggering substantial performance of a contract

2.83 Under SDLT a contract to be completed by a conveyance is substantially performed if the buyer takes possession of the whole, or substantially the whole, of the property, or a substantial amount of the consideration is paid, as described above for LBTT. However, under LBTT, there is an additional event which triggers substantial performance of a contract, and that is an assignation, sub-sale or other transaction as a result of which a person other than the original buyer becomes entitled to call for the property to be transferred, or the lease granted, to him (LBTT(S)A 2013, s 14(1)(c)).

Example 2.26 – Assignation of contract triggering substantial performance

On 1 July 2024 Bigbuilder Ltd enters into an agreement to acquire undeveloped land in Scotland from a local authority for a consideration of £2m including VAT. The purchase price is payable on the date of settlement and Bigbuilder Ltd has no rights to enter onto the land, or to any rent or profits from the land, until the date of settlement which is set for 31 March 2025.

Bigbuilder Ltd runs into financial difficulty and on 1 September 2024 assigns its rights and obligations under the agreement to an unrelated property developer, Black and White Ltd, for a consideration of £100,000.

The assignment triggers substantial performance of the agreement between the local authority and Bigbuilder Ltd and Bigbuilder Ltd must file a land transaction return, and pay LBTT of £80,250, by 1 October 2024, even though it has not taken possession of the property or paid any part of the purchase consideration. The LBTT liability is calculated as follows:

Purchase price	*Rate*	*LBTT*
£	%	£
150,000	0	NIL
100,000	1	1,000
1,750,000	5	87,500
2,000,000		88,500

It would seem that the agreement itself would be a 'chargeable interest' for the purposes of LBTT (LBTT(S)A 2013, s 4(2)) and therefore its assignment to Black and White Ltd would potentially be chargeable to LBTT with Black and White Ltd as the buyer. However, as the consideration paid of £100,000 is within the nil tax rate band no LBTT would be payable, and as the agreement is not a 'major interest' in land (LBTT(S)A 2013, s 60) there should be no requirement to file a land transaction return as the chargeable consideration does not exceed the nil rate tax band (LBTT(S)A 2013, s 30(1)(c)).

The substantial performance transaction, the assignment transaction and the completion transaction should not be linked transactions (see **2.79**) as they are not between the same buyer and seller.

When the agreement is completed on 31 March 2025 Black and White Ltd must file a land transaction return by 30 April 2025, however tax is only payable on this transaction to the extent, if any, that the tax chargeable on it is greater than the amount of the tax charged on the substantial performance of the agreement (LBTT(S)A 2013, s 10(3)). As the LBTT payable on the completion transaction should be the same as that on the substantial performance transaction (assuming no change in the LBTT rates and bands), no further tax is payable. As part of the agreement with Bigbuilder Ltd it is possible that Black and White Ltd may require a copy of the land transaction return filed on substantial performance of the contract, to support its land transaction return, filed following settlement of the transaction, showing no tax payable.

Where an agreement for lease (including missives of let not constituting a lease) is substantially performed without the lease having been executed, the provisions of LBTT(S)A 2013, Sch 19, para 25 (Agreement for lease substantially performed etc) apply rather than LBTT(S)A, s 10 (LBTT(S)A 2013, s 10(6) – see **4.84** et seq).

Sub-sale – substantial performance of a contract

2.84 If a sub-sale transaction (as opposed to the assignment of the existing contract) is entered into there will be two potential charges to LBTT, as a charge will potentially arise on the contract between the seller and the original buyer and on the sub-sale contract between the original buyer and the second buyer.

Example 2.27 – Sub-sale triggering substantial performance

The facts are as in **Example 2.26** except that instead of assigning the benefits and obligations of the agreement, Bigbuilder Ltd enters into a contract with Black and White Ltd under which Black and White Ltd agrees to purchase the undeveloped land for £2.1m.

The sub-sale transaction triggers substantial performance of Bigbuilder Ltd's agreement with the Local Authority (LBTT(S)A 2013, s14(1)(c)), and

Bigbuilder Ltd must file a land transaction return and pay LBTT of £88,500 by 1 October 2024. This is subject to the possibility of a claim being made for sub-sale development relief: see below.

On completion of the agreement between the Local Authority and Bigbuilder Ltd, a land transaction return will have to be filed by Bigbuilder Ltd, however no additional tax should be payable, as the liability should be the same as for the substantial performance transaction assuming no change in LBTT rates and bands.

On completion of the agreement between Bigbuilder Ltd and Black and White Ltd a land transaction return will have to be filed by Black and White Ltd, by 30 April 2025, and LBTT of £93,500 paid.

Bigbuilder Ltd may be able to claim sub-sale development relief

The Land and Buildings Transaction Tax (Sub-sale Development Relief and Multiple Dwellings Relief) (Scotland) Order 2015, SSI 2015/123 provides for a 'sub-sale development relief' (see **5.32**) to be available under LBTT, with the legislation to be found in LBTT(S)A 2013, Sch 10A (sub-sale development relief). Under LBTT(S)A 2013, Sch 10A, para 16 the original contract will not be treated as 'substantially performed' if the transaction by which the person other than the original buyer (in this case Black and White Ltd) becomes entitled to call for a conveyance of the property is a 'qualifying sub-sale' within the meaning of LBTT(S)A 2013, Sch 10A, para 3 and sub-sale development relief is to be given to the original buyer.

It is not clear what is meant when the legislation refers to sub-sale development relief being 'given', as LBTT is a self-assessment tax. It is assumed that 'given' should be interpreted as the relief being claimed in a land transaction return. However, if the original contract is not treated as having been 'substantially performed' on entering into the 'qualifying sub-sale' (LBTT(S)A 2013, Sch 10A, para 16) it is likely that Bigbuilder Ltd would have no obligation to file a land transaction at that time, and may not have such an obligation until completion of the contract, which may be months or years later. As a consequence sub-sale development relief would not be claimed by Bigbuilder Ltd at the time of entering into the 'qualifying sub-sale', which would mean that LBTT(S)A 2013, s 14(1)(c) would apply to treat the original contract as having been substantially performed! In the author's view this cannot be the intention behind the legislation. It would seem that where there is to be a time gap between entering into the 'qualifying sub-sale' and the substantial performance (other than by virtue of LBTT(S)A 2013, s14(1)(c)) and completion of the original contract, then Bigbuilder Ltd must assume that sub-sale development relief will be 'given' and only file a land transaction return on the substantial performance (other than under LBTT(S)A 2013, s14(1)(c)) and/or completion of the original contract.

A sub-sale is a 'qualifying sub-sale' if it is a contract under which the first buyer (ie the person who entered into the original contract – Bigbuilder Ltd) contracts to sell the whole or part of the chargeable interest (which is the subject of the original contract) to another person (the 'second buyer' – Black and White Ltd), and the second buyer (Black and White Ltd) becomes entitled to call for a conveyance of the whole or part of the chargeable interest which is the subject of the original contract. In addition, before the first buyer (Bigbuilder Ltd) entered into the sub-sale, the first buyer (Bigbuilder Ltd) must have been entitled to call for a conveyance of the whole or part of the chargeable interest. If sub-sale development relief is available, and is claimed by Bigbuilder Ltd, no LBTT should be payable by Bigbuilder Ltd. Sub-sale development relief can be withdrawn in full, or in part, in certain circumstances (see **5.39**).

TRANSITIONAL PROVISIONS

Disapplication of UK SDLT

2.85

> **Focus**
>
> - Certain land transactions with an effective date on or after 1 April 2015 will still be within the SDLT regime and will not be chargeable to LBTT (see **2.88**).
> - Transitional guidance dated 13 February 2015 ('Land transactions in Scotland – Transitional guidance on the introduction of Land and Buildings Transaction Tax') covering the move from SDLT to LBTT, in relation to land in Scotland, was issued by HMRC with input from Revenue Scotland. The guidance can be found on the Revenue Scotland website. In addition the Scottish Government has made an order known as The Land Buildings Transaction Tax (Transitional Provisions) (Scotland) Order 2014, SI 2014/377 (which was laid before the Scottish Parliament on 19 December 2014) dealing with the transition from an LBTT perspective. Both the transitional guidance and the Order should be consulted when considering the SDLT and LBTT implications of any land transaction which began under SDLT but which may have an 'effective date' (see **2.81**) on or after 1 April 2015.

The Scotland Act 2012 contains provisions at s 29 and Sch 3 for the disapplication of SDLT, in relation to transactions in land situated in Scotland, from a date to be appointed by the Treasury, and the appointed date was 1 April 2015.

The Scotland Act 2012, s 29(2) provides that a chargeable interest, for the purposes of SDLT (FA 2003, s 48) comprises an interest in land in England and Wales or Northern Ireland, but not in Scotland. Consequently, subject to the transitional provisions described below, a transaction in relation to an interest in land situated in Scotland, with an effective date (FA 2003, s 119) which is on or after 1 April 2015, will not be a land transaction for SDLT purposes but will, instead, be within the charge to LBTT (Scotland Act 2012, s 29(4)).

Linked transactions

2.86 Based on the Scotland Act 2012, s 29(2) and (4), and the transitional guidance published by HMRC with input from Revenue Scotland, transactions in land situated in Scotland with an effective date (FA 2003, s 119) on or after 1 April 2015, which would be linked (see FA 2003, s 108) for SDLT purposes, will no longer be linked for SDLT purposes with either:

- a transaction in land which is situated in England and Wales or Northern Ireland; or
- a transaction in land which is situated in Scotland but which is subject to SDLT (see **2.88**).

Example 2.28 – A transaction chargeable to SDLT is not linked to a transaction chargeable to LBTT

An Cala Ltd, as part of a single deal, agrees to acquire two commercial buildings one located in Inverness and the other in Derby, from the same company. The seller is based in Inverness and the effective date (see **2.81**) of the acquisition of both buildings is 28 April 2015.

The acquisition of the building located in Derby is chargeable to SDLT whereas the acquisition of the building in Inverness is chargeable to LBTT. Neither of the transactions is linked (see **2.79**) for the purposes of SDLT or LBTT.

As a separate deal An Cala Ltd also agrees to acquire two office blocks from a company based in London, with one of the office blocks being situated in Glasgow and one in Dundee. The effective date of the acquisition of the Glasgow property is 31 March 2005 whereas the property in Dundee is not acquired until later, the transaction having an effective date of 10 July 2015.

The acquisition of the Glasgow property is chargeable to SDLT whereas the acquisition of the Dundee property is chargeable to LBTT. Neither transaction is linked (see **2.79**) for the purposes of SDLT or LBTT.

Acquisition of land located in both Scotland and the rest of the UK

2.87 Where a transaction in land with an effective date (see **2.81** and FA 2003, s 119) on or after 1 April 2015 includes both land in Scotland and land in England and Wales or Northern Ireland, the acquisition of the land in Scotland is within the charge to LBTT, whereas the acquisition of the land in England and Wales or Northern Ireland is within the charge to SDLT, and the consideration given for the acquisitions should be apportioned on a just and reasonable basis (LBTT(S)A 2013, Sch 2, para 4 and FA 2003, Sch 4, para 4).

Example 2.29 – Apportionment of consideration – acquisition of properties in Scotland and in the rest of the UK

Super Retailer Ltd acquires a number of shops from Discount Retailer Ltd as a single transaction. Some of the shops are situated in England and Wales and some in Scotland. The effective date (see **2.81** and FA 2003, s 119) of the transaction (the date of settlement) is 31 October 2024.

The acquisition of the shops in Scotland is not chargeable to SDLT, but will be within the charge to LBTT. The acquisition of the shops in England and Wales will be within the charge to SDLT. The consideration given for the respective acquisitions should be apportioned on a just and reasonable basis.

Transitional provisions (Scotland Act 2012, s 29(5) and (6))

Land situated in Scotland – transactions to which SDLT continues to apply

2.88 SDLT continues to apply to any transaction in relation to land situated in Scotland, which has an effective date (FA 2003, s 119) on or after 1 April 2015, and which is:

(1) effected under a contract entered into and substantially performed (FA 2003, s 44(5)) on or before 1 May 2012 (the date the Scotland Act 2012 received Royal Assent); or

(2) effected under a contract entered into on or before 1 May 2012 (but not substantially performed on or before 1 May 2012) and not excluded by reason of falling into (a), (b) or (c) below:

   (a) the contract is varied, or there is an assignation of rights under the contract, after 1 May 2012;

   (b) the transaction is effected as a result of the exercise after 1 May 2012 of an option, right of pre-emption or similar right; or

   (c) after 1 May 2012 there is an assignation, sub-sale or other transaction relating to the whole or part of the land which is the subject of the contract, as a consequence of which a person other than the purchaser (buyer) under the contract becomes entitled to call for a conveyance.

The transitional guidance dated 13 February 2015, prepared by HMRC, with input from Revenue Scotland, covering the move from SDLT to LBTT in relation to land in Scotland, includes a useful table of the effect of the transitional provisions. The table is reproduced below.

4. Table to demonstrate the effect of the transitional provisions for land transactions in Scotland

On or before 1 May 2012	2 May 2012 – 31 March 2015	1 April 2015 and after	Tax charge
Conclusion of Missives		Settlement	SDLT on Settlement
Conclusion of Missives + Substantial Performance		Settlement	SDLT on Substantial Performance + SDLT on Settlement*
Conclusion of Missives + Substantial Performance	Variation	Settlement	SDLT on Substantial Performance + SDLT on Settlement*
Conclusion of Missives	Substantial Performance	Settlement	SDLT on Substantial Performance + SDLT on Settlement*
Conclusion of Missives	Variation	Settlement	LBTT on Settlement
Conclusion of Missives	Substantial Performance + Variation	Settlement	SDLT on Substantial Performance + LBTT on Settlement*
Conclusion of Missives		Substantial Performance + Settlement	SDLT on Substantial Performance + SDLT on Settlement*
Conclusion of Missives		Substantial Performance + Variation + Settlement	SDLT on Substantial Performance + LBTT on Settlement*
	Conclusion of Missives	Settlement	LBTT on Settlement
	Conclusion of Missives + Substantial Performance	Settlement	SDLT on Substantial Performance + LBTT on Settlement*
	Conclusion of Missives + Substantial Performance	Variation + Settlement	SDLT on Substantial Performance + LBTT on Settlement*
	Conclusion of Missives	Substantial Performance + Settlement	LBTT on Settlement
	Conclusion of Missives	Substantial Performance + Variation + Settlement	LBTT on Settlement

* An SDLT or LBTT charge on Settlement following Substantial Performance applies only to the extent (if any) that the amount of tax chargeable on it is greater than the amount of tax chargeable on the contract which was substantially performed.

2.89 HMRC have indicated (see transitional guidance issued by HMRC with input from Revenue Scotland dated 13 February 2015) that they will not regard the following post 1 May 2012 events as excluding a transaction from the SDLT regime under Scotland Act 2012, s 29(6) (see point (2) in **2.88**):

- a variation of the completion date specified in the contract;
- a transfer to the nominee or bare trustee of the purchaser (buyer) under the contract.

2.90 Each of the scenarios set out in the table in **2.88** are now considered in turn:

Contracts entered into on or before 1 May 2012

Scenario 1

The missives (exchange of contracts) are concluded on or before 1 May 2012, substantial performance and settlement (completion) take place at the same time but after 1 April 2015. The settlement transaction is within the SDLT regime (Scotland Act 2012, s 29(5)(b) and (6)).

Scenario 2

The missives (exchange of contracts) and substantial performance are concluded/takes place on or before 1 May 2012 and settlement (completion) takes place on or after 1 April 2015. The settlement transaction is within the SDLT regime (Scotland Act 2012, s 29(5)(a)).

Scenario 3

The missives (exchange of contracts) and substantial performance are concluded/takes place on or before 1 May 2012, however this time the contract is varied before 1 April 2015. The variation does not bring the settlement (completion) transaction into the LBTT regime, as the contract was substantially performed on or before 1 May 2012 (Scotland Act 2012, s 29(5)(a)). The settlement (completion) transaction is therefore within the SDLT regime.

Scenario 4

The missives (exchange of contracts) are concluded on or before 1 May 2012, substantial performance takes place after 1 May 2012 but before 1 April 2015, and settlement (completion) takes place after 1 April 2015. As the contract was entered into on or before 1 May 2012, and has not been varied, the settlement (completion) transaction on or after 1 April 2015 is within the SDLT regime (Scotland Act 2012, s 29(5)(b)). As substantial performance took place before 1 April 2015 it will also be within the SDLT regime.

Scenario 5

The missives (exchange of contracts) are concluded on or before 1 May 2012, the contract is varied after 1 May 2012 but before 1 April 2015, and settlement (completion) and substantial performance take place at the same time, but on or after 1 April 2015. As the contract has been varied after 1 May 2012 the settlement (completion) transaction is within the LBTT regime (Scotland Act 2012, s 29(5)(b) and (6)(a)).

Scenario 6

The missives (exchange of contracts) are concluded on or before 1 May 2012, the contract is substantially performed after 1 May 2012 but before 1 April 2015, the contract is then varied before 1 April 2015. Settlement (completion) of the contract takes place on or after 1 April 2015. The substantial performance transaction will fall within the SDLT regime, whilst the settlement (completion) transaction will be within the LBTT regime (Scotland Act 2012, s 29(5)(b)). However, LBTT will only be payable on the settlement (completion) transaction if, and to the extent that, the LBTT chargeable on that transaction exceeds the amount of the charge to SDLT, which was paid to HMRC, on the substantial performance of the contract (The Land and Buildings Transaction Tax (Transitional Provisions) (Scotland) Order 2014, SI 2014/377, art 3(4)).

Scenario 7

The missives (exchange of contracts) are concluded on or before 1 May 2012, there is no variation of the contract, and both substantial performance of the contract and settlement (completion) take place on or after 1 April 2015. Both the substantial performance transaction and the settlement (completion) transaction are within the SDLT regime (Scotland Act 2012, s 29(5)(b)).

Scenario 8

The missives (exchange of contracts) are concluded on or before 1 May 2012, the contract is substantially performed on or after 1 April 2015, but is subsequently varied, after which settlement (completion) takes place. The substantial performance transaction is within the SDLT regime as the missives were concluded on or before 1 May 2012 and there was no variation prior to substantial performance taking place (Scotland Act 2012, s 29(5)(b)). As the contract is then varied the subsequent settlement (completion) transaction is within the LBTT regime. However, LBTT will only be payable on the settlement (completion) transaction if, and to the extent that, the LBTT chargeable on that transaction exceeds the amount of the charge to SDLT, which was paid to HMRC, on the substantial performance of the contract (The Land and Buildings Transaction Tax (Transitional Provisions) (Scotland) Order 2014, SI 2014/377, art 3(4)).

2.91

Contracts entered into after 1 May 2012

Scenario 9

The missives (exchange of contracts) are concluded after 1 May 2012 but before 1 April 2015, and settlement (completion) and substantial performance take place at the same time after 1 April 2015. The settlement (completion) transaction is within the LBTT regime (Scotland Act 2012, s 29(2) and (4)).

Scenario 10

The missives (exchange of contracts) are concluded after 1 May 2012 but before 1 April 2015, the contract is then substantially performed before 1 April 2015, but settlement (completion) takes place after 1 April 2015. As substantial performance takes place before 1 April 2015 it is within the SDLT regime (Scotland Act 2012, s 28(2)). However, as the missives were concluded after 1 May 2012 the post 31 March 2015 settlement (completion) transaction is within the LBTT regime (Scotland Act 2012, s 29(2) and (4)). In these circumstances, LBTT is only payable to the extent that the amount of the LBTT chargeable on the settlement (completion) transaction exceeds the amount of the SDLT chargeable, and paid to HMRC, on substantial performance of the contract (The Land and Buildings Transaction Tax (Transitional Provisions) (Scotland) Order 2014, SI 2014/377, art 4(4)).

Scenario 11

The missives (exchange of contracts) are concluded after 1 May 2012 but before 1 April 2015, the contract is then substantially performed before 1 April 2015, however on or after 1 April 2015 the contract is varied. Sometime after the variation, settlement (completion) of the contract takes place. As substantial performance takes place before 1 April 2015, and prior to the variation of the contract, it is within the SDLT regime (Scotland Act 2012, s 28(2)). As the contract was entered into after 1 May 2012, the variation of the contract has no impact, since the settlement (completion) is in any event within the LBTT regime (Scotland Act 2012, s 29(2) and (4)). However, LBTT is only payable to the extent that the amount of the LBTT chargeable on the settlement (completion) transaction exceeds the amount of the SDLT chargeable, and paid to HMRC, on substantial performance of the contract (The Land and Buildings Transaction Tax (Transitional Provisions) (Scotland) Order 2014, SI 2014/377, art 4(4)).

2.92

Scenario 12

The missives (exchange of contracts) are concluded after 1 May 2012 but before 1 April 2015, and the contract is then substantially performed on or after 1 April 2015, after which settlement (completion) takes place.

Surprisingly the HMRC transitional guidance dated 13 February 2015 indicates that in these circumstances the substantial performance of the contract will not give rise to either SDLT or LBTT obligations. It is clear that the substantial performance of the contract does not fall within the SDLT regime as the contract was entered into after 1 May 2012, and therefore the transitional provisions within the Scotland Act 2012, s 29(5) have no application. However, as the 'effective date' of the land transaction deemed to be effected on substantial performance of the contract (LBTT(S)A 2013, s 10(1) and (2)) is on or after 1 April 2015, it would seem that the deemed transaction should be chargeable to LBTT. The transitional guidance however states that the substantial performance transaction is not chargeable to LBTT. The basis for the analysis set out in the technical guidance may be that LBTT(S)A 2013, s 10 (substantial performance without completion) only applies on the substantial performance of a contract for a 'land transaction' which is to be completed by a conveyance. As the contract was entered into prior to 1 April 2015 it was not a contract for a 'land transaction' for LBTT purposes, because when it was entered into the land in Scotland, which is the subject of the contract, was still a 'chargeable interest' for the purposes of SDLT, and had not become a 'chargeable interest' for LBTT purposes (Scotland Act 2012, s 29(2) and (4)). The subsequent completion of the contract would however give rise to LBTT obligations as that would be the acquisition of a 'chargeable interest' for LBTT purposes with an 'effective date' on or after 1 April 2015. Obviously there would be 'no credit' for any SDLT or LBTT arising from the earlier substantial performance of the contract, as no tax would have been paid.

If this analysis is correct it would mean that a contract for a land transaction, to be completed by a conveyance, could have been entered into before 1 April 2015 and substantially performed (but not completed) on or after 1 April 2015, with no liability to either SDLT or LBTT being crystallised. Whilst this may mean that the buyer would not be able to register title to the land, and may, in law, have no ownership or other rights in relation to the land, there may be circumstances, for example, where the seller and buyer are connected persons, where such a strategy would be feasible. The potential application of the general anti-avoidance rule (see **9.3**) would have to be considered.

The author would suggest that any buyer under a pre-1 April 2015 contract for a land transaction, which is to be completed by a conveyance, who substantially performs the contract (but does not complete the contract at the same time) on or after 1 April 2015, should specifically confirm with Revenue Scotland that no LBTT obligations arise as a consequence of the substantial performance of the contract, making reference to the transitional guidance.

Scenario 13

This scenario is the same as Scenario 12 except that following the substantial performance of the contract, a variation of the contract takes place, after which settlement (completion) occurs. As the contract was entered into after 1 May 2012, the variation has no impact, since the settlement (completion transaction) is in any event within the LBTT regime (Scotland Act 2012, s 29(2) and (4)). As discussed above in relation to Scenario 12 the HMRC transitional guidance states that the substantial performance of the contract should not give rise to any SDLT or LBTT obligations. The author would suggest that any buyer who finds themselves in this position should specifically confirm with Revenue Scotland that no LBTT obligations arise on the substantial performance of the contract.

2.93 The note to the table in **2.88** confirms that where the term 'variation' is used in the table it refers not only to a 'variation' but to any of the disqualifying events prescribed by Scotland Act 2012, s 29(6) (see **2.88**), including inter alia an assignation of rights under the contract or the exercise of an option.

Example 2.30 – Contract entered into post 1 May 2012 but before 1 April 2015 and completed post 31 March 2015

Caroline concludes missives for the purchase of a house in Prestwick on 21 March 2015. The agreement is not substantially performed before the date of settlement and the effective date (see **2.81** and FA 2003, s 119) of the transaction (the settlement date) is on 30 May 2015.

The purchase of the house is within the LBTT regime, and is not chargeable to SDLT, despite the fact that the missives were concluded prior to 1 April 2015. The transitional rules in the Scotland Act 2012, s 29(5) and (6) do not apply as the missives were not concluded on or before 1 May 2012.

Example 2.31 – Contract entered into before 1 May 2012 but completed post 31 March 2015

On 1 April 2012 Pamela concludes missives for the purchase of a completed office block, located in Scotland, before construction begins on 1 May 2012. Completion of the construction work is delayed and, by agreement between the parties, the date of settlement is changed to 1 May 2015. The agreement is not substantially performed before the date of settlement and the effective date (FA 2003, s 119) of the acquisition of the office block (the date of settlement) is 1 May 2015.

The acquisition is subject to SDLT since it falls within the transitional provisions (Scotland Act 2012, s 29(5)(b) and (6)), as the missives were concluded before 1 May 2012, and none of the exclusions in Scotland Act 2012, s 29(6) should apply. In particular the change in the date of settlement is not treated as a variation of the contract within Scotland Act 2012, s 29(6) (see HMRC transitional guidance dated 13 February 2015).

Example 2.32 – Substantial performance of a contract before 1 April 2015 with completion post 1 April 2015

Andrew concludes missives for the purchase of a retail unit in Dumfries on 28 February 2015, for a consideration of £300,000 and with the date of settlement agreed for 1 May 2015. The agreement is substantially performed (see FA 2003, s 44(5)(a)) on 14 March 2015 when Andrew goes into the retail unit to undertake the fit-out.

The substantial performance of the agreement will be within the charge to SDLT as the contract is treated as if it were the transaction governed by the contract and the effective date (FA 2003, s 119) of the transaction is when the contract is substantially performed, namely 14 March 2015.

However, as the date of settlement takes place on 1 May 2015, that transaction will have an effective date of 1 May 2015 (LBTT(S)A 2013, s 63(1)(a)) which means it will be within the LBTT regime, and will not be chargeable to SDLT. The transitional rules in the Scotland Act 2012, s 29(5) and (6) do not apply as the missives were concluded after 1 May 2012. However, Andrew is only required to pay LBTT in relation to the settlement transaction if, and to the extent that, the LBTT chargeable on the completion transaction exceeds the amount of the SDLT chargeable, and paid to HMRC, on substantial performance of the contract (Land and Buildings Transaction Tax (Transitional Provisions) (Scotland) Order 2014, SI 2014/377, art 4(4)).

However, even if no LBTT is payable, Andrew will have an obligation to file an LBTT land transaction return by 31 May 2015 (LBTT(S)A 2013, ss 6(a), 10(3)(a) and 30(1)).

Focus

- The Land and Buildings Transaction Tax (Transitional Provisions) (Scotland) Order 2014, SI 2014/377 and the HMRC transitional guidance issued on 13 February 2015 include transitional rules to deal with specific provisions within the SDLT and LBTT legislation.

Specific provisions

Contract providing for conveyance to a third party (FA 2003, s 44A and LBTT(S)A 2013, s 11)

2.94 Under SDLT FA 2003, s 44A applies where a contract is entered into pursuant to which a chargeable interest in land is to be conveyed by (A) at the request of (B), either to (B) or (C) in circumstances where only (A) and (B) are party to the contract.

If such a contract is substantially performed (FA 2003, s 44(5)) on or before 1 May 2012 (the day on which the Scotland Act 2012 came in force) and, at the request of (B), (A) becomes obliged to convey the land to (B), or a conveyance is made under a contract between (B) and (C), such transactions will be subject to SDLT even if the effective date (FA 2003, s 119) of the transaction is on or after 1 April 2015 (see paragraph 6.2 of the HMRC transitional guidance on the move from SDLT to LBTT and Scotland Act 2012, s 29(5)(a)).

Where such a contract is entered into on or before 1 May 2012, but not substantially performed by that date, a conveyance from (A) to (B), or a conveyance under a contract between (B) and (C) will be subject to SDLT if the effective date (FA 2003, s 119) of the transaction is on or after 1 April 2015, and none of the exclusions set out at **2.88** (Scotland Act 2012, s 29(6)) applies to the contract. However, if any of the exclusions set out at **2.88** do apply, and the effective date (see **2.81**) of the transaction is on or after 1 April 2015, a conveyance from (A) to (B), or a conveyance under a contract between (B) and (C), will be subject to LBTT (see paragraph 6.3 of the HMRC transitional guidance on the move from SDLT to LBTT and Scotland Act 2012, s 29(5)(b)). If the contract was substantially performed before 1 April 2015, and tax has been paid to HMRC in respect of that substantial performance, LBTT is only payable on the conveyance to the extent (if any) that the LBTT chargeable is greater than the SDLT chargeable, and paid to HMRC, on the substantial performance transaction (Land and Buildings Transaction Tax (Transitional Provisions) (Scotland) Order 2014, SI 2014/377, art 3(4)).

Finally, if such a contract is entered into after 1 May 2012, a conveyance from (A) to (B), or a conveyance under a contract between (B) and (C), will not be subject to SDLT if the effective date (see **2.81** and FA 2003, s 119) of the transaction is on or after 1 April 2015. Such transactions will be within the LBTT regime (see para 6.4 of the HMRC transitional guidance on the move from SDLT to LBTT). If the contract was substantially performed before 1 April 2015, and tax has been paid to HMRC in respect of that substantial performance, LBTT is only payable on the conveyance to the extent (if any) that the LBTT chargeable is greater than the SDLT chargeable, and paid to HMRC, on the substantial performance transaction (Land and Buildings Transaction Tax (Transitional Provisions) (Scotland) Order 2014, SI 2014/377, art 4(4)).

Pre-completion transactions (FA 2003, s 45 and Sch 2A)

2.95 FA 2003, Sch 2A applies where a person (the original purchaser) enters into a contract (the original contract) for the acquisition of an interest in UK land under which the acquisition is to be completed by a conveyance and, before that contract is substantially performed or completed, there is 'a pre-completion transaction'. For these purposes a 'pre-completion transaction' is a transaction which results in a person other than the original purchaser (the transferee) becoming entitled to call for a conveyance to him of the whole or part of the UK land interest to be acquired under the original contract. A pre-completion transaction can either be an 'assignment of rights' or a 'free standing transfer'. A pre-completion transaction will be 'an assignment of rights' if the entitlement of the transferee to call for the conveyance is made to him is an entitlement to exercise rights under the original contract ie the original contract has been assigned in whole or in part to the transferee. A pre-completion transaction which is not an assignment of rights is a 'free standing transfer', and this term would therefore include a sub-sale or a novation of the original contract.

The transitional rules in relation to such pre-completion transactions then operate as follows:

If the assignment or free standing transfer transaction is completed or substantially performed by the 'transferee' (ie the person other than the original buyer who is now entitled to call for a conveyance) on or after 1 April 2015 neither the completion of the assignment or free standing transfer transaction, nor a transaction (sub-sale) or notional transaction (for the purposes of FA 2013, Sch 2A on an assignment of rights) entered into by 'the transferor', will be subject to SDLT. For these purposes the transferor in relation to a pre-completion transaction is the party to the pre-completion transaction who immediately before the pre-completion transaction took place was entitled to call for a conveyance of the interest in UK land which was the subject matter of the pre-completion transaction ie in most cases the original purchaser (see para 7.2 of the HMRC transitional guidance on the move from SDLT to LBTT).

Unless the original contract was substantially performed on or before 1 May 2012, the assignment of rights or free standing transfer transaction will mean that the substantial performance and completion of the original contract on or after 1 April 2015 will be excluded from SDLT by virtue of the Scotland Act 2012, s 29(6)(c) (see **2.88**).

Instead, if the assignment of rights or free standing transfer transaction is entered into on or after 1 April 2015 LBTT will be chargeable both on the original buyer in relation to the substantial performance of the original contract, as that original contract will be treated as having been substantially performed under LBTT(S)A 2013, s 14(1)(c) (see **2.83** et seq), and on the substantial performance and completion of the further agreement ie the assignment, sub-sale or novation. This is subject to the availability of sub-sale development relief – see **5.32**.

This analysis seems contrary to the analysis in Scenario 12 in **2.92** as the substantial performance on or after 1 April 2015, of a pre-1 April 2015 contract, is stated to be chargeable to LBTT, whereas the analysis in Scenario 12 is that no charge to LBTT arises. Again any buyer in this position should seek specific confirmation of the LBTT analysis from Revenue Scotland.

If the pre-completion transaction (ie the assignment of rights or free standing transfer transaction) is entered into before 1 April 2015 it is considered that LBTT(S)A 2013, s 14(1)(c) should not apply, but the subsequent completion of both the original contract and the free-standing transfer transaction (sub-sale or novation), on or after 1 April 2015, will be chargeable to LBTT. This is subject to the availability of sub-sale development relief – see **5.32**.

Options (FA 2003, s 46 and LBTT(S)A 2013, s 12)

2.96 If an option or pre-emption right over land in Scotland is acquired before 1 April 2015, the exercise of the option or pre-emption right on or after 1 April 2015 will not be within the SDLT regime, regardless of whether or not the grant and exercise of the option would have been linked transactions (FA 2003, s 108) for SDLT purposes, but for the fact that land in Scotland is not a chargeable interest for the purposes of SDLT on or after 1 April 2015 (see **2.86**). The exercise of the option will potentially be chargeable to LBTT (see paragraph 8.2 of the HMRC transitional guidance on the move from SDLT to LBTT). As regards the treatment of the exercise of an option for LBTT purposes (see **2.10**).

If the option or pre-emption right is acquired on or after 1 April 2015 both the acquisition of that right, and any subsequent exercise, will be chargeable to LBTT and may be linked transactions (see **2.79**).

Exchanges (FA 2003, s 47 and LBTT(S)A 2013, s 57)

2.97 Where on or after 1 April 2015 land in England and Wales or Northern Ireland is exchanged for land in Scotland, the acquisition of the land in England and Wales or Northern Ireland will be within the SDLT regime, whilst the acquisition of the land in Scotland will be within the LBTT regime. As the acquisition of land in Scotland is not a land transaction for SDLT purposes, the SDLT exchange provisions (FA 2003, s 47 and Sch 4, para 5) will not apply, and SDLT will be charged on the consideration given for the land in England and Wales or Northern Ireland under the normal rules (FA 2003, Sch 4, paras 1 and 7) (see para 9.2 of the HMRC transitional guidance on the move from SDLT to LBTT).

Equally, as the acquisition of the land in England and Wales or Northern Ireland will not be a land transaction for LBTT purposes, the LBTT exchange provisions (LBTT(S)A 2013, s 13 and Sch 2, paras 5 and 6 – see **2.31**) will not apply. LBTT will be charged on the acquisition of the land in Scotland by reference to the market value of the land in England and Wales or Northern Ireland given as consideration (LBTT(S)A 2013, Sch 2, para 7), plus the amount of any equality money or other consideration given by the buyer of the land in Scotland (see paragraph 9.5 of the HMRC transitional guidance on the move from SDLT to LBTT).

2.98 Where the transfer of land in England and Wales or Northern Ireland takes place before 1 April 2015, and the transfer of the land in Scotland takes place on or after 1 April 2015, neither the SDLT nor the LBTT exchange provisions will apply (see paragraph 9.3 of the HMRC transitional guidance on the move from SDLT to LBTT).

2.99 In contrast, where the transfer of land in Scotland takes place before 1 April 2015 and the transfer of land in England and Wales or Northern Ireland takes place on or after 1 April 2015, both transactions will be within the SDLT regime, and the SDLT exchange provisions apply (FA 2003, s 47 and Sch 4, para 5) (see para 9.8 of the HMRC transitional guidance on the move from SDLT to LBTT).

Example 2.33 – Exchange of a property in England for one located in Scotland

A company (A Ltd) decides to relocate its head office from England to larger premises in Scotland, and enters into an agreement on 1 March 2015 with another unrelated company (B Ltd) to exchange A Ltd's offices in England for an office block in Scotland, and to pay £750,000 equality money. The agreement is not substantially performed (see **2.7**) before the date of settlement which takes place on 30 June 2015.

A Ltd's acquisition of the premises in Scotland is within the LBTT regime, however the LBTT exchange provisions (see **2.31**) do not apply as the sale of the English property is not a land transaction for LBTT purposes, as the right over the English property is not a chargeable interest for the purposes of LBTT(S)A 2013, s 4(2). The consideration chargeable to LBTT will be the market value of the property in England plus £750,000.

B Ltd's acquisition of the offices in England will be within the SDLT regime, however the SDLT exchange provisions will not apply as the sale of the Scottish property is not a land transaction for SDLT purposes (Scotland Act 2012, s 29(2) and (4)). The consideration chargeable to SDLT will be the market value of the property in Scotland given as consideration (FA 2003, Sch 4, para 7).

Contingent, uncertain or unascertained consideration (FA 2003, s 51 and LBTT(S)A 2013, ss 18 and 19)

2.100 If a transaction is within the SDLT regime, the obligation to adjust the chargeable consideration when, on or after 1 April 2015, a contingency ceases or consideration is ascertained (FA 2003, s 80) remains in place and is not affected by the introduction of LBTT. Similarly the provisions relating to the deferment of SDLT (FA 2003, s 90) remain unchanged. The contingency ceasing or the consideration becoming ascertained, in relation to such a transaction, will not be subject to LBTT (see para 10.1 of the HMRC transitional guidance on the move from SDLT to LBTT).

Sale and leaseback transaction (FA 2003, s 57A and LBTT(S)A 2013, Sch 3)

2.101 Where the effective date (FA 2003, s 119) of a sale (or lease) of land situated in Scotland is before 1 April 2015 but the effective date (see **2.81**) of the grant back of the lease (or sub-lease) is on or after 1 April 2015, the sale (or lease) transaction will be within the SDLT regime, however the lease (or sub-lease) back transaction will be within the LBTT regime. This means that neither the SDLT nor the LBTT exchange provisions will apply (see **2.97**).

For SDLT purposes the chargeable consideration for the sale (or lease) transaction will be the consideration given in money or money's worth for the sale (or lease), including the market value, if any, of the lease (or sub-lease) granted back.

For LBTT purposes the grant of the lease (or sub-lease) back on or after 1 April 2015 will potentially be within the LBTT sale and leaseback relief provisions in LBTT(S)A 2013, Sch 3 (see **5.23**) and therefore, provided all of the requisite conditions are satisfied, the grant of the lease back would be exempt from the charge to LBTT, despite the fact that the sale (or lease) transaction took place before 1 April 2015 (see paragraph 11.2 of the HMRC transitional guidance on the move from SDLT to LBTT).

Multiple dwellings relief (FA 2003, Sch 6B and LBTT(S)A 2013, Sch 5)

2.102 Where a transaction (or linked transactions) comprise multiple dwellings situated in both Scotland and England and Wales or Northern Ireland, the rate of SDLT payable on a claim for multiple dwellings relief is calculated according to the number of dwellings the acquisition of which is subject to SDLT (see para 12.1 of the HMRC transitional guidance on the move from SDLT to LBTT).

Similarly, the LBTT payable on a claim for multiple dwellings relief is calculated based on the number of dwellings the acquisition of which is subject to LBTT.

Example 2.34 – Claim for multiple dwellings relief where properties are acquired in both Scotland and in the rest of the UK

Property Investments Ltd acquires eight new houses from the same developer on 30 September 2024. It plans to let the eight houses out to a third party. Four of the houses are in Kendal with two costing £200,000 each and two costing £400,000 each. The other four houses are in Aberdeen with two costing £600,000 each and two costing £500,000 each.

Only the four houses in Kendal are chargeable to SDLT, a claim for multiple dwellings relief is made and therefore the rate of SDLT is determined by dividing the aggregate consideration for the Kendal houses of £1,200,000 by the number of dwellings chargeable to SDLT of four, giving an average price per dwelling of £300,000. As the purchaser is a company, and the 'chargeable consideration' is £40,000 or more, the additional 3% rate of SDLT applies to the acquisition of the four properties situated in England such that the SDLT charge per dwelling is calculated as follows:

Purchase Price	*Rate*	*SDLT*
£	%	£
250,000	3	7,500
50,000	8	4,000
300,000		11,500

Based on four dwellings the SDLT payable is therefore £46,000 (4 × £11,500). However, if this amount is less than 1% of the total dwellings consideration then the SDLT payable is that 1% amount.

Total dwellings consideration of £1,200,000 × 1% = £12,000.

Consequently the SDLT payable is £46,000.

Note: As none of the properties are acquired for chargeable consideration of more than £500,000 the 15% rate of SDLT in FA 2003, Sch 4A is not in point.

Similarly, if a claim for multiple dwellings relief is made, the LBTT chargeable on the purchase of the four houses in Aberdeen is determined by dividing the aggregate consideration for the Aberdeen houses of £2,200,000, by the number of dwellings chargeable to LBTT of four, such that the LBTT is determined based on an average consideration of £550,000. As the buyer is a company and the 'relevant consideration' (see **2.57**) is £40,000 or more, the ADS will apply to the acquisition of the four Scottish properties. The LBTT charge per dwelling is therefore calculated as follows:

Purchase Price	*Rate*	*LBTT*
£	%	£
145,000	6	8,700
105,000	8	8,400
75,000	11	8,250
225,000	16	36,000
550,000		61,350

Based on four dwellings the LBTT charge would be £245,400 (4 × £61,350)

This is subject to the 'minimum prescribed amount' being 25% of the LBTT which would have been payable if multiple dwellings relief had not been available (see **5.25**).

If multiple dwellings relief had not been available the LBTT charge would have been as follows:

Purchase price	*Rate*	*LBTT*
£	%	£
145,000	6	8,700
105,000	8	8,400
75,000	11	8,250
425,000	16	68,000
1,450,000	18	261,000
2,200,000		354,350
The 'minimum prescribed amount' is therefore 25% × £354,350		£88,587

In this instance therefore the minimum prescribed amount does not apply and the LBTT payable is £245,400.

2.103 If a claim for SDLT multiple dwellings relief was made in relation to a transaction which included land in Scotland, the 'Adjustment for change of circumstances' provisions in FA 2003, Sch 6B, para 6 continue to apply to the transaction even if the event which triggers the adjustment occurs on or after 1 April 2015 (see para 12.2 of the HMRC transitional guidance on the move from SDLT to LBTT).

Group relief, reconstruction and acquisition reliefs (FA 2003, s 62 and Sch 7)

2.104 Where group relief, reconstruction relief or acquisition relief have been claimed in relation to a transaction within the SDLT regime, and the transaction included land situated in Scotland, the provisions relating to the withdrawal of the relevant relief will continue to apply even if the event giving rise to the withdrawal takes place on or after 1 April 2015 (see paragraph 13.1 of the HMRC transitional guidance on the move from SDLT to LBTT). In these circumstances a further return must be submitted by letter to Birmingham Stamp Office in accordance with SDLTM50400 and any payment of SDLT made to HMRC.

Charities relief (FA 2003, s 68 and Sch 8)

2.105 Where charities relief has been claimed in relation to a transaction within the SDLT regime, and the transaction included land situated in Scotland, the provisions relating to the withdrawal of the relief will continue to apply even if the event giving rise to the withdrawal takes place on or after 1 April 2015 (see paragraph 14.1 of the HMRC transitional guidance on the move from SDLT to LBTT). In these circumstances a further return must be submitted by letter to Birmingham Stamp Office in accordance with SDLTM50400 and any payment of SDLT made to HMRC.

Shared ownership leases (FA 2003, s 70 and Sch 9)

2.106 Where the grant of a shared ownership lease in relation to a dwelling located in Scotland was subject to SDLT (and a market value election has not been made), any 'staircasing transaction' following which the lessee does not hold a total share of the dwelling which exceeds 80% is exempt from the charge to SDLT (see para 15.1 of the HMRC transitional guidance on the move from SDLT to LBTT).

Any 'staircasing transaction' in relation to a dwelling situated in Scotland which takes the lessee's total share of the dwelling over 80%, or the acquisition of the ownership of the land, will be exempt from SDLT if the effective date of the transaction is on or after 1 April 2015 (see para 15.2 of the HMRC transitional guidance on the move from SDLT to LBTT).

Alternative property finance (FA 2003, s 72 and s 72A and LBTT(S) A 2013, Sch 7)

2.107 The Scotland Act 2012, Sch 3, para 10 omitted from the SDLT legislation FA 2003, s 72 (alternative property finance in Scotland: land sold to financial institution and leased to person) and s 72A (alternative property finance in Scotland: land sold to financial institution and person in common) with effect from 1 April 2015. As a consequence, if the effective date (FA 2003, s 119) of the third transaction (s 72) or further transaction (s 72A) under arrangements falling within those sections is on or after 1 April 2015, those transactions will be neither chargeable to SDLT nor notifiable for the purposes of SDLT (see paragraph 16.1 of the HMRC transitional guidance on the move from SDLT to LBTT).

Alternative property finance relief is available under LBTT (see **5.30**). The Scottish Government has ensured that a party entering into a land transaction in connection with an alternative property finance arrangement prior to 1 April 2015, in relation to land situated in Scotland, is not disadvantaged by the move from SDLT to LBTT, by making subordinate legislation providing that neither a third transaction under FA 2003, s 72 nor a further transaction under FA 2003, s 72A, with an effective date on or after 1 April 2015, will be chargeable to LBTT, provided that the conditions mentioned respectively in FA 2003 s 72(4) and s 72A(4) have been met (Land and Buildings Transaction Tax (Transitional Provisions) (Scotland) Order 2014, SI 2014/377, art 5).

Alternative finance investment bonds (FA 2009, Sch 61 and FA 2003, s 73C and LBTT(S)A 2013, Sch 8)

2.108 A land transaction in relation to land located in Scotland and which is a 'first transaction' within the meaning of FA 2009, Sch 61, para 6 will be exempt from SDLT if the effective date (FA 2003, s 119) of the transaction is before 1 April 2015 and the conditions for the relief are satisfied. In such circumstances SDLT will become chargeable if the relief is withdrawn on or after 1 April 2015 under FA 2009, Sch 61, para 7(3) (see para 17.1 of the HMRC transitional guidance on the move from SDLT to LBTT).

A transaction which is a 'second transaction' for the purposes of FA 2009, Sch 61 para 8 will be exempt from SDLT if the 'effective date' of the transaction is before 1 April 2015 and the conditions in para 8 are satisfied (see para 17.2 of the HMRC transitional guidance on the move from SDLT to LBTT).

In either case the transaction will be not be subject to SDLT if the effective date (see **2.81**) is on or after 1 April 2015 (see para 17.3 of the HMRC transitional guidance on the move from SDLT to LBTT).

Relief for alternative finance investment bonds is also available under LBTT (LBTT(S)A 2013, Sch 8). The Scottish Government has ensured that a party entering into a land transaction in connection with an alternative finance investment bond prior to 1 April 2015, in relation to land situated in Scotland, is not disadvantaged by the move from SDLT to LBTT, by making subordinate legislation providing that the second transaction for the purposes of FA 2009, Sch 61, para 8 with an effective date on or after 1 April 2015 will not be chargeable to LBTT provided that the conditions in FA 2009, Sch 61, para 8(1)(a) and (b) have been met (Land and Buildings Transaction Tax (Transitional Provisions) (Scotland) Order 2014, SI 2014/377, art 6).

Anti-avoidance (FA 2003, s 75A)

2.109 The general anti-avoidance provision within the SDLT legislation will only apply to a disposal and acquisition of land in Scotland if the effective date of the notional transaction (FA 2003, s 75A(6)) is before 1 April 2015 (see para 18.1 of the HMRC transitional guidance on the move from SDLT to LBTT).

The effective date of the 'notional transaction' is the earlier of: (a) the last date of completion for the 'scheme transactions' (broadly the transactions which are involved in connection with the disposal and acquisition), and (b) the last date on which a contract in respect of the 'scheme transactions' is substantially performed.

Later linked transactions (FA 2003, s 81A and s 108)

2.110 Where a land transaction in relation to land situated in Scotland has an effective date (FA 2003, s 119) before 1 April 2015 but it is not notifiable for SDLT purposes (FA 2003, s 77) and the transaction becomes notifiable on or after 1 April 2015 by reason of a later linked transaction (FA 2003, s 108), which does not relate to land in Scotland, the pre 1 April 2015 transaction remains chargeable to SDLT and a land transaction return must be filed in accordance with FA 2003, s 81A (see para 19.1 of the HMRC transitional guidance on the move from SDLT to LBTT). In these circumstances a paper SDLT 1 form must be submitted to Birmingham Stamp Taxes notifying the pre 1 April 2015 transaction, with a covering letter (see SDLTM 50350, para 3), and the effective date of the transaction is the effective date of the later linked transaction. The special Code 8998 should be entered in Box 29 of the SDLT 1 form, and not a Scottish local authority code (see para 19.2 of the HMRC transitional guidance on the move from SDLT to LBTT).

If the pre 1 April 2015 transaction in relation to land situated in Scotland has been notified but SDLT, or more SDLT, becomes payable as a result of the post 1 April 2015 linked transaction in relation to land in England and Wales or Northern Ireland, then a further SDLT1 form must be submitted by letter to Birmingham Stamp Taxes in accordance with SDLTM 50350, paras 1 and 2 (see para 19.3 of the HMRC transitional guidance on the move from SDLT to LBTT).

Partnerships (FA 2003, s 104 and Sch 15 and LBTT(S)A 2013, Sch 17)

2.111 FA 2003, Sch 15, para 17 is an anti-avoidance provision which applies where land in the UK is contributed to a partnership (which is not a 'property-investment partnership') by a partner, or a person who becomes a partner as a consequence of the contribution, or a person connected with a partner or a person who becomes a partner as a consequence of the contribution and there is subsequently a transfer of an interest in that partnership under arrangements which were in place at the time the land was transferred to the partnership. Para 17 treats the transfer of the interest in the partnership as a land transaction chargeable to SDLT, whereas a transfer of an interest in a partnership, which is not a property-investment partnership, would not normally be chargeable to SDLT.

If, in these circumstances, the land transferred to the partnership includes land situated in Scotland, then to that extent the transfer of the interest in the partnership will not be subject to SDLT if the effective date of the transfer of the interest in the partnership is on or after 1 April 2015, even if the transfer of the land to the partnership took place before 1 April 2015 (see para 20.1 of the HMRC transitional guidance on the move from SDLT to LBTT).

However, the LBTT legislation includes a similar anti-avoidance provision (see **6.27**), and the Scottish Government have made subordinate legislation to ensure that the transfer of the interest in the partnership will be chargeable to LBTT, even if the contribution of the land in Scotland took place prior to 1 April, 2015. Consequently, where the effective date of the land transfer referred to in FA 2003, Sch 15 para 17(1)(a) is before 1 April 2015 and the transfer of the interest in the partnership referred to in FA 2003, Sch 15, para 17(1)(c) is on or after 1 April 2015, the earlier land transfer will be treated for the purposes of LBTT(S)A 2013, Sch 17, para 17 as though it were the land transfer referred to in LBTT(S)A 2013, Sch 17, para 17(1)(a), such that the provisions of LBTT(S) A 2013, Sch 17, para 17 will apply to the transfer of the partnership interest – see **6.27** (Land and Buildings Transaction Tax (Transitional Provisions) (Scotland) Order 2014, SI 2014/377, art 7).

2.112 In certain circumstances, where land is transferred by a partner or a person who becomes a partner as a consequence of the contribution or a person connected with a partner or a person who becomes a partner as a consequence of a contribution, to a partnership, and within three years of the land transfer the transferring partner withdraws money or money's worth from the partnership which does not represent income profit, or the partner (or a person connected with a partner) has made a loan to the partnership and that loan is to any extent repaid, or the partner withdraws money or money's worth which does not represent income profit, then a charge to SDLT can arise (FA 2003, Sch 15, para 17A).

Where the 'effective date' (FA 2003, s 119) of the later deemed land transaction (ie the date the money or money's worth is withdrawn or the loan is repaid) would be on or after 1 April 2015, the deemed land transaction will not be chargeable to SDLT, even if the transfer of land to the partnership took place before 1 April 2015 (see para 20.3 of the HMRC transitional guidance on the move from SDLT to LBTT). However, the Scottish Government has made subordinate legislation to ensure that such a deemed land transaction will be chargeable to LBTT.

The land transfer to the partnership which took place prior to 1 April 2015 will be treated for the purposes of LBTT(S)A 2013, Sch 17, para 18 as if it were the land transfer mentioned in LBTT(S)A 2013, Sch 17, para 18(1) and the withdrawal of money or money's worth which does not represent income profit, or the repayment of the loan on or after 1 April 2015, will be treated as though it were a 'qualifying event' for the purposes of LBTT(S)A 2013, Sch 17 para 18(2) (Land and Buildings Transaction Tax (Transitional Provisions) (Scotland) Order 2014, SI 2014/377, art 8.) As a consequence the provisions of LBTT(S)A 2013, Sch 17, para 18 will apply – see **6.17**.

LBTT(S)A 2013, Sch 17, paras 25 and 26 (see **6.23**) determine the partnership share attributable to a partner where an interest in land situated in Scotland is transferred from a partnership. It is provided that paras 25 and 26 will have effect even though the relevant date for the purposes of para 26(1) is prior to 1 April 2015. However, any references to obligations to pay tax under LBTT(S) A 2013, shall have no effect – see **6.23** (Land and Buildings Transaction Tax (Transitional Provisions) (Scotland) Order 2014, SI 2014/377, art 9).

Leases (FA 2003, s 120 and Sch 17A)

Leases that continue after a fixed term (FA 2003, Sch 17A, para 3 and LBTT(S)A 2013, Sch 19, para 20)

2.113 FA 2003, Sch 17A, para 3 provides that where a lease continues beyond its fixed term, it is treated as a lease for the original fixed term plus one year longer than the original fixed term and so on. Where, as a consequence of the deemed extension of the lease SDLT, or more SDLT, becomes payable, an SDLT land transaction return or further return must be filed within 30 days of the last day of the one year period concerned (FA 2003, Sch 17A, para 3(4)).

Where the lease which is treated as continuing beyond its fixed term as described above was granted before 1 April 2015, and is a lease over land situated in Scotland, the lease remains subject to SDLT, even if the period for which the lease is treated as having been extended includes a period on or after 1 April 2015 (see para 21.1 of the HMRC transitional guidance on the move from SDLT to LBTT).

If the deemed extension of the lease on or after 1 April 2015 causes the lease to become notifiable for the first time, an SDLT 1 form must be filed in the normal way (SDLTM 12050 para 1), the effective date of the transaction is the last day of the one-year period giving rise to the notification requirement and code 8998, and not a Scottish local authority code, must be entered at Box 29.

If the grant of the lease has already been notified but the deemed extension of the lease causes additional SDLT to become payable, notification should be made by way of a letter to Birmingham Stamp Taxes (see SDLTM 12050 para 2ff) and the additional SDLT should be paid.

Leases for an indefinite term (FA 2003, Sch 17A, para 4)

2.114 A lease for an indefinite term (for example a lease for life – see SDLTM 18715 or a lease the duration of which is subject only to a period of notice) is treated in the first instance as though it were a lease for a fixed term of one year and, if the lease continues beyond that first year it is treated as a lease for a fixed term of two years, and so on.

Where a lease of land in Scotland is for an indefinite term, and is granted before 1 April 2015, it will continue to be liable to SDLT even if its deemed term continues beyond 1 April 2015 (see para 21.2 of the HMRC transitional guidance on the move from SDLT to LBTT). In these circumstances the deemed extension of the lease will not be subject to LBTT.

Example 2.35 – Lease for an indefinite term treated as granted before 1 May 2012

George enters into a verbal contract for a lease of an office in Glasgow at a market rate rent. The verbal contract is 'substantially performed' (see **2.7**) by the first payment of rent on 1 April 2012. FA 2003, Sch 17A, para 19(3) treats the verbal contract as the grant of a lease, beginning on the date of substantial performance.

The grant of the lease is within the SDLT regime and it remains within that regime after 1 April 2015 so long as it continues from year to year, and an SDLT land transaction return must be filed, or notification given, if SDLT becomes payable or additional tax becomes due (FA 2003, Sch 17A, para 4).

Successive linked leases (FA 2003, Sch 17A, para 5 and LBTT(S)A 2013, Sch 19, para 23)

2.115 Where successive leases are granted of the same premises, and the grants of the leases are linked for SDLT purposes, SDLT applies as though there was a single lease granted at the time the first lease in the series was granted, for a term equal to the aggregate of the terms of all of the leases in the series, and in consideration of the rent payable under all of the leases in the series (FA 2003, Sch 17A, para 5).

Any lease over land in Scotland, where the effective date of the grant of the lease is on or after 1 April 2015 cannot be treated as successive to a lease over the same premises granted before 1 April 2015, as the later lease is not a land transaction for SDLT purposes (Scotland Act 2012, s 29(2) and (4)). However, the grant of the lease on or after 1 April 2015 will be within the LBTT regime (see para 21.3 of the HMRC transitional guidance on the move from SDLT to LBTT).

Adjustment where rent ceases to be uncertain (FA 2003, Sch 17A, para 8)

2.116 Where the rent payable under a lease subject to SDLT is contingent, uncertain or unascertained FA 2003, Sch 17A, para 8 provides for a reassessment of the SDLT chargeable on the lease to be made either: (a) at the end of the fifth year of the term of the lease, or (b) when the rent payable in respect of the first five years of the term of the lease ceases to be uncertain at an earlier date.

Where such a lease over land situated in Scotland is granted before 1 April 2015 and under the provision of para 8, SDLT, or more SDLT, becomes payable on or after 1 April 2015, the lease remains subject to SDLT. An SDLT1 form or further return, must be filed within 30 days of the end of the fifth year of the term of the lease or, if earlier, the date on which the amount of rent payable in the first five years ceases to be uncertain (see para 21.4 of the HMRC transitional guidance on the move from SDLT to LBTT).

If as a result the grant of the lease becomes notifiable for the first time, an SDLT 1 form must be submitted in the usual way, the effective date of the transaction is the date prescribed by FA 2003, Sch 17A, para 8(1) and (3) and code 8998, and not a Scottish Local authority code, must be entered at Box 29.

If the grant of the lease has already been notified but the effect of the reassessment of the SDLT payable is that additional tax becomes payable, notification should be made by letter to Birmingham Stamp Taxes – see SDLTM 18525.

Overlap relief (FA 2003, Sch 17A, para 9 and LBTT(S)A 2013, Sch 19, para 24)

2.117 Both the SDLT and LBTT legislation give overlap relief (see **4.92**) where A surrenders (renounces) an existing lease (the old lease) to B and in consideration of that surrender (renunciation) B grants a lease to A (the new lease) of the same or substantially the same premises.

Where a lease of land in Scotland which was granted before 1 April 2015, is renounced on or after that date and, as consideration for that renunciation, a new lease of the same or substantially the same premises is granted, the grant of the new lease will be within the LBTT regime, and will not be chargeable to SDLT (see para 21.5 of the HMRC transitional guidance on the move from SDLT to LBTT).

To ensure that the party entering into the new lease is not disadvantaged by the move from SDLT to LBTT the Scottish Government has made subordinate legislation which provides that where the old lease was granted before 1 April 2015, and the new lease is granted on or after 1 April 2015, the rent chargeable to LBTT on the grant of the new lease will be reduced by the rent which was charged to SDLT for the period of the overlap of the two leases – see **4.92** (Land and Buildings Transaction Tax (Transitional Provisions) (Scotland) Order 2014, SI 2014/377, art 10).

Backdated leases granted to tenant holding over (FA 2003, Sch 17A, para 9A and LBTT(S)A 2013, Sch 19, para 21)

2.118 For SDLT purposes where the tenant under a lease continues in occupation beyond the fixed term of the lease, the tenant is granted a new lease of the same premises, and the term of the lease is stated to begin immediately after the contractual termination date of the previous lease, the term of the new lease is treated as beginning on the stated date ie immediately following the termination of the previous lease.

Where the effective date of the grant of a new lease over land in Scotland, in circumstances where an earlier lease has continued beyond the fixed term, is on or after 1 April 2015, but the term of the new lease is stated to begin from the termination date of the previous lease, which date is before 1 April 2015, the new lease will not be subject to SDLT. However, the grant of the new lease over land in Scotland on or after 1 April 2015 will be within the LBTT regime (see para 21.6 of the HMRC transitional guidance on the move from SDLT to LBTT).

Assignment of a lease on or after 1 April 2015 where the lease was granted before 1 April 2015

2.119 Where a lease of land in Scotland was granted before 1 April 2015 and is assigned on or after 1 April 2015, the assignation is not chargeable to SDLT, but may be subject to LBTT if a premium is actually paid, or deemed to be paid (see **2.28** et seq regarding when a deemed premium might arise) for the assignation (see para 21.7 of the HMRC transitional guidance on the move from SDLT to LBTT).

Assignment of lease treated as the grant of a new lease (FA 2003, Sch 17A, para 11 and LBTT(S)A 2013, Sch 19, para 27)

2.120 Both the SDLT and LBTT legislation provide that where the grant of a lease is exempt from the charge to the respective taxes because one of a number of specified reliefs is claimed, the first assignation of that lease which is not so exempt, is taxed as though it were the grant of a new lease (see **4.35** et seq).

Where the lease of land in Scotland is granted before 1 April 2015, an assignation of the lease on or after 1 April 2015 will not be subject to SDLT and the provisions of FA 2003, Sch 17A, para 11 will not apply to tax the assignation as though it were the grant of a new lease (see para 21.8 of the HMRC transitional guidance on the move from SDLT to LBTT). However, the Scottish Government has made subordinate legislation to provide that where a lease of land in Scotland was granted before 1 April 2015 and it was relieved or exempt from SDLT as one of the reliefs specified in FA 2003, Sch 17A, para 11 applied, the first assignment of that lease, if it takes place on or after 1 April 2015, which is not exempt from LBTT as none of the reliefs specified in LBTT(S)A 2013, Sch 19, para 27(3) apply, will be charged to LBTT as though it were the grant of a new lease (Land and Buildings Transaction Tax (Transitional Provisions) (Scotland) Order 2014, SI 2014/377, art 11).

Variations of leases – increases of rent treated as grant of a new lease (FA 2003, Sch 17A, para 13)

2.121 Under SDLT, where a lease is varied so as to increase the amount of the rent payable as from a date before the end of the fifth year of the lease, the variation is treated for SDLT purposes as if it were the grant of a new lease in consideration of the additional rent now payable (FA 2003, Sch 17A, para 13). This rule does not apply to any increase in the rent payable as a consequence of a provision within the lease.

A variation of a lease of land in Scotland falling within the above provision will not be treated as the grant of a new lease for SDLT purposes where the effective date of the grant of the deemed new lease would be on or after 1 April 2015 (see para 21.9 of the HMRC transitional guidance on the move from SDLT to LBTT).

However, the Scottish Government has made subordinate legislation providing that where the effective date of the grant of the deemed new lease would have been on or after 1 April 2015, had the provisions of FA 2003, Sch 17A, para 13 continued to apply to the lease, that the increase in rent will be charged to LBTT as though it were the grant of a new lease and the chargeable consideration for LBTT purposes (other than in respect of any premium) will be the additional rent payable (Land and Buildings Transaction Tax (Transitional Provisions) (Scotland) Order 2014, SI 2014/377, art 12). The deemed new lease, if it is notifiable on grant, or it subsequently becomes notifiable, will then be subject to the three-yearly review process outlined at **4.17** et seq. In the author's view this should mean that any subsequent change to the additional rent which is treated as being the consideration given for the grant of the deemed new lease will be within the charge to LBTT. However, the rent payable under the lease, prior to the post 31 March 2015 variation to the lease, should not be within the charge to LBTT.

Revenue Scotland has confirmed this view in LBTT Technical Bulletin 1 issued on 14 October 2016. In that Bulletin Revenue Scotland give the following example:

> 'So, if the original lease started off at £1000 per month, but included terms for a rise to £1200 per month (or provided for rent reviews within parameters), and subsequently an amendment was made to the lease to set the rent at £1500 per month, the additional rent would be the difference between £1500 and the £1200, that is, £300.'

The author interprets this example as meaning that when the lease was granted prior to 1 April 2015, within the SDLT regime, it provided for a rent of £1,000 per month but the terms of the lease also provided for the rent to increase to £1,200 per month. On or after 1 April 2015 the terms of the lease were varied such that the rent was increased to £1,500 per month. The additional rent chargeable to LBTT is therefore £300 per month.

Missives of let (FA 2003, Sch 17A, para 19(2) and LBTT(S)A 2013, Sch 19, para 26)

2.122 FA 2003, Sch 17A, para 19(2) deals with the situation where a lease is initially constituted by concluded missives of let (the first lease) and at some later time a lease is executed (the second lease). The equivalent legislation within the LBTT regime is LBTT(S)A 2013, Sch 19, para 26 (see **4.81**).

Where the first lease is constituted by concluded missives of let before 1 April 2015, and the second lease is executed on or after that date, the provisions of FA 2003, Sch 17A, para 19(2) do not apply as the second lease is not subject to SDLT and cannot be linked with the first lease. However, the second lease will be subject to LBTT and LBTT(S)A 2013, Sch 19, para 26 will apply to the second lease despite the fact that the first lease was constituted by concluded missives of let prior to 1 April 2015 (see para 21.10 of the HMRC transitional guidance on the move from SDLT to LBTT).

Increase in the term of a lease or the extension of the land demised under the lease is treated as the grant of a new lease (FA 2003, s 43(3)(d)(i))

2.123 Where a lease of land in Scotland is granted prior to 1 April 2015, there is a variation of the lease on or after 1 April 2015 so as to increase the term of the lease or to extend the land demised under the lease (which under English property law is likely to be treated as the grant of a new lease) and, if that variation had taken place before 1 April 2015, it would have been treated as the grant of a new lease for SDLT purposes, then the variation of the lease is treated as the grant of a new lease for LBTT purposes (see para 21.9 of the HMRC transitional guidance on the move from SDLT to LBTT). The consideration chargeable to LBTT, other than in respect of a premium, is the amount of the additional rent payable over the increased term of the lease or the additional rent payable in relation to the additional land now demised under the lease (Land and Buildings Transaction Tax (Transitional Provisions) (Scotland) Order 2014, SI 2014/377, art 13). The deemed new lease, if it is notifiable on grant, or it subsequently becomes notifiable, will then be subject to the three-yearly review process outlined at **4.17** et seq. In the author's view this should mean that any subsequent change to the additional rent which is treated as being the consideration given for the grant of the deemed new lease will be within the charge to LBTT. However, the rent payable under the lease, prior to the post 31 March 2015 variation to the lease, should not be within the charge to LBTT.

Revenue Scotland has now confirmed this view in LBTT Technical Bulletin 1 issued on 14 October 2016. In that Bulletin Revenue Scotland give the following example:

> 'So, if the original lease started off at £1000 per month, but included terms for a rise to £1200 per month (or provided for rent reviews within parameters), and subsequently an amendment was made to the lease to set the rent at £1500 per month, the additional rent would be the difference between £1500 and the £1200, that is, £300.'

The author interprets this example as meaning that when the lease was granted prior to 1 April 2015, within the SDLT regime, it provided for a rent of £1,000 per month but the terms of the lease also provided for the rent to increase to £1,200 per month. On or after 1 April 2015 the terms of the lease were varied such that the rent was increased to £1,500 per month. The additional rent chargeable to LBTT is therefore £300 per month.

Agreement for lease substantially performed prior to 1 April 2015 but lease granted on or after 1 April 2015

2.124 LBTT Technical Bulletin 1 (para 5.3) issued on 14 October 2016 confirms that where an agreement for lease in relation to non-residential property situated in Scotland was 'substantially performed' for SDLT purposes before 1 April 2015, but the lease is then granted on or after 1 April 2015, the grant of the lease is potentially chargeable to LBTT. If the relevant notification criteria are satisfied (see **4.11** et seq) then there would be a requirement to file a land transaction return in relation to the grant of the lease and subsequently carry out three-yearly reviews of the LBTT chargeable (see **4.17** et seq). However, LBTT would only be chargeable on the grant of the lease to the extent that the LBTT payable was greater than the amount of the SDLT paid to HMRC on the 'substantial performance' of the agreement for lease (Land and Buildings Transaction Tax (Transitional Provisions) (Scotland) Order 2014, SI 2014/377, art 4).

General Anti-avoidance Rule (RSTPA 2014, s 62)

2.125 The general anti-avoidance rule (GAAR) applies in relation to any tax avoidance arrangement which is 'artificial' (see **9.3**) and which is entered into on or after 1 April 2015.The GAAR applies to the devolved taxes. Where the tax avoidance arrangement forms part of any other arrangements entered into before 1 April 2015, those other arrangements are to be ignored unless taking account of those arrangements would mean that the arrangement would not be 'artificial' (RSTPA 2014, s 72(2) and (3) – see **9.4**).

The UK general anti-abuse rule found in FA 2013, ss 206–215 will continue to apply to any land transaction within the SDLT regime but will not apply to any land transaction within the LBTT regime.

Chapter 3

Key Differences between LBTT and SDLT

SIGNPOSTS

Summarises the key differences between LBTT and SDLT which are as follows:

- Lower nil tax rate threshold for residential property under LBTT.
- Different tax rates and bands under LBTT compared to SDLT.
- Non-resident surcharge under SDLT.
- Differences between the 'additional dwellings supplement' under LBTT and the higher rates of SDLT on the acquisition of additional dwellings and dwellings purchased by companies and certain trusts.
- Registration of land transactions and payment of LBTT.
- No general sub-sale relief but there is a 'sub-sale development relief'.
- Leases – requirement for three-yearly review, and a review on assignation or termination, of the tax payable under LBTT.
- The grant, assignation or renunciation of a lease over residential property is exempt from LBTT unless it is an 'ultra-long lease' which was converted to ownership on 28 November 2015.
- Anti-Avoidance – SDLT specific anti-avoidance rule (FA 2003, s 75A) not imported into LBTT.
- Scottish general anti-avoidance rule wider in scope, with fewer safeguards, compared to the UK general anti-abuse rule.
- Potential charge to LBTT on transfers of shares in a 'residential property holding company'.
- Multiple Dwellings Relief can reduce the LBTT payable where two or more dwellings are acquired but not to less than 25% of the tax that would have been payable had the relief not been available.
- Acquisition relief reduces the LBTT charge to 12.5% of the tax that would have been payable had the relief not been available.

- The grant, assignation or renunciation of a licence to use or occupy land is an exempt transaction under LBTT whereas under SDLT such a licence is an exempt interest.
- The administration of the taxes – the period for launching and closing an enquiry, the period for raising a discovery assessment and penalties for non-compliance.

3.1 LBTT is similar to SDLT in many respects and the LBTT legislation borrows heavily from the corresponding SDLT law. In particular, LBTT is a self-assessment tax charged on the consideration given for land transactions. It is payable by the buyer, generally within 30 days of the 'effective date' (see **2.48**) of the transaction. The rules to determine the occasions of charge and the amount of consideration closely parallel those for SDLT. As with SDLT, any VAT payable will be included in the measure of consideration, thus increasing the effective rate of tax for a business which is able to recover VAT as input tax (see **2.21**). Most SDLT reliefs are imported into LBTT, normally with similar rules and conditions, although some have been omitted (for example, there is no general sub-sale relief).

There are however some significant differences between LBTT and SDLT and these are outlined in the following paragraphs and discussed throughout the book.

It should always be borne in mind that LBTT is not simply SDLT with a different name and that Revenue Scotland may take a different approach to the interpretation of the LBTT legislation, compared to the approach taken by HMRC in relation to SDLT, even where the legislation is the same or very similar.

LOWER NIL TAX RATE THRESHOLD FOR RESIDENTIAL PROPERTY

3.2 The nil rate tax band for transactions in relation to residential property, at or below which no tax will be charged, is £105,000 lower under LBTT (£145,000) than under SDLT (£250,000). The nil rate tax band is, however, only available if the additional dwellings supplement does not apply (see **2.37** et seq).

DIFFERENT TAX RATES AND BANDS UNDER LBTT COMPARED TO SDLT

3.3 It is understood that the Scottish government's original plans were to collect broadly the same amount of tax under LBTT as the UK government would have collected, in Scotland, under SDLT. However, the proposed tax rates and bands announced by the Scottish Government on 9 October 2014 were set at such a level that there would be winners and losers with purchases at the lower end of the market paying less tax, and those at the higher end of the market paying more tax, compared to SDLT. Subsequent to the release of the proposed LBTT tax rates and bands, the Chancellor of the Exchequer announced that with effect from 4 December 2014 a progressive tax structure would apply for the purposes of SDLT, in relation to the acquisition of residential property, and the new SDLT tax rates and bands would have resulted in an SDLT rate of 5% applying to that part of the purchase price above £250,000 compared to an LBTT rate of 10%. In response to the change in the SDLT tax structure and tax rates and bands, the Scottish Government announced on 21 January 2015 that the proposed LBTT tax rates and bands, in relation to residential property, would be revised. The revised tax rates and bands were specified in the Land and Buildings Transaction Tax (Tax Rates and Tax Bands) (Scotland) Order 2015, SSI 2015/126 and are set out at **2.35** above. The LBTT rates and bands for residential property remain unchanged; however the non-residential rates and bands were varied on 25 January 2019 by the Land and Buildings Transaction Tax (Tax Rates and Tax Bands etc) (Scotland) Amendment Order 2018, SSI 2018/372.

The SDLT nil-rate band was increased from £125,000 to £250,000 with effect from 23 September 2022. Therefore, for a purchase by individual(s) that does not attract the non-resident surcharge (see **3.3B**), there is no point at which the liability under LBTT is less than that under SDLT. If the purchase attracts the non-resident SDLT surcharge (which does not apply for LBTT purposes), then the LBTT liability will be less than the equivalent SDLT liability where the chargeable consideration is less than £471,668 or greater than £2,360,000.

As regards non-residential property, LBTT will never be more than the equivalent SDLT charge as the bands are the same for both taxes, but LBTT applies a 1% rate between £150,000 and £250,000, whereas SDLT applies a 2% rate. There will therefore always be a maximum of £1,000 difference in favour of LBTT.

Set out below are examples comparing the LBTT and SDLT liabilities, for both residential and non-residential property purchases, at different levels of purchase price. These examples demonstrate that at the higher end of the market the LBTT charge in relation to residential property is significantly higher than the equivalent SDLT charge, reflecting the Scottish government's view that purchases at that level should bear a higher tax burden.

Residential property

House purchase costing £250,000 – assumes that an individual is replacing their main residence so that neither the 'additional dwellings supplement' (LBTT) or the higher rate of SDLT on additional dwellings (SDLT) apply.

3.3 *Key Differences between LBTT and SDLT*

LBTT

Purchase Price	*Rate*	*LBTT*
£	%	£
145,000	0	NIL
105,000	2	2,100
250,000		2,100

SDLT

Purchase Price	*Rate*	*SDLT*
£	%	£
250,000	0	NIL
250,000		NIL

There is no basic SDLT charged on the first £250,000, whereas LBTT begins to be charged above £145,000.

House purchase costing £750,000 – this time the assumption is that both the 'additional dwellings supplement' (LBTT) and the higher rate of SDLT on additional dwellings apply.

LBTT

Purchase Price	*Rate*	*LBTT*
£	%	£
145,000	6	8,700
105,000	8	8,400
75,000	11	8,250
425,000	16	68,000
750,000		93,350

SDLT

Purchase Price	*Rate*	*SDLT*
£	%	£
250,000	3	7,500
500,000	8	40,000
750,000		47,500
=======		=====

The LBTT charge is 196% of the equivalent SDLT charge.

Non-residential property

Commercial property purchase costing £175,000

LBTT

Purchase Price	*Rate*	*LBTT*
£	%	£
150,000	0	Nil
25,000	1	250
175,000		250

SDLT

Purchase Price	*Rate*	*SDLT*
£	%	£
150,000	0	Nil
25,000	2	500
175,000		500

The LBTT charge is 50% of the equivalent SDLT charge.

Commercial property purchase costing £5,000,000

LBTT

Purchase Price	*Rate*	*LBTT*
£	%	£
150,000	0	NIL
100,000	1	1,000
4,750,000	5	237,500
5,000,000		238,500

SDLT

Purchase Price	*Rate*	*SDLT*
£	%	£
150,000	0	Nil
100,000	2	2,000
4,750,000	5	237,500
5,000,000		239,500

The SDLT charge is 0.4% higher than the equivalent LBTT charge.

Under SDLT a rate of 15% applies to the whole of the chargeable consideration where a company, or a partnership with one or more corporate members or a collective investment scheme acquires a dwelling for chargeable consideration of more than £500,000 (FA 2003, Sch 4A). There are however a number of exceptions from that penal rate where, for example, the dwellings are held by property traders and developers or for the purposes of a property development business. The LBTT rates for residential property, including the top rate of 15% (assuming the 'additional dwellings supplement' applies) apply, on a progressive basis, irrespective of the category of buyer.

RELIEF FOR FIRST-TIME BUYERS

3.3A The Scottish Government introduced a relief for first-time buyers of a dwelling in Scotland which applies to transactions in relation to which the contract is entered into on or after 9 February 2018 and where the 'effective date' (see **2.81**) of the transaction is on or after 30 June 2018. If the relief is available it effectively increases the zero tax threshold for first-time buyers from £145,000 to £175,000 (see **5.31A** et seq). First-time buyers acquiring a property for more than £175,000 can also claim the relief on the portion of the price up to £175,000. This means that all first-time buyers can benefit from the relief by up to £600 (£175,000 – £145,000 × 2%). The legislation dealing with the relief can be found in LBTT(S)A 2013, Sch 4A (introduced by the Land and Buildings Transaction Tax (First-Time Buyer Relief) (Scotland) Order 2018). The relief must be claimed in a land transaction return or in an amendment to a land transaction return.

Under SDLT, a relief is available where a first-time buyer purchases their first home and the 'chargeable consideration' is not more than £625,000. If the relief is available, the rate of SDLT on the first £425,000 of consideration is 0% and on any balance of the consideration up to £625,000 the rate of SDLT is 5%. If the chargeable consideration for the transaction (or a series of 'linked transactions') exceeds £625,000, no relief is available, and the normal rates of SDLT apply to the full amount of the chargeable consideration. The legislation dealing with the relief can be found in FA 2003, s 57B and Sch 6ZA (introduced by FA 2018, s 41). The relief must be claimed in a land transaction return or in an amendment to a land transaction return.

NON-RESIDENT SURCHARGE

3.3B From 1 April 2021, the rates of SDLT must be increased by 2% where residential property is acquired by a buyer who is not resident in the UK.

This surcharge applies to purchases of both freehold and leasehold property, as well as increasing the SDLT payable on rents on the grant of a new lease.

The surcharge also applies to certain UK resident companies that are controlled by non-UK residents.

The surcharge does not apply to purchases of non-residential property or mixed transactions unless Multiple Dwellings Relief is claimed.

There is no similar surcharge under LBTT.

GRANT OF A NEW LEASE – TAX PAYABLE ON RENT

3.4 In relation to the grant of a new lease, under both LBTT and SDLT, the net present value of the rent payable over the term of the lease is determined and that net present value amount is then subject to tax, however the rates and bands are different under LBTT compared to SDLT.

LBTT

Residential property

Exempt from LBTT – see **4.4** et seq.

Non-residential property

Net present value of rent payable	Rate of tax
Up to £150,000	Nil
Over £150,000 up to £2,000,000	1%
Above £2,000,000	2%

SDLT

Residential property

Net present value of rent payable	Rate of tax
Up to £250,000	Nil
Over £250,000	1%

Non-residential property

Net present value of rent payable	Rate of tax
Up to £150,000	Nil
Over £150,000 up to £5,000,000	1%
Over £5,000,000	2%

Loss of zero rate band on premium

Under LBTT if a lease of non-residential property is granted for both a premium and rent, and the annual rent amounts to £1,000 or more, the nil rate band for a premium of up to £150,000 is not available and is replaced with a 1% tax rate. This is no longer the case under SDLT as the equivalent SDLT provision was abolished for transactions with an 'effective date' on or after 17 March 2016.

DIFFERENCES BETWEEN THE 'ADDITIONAL DWELLINGS SUPPLEMENT' UNDER LBTT AND THE HIGHER RATES OF SDLT ON THE ACQUISITION OF ADDITIONAL DWELLINGS AND DWELLINGS PURCHASED BY COMPANIES AND CERTAIN TRUSTS

3.5 At the Autumn Statement 2015 the UK Chancellor of the Exchequer announced that on or after 1 April 2016 higher rates of SDLT (3% added to the tax rate for each tax band) would apply to purchases of additional residential properties, such as second homes and buy-to-let properties. In fact the SDLT legislation is much wider than the policy description and, for example, applies to first and subsequent purchases of residential properties by companies and certain trusts. In response to the Chancellor's announcement, and ostensibly to avoid distortions in the property market between Scotland and the rest of the UK, the Scottish government announced that it would also introduce a higher rate of LBTT (referred to below as the 'additional dwellings supplement' (ADS)) for purchases of additional residential properties but, like its SDLT equivalent, it is also much wider than the policy description and it applies to first and subsequent purchases of residential properties by:

- companies;
- individuals acquiring a dwelling as part of a business of investing or dealing in land (either conducting the business as a sole trader or as a partner in a partnership); and
- certain trusts.

There are however some important differences between the two regimes. The LBTT rates, if the ADS applies, are shown at **2.35** and the ADS regime is covered in detail at **2.37** et seq.

The principal differences between the two regimes are as follows:

- The broad thrust of both regimes is that neither the ADS nor the higher rates of SDLT apply to the acquisition of a dwelling by an individual if that transaction involves an individual replacing his or her only or main residence (see 2.44). However, under ADS, if the additional 6% tax rate is not to apply, an individual must either have sold his previous only or main residence within the 36-month period prior to the acquisition of the replacement only or main residence, or must sell that previous only or main residence within the period of 36 months following the acquisition of the replacement only or main residence. The equivalent period under SDLT is also three years before or three years after the acquisition of the replacement only or main residence.
- The ADS can apply to a non-residential property transaction (see 2.35), or a number of linked non-residential property transactions, if the transaction or transactions involve the acquisition of one or more dwellings (see 2.68 and Example 2.19). A common example of such a transaction is the acquisition of a shop with a residential flat above the shop. Where

the ADS does apply to a non-residential property transaction the 6% supplement is applied to that part of the 'relevant consideration' (see 2.57) attributable, on a just and reasonable apportionment, to the dwelling or dwellings acquired. The higher rates of SDLT do not apply to the acquisition of a dwelling as part of a non-residential property transaction (or a number of 'linked' non-residential property transactions), and such a transaction (or transactions) will be charged at the SDLT rates for non-residential property.

- Under the ADS regime, if six or more dwellings are acquired as part of a single transaction it is possible to make a claim in the land transaction return to exempt the transaction from the ADS, such that the transaction will be charged at the LBTT non-residential property rates (see 2.36 and 2.68). If a claim for multiple dwellings relief (see 5.25 et seq) is then made in relation to such a transaction, the calculation of the tax due in relation to a dwelling, based on the average consideration given for the dwellings, is made using the normal LBTT rates for residential property and the ADS does not apply (see 2.69 and Example 2.20). Under SDLT if six or more dwellings are acquired as part of a single transaction that transaction is automatically a non-residential property transaction (FA 2003, s 116(7)) and the SDLT rates for non-residential property transactions apply to calculate the SDLT liability. However, if a claim is then made for multiple dwellings relief in relation to such a transaction, the tax due in relation to a dwelling, based on the average consideration given for the dwellings, is calculated using the higher rates of SDLT for residential property (ie the additional 3% SDLT rates apply when making this calculation).

- When an individual acquires more than one dwelling as part of a single transaction, and one of the dwellings is a replacement of that individual's only or main residence (see 2.44), the ADS only applies to the other dwelling or dwellings acquired which are not replacements of the individual's only or main residence (see 2.57). In these circumstances the 'relevant consideration' (see 2.57) excludes so much of the 'chargeable consideration' (see 2.17 et seq) for the transaction as is attributable, on a just and reasonable apportionment, to the acquisition of ownership of the dwelling that the individual intends to use as their only or main residence. Under SDLT, where an individual acquires more than one dwelling as part of a single transaction, and assuming that the relevant conditions for the higher rates of SDLT to apply are satisfied, those higher rates of SDLT will apply to the acquisition of all of the dwellings, even if one of the dwellings being acquired is a replacement of the individual's only or main residence. The SDLT legislation does not allow there to be a combination of higher rates and normal residential rates applied to dwellings acquired under a single transaction, and the transaction will either be a 'higher rates transaction' (ie subject to the higher rates of SDLT) or it won't.

- Under SDLT where, for example, an individual is acquiring, as part of a single transaction, two dwellings one of which is 'subsidiary' (within the meaning of FA 2003, Sch 4ZA, para 5(5)) to the other, which means that it is within the grounds of, or within the same building as, the main dwelling, and the consideration apportioned to the 'subsidiary dwelling' is less than one third of the aggregate consideration given for both dwellings, the transaction will only be chargeable to the higher SDLT rates if the individual has another dwelling and is not replacing their main residence. This is the so called 'granny flat' exemption. There is no similar exemption under LBTT and therefore the ADS would be charged on the acquisition of the 'subsidiary' dwelling but not on the main dwelling, on the basis that the individual was replacing their main residence.

- The higher rates of SDLT do not apply to the acquisition of an interest in a dwelling if that interest is subject to a lease that has an unexpired term of more than 21 years as at the 'effective date' of the transaction under which the dwelling is acquired. There is no similar provision within the ADS legislation. However, it would be very rare in Scotland for a lease, with a term of more than 21 years, to be granted over residential property.
- Under LBTT, when deciding whether the buyer owns more than one dwelling at the end of the day which is the 'effective date' (see 2.81) of the transaction, any dwelling owned by a buyer's cohabitant is treated as owned by the buyer. For these purposes a person is a buyer's cohabitant if the two of them live together as though married to one another. This is not the case under SDLT as the purchaser is not treated as owning any dwelling owned by their cohabitant.
- If the relevant conditions are satisfied (see 2.37 et seq) the ADS applies to a chargeable transaction (see 2.12) where the missives for the transaction were concluded on or after 28 January 2016 if the 'effective date' (see 2.81) of the acquisition of the dwelling is on or after 1 April 2016. Under SDLT, if the relevant conditions are satisfied, the higher rates of SDLT will apply to the acquisition of a dwelling where the 'effective date' of the transaction is on or after 1 April 2016 (FA 2016, s 117(5)). However, the higher rates of SDLT do not apply where the contract for the acquisition of the dwelling was (a) entered into and 'substantially performed' before 26 November 2015, or (b) entered into before 26 November 2015 and not excluded by virtue of certain events occurring on or after 26 November 2015 (FA 2016, s 117(6)).

REGISTRATION OF LAND TRANSACTIONS AND PAYMENT OF LBTT

3.6 Whilst the collection and administration of LBTT is the responsibility of Revenue Scotland, the Keeper of the Registers of Scotland need not register title in relation to a notifiable transaction until the tax obligations (ie the land transaction return has been filed and any LBTT payable has been paid) have been dealt with by the buyer (LBTT(S)A 2013, s 43(1) and The Land and Buildings Transaction Tax (Ancillary Provision) (Scotland) Order 2014, SI 2014/376).

Differences in land law and practice between Scotland and the rest of the UK (in Scotland ownership of land does not pass until the registration of the ownership change has taken place) have historically meant that there was usually an impetus to register a change of owner of land in Scotland as soon as possible, frequently on the same day as the transaction. This should now be less of an issue following the Land Registration etc (Scotland) Act 2012 which came into force on 8 December 2014, and which, inter alia, introduced the concept of an 'advance notice' to provide protection, for a period of 35 days, for a deed that is intended to be registered in the Land Register (this is discussed further in the paragraph below). Despite this protection it is common for the land transaction return to be filed and LBTT to be paid immediately after, or very soon after, the 'effective date' (see **2.81**) of a transaction, (even though the tax need only be paid within 30 days of the 'effective date' of the transaction) although in relation to payment this only requires that 'arrangements satisfactory' to Revenue Scotland (see **8.25**) are in place at that date.

The technicalities of conveying land in Scotland are beyond the scope of this book. However, in a Scottish conveyancing transaction the seller receives the money (or other consideration) from the buyer in return for a personal right, and a real right is only created when the deed is registered in the land register. This means that there is likely to be a period of time (however short) between the settlement of the transaction and payment of the consideration and the registration of the deed in the land register. During that period the buyer is at risk of (a) the seller becoming insolvent, or (b) a competing deed over the same land being entered in the register first. The solution to this 'gap risk period' was the introduction by the Land Registration etc (Scotland) Act 2012, with effect from 8 December 2014, of the 'advance notice scheme'. Under this scheme an advance notice can be registered in the land register creating a 'protected period' of 35 days from (a) an inhibition registered against the seller in the Register of Inhibitions, and (b) a competing deed granted by the seller to a third party being registered before the deed granted to the buyer. The protected period begins the day after the advance notice is entered in the land register and continues in force for 35 calendar days. It is not possible to extend or renew the protected period and if it expires before settlement and registration of the deed a new advance notice would need to be sought. The advance notice does not have the effect of freezing the register in any way but instead gives preference to the protected deed. Where an advance notice has been registered this could in principle mean that there is not quite the same impetus to register a land transaction (and therefore file any land transaction return and pay any LBTT due); however, in practice, as ownership is not secured until registration takes place, it is likely that the registration application will be made at as early a date as possible

In general under SDLT, if the transaction is notifiable, the purchaser must file a land transaction return and obtain an SDLT 5 certificate from HMRC, before the effect of the transaction can be registered in the Land Registry. However, there is no requirement to pay the tax at the time the land transaction return is filed, as the tax need only be paid within the 14-day period from the 'effective date' of the transaction.

NO GENERAL SUB-SALE RELIEF BUT THERE IS A 'SUB-SALE DEVELOPMENT RELIEF'

3.7 Although most of the reliefs available under SDLT have been imported into LBTT, the one major omission is the relief which was most widely used for what was seen as being unacceptable tax mitigation – so called 'sub-sale relief' under FA 2003, s 45 and Sch 2A. By omitting the relief from the LBTT rules, the Scottish Government and Revenue Scotland have doubtless saved themselves a lot of trouble. However, sub-sale relief is not only relied upon for unacceptable tax mitigation. Under SDLT it has also been an important factor in arrangements to finance speculative development, which includes most private residential building, and in so called forward funding transactions where a developer identifies a site but then sells it on to an institutional investor or owner occupier prior to development. The omission of a general sub-sale relief may have a detrimental effect on this part of the Scottish economy.

Whilst there is no general sub-sale relief within LBTT the Scottish Government has introduced a much narrower relief known as 'sub-sale development relief'. The relief is only available where at the time of the filing of the land transaction return in relation to the substantial performance (see **2.7**) or completion of the first contract the first buyer has entered into a 'qualifying sub-sale' and a 'significant development' is to take place on the land, within five years of the date of the 'qualifying sub-sale' transaction. The relief will be withdrawn, or partially withdrawn, if the 'significant development' is not actually completed, or only part of the 'significant development' is completed, within the requisite five year period.

This relief is considered in detail at **5.32** et seq.

Assignment of a contract before substantial performance/completion

3.8 It should however be noted that there is a form of more general sub-sale relief within the LBTT legislation due to the fact that the assignation of a contract (which is to be completed by a conveyance), before its substantial performance and completion, triggers 'substantial performance' of that contract (LBTT(S)A 2013, s 14(1)(c)). As a consequence, the contract is treated as if it were the transaction provided for in the contract, and the 'effective date' of the deemed land transaction is the date of substantial performance (LBTT(S) A 2013, s 10(1) and (2)). Any LBTT payable in relation to the deemed land transaction will be payable by the original buyer within 30 days of the 'effective date' (see **2.81**) of the deemed land transaction (LBTT(S)A 2013, ss 29(3) and 40(2)). Following the assignation it will be the assignee who will complete the contract, and completion of the contract will also be a notifiable transaction, however LBTT will only be payable by the assignee to the extent (if any) that the LBTT payable on completion is greater than that which was paid by the original buyer on substantial performance of the contract (LBTT(S)A 2013, s10(3)). Therefore, if the consideration payable on completion is the same as that payable under the contract at the time of its assignation, and no LBTT reliefs applied at substantial performance but not at completion, and assuming no change in LBTT bands and rates, no further LBTT should be payable by the assignee. In such circumstances only one charge to LBTT will have arisen, although it will have been paid by the assignor (ie the original buyer) rather than the assignee. This is similar to the position had a general sub-sale relief been available, however here it is the assignee which has not incurred an LBTT liability, whereas under sub-sale relief it would have been the original buyer who would have been relieved from paying LBTT. See **2.83** and **Example 2.26**.

Whilst it may not always be commercially possible or acceptable to assign an existing contract, consideration could be given to such a strategy if a person other than the original buyer may look to get the benefit of the contract. In these circumstances it would be necessary to ensure that under the terms of the contract it is possible for the original buyer to assign the contract. If the prospective assignee is unhappy with some of the terms of the existing contract it may be possible to vary the terms of the contract, without giving rise to an LBTT liability, either before or after the assignment.

This does however mean that LBTT may become payable at a date earlier than that which might have been expected, and at a time when the assignor may not have the funds to pay the LBTT, as the assignee may not have made any payment for the assignation.

LEASES

3.9 The special rules for leases are contained in LBTT(S)A 2013, Sch 19. In principle, the manner of charging LBTT on the grant of a new lease will be similar to that under SDLT. Tax will be calculated separately on the rent and on any premium, and the two amounts added to give the initial tax bill for the lease. The rules relating to leases of indefinite term, leases for a fixed period which continue beyond that period and renewals are similar to those under SDLT (see **4.70** et seq).

3.10 However, under SDLT the tax liability on rents payable under a lease is usually finally determined by reference to the rent payable during the first five years of the term of the lease. Even if it is known that rents will increase after year five, this is not taken into account. There is no such rule in relation to LBTT – any **known** increases throughout the life of the lease will have to be taken into account in the initial assessment of tax, apart from increases in line with the retail price index, consumer price index or similar index of inflation. But even then, the position will not be finally determined. In addition, assuming the grant of the lease was notifiable or becomes notifiable, the tenant will be required to review the position every three years during the period of the lease, and again when either the lease is assigned or the lease comes to an end, to determine whether further tax is due – see **4.21** and **4.26**. The requirement for submission of new returns every three years (whether or not there is any further tax to pay) will be onerous for some lessees, especially those businesses which have numerous leased premises.

It is understood that the intention under LBTT is to adjust the tax payable at these three yearly intervals to take account of increases in rent or other changes in the lease. This is not entirely clear from the legislation. LBTT(S)A 2013, Sch 19, para 10(2) requires a further return to be made at each third anniversary of the effective date of the grant of the lease, if the grant of the lease was notifiable, or at each third anniversary of the event triggering notification of the lease (see **4.21**) assuming the lease has not been assigned or terminated. The further return must be made irrespective of whether there have been any changes affecting the amount of the tax payable. Paragraph 10(4) states that the return must include an assessment of the tax due on the basis of the information in the return. However, it is not stated in the legislation that such information should include any changes such as rent increases.

LEASES OF RESIDENTIAL PROPERTY

3.11 Generally in Scotland it is now not possible to grant a lease over residential property for more than 20 years (Land Tenure Reform (Scotland) Act 1974, ss 8–9). Although it should be noted that there are now exceptions to this general rule following the Housing (Scotland) Act 2010, ss 138 and 139 and the Private Rented Housing (Scotland) Act 2011, ss 36 and 37. Consequently, unlike in England, it is not common for leases of residential property to be granted for long periods. The Scottish Government therefore took the view that it was unlikely that the rent payable on the grant of a lease over residential property would be sufficient to breach the nil rate tax band for the NPV of the rent (£150,000) such that an LBTT liability arose. As a consequence the grant, assignation, or renunciation of a lease of residential property is exempt from LBTT unless it is an 'ultra-long lease' (see **4.4** et seq). Such 'ultra-long leases' were converted into ownership on 28 November 2015 hence their exclusion from the exemption from LBTT on leases over residential property.

There is no such exemption under SDLT. Currently a 20-year residential lease at a fixed rent of at least around £17,700 per annum would give rise to an SDLT liability, and at lower levels of annual rent there may be an obligation to submit an SDLT return even if no tax is due.

ANTI-AVOIDANCE PROVISIONS

SDLT specific anti-avoidance rule

3.12 The SDLT legislation contains a specific anti-avoidance rule (FA 2003, s 75A) which is extremely wide in its scope and, whilst its objective is clearly to counter-act SDLT avoidance, there is technically no requirement that an SDLT avoidance motive exists to fall within the rule. As a result wholly commercial transactions, perhaps structured in an SDLT efficient manner, potentially fall within the rule, which can lead to significant uncertainty for taxpayers.

The Scottish Government has very sensibly decided not to incorporate a similar type of rule into the LBTT legislation, meaning that taxpayers are spared the uncertainty which can arise under SDLT. Within the LBTT legislation the Scottish Government places reliance on targeted anti-avoidance provisions (see **9.14**) and the general anti-avoidance rule which applies to all devolved taxes (see **9.3**).

General anti-avoidance rule

3.13 The Scottish Government has introduced a general anti-avoidance rule (the Scottish 'GAAR') (Revenue Scotland and Tax Powers Act 2014, ss 62–72 – see **9.3**), which is specifically designed to be broader in scope than the UK general anti-abuse rule found in FA 2013, ss 206–215. The objective of the Scottish GAAR is to counteract 'tax advantages' arising from a 'tax avoidance arrangement' which is 'artificial'. The Scottish GAAR does not contain the safeguards of an advisory review panel, and the so called double reasonableness test, which apply to the UK general anti-abuse rule.

Residential property holding companies

3.14 The Scottish Ministers can, by regulation, provide that 'qualifying transfers' of interests in 'residential property holding companies' be treated as land transactions chargeable to LBTT (LBTT(S)A 2013, s 47 – see **9.15**). A 'residential property holding company' is a company whose shares are not listed on a recognised stock exchange, whose sole or main activity is holding interests in land (including interests in land located outside of Scotland) and whose assets include interests in residential property. A 'qualifying transfer' is a transfer of an interest in a 'residential property holding company' that results in the transferee (ie the buyer) acquiring the right to occupy some or all of the company's residential property. The Scottish Ministers have not yet made any such regulations and therefore this provision is not currently in force.

There is no similar provision under SDLT for transfers of shares in 'land-rich' companies to be treated as land transactions chargeable to tax.

MULTIPLE DWELLINGS RELIEF

3.15 The UK Government abolished multiple dwellings relief for SDLT with effect from 1 June 2024. The Scottish Government has not, at the time of writing, indicated whether it will follow suit.

Multiple dwellings relief in relation to LBTT is similar in most respects to the former relief under SDLT; however, it does not specify a lower rate of charge, but states that where the relief is available the tax payable on the acquisition of the dwellings cannot be less than a proportion (25%) of that due had the relief not been available (see **5.25**). This is stated by the Scottish government to be a consequence of LBTT being a progressive tax (see **3.3**).

Under LBTT if the 'additional dwellings supplement' applies to some but not all of the dwellings acquired, the basis upon which the LBTT payable is calculated, if a claim for multiple dwellings relief is made, is slightly different. The tax due in relation to a dwelling (DT – see Step 3 at **5.25**) is calculated in exactly the same manner; however, the calculation must be done separately for each dwelling acquired, with the 'additional dwellings supplement' being applied to the acquisition of those dwellings which fall within the provisions of LBTT(S)A 2013, Sch 2A, paras 2 or 3, and the normal rates of LBTT being applied to any dwelling which, for example, is replacing an individual's main residence so that the 'additional dwellings supplement' does not apply. Once the 'DT' (tax due in relation to a dwelling) has been calculated for each dwelling they must be added together to determine the LBTT chargeable in relation to the transaction(s). For transactions where the 'additional dwellings supplement' does not apply, once the DT (tax due in relation to a dwelling) has been calculated it is multiplied by the number of dwellings acquired to arrive at the LBTT payable.

Where six or more separate dwellings are acquired as part of a single transaction (ie a single contract between the same buyer and seller), and a claim is made to exempt the transaction from the 'additional dwellings supplement' (LBTT(S) A 2013, Sch 2A, paras 9 and 10 – see **2.68**), the calculation of DT (tax due in relation to a dwelling) in respect of the transaction is done on the basis that the ADS does not apply, and therefore the normal residential rates of LBTT are used in the calculation.

ACQUISITION RELIEF

3.16 Under SDLT a successful claim to acquisition relief reduces the rate of SDLT chargeable to 0.5% of the chargeable consideration for the transaction (FA 2003 Sch 7, para 8(1)).

A successful claim to acquisition relief in relation to LBTT reduces the tax payable to a proportion (12.5%) of that due had the relief not been available (see **5.14**). Again the fact that there is no single reduced rate of LBTT applied to the chargeable consideration is stated by the Scottish Government to be a consequence of LBTT being a progressive tax (see **3.3**).

CROFTING COMMUNITY RIGHT TO BUY RELIEF

3.17 Under SDLT, relief (FA 2003, s 75) for a transaction entered into by a crofting community body under Pt 3 of the Land Reform (Scotland) Act 2003 was provided by dividing the total chargeable consideration being given for the acquisition of the crofts by the number of crofts being acquired, calculating the SDLT chargeable on the amount so determined, and multiplying the amount of the SDLT charge per croft by the number of crofts being acquired to get the total SDLT payable. If that average consideration falls within the nil rate band no SDLT is payable as there is no minimum rate of tax payable under this relief as there is for multiple dwellings relief (see **3.15**).

In contrast, under LBTT (LBTT(S)A 2013, Sch 9), the acquisition of two or more crofts under a transaction, which is entered into pursuant to a crofting community right to buy, is wholly exempt from LBTT irrespective of the average consideration paid per croft (Land and Buildings Transaction Tax (Addition and Modification of Reliefs) (Scotland) Order 2015), draft SI 2015, article 2(4)).

LICENCES TO OCCUPY PROPERTY

3.18 Under LBTT, the grant, assignation or renunciation of a licence to use or occupy property is exempt from charge unless it is a 'prescribed non-residential licence', which is a licence of a description prescribed under regulations made by the Scottish Ministers (LBTT(S)A 2013, Sch 1, paras 3(1)(b), 3(4) and s 53(1)). Currently no such licences have been prescribed by the Scottish Ministers meaning that the grant, assignation or renunciation of a licence to use or occupy non-residential property, irrespective of the use to which the property is to be put, will be an exempt transaction for the purposes of LBTT – see **4.7** and **5.6** et seq.

In relation to SDLT a licence to use or occupy land is an exempt interest (FA 2003, s 48(2)(b)), so that any transaction in relation to such a licence will not be chargeable to SDLT.

The only practical impact of this difference in treatment should be that under LBTT the variation of a licence to use or occupy property may give rise to LBTT obligations to file a land transaction return and pay tax (LBTT(S) A 2013, s 6(1)(c), 3(c) and (4)(c)) if the chargeable consideration given for the variation exceeds the £150,000 nil rate tax band (LBTT(S)A 2013, s 30(1)(c)). In contrast, under SDLT, the variation of a licence to use or occupy land would be exempt.

ADMINISTRATION OF THE TAXES

3.19 There are a number of differences between LBTT and SDLT in relation to the administration of the respective taxes including the following:

- Under LBTT, Revenue Scotland must both launch and close an enquiry within the period of three years from the date upon which the LBTT return was due to be filed, or the actual date of filing if the return was late (see 8.38). In contrast, under SDLT, HMRC only have nine months from the date by which the SDLT return had to be filed to open an enquiry although there is no specified date by which the enquiry must be closed. This creates more uncertainty for a buyer of land in Scotland as their filing position is not certain for at least three years.
- The general rule is that, under LBTT, Revenue Scotland have five years from the date by which the LBTT return should have been filed in which to raise a discovery assessment, however this period is extended to

twenty years where the under-assessment to tax has been brought about deliberately by the buyer or a 'related person' (see 8.46). Under SDLT the time limit is generally four years from the 'effective date 'of the transaction, but extended to six years if the loss of tax is brought about carelessly by the purchaser or a 'related person', and to twenty years if it is brought about deliberately by the purchaser or a 'related person' or it is attributable to a failure to submit an SDLT return.

- The penalty regime under LBTT (see 8.55 et seq) is generally tougher than that under SDLT.

OTHER SDLT RELIEFS NOT AVAILABLE UNDER LBTT

3.20 The following SDLT reliefs are not available under LBTT:

- Relief for acquisition by an employer in a case of relocation of employment of an employee (FA 2003, Sch 6A, para 5).
- Relief for acquisition by a property trader from the personal representatives of a deceased person (FA 2003, Sch 6A, para 3).

Chapter 4

LBTT and Leases

SIGNPOSTS

- Consideration of the rules set out in the Land and Buildings Transaction Tax (Scotland) Act 2013, Sch 19 dealing with the LBTT obligations arising in relation to leases and licences to occupy land in Scotland.
- LBTT obligations can arise on the grant of a new lease and on the assignation, variation and renunciation of an existing lease.
- The grant, assignation or renunciation of most leases over 'residential property' is exempt from LBTT, provided the subject matter of the transaction (and any linked transactions) consists entirely of residential property.
- The grant, assignation or renunciation of a licence to occupy property is exempt from LBTT.
- The LBTT chargeable on a lease is generally subject to a three-yearly regular review and a review on assignation or termination of the lease.
- If certain LBTT reliefs have been claimed on the grant of a lease then a subsequent assignation of that lease, in relation to which none of the specified reliefs are available, may be taxed as the grant of a new lease.
- Variations to an existing lease may give rise to LBTT obligations in the following circumstances:
  - Reduction in rent payable – tenant is the buyer.
  - Reduction in the period (term) of the lease – landlord is the buyer.
  - Other variations where the tenant gives chargeable consideration – tenant is the buyer.
- The renunciation of a lease is the acquisition of a 'chargeable interest' by the landlord.
- The chargeable consideration for lease transactions, where the buyer is a company connected to the seller, is an amount not less than market value.

- Lease transactions may be 'linked' with other land transactions in relation to land in Scotland, which may impact LBTT obligations.
- There are special rules dealing with lease renewals and extensions.
- Consideration is given to when notification and payment obligations arise in relation to lease transactions.

4.1 Each of the grant, assignation and renunciation of a lease is a land transaction and therefore potentially gives rise to LBTT obligations as set out in **Chapter 2**. Under Scots property law the variation of a lease is not generally treated as the grant of a new lease. However, three types of variations to a lease are specifically treated as land transactions for LBTT purposes and these are as follows (LBTT(S)A 2013, Sch 19, para 29):

- A variation to reduce the amount of the rent payable – the tenant is the buyer.
- A variation to reduce the period (term) of the lease – the landlord is the buyer.
- Any other variation of a lease where the tenant gives consideration (other than an increase in rent) for the variation – the tenant is the buyer.

In addition, where a lease was not notifiable on grant, but the lease is then varied so as to extend its term or increase the amount of the rent payable, and the effect of the variation is that the grant of the lease would have been notifiable had it been granted for the term as now extended or for the rent as now increased, the buyer (ie the tenant) must file a land transaction return and pay any tax due (LBTT(S)A 2013, Sch 19, para 30).

As with other land transactions there may be obligations to make or amend LBTT returns even if no liability to LBTT arises. The detailed rules regarding leases are found in LBTT(S)A 2013, Sch 19 and these rules cover the following:

- Calculation of the tax chargeable in relation to rent (see **4.13–4.15** and **4.60** et seq).
- Calculation of the tax payable in relation to chargeable consideration other than rent, for example, a premium, which is sometimes referred to as a 'grassum' (see **4.58**).
- The requirement to carry out a review of the tax chargeable on a lease at periodic intervals (three-yearly) and on the occurrence of certain events (assignation and termination) (see **4.17** and **4.26**).
- What constitutes 'chargeable consideration' in relation to leases, including consideration consisting of rent, consideration other than rent, and consideration that is not treated as 'chargeable consideration' (see **4.54** et seq).
- How to determine the duration of a lease for LBTT purposes, the treatment of 'successive linked leases' and other rules specific to leases including lease renewals and extensions (see **4.67** et seq).

Obligations in relation to LBTT may arise at various times, and not only when the lease itself is granted but also, for example, on first occupation, when a payment of rent is made, when rent amounts are agreed or changed, and when a review is required to be made of the tax chargeable on a lease. It is, therefore, important to establish clearly the nature of the transaction being undertaken. The four key questions to address are the same as those for other transactions but, in relation to leases, the fourth question is likely to require most attention.

- What LBTT obligations may arise?
- At what time do LBTT obligations arise?
- What, if any, reliefs are available?
- What, if any, special rules may affect the transaction?

4.2 LBTT may be chargeable on both rent and any real or deemed premium (see **4.58**). LBTT obligations fall on the 'buyer'. In most cases this will be the tenant but, where a lease is either renounced or varied to reduce the term, the landlord will be the buyer (LBTT(S)A 2013, s 6(3)(b) and Sch 19, para 29(3)). The general rules relating to timing and notification of liability, availability of reliefs and disclosure of information apply to lease transactions. Specific rules for calculating the LBTT liability, and modifications to other general rules, are dealt with in detail by way of examples in the text which follows.

4.3 A liability to LBTT can arise at a future time on a lease granted at an earlier date, or currently as regards a lease granted some time previously. In particular, in certain circumstances, the legislation calls for a review of the LBTT payable on a lease on a regular basis (three-yearly) or on the occurrence of certain specified events (assignation and termination). It may, therefore, be important to obtain and retain the full detailed history of a lease, and of previous leases of the same premises if they are 'linked' with the current lease (see **4.66**).

RESIDENTIAL LEASES – EXEMPT TRANSACTIONS

4.4 The grant, assignation or renunciation of a lease of 'residential property' (see **2.36**), which is not a 'qualifying lease', is a transaction which is exempt from LBTT (LBTT(S)A 2013, Sch 1, para 3(1)(a)). A 'qualifying lease' has the same meaning as in the Long Leases (Scotland) Act 2012 (asp 9) (LBTT(S)A 2013, Sch 1, para 3(3)), being a lease which, immediately before the 'appointed day', which was 28 November 2015, is a right of lease in land which:

- is registered;
- is granted for a period of more than 175 years; and
- in respect of which the unexpired portion of that period is:
  - where the lease is wholly or mainly over a private dwelling house, more than 100 years;
  - in any other case, more than 175 years.

However, even where the above conditions are satisfied, a lease will not be a 'qualifying lease' where:

(1) the annual rent payable under the lease is over £100, (note: there are rules set out in the Long Leases (Scotland) Act 2012, s 2 for determining the amount of rent payable under a lease); or

(2) the lease is over land which includes a harbour, and in relation to which there is a harbour authority; or

(3) the lease is granted for the sole purpose of allowing the tenant to install and maintain pipes or cables; or

(4) the lease is one either of minerals or which include minerals and in respect of which a royalty etc. is payable by reference to the exploitation of those minerals.

4.5 In this paragraph a 'qualifying lease' (see **4.4**) is referred to as an 'ultra-long lease'. Thus the grant, assignation or renunciation of a lease of 'residential property' will be exempt from LBTT unless it is an 'ultra-long lease'. Even if the terms of the lease satisfy the requirements to be an 'ultra-long lease', if any of the exceptions (see (1) to (4) in **4.4** above) apply then it will not be an 'ultra-long lease' and the grant, assignation or renunciation of the lease will be exempt from LBTT. In particular, if the rent payable under the lease is more than £100 per annum, its grant, assignation or renunciation will be exempt from LBTT as a consequence of exception (1) in **4.4** above. Under the Long Leases (Scotland) Act 2012 (asp 9) such 'ultra-long leases' were converted into ownership on 28 November 2015, hence the reason they are not exempt from LBTT. After 28 November 2015, the acquisition of an 'ultra-long lease' became the acquisition of an ownership interest, and not the acquisition of a tenant's interest, and such a transaction is therefore potentially chargeable to LBTT at the standard rates for residential property and, if the relevant conditions are satisfied, the additional dwellings supplement (see **2.37** et seq) may apply.

4.6

Focus

- The grant, assignation or renunciation of a lease over residential property will not be exempt from LBTT if it is part of a single transaction which includes non-residential property, or it is one of a number of 'linked' transactions which include non-residential property.

The grant, assignation or renunciation of a lease of residential property (which is not an 'ultra-long lease' – see **4.5**) will only be exempt from LBTT if the main subject-matter of the transaction consists entirely of residential property (see **2.36**) or, where it is one of a number of linked transactions (see **4.66**), the main-subject matter of each of those transactions consists entirely of residential property (LBTT(S)A 2013, Sch 1, para 3(2)). This means that if, as part of a single transaction, a lease over residential property is granted, assigned or renounced, and a chargeable interest in relation to non-residential property is acquired, the transaction over the residential property would not be exempt as the main subject-matter of that transaction would not be comprised entirely of residential property. Similarly, if a lease over residential property is granted, assigned or renounced and that transaction is linked with one or more land transactions involving non-residential property, then again the transaction in relation to the lease over residential property would not be exempt as the main subject-matter of each linked transaction would not consist entirely of an interest in residential property. Care therefore needs to be taken to ensure that the grant, assignation or renunciation of a lease over residential property(ies) is exempt, and that it is not brought within the charge to LBTT by being part of the same transaction as, or linked with, a land transaction over non-residential property.

If the grant, assignation or renunciation of a lease over residential property is not exempt from LBTT, as it is part of a transaction which includes non-residential property, or it is one of a number of linked transactions which include non-residential property, the transaction(s) in relation to the lease over residential property will be taxed as a non-residential property transaction(s) (see **2.35**) and the LBTT tax rates and bands for non-residential property will apply to the transaction(s).

LICENCE TO OCCUPY PROPERTY

4.7

> **Focus**
>
> - The Scottish Ministers have the power to prescribe that the grant, assignation or renunciation of licences to occupy non-residential property are land transactions which are chargeable transactions for LBTT purposes, potentially giving rise to LBTT obligations.

In Scotland a lease generally requires all of the following elements:

- the parties to the contract;
- an exclusive right to occupy a specified property;
- a duration (although a duration of one year may be implied if the other characteristics are present); and
- rent payable.

If one or more of these characteristics is absent then the arrangement may comprise a licence to occupy property, rather than a lease. However, simply calling an arrangement a licence to occupy will not necessarily make it a licence to occupy, and if the characteristics described above are present it may well be a lease. Legal advice should therefore be taken to determine the true nature of any interest in land which is to be the subject of a transaction.

4.8 The grant, assignation or renunciation of a licence to occupy property will be exempt from LBTT unless it is a 'prescribed non-residential licence' (LBTT(S)A 2013, Sch 1 para 3(1)(b)). For these purposes a 'prescribed non-residential licence' means a licence of a description prescribed under regulations made by the Scottish Ministers (LBTT(S)A 2013, Sch 1, para 3(4) and s 53(1)).

In May 2014, the Scottish Government launched its consultation into proposed subordinate legislation which included a proposal to prescribe licences to occupy premises to be used as a retail shop such that the grant, assignation or renunciation of such licences would be 'land transactions' for LBTT purposes. However, the majority of those who responded to the consultation were opposed to the proposal, citing the view that licences were fundamentally different from leases, and highlighting the risk to Scotland's competitiveness, given that licences to occupy property are exempt interests for the purposes of SDLT. The Scottish Government took on board the respondent's views and decided not to use its power under LBTT(S)A 2013, s 53 to prescribe that the grant, assignation or renunciation of certain licences to occupy non-residential property would be land transactions for the purposes of LBTT.

This means that under current law the grant, assignation or renunciation of a licence to occupy all non-residential property, irrespective of the use to which the property is to be put, will be exempt from LBTT (LBTT(S)A 2013, Sch 1, para 3(1)(b)).

However, it would seem that the variation of a licence to occupy non-residential property may give rise to LBTT obligations to file a land transaction return and pay tax (LBTT(S)A 2013, s 6(1)(c), (3)(c) and (4)(c) if the chargeable consideration given for the variation exceeds the £150,000 nil rate tax band (LBTT(S)A 2013, s 30(1)(c)).

EVENTS GIVING RISE TO LBTT OBLIGATIONS AND LIABILITIES

New lease

4.9

> **Focus**
>
> - The grant of a new lease, including missives of let constituting a lease, is a land transaction for LBTT purposes and may give rise to LBTT obligations.
> - The criteria which trigger notification of the grant of a new lease are different depending upon whether the lease is for a term of seven years or more, or for less than seven years.

LBTT obligations may arise on entering into a lease including 'missives of let' which constitute a lease (LBTT(S)A 2013, s 6(1)(a)). In some transactions the parties will first enter into an agreement for lease or missives of let which do not constitute a lease, and the definitive lease may then be entered into at a later date. The agreement for lease, or missives of let not constituting a lease, may be acted on before the definitive lease is executed, for example, by payment of rent or the tenant having access to the premises. The general LBTT concept of 'substantial performance' (see **2.81**) applies to an agreement for lease or missives of let not constituting a lease. LBTT obligations may therefore arise when the agreement for lease or missives of let not constituting a lease are acted on (ie substantially performed) and when the definitive lease is entered into (see **4.82** et seq).

4.10 The LBTT legislation also makes provision for the circumstance where missives of let which constitute a lease are, some time later, followed by the execution of the definitive lease, and this is considered at **4.81** below.

New lease for seven years or more

4.11 For an acquisition of the ownership of land, there is no requirement to make an LBTT return if the chargeable consideration is less than £40,000 (LBTT(S)A 2013, s 30(1)(b)). Where a lease for seven years or more is granted, this exemption from making a return (ie where the chargeable consideration other than rent is less than £40,000) only applies if the annual rent is also less than £1,000 (LBTT(S)A 2013, s 30(2)(a)). This is logical for a lease involving both rent and premium because, if the annual rent is £1,000 or more, there is no 'nil rate tax band' for the premium (see **4.59**) and any premium payable will give rise to an LBTT liability (LBTT(S)A 2013, Sch 19, para 9). However, it does mean that, for example, a lease for seven years or more at rent, with no premium payable, will be notifiable if the rent is £1,000 or more per annum.

Example 4.1 – Rent below threshold, notifiable

On 1 January 2024 An Cala Ltd enters into a 175-year lease as tenant of a commercial building at a yearly rent of £5,200, subject to revision every five years in line with the movement in the Retail Prices Index. The tenant has the right to terminate the lease at any time after 1 January 2034. Increases in rent in line with the Retail Price Index are ignored for LBTT purposes (see **4.49**), so that the transaction is treated as a lease at a fixed rent of £5,200 per annum. The NPV of the rent is £148,209, which is below the threshold of £150,000 so that no LBTT is payable. Nonetheless, an LBTT return must be submitted within 30 days of execution of the lease or earlier substantial performance of any agreement for lease (or missives of let not constituting a lease). An LBTT return must be submitted because, whilst the chargeable consideration other than rent is less than £40,000 (in this instance it is nil as no premium is payable), the second part of the condition is not satisfied, as the annual rent exceeds £1,000. It will also mean that the lease is subject to a three-yearly review of the LBTT chargeable and a review on any assignment and on termination (see **4.21** and **4.26**).

New lease for less than seven years

4.12 The grant of a lease for less than seven years does not have to be notified unless the chargeable consideration (rent and/or premium) exceeds the 'nil rate tax band' applicable to the transaction (LBTT(S)A 2013, s 30(2)(c)). However, where the annual rent is £1,000 or more, the absence of a nil rate tax band in respect of any premium (see **4.59**) means that even a very small premium will be sufficient to make the grant of the lease notifiable.

Example 4.2 – Rent below threshold, not notifiable

Highlighter Ltd grants a five-year lease of a commercial building for a premium of £130,000 and an annual rent of £900 per annum. The NPV of the rent is clearly below the nil rate threshold for rent of £150,000. As the annual rent is not £1,000 or more, the £150,000 nil rate tax band for the premium is available (see **4.59**). Since the lease is for less than seven years, and no tax is payable on either rent or premium, no LBTT return or other notification is required.

Example 4.3 – Liability on small premium

On 1 March 2024, John agrees to grant a five-year lease of a shop to Dominic for rent of £12,000 per annum, payable quarterly in advance and a premium of £2,000. It is agreed that the lease will commence on 1 April 2023 and the lease is granted on that date. Dominic makes the first rent payment, for the period 1 April to 30 June 2024 on 1 April 2024 and takes possession of the shop on the same day. Since nothing happens to cause the agreement to be substantially performed before the lease is executed, the lease is deemed to commence on the date of execution and so, for LBTT purposes this is a five-year lease commencing on 1 April 2024. The lease is at a yearly rent of £12,000, and so there is no zero rate tax band for LBTT on the premium (see **4.59**). The £2,000 premium is chargeable at 1% and this £20 LBTT liability is sufficient to trigger an obligation to submit an LBTT return. It will also mean that the lease is subject to a three-yearly review of the LBTT chargeable and a review on any assignment and on termination (see **4.21** and **4.26**).

The NPV of the rent payable under the lease will be below the £150,000 nil rate tax band for rent and therefore no LBTT will be payable in relation to the rent.

Amount of tax chargeable in respect of rent

4.13 The amount of the tax chargeable on that part of the chargeable consideration comprising rent is determined as follows (LBTT(S)A 2013, Sch 19, para 4):

Step 1

The net present value (NPV) of all of the rent payable over the term of the lease is calculated.

Firstly, it is therefore necessary to establish the rent payable over the period (term) of the lease. If the rent payable is not determined at the 'effective date' of the grant of the lease, a reasonable estimate of the rent must be made (see **4.49**). However, no account is to be taken of any provision to adjust the rent in line with the Retail Prices Index, Consumer Prices Index or any similar index (LBTT(S)A 2013, Sch 19, para 13(5)). However, the rent, as adjusted for any increase in the index, should be used for the purposes of any further land transaction return which has to be filed, for example, under the three-yearly review procedure (see **4.17** et seq), and the review on assignation or termination (LBTT60031). If the rent payable under the lease is subject to an open market rent review it should be acceptable to estimate the rent payable after the review date as being the same as the rent payable before the rent review (LBTT60031). Once the rent for each year is established (or estimated if uncertain at the outset), the NPV of that rent over the life of the lease must be calculated, using the formula and discount rate specified in the legislation (LBTT(S)A 2013, Sch 19, paras 6 and 7). The annual discount rate to be applied is currently 3.5%, however this may be varied by an order of the Scottish Ministers. For these purposes the length of the lease is taken to be the term specified in the lease ignoring any break clauses, or any right of either the landlord or the tenant to terminate the lease early or to renew it (LBTT(S)A 2013 Sch 19, para 19). However, if any right to renew is subsequently exercised, the resulting further lease may be 'linked' with the original lease, whether successively or not; see **4.66** et seq.

In simple terms, the rent for the first 12 months is divided by 1.035 to give its discounted value, the rent for the second 12 months is divided by $(1.035)^2$, and so on to the end of the term of the lease. The discounted rents for all years are then totalled. This is the NPV of the rent payable over the term of the lease.

Step 2

For each tax band applicable to chargeable consideration which consists of rent, multiply so much of the NPV as falls within each band by the tax rate for that band.

Step 3

Total each of the amounts calculated in Step 2 above and the resultant amount is the total amount of the LBTT payable in respect of rent.

4.14 Where the grant of the new lease is one of a number of 'linked transactions' in relation to which the 'chargeable consideration' consists of or includes rent the amount of LBTT chargeable in respect of rent is calculated as follows (LBTT(S)A 2013, Sch 19, para 5):

Step 1

The NPV of all of the rent payable over the period (term) of each of the leases is calculated in the same manner as described in **4.13,** and all of the NPVs are totalled. The total of the NPVs is referred to as 'TNPV'.

Step 2

For each tax band applicable to chargeable consideration which consists of rent, multiply so much of the TNPV as falls within each band by the tax rate for that band.

Step 3

Total each of the amounts calculated in Step 2 above and the resultant amount is the total amount of LBTT payable in respect of rent.

Step 4

For each lease in question divide its NPV of rent payable over the term of that lease by the TNPV (see **Step 1** above).

Step 5

Multiply the total LBTT payable in respect of rent calculated in Step 3 by the fraction determined in Step 4. The result is the amount of tax chargeable in respect of rent for the lease in question.

4.15 It should be possible to create a spreadsheet to perform LBTT calculations for leases. However, an LBTT calculator for this purpose can be found on the Revenue Scotland website. The calculator works for most cases, provided the correct information is input, and its use is recommended. However, it is purely a mechanical aid. It will not detect whether the correct information is entered and it is therefore important to have a full understanding of the nature of the transaction and the consideration that is chargeable to LBTT when entering information into the calculator, to guard against errors. A copy of the output (printed or electronic) should be retained in case of any future enquiry by Revenue Scotland.

Example 4.4 – Calculation of LBTT payable on rent and a premium

On June 1 2024, Elizabeth agrees to grant John a ten year lease of a hotel at an annual rent of £50,000 including VAT and for a premium of £425,000. There is an upwards-only market rent review on the fifth anniversary of the grant of the lease. The lease is granted on 1 July 2024 without the agreement having been previously substantially performed. The effective date of the grant of the lease is therefore 1 July 2024 and the rent review is due on 1 July 2029. The LBTT payable can be calculated manually as follows:

Year	*Actual rent for LBTT purposes*	*Discounted rent*
1	£50,000	£48,308
2	£50,000	£46,674
3	£50,000	£45,096
4	£50,000	£43,572
5	£50,000	£42,098
6	£50,000	£40,674
7	£50,000	£39,298
8	£50,000	£37,970
9	£50,000	£36,686
10	£50,000	£35,444
Total discounted rent		£415,820
Less zero rate band		(£150,000)
LBTT charged at 1% on		£265,820
LBTT on rent		£2,658
LBTT on premium	1% × £250,000 = £2,500	
	5% × £175,000 = £8,750	
		£11,250
Total LBTT (on rent and premium)		£13,908

Note: As the rent payable is £1,000 per annum or more there is no nil rate band in relation to the premium (see **4.59**).

Alternatively, the Revenue Scotland calculator may be used.

Grant of a lease for an indefinite term

4.16 Where a lease is entered into which has no term specified (ie it is for an indefinite period of time, for example, a lease for life, or a lease which terminates on notice being given) it is treated initially as though it were a lease for a fixed term of one year (LBTT(S)A 2013, Sch 19, para 22(1)). If it continues beyond the end of the first year it is treated as having been a lease for two years from the outset. At the start of each successive year thereafter, it is treated as having been, from the outset, a lease for one year longer than at the commencement of the previous year. For the purpose of determining whether a lease for an indefinite term requires to be notified it is always treated as being for a term of less than seven years (LBTT(S)A 2013, Sch 19, para 22(3)). This means that the lease will only be notifiable if the NPV of the rent exceeds £150,000, or if any premium exceeds £150,000, or if the annual rent is £1,000 per annum or more and any amount of premium is payable (LBTT(S)A 2013, s 30(2)(c)). It is therefore necessary, at the beginning of each year, to consider what LBTT obligations arise. Initially the rent may not be high enough to produce any LBTT liability. However, as time passes, and the lease 'grows' in length, LBTT obligations may arise.

If the extension of the lease by a further year causes the lease to become notifiable, where it was not previously notifiable, the tenant must make a return in respect of the grant of the 'extended' lease before the end of the period of 30 days after the expiry of the last notional term of the lease (see **Example 4.5**). The return must include an assessment of the tax payable, and the tax is charged by reference to the tax rates and tax bands in force at the 'effective date' of the transaction. The 'effective date' of the transaction will be the date the lease was originally executed (LBTT(S)A 2013, Sch 19, para 22(2)).

Once the lease has been notified under Sch 19, para 22(2) it will then be subject to a three-yearly periodic review, and a review on assignment or termination (LBTT(S)A 2013, Sch 19, para 10(1)(b)(iii) and para 11(1)) as described below at **4.21** and **4.26**.

Example 4.5 – Lease for an indefinite term

On 1 September 2023 Rosco Ltd took on a tenancy of a commercial unit. Under the terms of the tenancy Rosco Ltd paid a quarterly rental of £7,500 including VAT, rent to be increased at each anniversary of the tenancy in line with the Retail Prices Index. The tenancy may be terminated by either party on giving one quarter's notice on the due date of the rental payment.

The tenancy was initially treated as a lease for one year at an annual rent of £30,000. No LBTT was due as the NPV of the rent was within the nil rate tax band being below £150,000 and no premium was payable. There was no obligation to make a return because the lease was for less than seven years and no tax was due. On 1 September 2024 the continuing tenancy will be treated as having been a lease for two years from the outset, at an annual rent of £30,000. The increase in rent in line with the RPI is ignored (LBTT(S)A 2013, Sch 19, para 13(5)). Again no LBTT liability arose and no return was required. The same applied at 1 September in each of 2025, 2026 and 2027. At 1 September 2028, the lease was deemed to have been for 6 years from 1 September 2023 to 31 August 2029. The NPV of the rent (at £30,000 per year ignoring RPI increases) on the deemed six-year lease will be £159,856. As this will be over the £150,000 threshold for an LBTT liability to arise, a land transaction return will be submitted and LBTT paid at a rate of 1% giving rise to a liability of £98 (see **Example 4.4** for calculation principles). The return and payment will be due by 30 September 2028 – 30 days after the end of the fifth year (LBTT(S) A 2013, Sch 19, para 22(2)(a)).

If the tenancy had then been terminated during the sixth year – say on 28 February 2029, so that in total it had lasted five years and six months – there would have been no refund of the LBTT. This is the case even though a fixed term lease for the same period and rent would not have given rise to any LBTT liability, as the NPV of the rent would have been below the £150,000 threshold.

Review of tax chargeable on lease on three-yearly basis and on termination (see 4.17 et seq)

The tenancy continues. At 1 September 2031 it is regarded as becoming a lease for nine years (from 1 September 2023 to 31 August 2032). A three year periodic review date will arise on 31 August 2031 (LBTT(S)A 2013, Sch 19, para 10(7)(d)), being the third anniversary of the date on which the deemed fixed term ended prior to notification of the transaction being triggered, and Rosco Ltd must make a further return in relation to the lease by 30 September 2031. This further return will result in LBTT being charged on the rent payable for the two year period to 31 August 2031. The NPV of the rent is £228,230. An LBTT liability arises on the increase in NPV of the rent in comparison with that included in the first land transaction return filed by 30 September 2029. The LBTT payable is 1% of £228,230 – £159,856, being £683, and a land transaction return is required to be filed.

However, in January 2033 Rosco Ltd and the landlord enter into negotiations to replace the tenancy with a new ten year lease. Terms are agreed and the new lease is executed (with no prior agreement) on 28 February 2033. On termination of the tenancy, Rosco Ltd must make a further return by 30 March 2033 (30 days after the termination of the tenancy) which will result in the rent for the period 1 September 2031 to 28 February 2033 being charged to LBTT (LBTT(S)A 2013, Sch 19, para 11(1)(b)(ii)) and the LBTT payable is 1% of £238,776 – £228,230, being £105. Separately, a Land Transaction Return and payment of any LBTT in respect of the new lease are due by 30 March 2033. The grant of a new ten-year lease should not be linked (see **2.79**) with the existing lease, as it was negotiated as a completely separate deal in January 2033.

Review of tax chargeable on a lease

4.17 In a departure from the treatment of leases under SDLT, the LBTT legislation deals with the fact that the rent payable under a lease may change during its term (for example as a result of rent reviews or the amount of the rent becoming ascertained etc), by requiring that in certain circumstances reviews are made of the LBTT chargeable (LBTT(S)A 2013, Sch 19, paras 10 and 11). The reviews are made every three years, referred to as a 'regular review', and on the occurrence of certain events being either: (a) the assignation of the lease, or (b) the termination of the lease. It is irrelevant for these purposes whether the termination is as a consequence of the lease coming to the end of its term or as a result of an early termination.

4.18 It should however be noted that the obligation to carry out a regular review only applies in relation to a 'chargeable transaction' (LBTT(S)A 2013,

Sch 19, para 10(1)). A 'chargeable transaction' (LBTT(S)A 2013, s 15) is a land transaction which is not: (a) an exempt transaction (see **5.6**), or (b) a transaction which is otherwise exempt from charge (see **5.2**).

This therefore means that, for example, if a lease is granted and LBTT group relief (or another LBTT relief) is available to exempt the transaction from the charge to tax, there will be no requirement for the buyer to carry out subsequent reviews of the LBTT chargeable, even if, say, rent which was uncertain becomes ascertained, and at the time it becomes ascertained LBTT group relief would not be available.

However, if the grant of a lease was exempt from the charge to LBTT because, for example, group relief was available, and that lease is subsequently assigned to an unrelated party, the assignment will be taxed as though it were the grant of a new lease (see **4.35**), and, if the transaction is notifiable, the assignee will then have to carry out a three-yearly review based on the rules discussed below (see **4.21**).

4.19 The obligation to carry out a regular review of the LBTT chargeable can therefore arise not only when the grant of the actual lease is a chargeable transaction, but also when the assignation of a lease is treated as the grant of a new lease under LBTT(S)A 2013, Sch 19, para 27 (see **4.35**).

4.20 In addition, where the grant of a lease is not initially notifiable, but becomes notifiable because: (a) a contingency in relation to the rent ceases or rent which was uncertain is ascertained (see **4.49**), or (b) a lease for a fixed term continues after the end of the term (see **4.77**), or (c) a lease for an indefinite term is treated as continuing for a further year(s) (see **4.16**), or (d) of a variation of the lease to increase the rent payable or to extend the term of the lease (see **4.41**), then there is a requirement to carry out subsequent regular (three-yearly) reviews of the LBTT chargeable (LBTT(S)A 2013, Sch 19, para 10(1)(b)), and a review on assignation or termination of the lease (LBTT(S)A 2013, Sch 19, para 11(1)).

Regular review of tax chargeable

4.21 The 'buyer' must file a further land transaction return if on a 'review date' (see below for the meaning of this term) the lease has: (a) not been assigned, and (b) not been terminated (whether because the term has expired or because of an early termination) (LBTT(S)A 2013, Sch 19, para 10(2)). The further land transaction return must be filed irrespective of whether additional (or less) LBTT is payable or not. In this context the 'buyer' will not only be the person to whom the lease was granted but will also include the assignee (and any further assignee) of a lease which has been assigned. LBTT(S)A 2013, Sch 19, para 28(1) and (2)(c) provides that, where a lease is assigned, any three-yearly reviews required to be undertaken by the assignor must, if the 'review date' occurs after the 'effective date' of the assignation, be carried out instead by the assignee. It is important to note that the assignment of the lease does not 'reset the clock' in relation to the timing of the three-yearly reviews and therefore, where a lease is assigned two years after the 'effective date' (see **2.81**) of its grant, the assignee will be required to carry out a review of the LBTT payable at the end of year three.

There are five different scenarios which trigger a requirement to carry out a regular review and file a further land transaction return, and these are set out below (LBTT(S)A 2013, Sch 19, para 10(1)). The meaning of 'review date' for each scenario is also detailed below:

(1) *Buyer filed a land transaction return on the grant of the lease* (LBTT(S)A 2013, Sch 19, para 10(1)(a)).

If the buyer (ie the tenant) filed a land transaction return either: (a) on the grant of an actual lease (or deemed grant of a new lease – see **4.35**), or (b) on the substantial performance, before a lease is executed, of an agreement for lease (including missives of let not constituting a lease) so that the agreement is treated as if it were the grant of a notional lease, then the buyer must carry out a review of the LBTT chargeable in relation to that transaction on the third anniversary of the 'effective date' (see **2.81**) of the transaction, and on each subsequent third anniversary of that date. Each of these third anniversary dates is a review date in relation to such a lease (LBTT(S)A 2013, Sch 19, para 10(7)(a)).

(2) *No land transaction return filed on grant of lease but land transaction return subsequently filed.*

Where the buyer (ie the original tenant or a subsequent assignee) did not file a land transaction return on the grant of the actual lease, or on the deemed grant of a notional lease following the substantial performance of an agreement for lease (including missives of let not constituting a lease) before the lease is executed, but subsequently the first land transaction return is filed in any of the circumstances outlined below, a regular review of the LBTT chargeable in relation to the transaction must be carried out on each review date.

(a) *Contingency ceases or consideration ascertained* (LBTT(S)A 2013, Sch 19, para 10(1)(b)(i)).

The buyer (ie the original tenant or a subsequent assignee) makes a return under LBTT(S)A 2013, s 31 (see **4.51**), in which case the review must be carried out, where the return made under section 31 is the first return made in relation to the transaction, on the third anniversary of the date on which, in the case of contingent consideration, the contingency occurred, or it became clear that the contingency would not occur, and in the case of uncertain or unascertained consideration, the consideration, or an instalment of consideration, becomes ascertained. This third anniversary date is the review date in relation to such a lease (LBTT(S)A 2013, Sch 19, para 10(7)(b)).

It should be noted that the legislation does not provide for any further reviews to be carried out of the LBTT chargeable in relation to such a transaction. It is not clear why there are no further reviews required to be carried out, particularly given that it may only be an instalment of consideration which becomes ascertained, leaving part of the consideration still to be ascertained, possibly beyond the review date. This may result in subsequent changes to the amount of rent not being brought into account for LBTT purposes.

(b) *Leases that continue after a fixed period* (LBTT(S)A 2013, Sch 19, para 10(1)(b)(ii)).

The buyer (ie the original tenant or subsequent assignee) makes a return under LBTT(S)A 2013, Sch 19, para 20 (see **4.77**), in which case the review must be carried out, where the return made under para 20 is the first return made in relation to the transaction, on the third anniversary of the date on which the one year period ended which triggered notification of the transaction under LBTT(S)A 2013, Sch 19, para 20(3) and on each subsequent third anniversary of that date. Each of these third anniversary dates is a review date in relation to such a lease (LBTT(S)A 2013, Sch 19, para 10(7)(c)).

(c) *Leases for an indefinite term* (LBTT(S)A 2013, Sch 19, para 10(1)(b)(iii))

The buyer (ie the original tenant or subsequent assignee) makes a return under LBTT(S)A 2013, Sch 19, para 22 (see **4.16**) in which case the review must be carried out, where the return made under Sch 19, para 22 is the first return made in relation to the transaction, on the third anniversary of the date on which the deemed fixed term mentioned in Sch 19, para 22(2) ended, and on each subsequent third anniversary of that date. Each of these third anniversary dates is a review date in relation to such a lease (LBTT(S)A 2013, Sch 19, para 10(7)(d)).

(d) *Variation to a lease to increase the rent payable or to extend the period (term) of the lease* (LBTT(S)A 2013, Sch 19, para 10(1)(b)(iv)).

The buyer (ie the original tenant or subsequent assignee) makes a return under LBTT(S)A 2013, Sch 19, para 30 (see **4.41**) in which case the review must be carried out, where the return made under Sch 19, para 30(2) is the first return made in relation to the transaction, on the third anniversary of the date on which the variation to the lease takes effect, and on each subsequent anniversary of that date. Each of these third anniversary dates is a review date in relation to such a lease (LBTT(S)A 2013, Sch 19, para 10(7)(e)).

Requirement to file a further land transaction return

4.22 Provided that the buyer (ie the original tenant or a subsequent assignee) has not assigned the lease, and the lease has not terminated, then on each 'review date' (see **4.21**) the buyer must file a further land transaction return. The further land transaction return must be filed in the 30 day period commencing on the day after the 'review date' and must be filed irrespective of whether additional LBTT is payable (LBTT(S)A 2013, Sch 19, para 10(2) and (3)).

4.23 The further return must include an assessment of the amount of the LBTT payable in respect of the transaction, based on the information available at the 'review date' (LBTT(S)A 2013, Sch 19, para 10(4)). The return can be filed online, using Revenue Scotland's 'online portal for taxpayers' (for unrepresented tenants) or SETS (for agents and solicitors).

4.24 In calculating the LBTT chargeable the tax rates and tax bands to be used are those which were in force at the 'effective date' of the transaction (LBTT(S)A 2013, Sch 19, para 10(5)). This means that the tax rates and tax bands to be used will be those in force when the lease was originally granted, or deemed to be granted (in the case of the substantial performance of an agreement for lease before the lease is executed or in the case of the assignment of a lease which is treated as the grant of a new lease), and not those in force at the review date.

4.25 If the further land transaction return shows that additional LBTT is payable, the tax must be paid at the same time as the further return is made (LBTT(S)A 2013, s 40(2)(e)(i)). Where the tax payable is less than that already paid, the tax authority is required to repay the amount of the overpayment (LBTT(S)A 2013, Sch 19, para 10(6)).

Review of tax chargeable on assignation or termination of the lease

4.26 Where an obligation has arisen under LBTT(S)A 2013, Sch 19, para 10 to carry out a regular review of the LBTT chargeable in relation to a lease (see **4.21** et seq) and the lease is either: (a) assigned, or (b) terminated (whether by virtue of the term of the lease coming to an end or as a result of an early termination) the buyer (ie the original tenant or a subsequent assignee) must make a further land transaction return (LBTT(S)A 2013, Sch 19, para 11).

4.27 The further return must be made before the end of the 30 day period beginning with the day after the day (the 'relevant day') on which the lease is assigned or terminated (LBTT(S)A 2013, Sch 19, para 11(3)).

4.28 The further return must include an assessment of the amount of the tax chargeable based on the information available at the date of assignment or termination (LBTT(S)A 2013, Sch 19, para 11(4)). In calculating the LBTT chargeable, the tax rates and tax bands to be used are those which were in force at the 'effective date' of the transaction, being the tax rates and tax bands in force when the lease was originally granted or deemed to be granted (in the case of the substantial performance of an agreement for lease before the lease is executed or in the case of the assignment of a lease which is treated as the grant of a new lease), and not those in force when the lease is actually assigned or terminated (LBTT(S)A 2013, Sch 19, para 11(5)).

It seems that Revenue Scotland consider that no account is to be taken of a reduction in term of the lease as a consequence of the lease being renounced or otherwise terminated early.

4.29 If the further land transaction return shows that additional LBTT is payable, the tax must be paid at the same time that the further return is made (LBTT(S)A 2013, s 40(2)(e)(ii)). Where the tax payable is less than that already paid, the tax authority is required to repay the amount of the overpayment (LBTT(S)A 2013, Sch 19, para 11(6)).

Example 4.6 – Regular review of tax chargeable on a lease – buyer filed a land transaction return on the grant of the lease

The facts are as set out in **Example 4.4**. The rent review takes place on 1 July 2029 and the annual rent is increased to £65,000 per annum including VAT. John retains the lease until 30 June 2034 when it terminates.

John is required to review the LBTT chargeable on the lease on each of the following dates, and to file a land transaction return irrespective of whether any additional tax may be payable.

Review date	*Due date by which the land transaction must be filed*
1 July 2027 – no additional LBTT payable as premium and rent remain unchanged from that assessed in the original return	31 July 2027
1 July 2030 – additional LBTT payable as the rent review took place on 1 July 2029 and the annual rent was increased to £65,000 including VAT per annum for the remaining five years of the lease	31 July 2030

Year	*Actual rent for LBTT purposes*	*Discounted rent*
1	£50,000	£48,308
2	£50,000	£46,674
3	£50,000	£45,096
4	£50,000	£43,572
5	£50,000	£42,098
6	£65,000	£52,876
7	£65,000	£51,087
8	£65,000	£49,361

9	£65,000	£47,692
10	£65,000	£46,077

Revised total discounted rent	£472,841
Less zero rate band	(£150,000)
LBTT charged at 1% on	£322,841
LBTT on rent	£3,228
LBTT on premium – see **Example 4.4**	£11,250
Total LBTT payable	£14,478
LBTT paid with original return	£13,908
Additional LBTT payable	£570

Review date	*Due date by which the land transaction must be filed*
1 July 2033 – no additional LBTT payable as premium and rent remain unchanged from the return filed by 31 July 2023	31 July 2033
30 June 2034 – no additional LBTT payable as premium and rent remain unchanged from the return filed by 31 July 2026	30 July 2034

It can therefore be seen that the requirement to carry out subsequent reviews of the LBTT chargeable on a lease imposes a significant administrative burden on the taxpayer. In all John has to file five land transaction returns in relation to a ten year lease. Taxpayers would be well advised to put a system in place to ensure that filing deadlines are not missed.

Focus

- Normally the assignation of an existing lease to a new tenant is taxed in the same way as the transfer of any other interest in land in Scotland. However, if any of a number of specified reliefs was claimed on the grant of the lease, the first assignment of that lease, which is not exempt from LBTT on the basis that one of those same reliefs applies, is taxed as the grant of a new lease. This can give rise to a higher than expected LBTT liability.

Assignation of a lease or agreement for lease (including missives of let which do not constitute a lease)

4.30 From the perspective of the buyer (ie the assignee), the assignation (transfer) of an existing lease to a new tenant (with no other change in terms and conditions) will be subject to LBTT in the same way as the transfer of any other interest in land in Scotland. The new tenant will be subject to LBTT on any consideration given: (a) to the outgoing tenant, and (b) the landlord (apart from ordinary rent) – eg, a lump sum to be paid to the landlord to persuade the landlord to consent to the assignation. However, neither the rent payable under the lease, nor the assumption by the assignee of the obligation to perform or observe any other undertaking of the tenant under the lease will be chargeable to LBTT in relation to an assignment (LBTT(S)A 2013, Sch 19, para 16). In addition any premium paid to the landlord by the outgoing tenant (provided the outgoing tenant is not 'connected' with the assignee), for example, in return for the landlord agreeing to release the tenant from the lease, (LBTT(S)A 2013, Sch 2, para 1 – in these circumstances the outgoing tenant would be the seller and not the buyer and would not be connected with the buyer) will not figure in the calculation of the new tenant's LBTT liability.

4.31 Where an agreement for lease (including missives of let not constituting a lease) which has not previously been substantially performed (see **2.81**) is assigned without the lease having been executed, the assignation will constitute 'substantial performance' of that agreement (see **4.82**) as the assignee will become entitled to call for the grant of the lease (LBTT(S)A 2013, s 14(1)(c)). The consequences of the agreement having been 'substantially performed' will be that the agreement is treated as if it were the grant of a lease in accordance with the agreement ('the notional lease'), for a term beginning with the date of the substantial performance ie the date of the assignment of the agreement for lease (LBTT(S)A 2013, Sch 19, para 25(1)). The 'effective date' of the grant of the notional lease will be the date when the agreement is assigned (LBTT(S) A 2013, Sch 19, para 25(2)). The notional lease will be between the parties to the agreement, being the landlord and the original person who was to become the tenant. As a consequence, LBTT will potentially be payable by the original intended tenant in relation to any rent due under the terms of the agreement (see **4.13**), and in relation to any other chargeable consideration (ie other than rent) to be given under the terms of the agreement (see **4.58**). Assuming that the grant of the notional lease is notifiable (see **4.11** and **4.12**) the intended tenant under the agreement (ie the assignor) will have to file a land transaction return within the 30 day period starting on the day after the date of substantial performance of the agreement for lease, and pay any LBTT due at the same time (LBTT(S)A 2013, s40(2)(a)). This means that any LBTT liability will be paid by the intended tenant, even though he will not have taken possession of the property or paid rent in relation to the property, otherwise these events would have triggered substantial performance.

4.32 The assignee of the agreement for lease should be treated as taking an assignment of the 'notional lease', and any consideration which the assignee, or a person connected to the assignee, gives for the assignment will be chargeable to LBTT in the normal way (see **4.30**).

4.33 For details of the LBTT implications if the actual lease is granted pursuant to the agreement for lease (or missives of let not constituting a lease) which has been substantially performed, see **4.86**.

Review of tax chargeable on assignation of a lease

4.34 As discussed at **4.26** above where an obligation arose under LBTT(S) A 2013, Sch 19, para 10 for a regular review of the LBTT chargeable in relation to a lease to be carried out, the assignation of the lease to a new tenant will mean that the existing tenant must file a further land transaction return in relation to the lease (LBTT(S)A 2013, Sch 19, para 11) and the new tenant must file any further land transaction returns under the three-yearly review requirement (see **4.21**) that the existing tenant would have been required to file (see **4.40**).

Assignation of lease treated as grant of a new lease

4.35 However, some assignations of a lease are not straight forward and a new tenant may incur unexpected LBTT liabilities where one of a specified list of reliefs (see **4.38**) was claimed when the lease was originally granted (LBTT(S) A 2013, Sch 19, para 27). If nothing has happened to cause a clawback of that relief (see **5.17**, **5.20** and **5.27**), the first assignation of the lease which does not itself qualify for one of the specific reliefs on the list (see **4.38**) is treated as the grant of a new lease for the remaining term of the actual lease and at the rent payable by the assignee. LBTT is also payable, in the normal way, on any premium which the new tenant pays to the landlord, for example, to persuade the landlord to agree to the assignation. It is understood that any amount paid by the new tenant to the outgoing tenant in respect of the assignation is also within the charge to LBTT, as would be the case for a straightforward transfer of an existing lease on which none of the specified reliefs had previously been claimed. Whilst it may be logical that this should be the case, it is by no means clear that the wording of the legislation supports this view.

4.36 Where the assignation of a lease is treated as the grant of a new lease LBTT is chargeable on the assignee, and not on the original lessee who claimed the relief. Therefore, strictly, this is not a clawback of the relief originally granted, it is merely a modification of the normal rules for determining a buyer's LBTT liability. However, as **Example 4.7** below demonstrates, in practice the rules do lead to the effective clawback of part of the relief previously claimed, even though it is the new tenant who is liable for the resulting LBTT.

4.37 This rule is not subject to any time limitation so that it applies on a disposal of the lease at any time in its life. Anyone acquiring an existing lease by way of assignation should check whether it will be subject to this special rule and should seek protection from unexpected LBTT liabilities by way of warranties, indemnities, retentions or whatever other protection is thought appropriate.

4.38 This special rule applies where any of the following reliefs have been claimed on the grant of a lease (LBTT(S)A 2013, Sch 19, para 27(3)):

- Sale and leaseback relief (see **5.23**).
- Relief for alternative finance investment bonds (see **5.29**).
- Group relief (see **5.10**).
- Reconstruction relief or acquisition relief (see **5.13** and **5.14**).

- Charities relief (see **5.26**).
- Green freeports relief (see **5.39A**).
- Public bodies relief (see **5.46**).

4.39 However, as highlighted at **4.35** above, the special rule does not apply if the assignation to the new tenant itself qualifies for any of the reliefs listed in **4.38** (not necessarily the same relief as that previously claimed by the original lessee), provided the assignee claims the relief in an LBTT return.

Example 4.7 – Transfer of a lease after relief claimed

On 1 July 2023, A plc granted a 25 year lease over non-residential property to its subsidiary B Ltd at a rent of £200,000 per annum, subject to five-yearly upwards-only market rent reviews. Group relief was claimed by B Ltd.

B Ltd assigns the lease to an unrelated company X Ltd on 1 July 2027. X Ltd pays B Ltd £140,000 for the assignation and takes over all of the other terms and conditions of the lease.

X Ltd is not entitled to any of the reliefs set out in **4.38** above, so the assignation is treated as the grant of a new lease for the remaining 21 years of the term at an initial yearly rental of £200,000 per annum. This charge effectively claws back part of the group relief claimed by B Ltd when the lease was first granted. In addition, in this example, X Ltd pays £140,000 to B Ltd for the assignation, and this will be subject to LBTT as if it was a premium. Since the annual rent payable under the lease is £1,000 per annum or more, there is no 'zero rate tax band' for the premium (see **4.59**), and LBTT will be charged on the £140,000 at 1%.

The original grant of the lease by A plc to B Ltd was not a chargeable transaction as group relief was available (LBTT(S)A 2013, s 15(b) and Sch 10, para 2), and therefore B Ltd is not required to review the tax chargeable on the lease, on its assignation to X Ltd. However, as the assignation is treated for LBTT purposes as though it were the grant of a new lease, and X Ltd as buyer files a land transaction return in relation to the transaction, X Ltd will be required to file further land transactions on each third anniversary of the 'effective date' of the assignation (LBTT(S)A 2013, Sch 19, para 10(1)(a) and (2)).

Assignation of lease: responsibility of assignee for returns etc

4.40

Focus

- The assignee of a lease 'stands in the shoes' of the assignor and must, in certain circumstances, file an LBTT return or further return and pay any LBTT due, where the 'event' giving rise to the adjustment or return occurs after the 'effective date' of the assignation.

Where a lease is assigned, anything that would have been required under the provisions detailed below, to have been done by the assignor, absent the assignation, must, if the 'event' giving rise to the adjustment or return occurs after the 'effective date' of the assignation, be done instead by or in relation to the assignee (LBTT(S) A 2013, Sch 19, para 28(1)). It would seem that the word 'event' should be given a wide meaning so as to include, for example, a 'review date' in relation to a regular review of the LBTT chargeable on a lease (see **4.21**) falling after the effective date of an assignation. In effect the assignee assumes the assignor's obligations to file future land transaction returns in relation to the following:

- Land transaction return to be filed where a contingency ceases or consideration is ascertained (LBTT(S)A 2013, s 31).
- Land transaction return or further return to be made in consequence of a later 'linked transaction' (LBTT(S)A 2013, s 34).
- Land transaction return on three-yearly review (LBTT(S)A 2013, Sch 19, para 10).
- Land transaction return on review to be carried out on assignation or termination of a lease (LBTT(S)A 2013, Sch 19, para 11).
- Land transaction return or further return where a lease for a fixed term continues after the end of that term (LBTT(S)A 2013, Sch 19, para 20).
- Land transaction return or further return in relation to a lease for an indefinite term (LBTT(S)A 2013, Sch 19, para 22).
- Land transaction return where a land transaction becomes notifiable as a consequence of a variation to a lease which results in the extension of the period (term) of a lease and/or an increase in the rent payable under the lease (LBTT(S)A 2013, Sch 19, para 30).

For the purpose of the above mentioned returns, or further returns, anything previously done by, or in relation to, the assignor is to be treated as done by, or in relation to, the assignee (LBTT(S)A 2013, Sch 19, para 28(3)).

However, if the assignation of the lease is treated as the grant of a new lease under LBTT(S)A 2013, Sch 19, para 27 (see **4.35**) then the above rule that the assignee effectively 'stands in the shoes' of the assignor does not apply (LBTT(S)A 2013, Sch 19, para 28(4)). This means that, in these circumstances, the LBTT obligations are determined as though the 'grant' of the deemed lease under para 27 is the original grant of the lease. Therefore, for example, whether or not the assignee has an obligation to carry out a three-yearly periodic review (see **4.21**) is determined based on the 'grant' of the deemed lease.

Variation of an existing lease

4.41

> **Focus**
>
> - The variation of an existing lease may cause the grant of a lease, which was not previously notifiable, to become notifiable.

Under Scots law the variation of a lease does not generally create a new lease. However, under LBTT the variation of an existing lease may give rise to LBTT obligations in the following circumstances:

- The lease is varied so as to reduce the amount of the rent payable – see **4.42** (LBTT(S)A 2013, Sch 19, para 29(1)).
- Where any consideration in money or money's worth is given by the tenant for the variation, other than for a variation of the amount of the rent payable or of the term of the lease – see **4.44** (LBTT(S)A 2013, Sch 19, para 29(2)).
- The lease is varied so as to reduce its term – see **4.43** (LBTT(S)A 2013, Sch 19, para 29(3)).
- Where the original grant of the lease was not notifiable to Revenue Scotland under LBTT(S)A 2013, s 30 (see **4. 11** and **4.12**), and the lease is varied so as to: (i) extend its term, or (ii) increase the amount of the rent payable, and the effect of the variation is that the grant of the lease would have been notifiable under LBTT(S)A 2013, s 30 had the lease originally been granted for its now extended term, or granted for the rent now payable – see **4.45** (LBTT(S)A 2013, Sch 19, para 30).

Reduction of rent

4.42 Where a lease is varied so as to reduce the amount of the rent payable, there is the acquisition of a chargeable interest by the tenant (LBTT(S)A 2013, Sch 19, para 29(1)). Consequently, if the tenant gives, or is deemed to give (see **4.65**), any chargeable consideration, the variation will be within the charge to LBTT.

Decrease in term

4.43 If a lease is varied so as to decrease the term this is specifically treated as the acquisition of a chargeable interest by the landlord (LBTT(S)A 2013, Sch 19, para 29 (3)). If the landlord gives, or is deemed to give (see **4.65**) any chargeable consideration, the variation will be within the charge to LBTT. However, if the tenant gives consideration, for example in order to have the term of an onerous lease reduced, that consideration will not be subject to LBTT, as in that case the consideration is being given by the seller (tenant) and not the buyer (landlord).

Other variations

4.44 All other variations, other than those considered in **4.42** and **4.43**, will only be treated as the acquisition of a chargeable interest by the tenant if the tenant gives (or is deemed to give – see **4.65**) consideration in money or money's worth (other than an increase in rent) for the variation (LBTT(S) A 2013, Sch 19, para 29(2)).

Increase of rent or term: notification

4.45 Where the original grant of the lease (or substantial performance of an agreement for lease or missives of let not constituting a lease) was not notifiable to Revenue Scotland under LBTT(S)A 2013, s 30 (notifiable transactions – see **4.11** and **4.12**), and the lease is subsequently varied so as to: (i) extend its term, and/or (ii) increase the amount of the rent payable, and the effect of that variation is that the grant of the lease would have been notifiable to Revenue Scotland (under LBTT(S)A 2013, s 30) had the lease originally been granted for its now extended period and/or granted for the rent now payable, then the buyer (ie the tenant) must make a land transaction return to Revenue Scotland. The LBTT return must be made within 30 days from the day after the date upon which the variation to the lease takes effect (LBTT(S)A 2013, Sch 19, para 30(2)(a) and (3)). The LBTT return must include a self-assessment of the tax, if any, which is payable based on the extended term and/or the increased rent (LBTT(S)A 2013, Sch 19, para 30(2)(b)). Any LBTT payable is to be calculated by reference to the tax rates and tax bands in force at the 'effective date' of the original grant of the lease (or the substantial performance of the agreement for lease or missives of let not constituting a lease) (LBTT(S) A 2013, Sch 19, para 30(2)(c)).

For the purposes of determining whether a lease which has been varied to extend its term has become notifiable, the lease is treated for the purposes of LBTT(S) A 2013, s 30 as being a lease for the extended term (LBTT(S)A 2013, Sch 19, para 30(4)(a)). Thus if a lease is originally granted for a term of five years, the notification criteria will then be whether the chargeable consideration exceeds the nil rate band applicable to the transaction (LBTT(S)A 2013, s 30(2)(c)). However, if the term of that lease is then extended to ten years, the notification criteria will then become whether any chargeable consideration other than rent is £40,000 or more, or the rent payable is £1,000 or more (LBTT(S)A 2013, s 30(2)(a)).

Similarly, for the purposes of determining whether a lease which has been varied to increase the rent payable is notifiable, the lease is taken to have been granted for the rent as so increased (LBTT(S)A 2013, Sch 19, para 30(4)(b)).

Example 4.8 – Increase in rent results in notification of the grant of the lease

On 1 September 2023 Adam agrees to grant a lease of commercial premises to Rearguard Action Ltd at a yearly rent of £28,000, including VAT, for a term of six years. No premium is payable and there is an upwards-only market rent review on the fourth anniversary of the grant of the lease. The lease is granted on 1 October 2023 without the agreement having been previously substantially performed. The effective date of the grant of the lease is therefore 1 October 2023.

The NPV of the rent payable under the lease is £149,199, which is below the £150,000 zero rate band for rent payable on a lease. As the lease is for a period of less than seven years, and as no premium is payable, there is no requirement for Rearguard Action Ltd to file a land transaction return (LBTT(S)A 2013, s 30(2)(c)).

The lease restricted activities in the premises to storage, repackaging and distribution. Adam always intended, in due course, to carry out repairs of faulty goods returned to the depot (and had mentioned this to the landlord when taking the lease on). The landlord agrees to vary the lease to permit the repair work to be carried on in return for an increase in the annual rent to £32,000, including VAT, from 1 October 2025. The NPV of the rent payable is now £162,914, which exceeds the zero rate band for rent, and Rearguard Action Ltd is now required to file a land transaction return by 31 October 2025 and pay the LBTT due of £129 (LBTT(S)A 2013, Sch 19, para 30(2)(a) and (3)).

A rent review takes place on 1 October 2027 at which point the rent is increased to £35,000 per annum including VAT. However, this increase in rent does not result in Rearguard Action Ltd having to submit a further land transaction as a result of the rent increase, as the grant of the lease has already been notified to Revenue Scotland.

Rearguard Action Ltd is, however, required to carry out a review of the LBTT chargeable on the lease on 1 October 2028 (LBTT(S)A 2013, Sch 19, para 10(1)(b)(iv) and para 10(7)(e)) and on 30 September 2029 when the lease terminates (LBTT(S)A 2013, Sch 19, para 11).

In the further return to be filed by 31 October 2028 (ie 30 days after the review date) the NPV of the rent is £167,881 and the tax payable has increased to £179, meaning that Rearguard Action Ltd is required to pay a further £50.

Finally, Rearguard Action Ltd is required to file a further return by 30 October 2029, being 30 days after the date upon which the lease terminated. As there will have been no further change to the rent payable since the return filed by 31 October 2028, no further tax would be payable.

It can therefore be seen that a significant administration burden is placed on Rearguard Action Ltd as it has to file three land transaction returns in relation to a six-year lease.

Renunciation or release of a lease

4.46 The renunciation or release of a lease is the acquisition of a 'chargeable interest' by the landlord (LBTT(S)A 2013, s6(3)(b)). Therefore, if the landlord gives, or is deemed to give (see **4.65**), chargeable consideration for the renunciation or release, such consideration will be within the scope of LBTT.

Renunciation of existing lease in return for new lease

4.47 Where the landlord grants a new lease to the tenant in consideration of the renunciation of the existing lease between the same parties, the following rules apply (LBTT(S)A 2013, Sch 19, para 18(1)(a) and (b)):

- the grant of the new lease does not count as chargeable consideration given by the landlord for the renunciation of the existing lease; and
- the renunciation of the existing lease does not count as chargeable consideration given by the tenant for the grant of the new lease.

Equally the LBTT exchange provisions (see **2.31**) do not apply (LBTT(S) A 2013, Sch 19, para 18(2)).

In such circumstances therefore the landlord will be charged to LBTT based on any chargeable consideration he gives (or is deemed to give – see **4.65**) for the renunciation, but taking no account of the value of the new lease granted. Similarly, the tenant will be taxed based on the 'chargeable consideration' he gives (or is deemed to give – see **4.65**) for the grant of the new lease, ignoring any value in the existing lease which is renounced.

Lease renewal

4.48 An alternative to varying a lease to extend its term may be for the parties to enter into a new lease of the land, covering the period from expiry of the current lease to the desired later expiry date. When this happens, the lease may be granted before its start date. The 'effective date' for LBTT purposes will be the date of grant, not the date upon which the lease starts. However, the start date is used in calculating the NPV of the rents, so no benefit is gained from the fact that the rent will not become payable under the new lease until some future date. The original and new leases may be 'successive linked leases' if the new lease was contemplated when the original lease was entered into (see **4.67**). However, this is a question of fact and the leases are not necessarily linked.

Example 4.9 – New lease to commence on expiry of old lease

Pamela occupies an office unit under a ten-year lease which expires on 30 September 2026. She wants to remain in occupation beyond this date and, on 1 October 2023, a new lease is executed for a further ten years from 1 October 2026 at a rent of £40,000 per annum, including VAT. Pamela must submit an LBTT return no later than 31 October 2023 and pay any LBTT due at the same time. The NPV of the rents, calculated using 1 October 2026 as the start date, is £332,664. The new lease was not contemplated at the time the original lease was entered into, and therefore the new lease is not linked with the existing lease, and the LBTT payable is 1% of £182,664, which is £1,826.

As the existing lease and the new lease were not linked, Pamela gets the benefit of two 'zero rate bands' when calculating the LBTT payable on the existing lease and the new lease.

Variable or uncertain rent

4.49

> **Focus**
>
> - Where when a lease is granted the rent payable is subject to a contingency, or it is uncertain or unascertained, the effect of that contingency ceasing, or the rent becoming certain or ascertained, may be that a lease which was not notifiable becomes notifiable.

Sometimes, when a lease is granted, the rent is actually or potentially variable or uncertain – for example, because the rent depends on the tenant's business results or it is subject to a rent review. In such cases the following rules apply (LBTT(S)A 2013, Sch 19, para 13(2)):

- If the rent payable is contingent it is to be determined on the assumption that the outcome of the contingency will be such that the rent is payable or, as the case may be, the rent does not cease to be payable (LBTT(S) A 2013, s 18(2)). For these purposes the rent will be contingent in the following circumstances (LBTT(S)A 2013, s 18(3)):
  - the rent is to be paid or provided only if some uncertain future event occurs; or
  - the rent is to cease to be paid or provided if some uncertain future event occurs.
- If the rent is uncertain or unascertained it is to be determined on the basis of a reasonable estimate (LBTT(S)A 2013, s 19(2)). For these purposes the rent will be uncertain if the amount depends on uncertain future events (LBTT(S)A 2013, s 19(3)). In the case of an open market rent review, it is normally acceptable to estimate the rent payable after review as being the same as the previous rent (LBTT60031). Any provision for rent to be adjusted in line with the Retail Prices Index, the Consumer Prices Index or any other 'similar' index is to be ignored in determining the rent payable for the purposes of LBTT (LBTT(S)A 2013, Sch 19, para 13(5)). However, when an adjustment of the rent in line with, say, the Retail Prices Index actually takes place, it would seem that the adjusted rent should then be used in calculating the LBTT on any subsequent three-yearly review (see **4.21**) and on any review on assignation or termination of the lease (see **4.26**). This is on the basis that LBTT(S)A 2013, Sch 19, para 13(5) only applies for determining the amount of the rent payable under a lease where the rent varies in accordance with a provision in a lease or it is contingent, uncertain or unascertained. Essentially it provides that the rent which is uncertain must be determined on the basis of a reasonable estimate. However, when the rent has actually been adjusted in line with, say, the Retail Prices Index, it would seem that it would no longer vary with a provision in the lease or be uncertain,

and therefore the adjustment in line with Retail Prices Index would be brought into account in determining the LBTT payable on a subsequent three-yearly review or on an assignation or termination of a lease. The adjusted annual rent at the time of the lease review may also be used as an estimate of the rent payable for the remaining lease term. This would seem to be the view of Revenue Scotland in LBTT60031.

4.50 The general rule is that if the grant of the lease is notifiable to Revenue Scotland under LBTT(S)A 2013, s 30 then there is no requirement for the buyer (ie the original tenant or a subsequent assignee) to make an LBTT return when the contingency to which the rent is subject ceases or the rent becomes certain or ascertained. This is because the LBTT chargeable on the lease will then be subject to the three-yearly regular review and a review on assignation or termination (see **4.21** and **4.26**), and therefore any change in the rent payable as a consequence of the contingency ceasing, or the rent becoming certain or ascertained, should be taxed under that review process. This is the case whether the change in rent payable occurs whilst the lease is held by the original tenant or by a subsequent assignee (LBTT(S)A 2013, Sch 19, para 28(2)(c)).

4.51 However, if the grant of the lease was not notifiable to Revenue Scotland under LBTT(S)A 2013, s 30, but the effect of the rent ceasing to be subject to the contingency, or the rent becoming certain or ascertained, is that the grant of the lease becomes notifiable, then the buyer (ie the original tenant or a subsequent assignee) must make a return to Revenue Scotland (LBTT(S)A 2013, s 31(6) and Sch 19, para 28(2)(a)). The return must be made within the 30 day period commencing on the day after the rent ceased to be subject to the contingency or became certain or ascertained, and the return must include a self-assessment of any LBTT payable (LBTT(S)A 2013, s 31(3) and (4)). The LBTT chargeable, if any, is to be calculated by reference to the tax rates and tax bands in force at the 'effective date' of the grant of the lease (or earlier 'substantial performance' of the agreement for lease) (see **4.84** et seq) (LBTT(S)A 2013, s 31(5)).

4.52 For these purposes the circumstances where rent is uncertain or unascertained include those where the rent payable may vary under either of the following provisions (LBTT(S)A 2013, Sch 19, para 13(4)):

- section 13, 14, 15 or 31 of the Agricultural Holdings (Scotland) Act 1991 (c.55); or
- section 9, 10 or 11 of the Agricultural Holdings (Scotland) Act 2003 (asp 11).

Example 4.10 – Variable or uncertain rent

On 14 August 2023 Kenneth grants Ryan a 20-year lease of a site for a theme park. The lease requires Ryan to construct and open the theme park within two years of grant. No premium is payable. Rent is set at a base level of £15,000 per year, but from Year 4 onwards the rent is to be 5% of the turnover of the park if this is higher than £15,000 (additional rent based on turnover to be estimated and paid quarterly with adjustment at the year-end). Prudent projections indicate that 5% of turnover will be £12,000, including VAT, in Year 4 and £16,000 in Year 5, rising by £2,000, including VAT, per annum thereafter.

By 13 September 2023, Ryan must submit an LBTT return on the basis of a reasonable estimate of rent, and it seems that the following would be justifiable:

Year	*Rent for LBTT*	*Discounted rent*
1	£15,000	£14,492
2	£15,000	£14,003
3	£15,000	£13,529
4	£15,000	£13,071
5	£16,000	£13,472
6	£18,000	£14,643
7	£20,000	£15,719
8	£22,000	£16,707
9	£24,000	£17,609
10	£26,000	£18,432
11	£28,000	£19,178
12	£30,000	£19,853
13	£32,000	£20,461
14	£34,000	£21,005
15	£36,000	£21,488
16	£38,000	£21,915
17	£40,000	£22,288
18	£42,000	£22,611
19	£44,000	£22,886
20	£46,000	£23,118
Total discounted rent		£366,480
Less zero rate band		(£150,000)
LBTT charged at 1% on		£216,480
LBTT on rent		£2,164

Ryan will then have to carry out a regular review of the LBTT chargeable on the lease, assuming he remains the tenant until it expires, on 13 August 2043, on each of the following dates:

14 August 2026

14 August 2029

14 August 2032

14 August 2035

14 August 2038

14 August 2041

13 August 2043

This means that Ryan would file eight land transaction returns in relation to the 20-year lease, however there would be no requirement to file a further return as each annual rent was ascertained, at each of years 5 through to 20, as this is dealt with through the regular review procedure.

MAKING AND AMENDING LBTT RETURNS

4.53 LBTT returns relating to lease transactions are made and amended in the same way as for other transactions relating to land in Scotland: see **Chapter 8**. Some sections of the LBTT return only apply to transactions involving leases. If the return is completed online, the lease-specific questions will only appear if, in the 'About the Transaction' section of the online return, 'lease' is chosen as the 'Description of the transaction'. An LBTT return filed online can be amended by selecting the relevant return from the list of returns within the 'All returns' selection from the 'Dashboard' page, and then selecting the 'Amend' option below the relevant return. This should then take you into the LBTT return where amendments can be made to that return. Where a paper LBTT return was filed, or the taxpayer no longer has access to the online return, the return can be amended by writing to Revenue Scotland at the address set out in **Appendix A.** The request for the amendment should set out for each section ('field') within the paper return that is to be amended:

- the current entry in the return which has been filed; and
- the amended entry.

It is not possible to amend an LBTT return more than 12 months after the 'filing date', which will generally be the date which is 30 days after the 'effective date' (see **2.81**) of the transaction. The amendment of LBTT returns is discussed further at **8.17**.

Calculating the liability

What is consideration?

4.54 LBTT is charged on 'chargeable consideration', which is defined for leases, as it is for other transactions, as '...any consideration in money or money's worth given for the subject-matter of the transaction, directly or indirectly, by the buyer or a person connected with the buyer'. (LBTT(S)A 2013, Sch 2, para 1). In relation to the grant or variation of a lease, consideration may be in the form of rent and/or premium. Since the tax treatments of the two forms of consideration differ, it is important to distinguish between them (see **4.58**). In relation to both rent and premium, the usual valuation rules apply to consideration other than in cash, and to non-sterling consideration (see **2.17**), or to the limited exemption where the consideration includes the carrying out of works (see **2.25**).

4.55 When a lease is renounced in consideration for the grant of another lease between the same parties, the renunciation and grant do not count as consideration for each other (LBTT(S)A 2013, Sch 19, para 18(1)). In addition, the exchange provisions (see **2.31**) in LBTT(S)A, Sch 2, para 5 do not apply (LBTT(S)A 2013, Sch 19, para 18(2)). The acceptance of normal tenant's obligations other than payment of rent and premium does not count as chargeable consideration when a lease is granted (LBTT(S)A 2013, Sch 19, para 15). The acceptance of such obligations, including the obligation to pay rent, does not count as chargeable consideration for the assignation of a lease (LBTT(S)A 2013, Sch 19, para 16).

Rent

4.56

> **Focus**
>
> - To minimise LBTT payable on the grant of a lease it will be important to ensure that 'inclusive rents' (ie those covering items such as insurance, cleaning, maintenance etc.) are overtly apportioned in the lease, on a just and reasonable basis, so that LBTT is only charged on the amount apportioned to rent.

There is no comprehensive definition of rent, so it must take its ordinary commercial meaning of consideration paid by a tenant, usually periodically, for the use or occupation of the property. Where rent is payable other than in sterling cash, it must be valued in the same way as other consideration, at the 'effective date' of the lease (see **2.17**). A single sum expressed as payable in respect of rent and other matters, without apportionment, is to be treated as entirely rent (LBTT(S)A 2013, Sch 19, para 12(1)). To minimise the LBTT payable, it may therefore be important to ensure that 'inclusive' rents are overtly apportioned in the terms and conditions of the lease between what is truly rent and other items such as insurance, cleaning, maintenance etc. The apportionment to the rent and other items must be on a just and reasonable basis (LBTT(S)A 2013, Sch 2, para 4(1)).

Example 4.11 – What is chargeable to LBTT as rent?

Caroline leases an office suite in a larger building owned by Big Office Co Ltd on a ten-year lease, terminable by either party on one year's notice. The rent is

£30,000 per annum, plus a proportionate share of an insurance premium paid by Big Office and covering the whole building. The rent includes heating/air conditioning and regular cleaning, but amounts are not allocated to these in the lease. Light and power are separately metered and charged. The insurance premium is clearly identified and, since it merely passes on actual cost, is presumably 'just and reasonable', so it will not form part of the rent for LBTT purposes. Since the remaining rent is not allocated between real rent and matters such as cleaning and heating, strictly it is all rent for LBTT purposes. The parties would be well advised to insert a reasonable allocation into the lease. However, even in the absence of numbers in the lease itself, Revenue Scotland may be persuaded to accept an allocation. They may require evidence from Big Office to support amounts allocated to non-chargeable items.

4.57 An anti-avoidance provision at LBTT(S)A 2013, Sch 19, para 17 is designed to prevent a premium being disguised as a loan or deposit on the grant of a new lease. If, in connection with the grant of a lease, the tenant makes any loan or pays any deposit and the repayment of all or part of the loan or deposit is contingent on anything done or omitted to be done by the tenant, or is contingent on the death of the tenant, the amount of the loan or deposit (disregarding any amount which has been repaid) is to be treated for LBTT purposes as though it were a premium given for the grant of the lease (LBTT(S) A 2013, Sch 19, para 17(1)). However, this rule does not apply to a deposit if the amount of that deposit is not more than twice the highest amount of rent payable in respect of any consecutive 12 month period during the term of the lease (LBTT(S)A 2013, Sch 19, para 17(3) and 4(a)).

In determining the highest amount of rent in respect of any 12 month period during the term of the lease, account is taken of: (a) any rent which is subject to a contingency (ie it is assumed that the outcome of the contingency will be that the rent is payable or that the rent does not cease to be payable), and (b) a reasonable estimate of any rent which is uncertain or unascertainable. However, where there is a renunciation of an existing lease, and in consideration a new lease is granted to the tenant, no account is to be taken of the reduction of rent for the period of any overlap between the two leases, as a consequence of overlap relief being available (see **4.92**) (LBTT(S)A 2013, Sch 19, para 17(5)).

The anti-avoidance provision also applies on the assignation of an existing lease, where the assignee pays a deposit or makes a loan which is contingent on anything done or omitted to be done by the assignee or on the death of the assignee (LBTT(S)A 2013, Sch 19, para 17(2)). This provision is presumably aimed at a premium being disguised as a loan or deposit which may never be repaid. In this case, the rule does not apply if the amount of any deposit is not more than twice the highest amount of rent payable in respect of any consecutive 12 month period during the term of the lease which remains outstanding at the date of the assignation (LBTT(S)A 2013, Sch 19, para 17(4)(b)). The highest amount of rent payable in any 12 month period during the term of the lease which remains outstanding at the date of the assignation is determined on the same basis as described above in relation to the grant of a lease (LBTT(S)A 2013, Sch 19, para 17(5)).

However, tax is not chargeable under this anti-avoidance provision in relation to either the grant of a new lease or the assignation of an existing lease, if the amount of the deposit or loan (plus the amount of any actual premium payable) is equal to or less than the amount of the nil rate tax band for consideration other than rent, namely £150,000, but the rent payable under the terms of the lease is £1,000 or more, so that tax would only be chargeable under this rule due to the removal of the nil rate band by virtue of LBTT(S)A 2013, Sch 19, para 9 (LBTT(S)A 2013, Sch 19, para 17(6)).

New leases

4.58 When a new lease is granted or deemed to be granted, LBTT must be calculated separately on any rent and on any premium or deemed premium (LBTT(S)A 2013, Sch 19, para 2). The two components are then simply added to give the LBTT liability. As in other cases, any VAT chargeable must be included in both rent and premium. However, if VAT arises as a result of the landlord exercising the 'option to tax' after the effective date of the transaction, this does not have to be taken into account (LBTT(S)A 2013, Sch 2, para 2). Where a tenant pays a landlord's reasonable legal fees in connection with the grant of a lease, that payment will not be treated as a premium for LBTT purposes.

Loss of zero rate band on premium

4.59

Focus

- If a lease of non-residential property is granted for both a premium and rent, and the annual rent amounts to £1,000 or more, the nil tax rate for a premium up to £150,000 is replaced by a 1% rate.

The premium on the grant of a lease over non-residential property is subject to LBTT at normal rates up to 5% on the same 'progressive' system as any other lump sum payment for an interest in land (see **2.35**) but with one important change. If there is both rent and consideration other than rent (ie a premium or deemed premium) being given for the grant of a lease, and the rent amounts to £1,000 or more per annum, the nil tax rate for a premium up to £150,000 is replaced by a 1% rate (LBTT(S)A 2013, Sch 19, para 9(2)). Rent for these purposes is the average annual rent payable over the term of the lease or, if different amounts of rent are payable for different parts of the term of the lease, and these amounts are ascertainable at the effective date (see **2.81**) of the transaction, then the average annual rent over that part of the term for which the highest ascertainable rent is payable, should be taken (LBTT(S)A 2013, Sch 19, para 9(7)).

If the transaction is one of a number of 'linked transactions' comprising both residential and non-residential property, and the annual rent attributable to the non-residential property, on a just and reasonable apportionment, is at least £1,000 then for the purposes of determining the tax chargeable in relation to the premium, the transactions are treated as if there were two sets of transactions, one consisting entirely of residential property and the other consisting entirely of non-residential property (LBTT(S)A 2013, Sch 19, para 9(4)). The aggregate rent and premium payable for each of the linked transactions is attributed to the two sets of notional transactions, one consisting of all of the residential property and the other consisting of all of the non-residential property, on a just and reasonable basis (LBTT(S)A 2013, Sch 19, para 9(5)). The amount of the rent apportioned to the notional transaction for non-residential property is then used to determine whether the £1,000 or more per annum threshold has been breached in relation to that notional transaction. If it has, any premium apportioned on a 'just and reasonable' basis to the notional non-residential transactions will then be taxed on the basis that the nil tax rate for a premium up to £150,000 is replaced by a 1% rate (LBTT(S)A 2013, Sch 19, para 9(2)).

Surprisingly, the legislation says nothing about treating the two notional sets of transactions as being linked. There is a reference to 'linked transactions' in LBTT(S)A 2013, Sch 19, para 9(3)(a) but this merely says that if there are two or more real transactions which are linked, for the purposes of determining the tax payable on the non-residential lease(s), the real transactions are to be treated as two sets of transactions, one comprising wholly residential property and the other wholly non-residential property. Therefore it would appear that there is a notional separation into two independent transactions which do not have to be treated as linked in determining the rate of LBTT to be charged on each part of the premium. However, treating one set of the notional transactions as comprising wholly residential property, should mean that no LBTT is payable in relation to the premium apportioned to the residential property by virtue of LBTT(S)A 2013, Sch 1, para 3(1)(a), unless the lease is a 'qualifying lease' – (see **4.4**). It would seem that LBTT would still be chargeable on the rent payable apportioned to the residential property, as the treatment as an independent transaction only applies for the purposes of determining the tax chargeable in relation to the consideration other than rent ie the premium (LBTT(S)A 2013, Sch 19, para 9(4)). Therefore for the purposes of determining the tax chargeable on rent, the linked transactions would not consist entirely of residential property, and consequently the rent on the residential properties would still be chargeable to LBTT (see **4.6**).

Example 4.12 – Loss of zero rate band on premium

On 1 April 2024 Benmore Ltd grants a five-year lease of commercial property to Rangefinder Ltd for a premium of £500,000 including VAT and an annual rent of £1,500 per annum. The NPV of the rent is clearly below the nil rate threshold for rent of £150,000, and therefore no LBTT is payable on the rent. However, as the annual rent exceeds £1,000 the £150,000 nil rate band for the premium is not available and the LBTT on the premium is calculated as follows:

Premium	*Rate*	*LBTT*
£	%	£
250,000	1	2,500
250,000	5	12,500
500,000		15,000

LBTT on rent

4.60 As set out at **4.13** to determine the LBTT chargeable on the rent payable under a lease the steps are as follows:

- Step 1 – Establish the rent payable over the term of the lease. If the rent is subject to a contingency assume that the contingency will be such that the rent is payable or, as the case may be, does not cease to be payable. If the rent is uncertain or unascertained make a reasonable estimate of the rent payable (see **4.49** et seq).
- Step 2 – Calculate the NPV of the rent payable over the term of the lease, as established in Step (1), using the formula and discount rate specified in the legislation (LBTT(S)A 2013, Sch 19, paras 6 and 7). The term of the lease is that specified in the lease, ignoring any break clauses, or any right of either the landlord or the tenant to terminate the lease early or renew it.
- Step 3 – The discounted rent amounts for each year are then totalled. If this total does not exceed the threshold for the nil tax rate band (currently £150,000) no LBTT is chargeable on the rent. If the total NPV does exceed the threshold for the nil tax rate band, only the excess is chargeable to LBTT. The rate of LBTT is 1% until the total NBV exceeds £2,000,000, when the rate increases to 2%.

The calculation of the LBTT charge on rent is considered in more detail at **4.13–4.15** and **Example 4.4**.

4.61 The NPV of the rent payable over the term of the lease can be calculated manually, however an LBTT calculator for this purpose can be found on the Revenue Scotland website. This is discussed in more detail at **4.15**.

Example 4.13 – Calculation of NPV of a lease at rent

On 1 May 2024, John agrees to grant Kate a ten year lease of a hotel at an annual rent of £25,000 and for a premium of £260,000, both amounts inclusive of VAT. There is an upwards-only market rent review on the fifth anniversary. The lease is granted on 1 July 2024 without the agreement previously having been substantially performed. The effective date of the grant of the lease is therefore 1 July 2024, and the rent review is due on 1 July 2029. The LBTT can be calculated manually as follows:

Year	*Actual rent for LBTT purposes*	*Discounted rent*
1	£25,000	£24,154
2	£25,000	£23,337
3	£25,000	£22,548
4	£25,000	£21,786
5	£25,000	£21,049
6	£25,000	£20,337
7	£25,000	£19,649
8	£25,000	£18,985
9	£25,000	£18,343
10	£25,000	£17,722
Total discounted rent		£207,910
Less zero rate band		(£150,000)
LBTT charged at 1% on		£57,910
LBTT on rent		£579
LBTT on premium: £250,000 @ 1% £10,000 @ 5%		£3,000
Total LBTT (on rent and premium)		£3,579

Note: As the annual rent is £1,000 or more the nil rate band is not available in relation to the lease.

4.62 Alternatively, the Revenue Scotland calculator for non-residential leases may be used. The calculator can be found on the Revenue Scotland website.

The effective date of the transaction, the lease start date and the lease end date must be entered in the relevant boxes, as must the chargeable consideration other than rent (ie any premium payable). The number of input boxes for rent will then automatically adjust to reflect the actual duration of the lease. The rent for each year of the lease must be entered in the relevant boxes. If the grant of the lease is linked with the grant of any other leases, the rent to be entered is the aggregate rent for all of the linked leases for each year. The calculator will then calculate the net present value of the rent, the LBTT on the consideration other than rent, the LBTT on the rent, and the aggregate of these two amounts being the LBTT payable on the transaction.

4.63 The 'relevant rent' must be entered in the box below the annual rental boxes and is as set out in LBTT(S)A 2013, Sch 19, para 9(6). For a lease not linked with any other, the figure is the average annual rent payable over the term of the lease. However, if different amounts of rent are payable for different parts of the term of the lease, and these amounts are ascertainable at the effective date (see **2.81**) of the transaction, then the average annual rent over that part of the term for which the highest ascertainable rent is payable, should be taken (LBTT(S)A 2013, Sch 19, para 9(6) and (7)). If the lease is linked with any other leases at rent, the figure is the aggregate of such figures for all of the leases (again, apportioned to non-residential parts where appropriate). However, the 'relevant rent' influences the output from the calculator in only one respect, and that is to deny the benefit of the zero rate band on any premium if the rent (ie the relevant rent) is £1,000 or more (see **4.59**).

Example 4.14 – Use of Revenue Scotland calculator

Using numbers from **Example 4.13** above, the output from the calculator is:

News About Us Legislation Compliance and Dispute Resolution Contact Us

Revenue Scotland
Teachd-a-steach Alba

Land and Buildings Transaction Tax

Search

Home > Land and Buildings Transaction Tax > Tax Calculators > LBTT on Lease Transactions Calculator

LBTT on Lease Transactions Calculator

This calculator provides the amount of liability of LBTT on Lease Transactions, based on the rates and bands approved by the Scottish Parliament. For assignations of leases (other than those treated as the grant of a new lease), you should use the LBTT on Property Transactions Calculator. See the Guidance section for more information.

Tax Calculators

LBTT on Property Transactions Calculator

View More

Values Entered:

Effective Date:	01/07/2016
Lease Start Date:	01/07/2016
Lease End Date:	30/06/2026
Chargeable consideration other than rent:	£260,000.00
Year 1 Rent:	25000.00
Year 2 Rent:	25000.00
Year 3 Rent:	25000.00
Year 4 Rent:	25000.00
Year 5 Rent:	25000.00
Year 6 Rent:	25000.00
Year 7 Rent:	25000.00
Year 8 Rent:	25000.00
Year 9 Rent:	25000.00
Year 10 Rent:	25000.00
Relevant rental figure:	£25,000.00

4.64 Note that the calculator output shows all of the entries made on the input screens, so it is easy to check there have been no transcription errors.

Connected company rule

4.65

> **Focus**
>
> - If a land transaction in relation to a lease takes place where the buyer is a company and the seller is connected with that company, the consideration chargeable to LBTT is deemed to be at least equal to market value.

The normal rule applies (see **2.29**), that if the 'buyer' (the tenant on the grant of a new lease or, in the case of a renunciation, the landlord or in the case of an assignation the assignee) is a company connected with the seller, the chargeable consideration is taken to be at least equal to the market value of the subject matter of the transaction in question, plus the actual rent payable if the transaction is the grant of a lease (LBTT(S)A 2013, s22). Note that it does not matter whether the 'seller' is a company, individual or other entity. Application of the rule depends only on the 'buyer' being a company which is 'connected' with the 'seller'. This is subject to the same exceptions as apply to other transactions (see **2.29**). Where this rule applies to the grant of a lease, it does not lead to any deemed adjustment of the actual rent. If the rent charged under the lease is less than a full market rent, it is assumed that the lease will have a capital value. The amount of this capital value is taxed as a deemed premium.

Example 4.15 – Lease to connected company

Amanda grants to her family trading company, PPM Ltd, a ten year lease of a barn on her farm, for use as a storage facility. The lease is at a flat rent of £5,000 per annum with no provision for rent reviews. The NPV of rent over the life of the lease is clearly below the £150,000 nil tax rate threshold. However, it is acknowledged that a current annual market rent would be £7,500 and a lease at the actual rent of £5,000 would command a market premium of £20,000. The lease is therefore subject to LBTT on this premium. Because the yearly rent is £1,000 or more, there is no zero rate band for the premium and this is chargeable at 1%. LBTT of £200 is payable. It is worth noting that, if the rent had been set at a market level of £7,500, so that there was no deemed premium, the NPV of the rent would still have fallen below the £150,000 threshold and no LBTT would have been payable. However, an LBTT return would still have been required (LBTT(S)A 2013, s 30(2)(a)); see **8.2**).

> **Focus**
>
> - Successive leases of the same premises may be treated as linked so that the second and any subsequent leases are effectively treated as extending the first lease. This may result in a requirement to file a land transaction return either because the first lease becomes notifiable when it was not previously notifiable, or additional tax becomes payable, or tax is payable where it was previously not payable.

Linked transactions

4.66 Lease transactions may be 'linked' with other transactions in relation to land located in Scotland (whether or not involving other leases) if they form part of a single scheme, arrangement or series of transactions between the same seller and buyer or persons connected with them (LBTT(S)A 2013, s 57 – see **2.79**). There are two distinct ways (successive linked leases and other linked leases) in which lease transactions may be linked, and each has its own implications. These are discussed in **4.67** and **4.68** et seq.

Successive linked leases

4.67 If successive leases of the same or substantially the same premises are granted, (irrespective of whether the leases are granted at the same time or at different times) and if those leases are linked, the second and subsequent leases are effectively treated as extending the first lease (LBTT(S)A 2013, Sch 19, para 23(1) and (2)). The 'extended' lease is treated as granted when the first lease in the series was granted, for a period (term) equal to the aggregate of the periods of all of the leases and in consideration of the rent payable under all of the leases.

The grant of the second and any subsequent leases is ignored for the purposes of LBTT except where the effect of the grant of that second or subsequent lease is any of the following (LBTT(S)A 2013, Sch 19, para 23(3) and s 34):

(a) the grant of the first lease in the series, as extended by the subsequent lease(s), becomes notifiable when it was not previously notifiable; or

(b) additional tax is payable in respect of the first lease as extended by the subsequent lease(s); or

(c) tax is payable in relation to the first lease where none was payable prior to the extension by the subsequent lease.

If any of (a), (b) or (c) above apply then the buyer in relation to the first lease (ie the original tenant or any subsequent assignee (LBTT(S)A 2013, Sch 19, para 28(2)(b)) must file a land transaction return in relation to that lease, and the return must be filed within the 30 day period beginning with the day after the effective date (see **2.81**) of the later transaction (ie the date upon which the second or subsequent lease was granted or the agreement for lease substantially performed) (LBTT(S)A 2013, s 34(2) and (3)). This return will either be the first notification of the transaction or notification that tax is now payable (where none was payable before) or notification that additional tax is payable.

If the grant of the first lease in the series was notifiable then the grant of the second and any subsequent leases may lead to LBTT becoming payable for the first time, or to additional LBTT becoming payable, so that there may be a requirement for a land transaction return to be filed (LBTT(S)A 2013, s 34(1)(b) and (c)). The increase in term and rent payable caused by the deemed extension of the first lease, on the grant of the second or subsequent leases, will be brought into account for LBTT when that further land transaction return is filed. The lease will continue to be subject to the three-yearly review in the normal way (see **4.17** et seq). Alternatively, if the grant of the first lease was not notifiable, but its deemed extension by the grant of the second or subsequent lease causes it to become notifiable, then a land transaction return will have to be filed by the buyer as described above. The rent payable under the 'extended' first lease will therefore be brought into account for the purposes of LBTT when that land transaction return is filed, and the lease will then be subject to the three-yearly review (LBTT(S)A 2013, Sch 19, para 10(1)(a)) and the review on assignation or termination (LBTT(S)A 2013, Sch 19, para 11).

It is assumed that where a further LBTT return is filed because additional tax was payable, or tax became payable where none was payable prior to the extension by the subsequent lease, account will be taken of the tax paid based on that further return, in assessing the LBTT liability on any subsequent three-yearly review (see **4.21**).

LBTT may become payable, or additional LBTT may arise, in relation to rent (the NPV of the rent will have increased because the deemed lease is for a longer period) and/or premium (if a further premium is paid, the premiums must be aggregated to calculate the amount of tax payable).

However, successive leases are not necessarily linked. If, when the first lease was granted, there was no agreement (explicit or implied) that the next lease would be granted, and if the next lease was negotiated independently of the first, they are not likely to be linked. However, if the first lease contained an option for the grant of a further lease, they probably are linked. Revenue Scotland may assume that successive leases are linked unless there is clear evidence to the contrary.

Example 4.16 –Successive linked leases

Amanda granted Ian a five-year lease of a warehouse commencing 1 September 2023 for a premium of £130,000 and a yearly rent of £50,000. The lease was executed on the start date without prior substantial performance of any agreement. The lease terms included an option for Ian to take a further five year lease commencing on 1 September 2028 at the same rent, on payment of a further premium of £130,000. Ian exercises the option; the second lease is executed on 1 August 2028 (ie one month before commencement) and the additional premium is paid on 1 September 2028.

During September 2023, Ian submitted an LBTT return for the five year lease, with premium £130,000 and yearly rent of £50,000. The total LBTT paid was £2,058, comprising £1,300 on the premium (charged at 1% because the rent is £1,000 or more (see **4.59**)) and £758 on the rent. A three-yearly review of the grant of the original lease must be carried out by Ian on 1 September 2026 and a return filed by 1 October 2026. However, as there was no change to the rent or premium payable at that date, no further tax is payable. As the second lease is executed on 1 August 2028, prior to the termination of the original lease on 31 August 2028, there is no requirement for Ian to file a land transaction on termination of the original lease under LBTT(S)A 2013, Sch 19, para 11. This is because the leases are linked and LBTT applies as if the two leases were a single lease, for a term of ten years, and in consideration of the rent payable under both leases (LBTT(S)A 2013, Sch 19, para 23(2) and (3)). As the leases are linked, there is deemed to be a ten year lease at a flat rental of £50,000 per annum and a premium of £260,000, commencing 1 September 2023. The LBTT on such a lease is £5,658, comprising £3,000 on the premium and £2,658 on the rent. The LBTT paid on the original lease is deducted, leaving £3,600 payable as a result of the grant of the second lease. As additional tax is payable Ian is required to file a land transaction return by 31 August 2028 and pay the additional tax due of £3,600. Although the second lease is not 'substantially performed' early, it is executed one month before commencement, so the further LBTT return and payment are due 30 days after the date of execution, that is no later than 31 August 2028.

Ian will therefore be required to carry out further three-yearly reviews of the LBTT chargeable on the lease on each of 1 September 2029 and 1 September 2032, and a review on 31 August 2033 when the extended lease terminates. This assumes that Ian holds the lease until expiry of the period of the lease.

Other linked leases

4.68 Leases of **different** premises may be linked – for example, a tenant may take on leases of two shops in different towns from the same landlord, negotiated as a single deal.

4.69 Where leases are linked and the 'successive leases' rules do not apply (for example, leases of two properties agreed between the same parties as part of a single transaction), any premiums are aggregated to determine the LBTT chargeable, and that chargeable amount is then apportioned between each premium. To determine the LBTT payable on the aggregate premiums, multiply that part of the aggregate premiums falling into each tax band by the tax rate for that band and then calculate the sum of each of these amounts (LBTT(S) A 2013, s 26(1) and (2)). This amount is the total LBTT chargeable in relation to the aggregate of the premiums payable which is then apportioned, using the fraction arrived at by dividing the amount of any particular premium by the total amount of the aggregate premiums, to arrive at the LBTT chargeable for each premium. The NPV of the rents under the leases are also aggregated to give a figure for total NPV (TNPV). Multiply that part of the TNPV falling into each tax band by the tax rate for that band and then calculate the sum of each of these amounts to give you the LBTT payable in relation to the TNPV (LBTT(S)A 2013, Sch 19, para 5). The tax on rent applicable to each lease is then calculated by applying the fraction obtained by dividing the NPV (for the individual lease) by the TNPV, to the overall tax on rent.

Example 4.17 – Non-successive linked leases calculation

The facts are as in **Example 4.13**. However, also on 1 May 2024 John agrees to grant Kate a ten year lease of another hotel at an annual rent of £50,000 and for a premium of £300,000, both amounts inclusive of VAT. There is an upwards only market rent review on the fifth anniversary. This second lease is not granted until 1 September 2024 without the agreement having been previously substantially performed. The leases are linked as they form part of a single arrangement between the same seller and buyer, so that the premiums and rent payable must be aggregated in determining the LBTT payable. The NPV of rent under the first lease is £207,910 and the LBTT paid was £579. The NPV of rent under the second lease is £415,820, so the aggregate NPV is £623,730. The LBTT payable on a lease with this NPV of rent is 1% of (£623,730 – £150,000), which is £4,737. The revised LBTT attributable to the rent on the first lease is £4,737 × £207,910/£623,730, which is £1,579, and the LBTT attributable to the rent on the second lease is £4,737 × £415,820/£623,730, which is £3,158.

The aggregate of the premiums payable under the first and second leases is £560,000, and the LBTT payable on consideration other than rent of that amount is £19,950.

This is calculated as follows:

Aggregate Premiums	*Rate*	*LBTT*
£	%	£
250,000	1	2,500
310,000	5	15,500
560,000		18,000

Note: As the annual rent is £1,000 or more the nil rate band is not available in relation to the lease.

The revised LBTT attributable to the premium on the first lease is £18,000 × £260,000/£560,000, which is £8,357, and the LBTT attributable to the premium on the second lease is £18,000 × £300,000/£560,000, which is £9,643.

LEASE RENEWALS AND EXTENSIONS

4.70

> **Focus**
>
> - There is a special rule to deal with the situation where a lease for a fixed term continues beyond that term, with the lease being treated as growing by one year at a time. The deemed extension of the lease may cause it to become notifiable where it was not previously notifiable.
> - If a new lease is subsequently issued within one year of the end of the fixed term then the rent payable during the gap period is treated as payable under the new lease. The allocation of the rent between the new and old lease is different if the new lease is granted more than one year after the end of the fixed term.

The LBTT legislation includes special rules to deal with the following situations:

- A lease for a fixed term which continues beyond that fixed term either as a result of the action of the parties or by operation of law.
- A lease for a fixed term which continues beyond that term after which a new lease of the same or substantially the same premises is granted.
- A lease for an indefinite term.

The LBTT rules which apply when a lease is renewed, or where a lease for an indefinite term (see **4.16**) is replaced by a fixed term lease are also considered below. In some cases the costs of compliance may be greater than the amount of tax payable. Inevitably, the tax payable will depend on the rent (and premium, if any) payable under the new lease and its length. However, the tax payable may also depend on matters such as:

- whether the old lease had a fixed term and if so;
- whether there has been a gap between expiry of the old lease and finalisation of the new lease.

Such a gap occurs when the tenant remains in occupation after a lease has expired, usually while a new lease is negotiated (ie if proper notice is not given by either landlord or tenant the lease continues by 'tacit relocation', effectively by implied re-lease).

Information required

4.71 The answers to the following questions will be important in determining the LBTT consequences of the renewal of a lease:

- Did the new lease take effect before expiry of the old (ie is there an overlap in the periods of the leases)?
- Did the parties enter into an agreement for lease or missives of let not constituting a lease, which was substantially performed before the new lease was finally executed?
- When is the new lease stated to begin?
- Was there a gap between the end of the old lease and the finalisation of the agreement for the new lease (or execution of the new lease if there was no pre-execution agreement), during which the tenant remained in occupation?
- If there was a gap, was it less than one year, or alternatively a year or more?
- Are the old and new leases linked (see **4.66**)?

The following paragraphs and examples deal with the LBTT consequences based on certain possible answers to these questions.

New lease granted on or before expiry of old fixed term lease

4.72 If the new lease is stated to take effect immediately after the end of the old, is executed before or immediately on expiry of the old and is not linked with the old lease (see **4.66**), LBTT is payable as if the new lease is a stand-alone lease for the period (term) and consideration stated in the lease. If the new lease is linked with the old, this affects the calculation of the LBTT payable (see **4.67** and **Example 4.16**) but not the timing of the LBTT obligations.

If the new lease is executed before the end of the old, it is important to consider timing – LBTT obligations arise 30 days after the date of execution of the new lease, not 30 days after the start date of the new lease (see **Example 4.18A**).

If the new lease takes effect before the end of the old, the rent chargeable to LBTT on the new lease may be reduced by the rent payable under the old lease for the overlap period. In addition, if the old lease is an SDLT lease the rent chargeable to LBTT on the new lease may be reduced by the rent payable under the old lease, and charged to SDLT, in respect of the overlap period. (see **Example 4.18B** and **4.92**. Also see The Land and Buildings Transaction Tax (Transitional Provisions) (Scotland) Order 2014, SI 2014/377, article 10.)

New lease granted after expiry of old fixed term lease

4.73 Provided the new lease is granted at some time during the one year period beginning with the date of expiry of the old fixed term lease, it will still be treated for LBTT purposes as beginning immediately on expiry of the old lease (LBTT(S)A 2013, Sch 19, para 21(3)). In other words any period before the new lease is granted, amounting to less than one year, will be added to the period (term) of the new lease for LBTT purposes. Accordingly, no separate land transaction return will be required for the period between the expiry of the old lease and the commencement of the new lease.

The most likely scenario is that a new lease will be executed within one year after the date of expiry of the old lease.

However, if the new lease is not executed until more than one year after expiry of the old, any complete years will be dealt with as explained in **4.78**. Once the new lease is finally executed, it is treated for LBTT purposes as beginning immediately after the end of the last complete year by which the lease is treated as having been extended (LBTT(S)A 2013, Sch 19, para 21(5)). Accordingly, no LBTT obligations arise in respect of the final part year before the grant of the new lease, but that part year is added to the term of the new lease for the purpose of calculating the LBTT on the new lease. The LBTT obligations in respect of the new lease arise 30 days after the date on which the new lease is executed.

New lease superseding old lease for indefinite term

4.74 The new lease will be subject to LBTT as a stand-alone lease for a term commencing on the date of execution or later stated start date or, if earlier, the date of substantial performance of any agreement for lease (or missives of let not constituting a lease). It should, however, be noted that occupation of the property under the earlier lease for an indefinite term will not cause substantial performance of any agreement for the new lease. If LBTT has been paid on the lease for an indefinite term for a period which is partly included in the term of the new lease, it should be possible to claim overlap relief in respect of that part – see **4.92**.

Lease renewal examples

4.75 The following examples relate to the rules described in paras **4.72** and **4.73**.

General fact pattern – ServiceCo occupies a commercial unit under a lease from unrelated Propco. When the old lease was granted (prior to 1 April 2015), there was no agreement between the parties as to whether the lease would be renewed and the old lease does not include any option to renew. The lease expires on 31 December 2023, at which time the annual rent is £100,000 including VAT. A new lease is negotiated, the commercial terms being for seven years from 1 January 2024 (except where noted below) at yearly rent of £120,000 including VAT. No premium is payable. There is a market rent review due on 1 January 2029.

Example 4.18A – New lease executed before existing lease expires but takes effect immediately after the end of the old lease

A new lease is negotiated in advance and executed on 1 December 2023 to take effect on 1 January 2024. There are no complications, the Revenue

Scotland calculator gives the NPV of the rent as £733,745, and the LBTT payable as £5,837. The calculation of LBTT is based on the lease commencing on 1 January 2024. However, because the lease was executed on 1 December 2023, the LBTT return and tax payment are due within 30 days of this date, ie by 31 December 2023, which is before the lease period commences. It does not matter whether the old lease was subject to SDLT.

Example 4.18B – New lease executed, and takes effect, before existing lease expires

As **Example 4.18A**, except the lease was executed on 1 July 2023 and took immediate effect, displacing the old lease. The new lease is again for seven years (that is, it expires in this case on 30 June 2030). The LBTT return and tax payment are due by 31 July 2023.

Despite the fact that the old lease was an SDLT lease, allowance is given in the LBTT calculation for the £50,000 rent which would have been paid under the old lease for the period from 1 July to 31 December 2023 and which was taken into account in determining the SDLT chargeable in respect of the old lease (The Land and Buildings Transaction Tax (Transitional Provisions) (Scotland) Order 2014, SI 2014/377, article 10). The rent for the first year of the new lease is therefore taken to be £70,000 with 'allowance' for the £50,000 rent payable being given under the old lease which was subject to SDLT. The Revenue Scotland calculator gives the NPV of the rent as £685,436 and the tax payable as £5,354.

Example 4.18C – New lease executed after old lease has expired, but within one year of the date of expiry

The new lease is finally executed on 1 July 2024, stated to be for seven years from 1 January 2024 at yearly rent of £120,000 but silent on the matter of payment of rent for the period before execution. ServiceCo has continued paying rent at the yearly rate of £100,000, but pays an extra £10,000 immediately before the lease is executed, to bring the yearly rate for the period 1 January to 30 June 2024 up to the new rent.

From an SDLT perspective the new lease would be treated as commencing on 1 January 2024 by virtue of FA 2003, Sch 17A, para 9A, however as that is on or after 1 April 2015 the new lease will no longer be chargeable to SDLT, but will be within the charge to LBTT.

The term of the new lease is treated for the purposes of LBTT as beginning on 1 January 2024 (LBTT(S)A 2013, Sch 19, para 21(3)) and the rent payable under the original lease for the period 1 January 2024 to 30 June 2024 is treated as being payable under the new lease, in calculating the LBTT payable on the grant of that new lease (LBTT(S)A 2013, Sch 19, para 21(4)).

The rent chargeable to LBTT on the new lease is therefore as follows:

Year to 31 December 2024	£120,000
Year to 31 December 2025	£120,000
Year to 31 December 2026	£120,000
Year to 31 December 2027	£120,000
Year to 31 December 2028	£120,000
Year to 31 December 2029	£120,000
Year to 31 December 2030	£120,000

The NPV of the rent is £733,745 and the LBTT payable is £5,837 as in **Example 4.18A**. However, in this case the LBTT return and tax payment are due within 30 days of the execution of the new lease being by 31 July 2024.

Example 4.18D – New lease executed more than one year after the old lease has expired

The new lease is finally executed on 1 July 2025, stated to be for seven years from 1 July 2025, so there is an 18-month gap between expiry of the old lease and the grant of the new lease. Yearly rent is £120,000 but the lease is silent on the matter of payment of rent for period before execution. ServiceCo has continued paying rent at yearly rate of £100,000, but pays an extra £30,000 immediately before the lease is executed, to bring the yearly rate for the period 1 January 2024 to 30 June 2025 up to the new rent.

As the existing lease is an SDLT lease it will be treated as if it were a lease for a fixed term of one year longer than its original term ie a lease to 31 December 2024 (FA 2003, Sch 17A, para 3).

The lease remains chargeable to SDLT (see paragraph 21.1 of the HMRC transitional guidance dated 13 February 2015 on the move from SDLT to LBTT) and additional tax will be payable, given that its term is treated as having been extended by one year to 31 December 2024 (FA 2003, Sch 17A, para 3(2)). Service Co will therefore be required to give notification by letter to Birmingham Stamp Taxes (see SDLTM 12050 para 2ff), and pay the additional SDLT due in relation to the deemed extension. The letter should be sent to Birmingham Stamp Taxes by 30 January 2025, being 30 days after the last day of the one year period (ie 31 December 2024) for which the lease is deemed to continue (FA 2003, Sch 17A, para 3(4)). As the new lease is granted during the year to 31 December 2025, and the term of the new lease is not expressed to begin until 1 July 2025 so that FA 2003, Sch 17A, para 9A does not apply, the term of the new lease will be treated as beginning immediately after the end of the original term as previously extended, namely it will be treated as commencing on 1 January 2025 (FA 2003, Sch 17A, para 3A). As the term of the new lease is treated as commencing on or after 1 April 2015, the lease will no longer be chargeable to SDLT, but will come within the charge to LBTT.

The term of the new lease is treated for the purposes of LBTT as beginning on 1 January 2025 (for LBTT purposes it is treated as a lease for 7 years 6 months to 30 June 2032) and the rent payable under the original lease for the period 1 January 2025 to 30 June 2025 is treated as being payable under the new lease, in calculating the LBTT payable on the grant of that new lease (LBTT(S) A 2013, Sch 19, para 21(4) and (5)).

No overlap relief (see **4.92**) will be available as there is no period between the deemed date of grant of the new lease (1 January 2025) and the deemed end of the term of the old lease (31 December 2024).

The rent chargeable to LBTT in respect of the new lease is therefore as follows:

Year to 31 December 2025	£120,000
Year to 31 December 2026	£120,000
Year to 31 December 2027	£120,000
Year to 31 December 2028	£120,000
Year to 31 December 2029	£120,000
Year to 31 December 2030	£120,000
Year to 31 December 2031	£120,000
Six months to 30 June 2032	£60,000

The NPV of the rent is £779,309 and the LBTT payable is £6,293. The LBTT return and tax payment are due within 30 days of the execution of the new lease being by 31 July 2025.

LEASE EXTENSIONS

Leases that continue after a fixed term and leases for an indefinite term

4.76 A lease for a fixed term, which continues beyond that term (whether by operation of law (tacit relocation) or otherwise, for example, by agreement between the parties) is initially treated as if it was a lease for a fixed term of one year longer than the original fixed term, and if the lease continues beyond that additional one year it is treated as if it were a lease for a fixed term which is two years longer than the original term, and if the lease continues beyond that additional two year period it is treated as a lease for a fixed term which is three years longer than the original term and so on (LBTT(S)A 2013, Sch 19, para 20(2)). If under this provision a lease is treated as continuing for a period of an additional one year, or a further additional period of one year, and the lease actually terminates during a one year extension period, the lease is treated as continuing only until the time it actually terminates (LBTT(S)A 2013, Sch 19, para 20(6)).

4.77 If the lease has previously been notified to Revenue Scotland, the tenant will not be required to file a further land transaction return each time the lease is treated as being extended by a further year, as the chargeable consideration for such additional periods will be taxed under the three-yearly review process (see **4.21**). If the deemed extension of the lease by one year (meaning both the first one year extension and any subsequent one year extension, or part of a year extension) causes the transaction to become notifiable, the buyer must file an LBTT return within 30 days of the day after the end of the one year period which triggered the notification and, as normal, the return must show the amount of any LBTT payable, with any liability being calculated using the tax rates and tax bands in force on the date the lease was executed (LBTT(S)A 2013, Sch 19, para 20(3)). However, for the purposes of LBTT(S)A 2013, s 30 ('Notifiable transactions') a lease which continues beyond its fixed term is still treated as a lease for its original fixed term (LBTT(S)A 2013, Sch 19, para 20(5)). This means that, for example, a lease which is originally granted for a fixed term of five years, which is subsequently treated as extended by a further two years because the tenant has remained in occupation for more than one year beyond the fixed five year term, is not then treated as a lease for a term of seven years in determining whether the lease becomes notifiable. It is still treated as a lease for a fixed five year term and it will only become notifiable if, as a result of the deemed extension, the chargeable consideration exceeds the nil rate tax band applicable to the transaction (LBTT(S)A 2013, s 30(2)(c)).

4.78 As discussed at **4.73** where a lease for a fixed term continues beyond that term, so that it is treated as extended by a one year under LBTT(S)A 2013, Sch 19, para 20(2), and during that one year extension period the tenant is granted a new lease of the same or substantially the same premises, and the term of the new lease commences during that one year period, then the original lease is not treated as continuing beyond its original fixed term and the term of the new lease is treated as beginning immediately after the end of the original fixed term (LBTT(S)A 2013, Sch 19, para 21(3)). If the new lease is not granted during the first one year extension under para 20(2), but is granted during the second or any subsequent one year extension, the term of the new lease is treated as beginning immediately after the end of the fixed term as previously extended, immediately prior to the year in which the actual lease is granted (LBTT(S)A 2013, Sch 19, para 21(3) and (5)).

4.79 Any rent due under the original lease in relation to the one year period after the expiry of the original lease and during which the new lease is granted is treated as being payable under the new lease when calculating any LBTT payable in relation to that new lease (LBTT(S)A 2013, Sch 19, para 21(4)).

4.80 As set out at **4.16**, a lease for an indefinite term is initially regarded as a lease for one year (LBTT(S)A 2013, Sch 19, para 22(1)(a)). However, if the term of the lease can be determined from the lease document or the agreement for lease it will not be a lease for an indefinite term. If the annual rent, or any premium, exceeds the relevant nil rate threshold, LBTT obligations arise 30 days after the effective date (see **2.81**) of the transaction. If the lease continues beyond one year, it is treated as a lease for two years, then three years and so on

(LBTT(S)A 2013, Sch 19, para 22(1)(b) and (c)). However, for the purposes of LBTT(S)A 2013, s 30 ('Notifiable transactions') a lease for an indefinite term is always treated as a lease which was originally granted for a term of less than seven years (LBTT(S)A 2013, Sch 19, para 22(3)). At the end of each further year, it is necessary to consider whether the cumulative rent is sufficient to give rise to LBTT notification or payment obligations. If so, those obligations arise 30 days after the end of the year in question.

It may be difficult to establish when LBTT obligations arise in cases of informal occupation and in such circumstances it will be essential to establish the precise legal nature of the occupation.

Missives of let constituting a lease followed by execution of formal lease

4.81 Where missives of let have been concluded which constitute a lease ('the First Lease'), and at some later time a formal lease ('the Second Lease') is executed relating to substantially the same premises, and for substantially the same term, as the missives of let, then the First Lease is treated as though (LBTT(S)A 2013, Sch 19, para 26(1)):

- it was granted on the date the missives of let were concluded;
- it was for a term which begins with the date the missives of let were concluded and ends when the term of the Second Lease ends ('the Deemed Term');
- it was granted in consideration of the total rent payable over the Deemed Term of the First Lease (under the First lease and the Second Lease), and any other consideration other than rent given for the First Lease or the Second Lease.

The grant of the First Lease and the Second Lease are treated as linked for the purposes of LBTT(S)A 2013, s 34 (return or further return in consequence of later linked transaction) whether or not they would actually be linked transactions under the normal rule in LBTT(S)A 2013, s 57 (LBTT(S)A 2013, Sch 19, para 26(4)(a)).

The grant of the Second Lease is ignored for LBTT purposes unless the effect of treating the First Lease as described above is any of the following:

(a) that the First Lease becomes notifiable in circumstances where it was not previously notifiable; or

(b) that additional tax becomes payable in respect of the grant of the First Lease; or

(c) that tax is payable in respect of the grant of the First Lease where none was payable before (LBTT(S)A 2013, Sch 19, para 26(2) and s 34).

If any of (a), (b) or (c) above apply then the tenant under the Second Lease (ie the tenant under the formal lease) must make a land transaction return in respect of the grant of the extended First Lease, and the return must be made within 30 days of the date of execution of the Second Lease (LBTT(S)A 2013, Sch 19, para 26(2) and s 34(2) and (3)). This return will either be the first notification of the transaction (if the grant of the First Lease was not notifiable) or notification that tax is now payable (where none was payable before) or notification that additional tax is payable. The tenant under the Second Lease is liable for any tax or additional tax which is payable (LBTT(S)A 2013, Sch 19, para 26(4)(b)). Any tax payable is calculated by reference to the tax rates and tax bands in force when the missives of let constituting a lease were concluded (LBTT(S)A 2013, Sch 19, para 26(2) and s 34(5)).

If the First Lease was notifiable then there will already be a requirement for the buyer to carry out a three-yearly review (see **4.21**) of the LBTT chargeable on the lease by reference to the third anniversary of the effective date (see **2.81**) of the conclusion of the missives of let which constituted a lease, and this obligation will continue following the execution of the formal lease. However, if the First Lease was not notifiable, but the execution of the Second Lease causes it to become notifiable, then it is assumed that the three-yearly review of the LBTT chargeable on the lease will still be carried out by reference to the third anniversary of the date on which the missives of let were executed, but only on those review dates falling after the date of execution of the Second Lease (LBTT(S)A 2013, Sch 19, para 10(1)(a)).

Example 4.19 – Missives of let followed by execution of formal lease

On 1 September 2023 George concluded missives of let (constituting a lease) with Estates Ltd over commercial premises for a term of five years and at a yearly rent of £100,000. No premium was payable. Subsequently, on 1 September 2024, a formal lease was granted by Estates Ltd to George over the same premises, and for the same term, as that covered by the missives of let. The formal lease clarified and improved, from the perspective of the tenant, certain of the terms included in the missives of let from 1 September 2024, and increased the rent by £5,000 per annum from that date.

George filed a land transaction return, in relation to the conclusion of the missives of let, by 1 October 2023. The NPV of the rent over the term of the missives of let was £451,505 and the LBTT payable was £3,015. On the grant of the formal lease the missives of let are treated as though they have been concluded in consideration of the following rent:

Year to 31 August 2024	£100,000
Year to 31 August 2025	£105,000
Year to 31 August 2026	£105,000
Year to 31 August 2027	£105,000
Year to 31 August 2028	£105,000

The increased NPV of the rent over the term of the lease is £469,249 and the revised LBTT liability is £3,192, meaning that additional tax of £177 must be paid. George must therefore file a land transaction tax return by 1 October 2024 and pay the additional LBTT of £177.

George will also be required to carry out a three-yearly review of the LBTT chargeable on the lease on 1 September 2026 and on the termination of the lease on 31 August 2028.

WHEN DO LBTT OBLIGATIONS ARISE?

Grant of a lease

4.82 The concepts of 'substantial performance' and 'effective date' (see **2.7** and **2.81**) apply to transactions involving leases, but with some specific 'trigger points'. In the case of the grant of a new lease, there may be several stages which may occur at different times. The first LBTT liability and obligation to submit a land transaction return will arise 30 days after the earlier of:

- the formal lease (or missives of let constituting a lease) being granted; and
- the agreement for lease (or missives of let not constituting a lease) being substantially performed.

In Scotland the date upon which a lease is granted is the date of the last execution of the lease. It is common for both parties to sign the same final lease document. Consequently, unless both parties are present at the same meeting, which would be unusual, one party to the lease will often sign the lease after the other party has signed it. In these circumstances the lease is granted when it has been signed by the last party to sign it. Where a lease is to be constituted by missives of let, and is not to be followed by the grant of a formal lease, the date of conclusion of the missives is the date on which the lease is granted.

Substantial performance of an agreement for lease (or missives of let not constituting a lease) occurs on the earliest of (LBTT(S)A 2013, s 14):

- the first payment of rent being made;
- substantially the whole of any consideration other than rent (eg a premium) being paid;
- the tenant (or a person 'connected' with the tenant) taking possession of the whole or substantially the whole of the premises. For these purposes, taking possession refers not only to taking physical possession, but includes the receipt of rent, or the right to receive rent, in relation to the property; and
- an assignation, sub-sale or other transaction (relating to the whole or part of the land which is the subject-matter of the agreement for lease/missives of let) as a result of which a person other than the original intended tenant becomes entitled to call for the grant of the lease to that person.

The date by which the land transaction return must be submitted is known as the filing date (RSTPA 2014, s 82).

4.83 The tenant is likely to be regarded as taking possession if he occupies the premises, including for the purpose of fitting out, or if he becomes entitled to enjoy other benefits of tenancy such as receipt of rent from a sub-tenant (see **2.7**).

AGREEMENT FOR LEASE IS SUBSTANTIALLY PERFORMED BEFORE THE LEASE IS GRANTED

4.84 Where an agreement for lease (or missives of let not constituting a lease) is substantially performed before the lease is granted, this is deemed to be the grant of a notional lease on the terms provided for in the agreement, and beginning on the date upon which substantial performance took place (LBTT(S)A 2013, Sch 19, para 25(1)). The 'effective date' of the transaction is when the agreement is substantially performed (LBTT(S)A 2013,Sch 19, para 25(2)). If, following substantial performance of the agreement, the agreement is to any extent rescinded, annulled or not carried into effect, the tax paid on the notional lease is, to that extent, to be repaid (LBTT(S)A 2013, Sch 19, para 25(6)). The repayment of the tax must be claimed by filing an amended return in respect of the notional lease (LBTT(S)A 2013, Sch 19, para 25(7)). Consequently, if the agreement for lease (or missives of let not constituting a lease) is (are) rescinded or annulled more than 12 months after the date by which the land transaction return in relation to the substantial performance transaction had to be filed, it is not clear that it will be possible to reclaim any tax paid. This is because a land transaction return must be amended within 12 months of the date by which the return had to be filed (RSTPA 2014, 83(2)).

4.85 When LBTT obligations have arisen on a notional lease as a result of substantial performance of the agreement for lease (or missives of let not constituting a lease), the subsequent grant of the actual lease in conformity with, or relating to substantially the same premises and for the same period (term) as in the agreement, may also give rise to LBTT obligations (LBTT(S)A 2013, Sch 19, para 25(3)).

4.86 When the actual lease is granted, the notional lease is deemed to be a lease granted on the date of substantial performance of the agreement and ending on the end date of the actual lease. The rent and premium are as given in the agreement for lease or actual lease. For the purposes of LBTT(S)A 2013, s 34 (return or further return in consequence of later linked transaction – see **4.67**) only, the grant of the notional lease and the grant of the actual lease are treated as linked (irrespective of whether they would actually be linked for the purposes of LBTT(S)A 2013, s 57). A further return is only required under LBTT(S)A 2013, s 34, if the effect of the grant of the actual lease is that the notional lease becomes notifiable, in circumstances where it was not previously notifiable, or that additional tax is payable, or tax becomes payable where none was payable before, because, for example, the rent, premium or period (term) of the actual lease are greater than was taken into account under the notional lease. The tenant under the actual lease (rather than the tenant under the notional lease if they are different) must make any return or further return, and is liable for any tax or additional tax payable as a consequence of the grant of the actual lease (LBTT(S)A 2013, Sch 19, para 25(5)(c)).

4.86A In accordance with LBTT(S)A 2013, s 40(2)(d) any tax due must be paid at the same time that the return is filed and, where a lease is to be registered (The Registration of Lease (Scotland) Act 1857 provides that only leases of over 20 years can be registered), this cannot take place until both the return has been filed and the tax paid. As is the case for other land transactions, tax is treated as having been paid if "arrangements satisfactory" to Revenue Scotland have been made for the payment of the tax (LBTT(S)A 2013, s 40(4) – see **8.25**). A tenant will become liable to a penalty if the land transaction return is not submitted by the filing date, if the return contains an error or if the tenant fails to pay the tax by the due date (see **Chapter 8**).

Deferral of LBTT

4.87 If (perhaps unusually) any amount of a premium is contingent or uncertain at the effective date (see **2.81**) of the grant of the lease, and will not be payable until more than six months after that effective date, the lessee may apply to Revenue Scotland to defer payment of an appropriate amount of LBTT in the same way as for other land transactions (LBTT(S)A 2013, s 41 – see **8.29**). However, it is not possible to apply to defer payment of LBTT arising in respect of rent (unless the Scottish Ministers provide otherwise by an order which they have not currently done), even if the amount of rent is uncertain at the effective date (LBTT(S)A 2013, s 41(5)). There is, however, no requirement for the lessee to file a return in circumstances where the contingency in relation to the rent occurs or it becomes clear it will not occur, or an amount relevant to the calculation of the rent becomes ascertained, unless the effect of these events is to make the transaction notifiable in circumstances where it was not previously notifiable (LBTT(S)A 2013, s 31(6)). The reason that there is no requirement to file a further return when the rent becomes known, where the transaction has previously been notified, is that any adjustment to the rent payable, which leads to an adjustment to the LBTT payable, will be brought into account when further returns are filed in relation to the lease under the provisions for a three-yearly review, or a review on the assignment or termination of the lease, of the tax chargeable in relation to the lease, see **4.21** and **4.26**.

Variation, renunciation or assignation of a lease

4.88 There are no special rules relating to the time for notifying and paying LBTT on the variation (see **4.41**), renunciation (see **4.46**) or assignation of a lease (see **4.30**). The obligations arise 30 days after the earlier of:

- the completion of the legal formalities giving effect to the variation, renunciation or assignation (for example, the parties executing the relevant document); and
- 'substantial performance' of the variation, renunciation or assignation.

Substantial performance has the same meaning as set out in **2.7**.

However, substantial performance will only be relevant to a variation, renunciation or assignation if a contract is entered into to give effect to that transaction, and that contract is to be completed by a conveyance (LBTT(S) A 2013, s 8). For these purposes a conveyance simply means any instrument (LBTT(S)A 2013, s 65), which in turn means that the contract must be completed by the execution of a formal legal document. For example, on a variation of a lease, if the agreement between the parties is not to be completed by execution of a legal document then any LBTT obligations will arise 30 days after the agreement is entered into, and 'substantial performance' of the agreement will not be relevant.

RELIEFS

4.89 In general, reliefs and exemptions available for other transactions in relation to land in Scotland also apply to transactions involving leases – see **Chapter 5**. Some of the reliefs are modified for lease transactions, particularly in relation to possible future clawback of the relief. There are, however, two reliefs which only apply to lease transactions.

Focus

- The leaseback element of a sale and leaseback transaction may be exempt from LBTT, but care has to be taken to ensure that the conditions for the relief to apply are satisfied.

Sale (or lease) and leaseback relief

4.90 Where a seller ('A') sells or leases a 'major interest' (see **2.9**) in a property to a buyer ('B') and, in consideration (wholly or partly), the buyer grants a lease (the 'leaseback') to the seller out of that 'major interest', the leaseback will be exempt from LBTT (LBTT(S)A 2013, Sch 3, paras 1 and 2) provided certain conditions are satisfied. The conditions which must be satisfied are as follows:

(a) the sale (or lease) transaction to B must be entered into wholly or partly in consideration of the lease (or sub-lease) being granted back to A;

(b) the only other consideration permitted for the sale/lease transaction to B is the payment of money (whether in sterling or another currency) and/or the assumption, satisfaction or release of a debt; and

(c) A and B must not be companies in a group relationship, such that the transaction could qualify for LBTT group relief.

4.91 A fairly commonplace commercial arrangement is for an owner to transfer a property to a developer in return for the developer redeveloping the site and granting the owner a long lease of part of the new development. The developer recoups his cost, and makes a profit, by selling the rest of the development to third parties. The lease back to the owner is unlikely to qualify for sale and leaseback relief, because the developer's agreement to redevelop the site is likely to amount to non-qualifying consideration. This will be the case even if the value of the works to redevelop the site is not chargeable to LBTT because the exemption in LBTT(S)A 2013, Sch 2, para 11 applies (see **2.25**), as that exemption only excludes the value of the works from being 'chargeable consideration', and does not exclude it from being consideration. In these circumstances LBTT is therefore likely to be due on both the original sale to the developer and the lease back to the original owner.

Overlap relief

4.92 This relief applies if A renounces an existing lease to B ('the old lease') and in consideration of that renunciation B grants a lease ('the new lease') of the same or substantially the same premises to A (LBTT(S)A 2013, Sch 19, para 24(1)(a)). In calculating LBTT on the new lease, the rent for the 'overlap period' (that is, the period which would have been covered by the old lease but is now covered by the new lease) is reduced by the rent which would have been paid under the old lease if that had been left to run its course (LBTT(S)A 2013, Sch 19, para 24(2)). The rent which would have been paid under the old lease is taken to be that rent for the overlap period which was actually taken into account in determining the LBTT payable in respect of the grant of the superseded lease (LBTT(S)A 2013, Sch 19, para 24(4)). This is not strictly a relief; it is a statutory treatment – see **Example 4.18B**. Therefore, it is not necessary to claim the 'relief' in the LBTT return. It is sufficient, when calculating LBTT on the new lease, to reduce the rent on the new lease by the rent which would have been paid under the old lease. The relief may also apply where the new lease is granted to someone who acted as guarantor under the original lease, or in certain circumstances where the new lease is granted to someone who was a sub-tenant of the original lessee (LBTT(S)A 2013, Sch 19, para 24(1)(b) and (c)).

This relief is in addition to the general principle set out in LBTT(S)A 2013, Sch 19, para 18 (see **4.47**) that, where a lease is renounced in consideration of the grant of another between the same parties, neither the renunciation nor the grant counts as chargeable consideration for the other.

Under the transitional provisions, on the move from SDLT to LBTT, overlap relief will also be available where the superseded lease was granted under the SDLT regime. The rent payable under the new lease, in respect of any period falling within the overlap period (that is, the period which would have been covered by the superseded lease but is now covered by the new lease), which is chargeable to LBTT, is reduced by the rent payable under the superseded lease, for that overlap period, which was taken into account in determining the SDLT chargeable on the grant of the superseded lease (Land and Buildings Transaction Tax (Transitional Provisions) (Scotland) Order 2014, SI 2014/377, art 10).

Chapter 5

LBTT Exempt Transactions and Reliefs

SIGNPOSTS

- An outline of those transactions which are automatically exempt from LBTT without the need to make a claim in a land transaction return ('Exempt Transactions');
- Detailed coverage of those reliefs which have wide application, and in relation to which a claim must be made in a land transaction return including, where appropriate, the anti-avoidance provisions which may deny the availability of the relief, and the provisions which may result in the claw-back of a relief already obtained:
  - group relief;
  - reconstruction and acquisition relief;
  - sale and leaseback relief;
  - multiple dwellings relief;
  - charities relief;
  - alternative finance reliefs;
  - sub-sale development relief;
  - green freeports relief.
- Commentary on certain specialist reliefs:
  - arrangements involving public or educational bodies;
  - certain acquisitions by registered social landlords;
  - house trader reliefs;
  - incorporation of a limited liability partnership;
  - public bodies relief;
  - crofting community right to buy relief;
  - relief for certain compulsory purchases;
  - relief for compliance with planning obligations.

5.1 Some transactions in land are automatically exempt from the obligation to notify Revenue Scotland and do not give rise to any LBTT charge. The legislation labels these as 'exempt transactions' and the same term has been used throughout this book when referring to such a transaction. Registers of Scotland should agree to register exempt transactions on the basis of a statement by the buyer that the transaction is exempt from LBTT, provided they and/or Revenue Scotland are satisfied that the documentation/information accompanying the registration application supports the view that the transaction is exempt.

5.2 In contrast, LBTT(S)A 2013, s 27 sets out a number of reliefs reducing or eliminating LBTT liabilities which would otherwise arise. Such reliefs do not apply automatically (despite the fact that the legislation describes qualifying transactions as 'exempt from charge'), but must be claimed in the first land transaction return filed in relation to the transaction or in an amendment to that return (see **8.1** – LBTT(S)A 2013, s 27(2)). The relief being claimed must be specified in the land transaction return. Many reliefs are subject to complex anti-avoidance rules, which can create genuine uncertainty as to their availability, and these are discussed in some detail in this chapter.

5.3 It will often be desirable to provide further information in order to ensure full disclosure and reduce the risk that Revenue Scotland may reject the claim for the relief and make a 'discovery' assessment up to five years later – see **8.46** et seq. There is no 'white space' included in the land transaction return to allow additional information to be provided. As a result, it may be appropriate to submit further information by way of letter when the LBTT land transaction return is completed (see **8.48**).

5.4 There are several reliefs which are subject to retrospective withdrawal ('clawback') if certain events occur, as explained below in the descriptions of the reliefs. In these cases, it is necessary to keep track of both the property and the owner(s), in order to be able to make the necessary returns and payments should clawback apply. It is the obligation of the buyer to both identify when a clawback occurs and to make the requisite notification to Revenue Scotland. Special rules apply where the interest assigned is a lease, on the grant of which group relief (or one of a list of other reliefs) was claimed. If no event has occurred to cause clawback of that relief, the first assignation of the lease which does not itself qualify for one of the reliefs on the list is treated as the grant of a new lease, for the remaining term of the actual lease, and at the rent payable by the new tenant. Consequently, LBTT is chargeable on the new tenant as though the transaction were the grant of a new lease (LBTT(S)A 2013, Sch 19, para 27) – see **4.35** et seq for an explanation of this special rule and an example.

5.5 In this chapter, reliefs with a wide application are dealt with in some detail, but those with relatively narrow or specialised application are dealt with only briefly. A few reliefs which apply specifically to leases are dealt with in **Chapter 4** (see **4.89** et seq).

EXEMPT TRANSACTIONS

5.6

> **Focus**
>
> - An exempt transaction is not chargeable to LBTT and there is no requirement to notify such a transaction to Revenue Scotland.

The exempt transactions are detailed in LBTT(S)A 2013, Sch 1, and are as follows:

No chargeable consideration:

(1) A transaction for which there is no chargeable consideration is exempt (LBTT(S)A 2013, Sch 1, para 1). Chargeable consideration is defined in LBTT(S)A 2013, Sch 2 (see **2.17**). If there is no actual consideration in money or money's worth, there will be no chargeable consideration unless LBTT(S)A 2013, s 22 (buyer is a company connected with the seller; see **2.29**) or LBTT(S)A 2013, Sch 2, para 13 (land transaction entered into by reason of a person's employment**; see 2.28**) or LBTT(S) A 2013, Sch 17 (transactions involving partnerships; see **Chapter 6**) apply. Additionally, LBTT(S)A 2013, Sch 2 provides for certain amounts of consideration to be ignored where they might otherwise be regarded as chargeable consideration – see **2.25** and **2.34**.

Acquisitions by the Crown:

(2) A transaction under which the buyer is any of the following is exempt (LBTT(S)A 2013, Sch 1, para 2).

- The Scottish Ministers.
- The Scottish Parliamentary Corporate Body.
- A Minister of the Crown.
- The Corporate Officer of the House of Lords.
- The Corporate Officer of the House of Commons.
- A Northern Ireland department.
- The Northern Ireland Assembly Commission.
- The Welsh Ministers, the First Minister for Wales and the Counsel General to the Welsh Assembly Government.
- The National Assembly for Wales Commission.
- The National Assembly for Wales.

Residential leases and licences to occupy land:

(3) The grant, assignation or renunciation of a lease of residential property (which is not a 'qualifying lease' – see **4.4**) is exempt but only if the chargeable interest (see **2.12**) which is the subject of the transaction consists entirely of an interest in land that is residential property (see **2.36**) or, if the transaction is one of a number of linked transactions (see **2.79**) the chargeable interest which is the subject of each of those transactions must consist entirely of residential property (LBTT(S) A 2013, Sch 1, para 3(1)(a) and (2) – see **4.4**–**4.6**).

It would seem that a variation of a lease of residential property, so as to reduce the amount of rent payable or to reduce the term of the lease, or where any consideration in money or money's worth (other than an increase in rent) is given by the tenant for the variation (other than a variation of the amount of the rent or of the term of the lease), will be the acquisition of a chargeable interest potentially giving rise to LBTT obligations (LBTT(S)A 2013, s 6(2) and Sch 19, para 29).

(4) The grant, assignation or renunciation of a licence to occupy property other than a prescribed non-residential licence is exempt (LBTT(S) A 2013, Sch 1, para 3(1)(b) and (4) – see **4.7** et seq).

It would seem that any variation of a licence to occupy property will be the acquisition of a chargeable interest potentially giving rise to LBTT obligations (LBTT(S)A 2013, s 6(1)(c)) if the chargeable consideration given for the variation exceeds the nil tax rate threshold for the transaction (LBTT(S)A 2013, s 30(1)(c)). For further discussion of this point see **4.8.**

Transactions in connection with divorce etc:

(5) A transfer between parties to a marriage or civil partnership in connection with the dissolution or annulment of the marriage or partnership or separation of the parties (whether in pursuance of a court order or by agreement) is exempt (LBTT(S)A 2013, Sch 1, paras 4 and 5).

Assents and appropriations by personal representative:

(6) A transfer of property to a beneficiary under a will, or intestacy, of a deceased person is exempt, provided the beneficiary gives no consideration other than the assumption of any debt secured on the property (LBTT(S) A 2013, Sch 1, para 6). If consideration other than the assumption of debt secured on the property is given, it is only that other consideration that is chargeable to LBTT, and the amount of any assumption of secured debt does not count as consideration in calculating the LBTT charge (LBTT(S)A 2013, Sch 2, para 9(1)).

Variations of dispositions under the will or intestacy of a deceased person:

(7) Similarly, a variation of a disposition of property, (whether the disposition is effected under the will or intestacy of the deceased person) within two years of death is exempt, provided no consideration is given other than an agreement to make variations to other dispositions under that will or intestacy (LBTT(S)A 2013, Sch 1, para 7). If other consideration is given

then the consideration chargeable to LBTT does not include the value of the making of any variations to those other dispositions (LBTT(S) A 2013, Sch 2, para 9(3)).

The Scottish Ministers can, by regulations, add further categories of transaction to the list of exempt transactions, provide that a transaction which is currently exempt is no longer to be exempt and vary the description of an exempt transaction (LBTT(S)A 2013, Sch 1, para 8).

GROUP, RECONSTRUCTION AND ACQUISITION RELIEFS

5.7 These reliefs are dealt with together because they appear alongside each other in LBTT(S)A 2013, Schs 10 and 11 and many of the conditions and anti-avoidance provisions are similar. The basic operation of each relief is outlined separately below, with an account of the conditions which apply to the particular relief. This is followed by a discussion of an anti-avoidance provision which is common to all three reliefs. Finally, there is a review of the circumstances in which each relief may be retrospectively withdrawn ('clawed back') as a result of events after the initial transaction.

5.8 The reliefs apply to transactions involving 'companies' (LBTT(S) A, Sch 10, para 1(1) and Sch 11, para 1(1)). There are no restrictions as to residence or place of incorporation of the companies, provided they can be recognised as bodies corporate. For the purposes of group relief a 'company' is any body corporate, including a partnership which is a body corporate (LBTT(S)A 2013, Sch 10, para 49), however for the purposes of reconstruction relief and acquisition relief a 'company' is any body corporate but excluding a partnership which is a body corporate (LBTT(S)A 2013, s 65). In all cases, with the possible exception of the top company of a group, the company must have 'issued ordinary share capital' or its equivalent. This can cause difficulties in relation to some overseas entities, as their 'corporate' nature may be open to question or the overseas jurisdiction may have no concept of shares or share capital. In any case of doubt, it is possible to ask the opinion of Revenue Scotland (see **8.49**). However, if it is not a type of body which they have previously considered, Revenue Scotland are likely to request an appropriate legal opinion from a lawyer in the relevant country. HMRC have published a list of foreign entities which they will accept as being bodies corporate for the purposes of UK stamp duty group relief (STSM042260 – Exemptions and reliefs: reliefs: stamp duty group relief – foreign companies). This list may be useful in any discussions with Revenue Scotland as to whether a foreign entity is a body corporate for the purposes of LBTT group relief, reconstruction relief or acquisition relief. The list does not, however, consider whether the foreign entity has the equivalent of 'ordinary share capital'.

5.9 Relief may not be due or, if it is due, may subsequently be withdrawn, if there are 'arrangements' for certain events to happen – the specific events are mentioned in relation to each relief below. The legislation makes it clear that 'arrangements' may exist even though there is no legal commitment by the parties (LBTT(S)A 2013, Sch 10, para 49 and Sch 11 para 42). In relation to stamp duty, HMRC gave their view that arrangements exist where it is intended that the event will happen and there is no likelihood in practice that it will not (see HMRC SP 3/98, para 6). It is not known whether Revenue Scotland will apply similar criteria in relation to LBTT as the relevant guidance is silent on the matter (LBTT3025).

Group relief

5.10 Group relief removes any LBTT charge on land transactions between companies (ie bodies corporate: see **5.8**) which, at the effective date (see **2.81**) of the transaction, are members of the same group (LBTT(S)A 2013, Sch 10, para 2). To be members of the same group, one company must be the 75% subsidiary (direct or indirect) of the other, or each must be the 75% subsidiary (direct or indirect) of a third company (LBTT(S)A 2013, Sch 10, para 43). For A to be the 75% subsidiary of B, B must be (LBTT(S)A 2013, Sch 10, para 44):

- the beneficial owner of not less than 75% of the issued 'ordinary share capital' of A;
- beneficially entitled to at least 75% of any profits of A available for distribution to 'equity holders' of A; and
- beneficially entitled to at least 75% of any assets of A available for distribution to 'equity holders' of A on a winding up.

'Ordinary share capital' of a company consists of all of the issued share capital of a company, no matter what name is given to the share capital, other than share capital which has a right to a dividend at a fixed rate but no other right to share in the profits of the company (LBTT(S)A 2013, Sch 10, para 46). Thus, for example, fixed rate preference shares are not normally included within the meaning of ordinary share capital.

Where ownership is indirect, proportions are to be calculated in the normal algebraic manner under the Corporation Tax Act 2010 (CTA 2010), ss 1155–1157 (LBTT(S)A 2013, Sch 10, para 45). Rights of 'equity holders' are measured in accordance with CTA 2010, Pt 5, Chapter 6 (omitting references to arrangements which might affect future rights if put into effect). If shares in a particular company are not identical as to par value and rights, or if creditors have greater rights than payment of the relevant debts, it will be necessary to consider the impact of CTA 2010, Pt 5, Chapter 6 (LBTT(S)A 2013, Sch 10, paras 47 and 48).

Example 5.1 – What constitutes a group for the purposes of LBTT group relief?

Fred, an individual, owns 100% of the shares of Gill Ltd and 100% of the shares of Irene Ltd. Gill Ltd owns 90% of the shares of Jack Ltd and 75% of the shares of Kerri Ltd. Irene Ltd owns the other 10% of Jack Ltd and 20% of Harry Ltd. Jack Ltd owns the remaining 80% of Harry Ltd. Fred's business partner Leo owns the remaining 25% of shares in Kerri Ltd. All shares are ordinary, same class and denomination, and there are no share options or other instruments which might change relative entitlement to dividends or asset distribution in a winding up. The structure is therefore as follows:

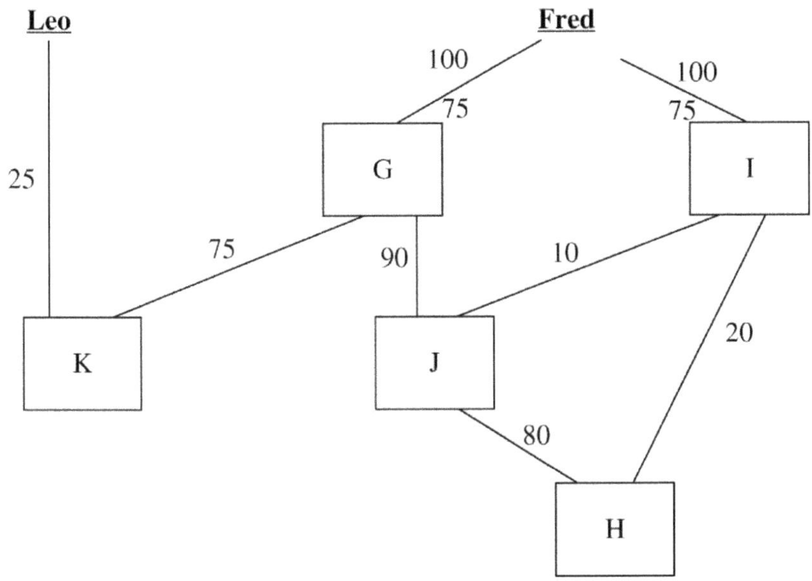

Clearly, Fred ultimately controls all of the companies, so they are connected for the purposes of CTA 2010, s 1122. This has implications for the measurement of consideration for any land transactions between them as the market value rule will apply (see **2.29**). However, they are not all members of the same group for LBTT purposes. J and H form an LBTT group, so that transfers between them are capable of qualifying for group relief. Equally G, J and K form an LBTT group, and transfers between them may qualify for relief. However, H is not grouped with G or K. This is because G has (indirect) beneficial ownership of only 72% (90% × 80%) of H, the other 28% being owned directly and indirectly by I (and I is not grouped with any of the other companies). Note that J is separately grouped with both H, and G and K. In contrast with some UK direct tax provisions, it is acceptable for LBTT purposes for a company to be a member of more than one group in this way. Although H and G (or K) are not directly grouped, it appears at first glance that it should be possible to transfer land between them free of LBTT, for example by G making the transfer first to J, and then J transferring onwards to H. However, group relief is surrounded by anti-avoidance provisions (see **5.15**), and it is possible that these would apply to such a sequence, potentially denying relief on both transfers and leading to a higher charge than would have applied to a direct transfer.

Treatment of LLP – company or partnership? Scottish Partnerships – break an LBTT group

5.11

> **Focus**
>
> - A limited liability partnership (LLP) breaks any group for LBTT group relief purposes isolating those companies above the LLP in the corporate structure, from those below the LLP. Care must therefore be taken in determining whether LBTT group relief is available where a group structure includes an LLP.

There is a conflict between the possible treatments of an LLP. For most purposes, an LLP is regarded as a body corporate and on this basis it is a 'company' for the purposes of LBTT group relief (LBTT(S)A 2013, Sch 10, para 49). Consequently, it can be the top company of a group for LBTT group relief purposes, and transfers between companies owned (75% or more) by the LLP may qualify for LBTT group relief. An LLP cannot be a subsidiary within a group, because it does not have issued ordinary share capital; it therefore breaks any group structure, isolating companies above it in the structure from those below. Therefore, group relief cannot be available for a transfer to (or from) a subsidiary company of an LLP, from (or to) a partner or other company above the LLP in the structure, even if all companies are substantively in the same corporate group.

However, the special rules governing the application of LBTT to partnerships (see **Chapter 6**) state that any chargeable interest held by a partnership (which includes an LLP) is regarded as held by the partners. Therefore, group relief is not available for a transfer of property from (or to) an LLP to (or from) a corporate partner, because this is regarded as a transfer from (or to) all of the partners, unless the partners are all members of the same LBTT group. A transfer of property from a subsidiary of the LLP to the LLP itself cannot qualify for group relief even if the partners in the LLP are all members of the same group. This is because such a transfer is regarded as a transfer to the partners, and the partners cannot be grouped with the subsidiary of the LLP because the presence of the LLP breaks the group relationship. The provisions at LBTT(S)A 2013, Sch 17, para 3(1)(a) which treat chargeable interests held by the partnership as owned by the partners, do not apply to treat shares in subsidiary companies held by the LLP as owned by the partners. HMRC set out their views on these matters at www.hmrc.gov.uk/so/group-rel-sdlt-sd.htm in relation to SDLT. Revenue Scotland appear to take a similar view in the LBTT legislation guidance at LBTT7012. If there is doubt as to whether LBTT group relief would be available where the ownership structure includes an LLP it is suggested that a formal opinion be requested from Revenue Scotland (see **8.49**).

Whilst Scottish partnerships and Scottish limited partnerships do have separate legal personality, so that they can hold shares in their own name, they are not bodies corporate and do not have the equivalent of ordinary share capital. This means that a Scottish partnership, and a Scottish limited partnership, will break an LBTT group and cannot, themselves, be the parent of an LBTT group (unlike an LLP) as they are not bodies corporate.

Example 5.2 – A limited liability partnership breaks an LBTT group

Companies B and C are 100% owned by company D. B and C are equal partners in an LLP. The LLP owns 100% of the shares in company E. The presence of the LLP means that, for LBTT purposes, E is not grouped with B, C or D. A transfer of property from E to the LLP will not qualify for group relief because it will be treated as a transfer to B and C. Similarly a transfer from E to any of B, C or D will not qualify for group relief. However, a transfer between any pair of B, C, D or the LLP (as this will be treated as a transfer to either C or B) may qualify for relief.

Arrangements

5.12

Focus

- LBTT group relief will not be available if at the effective date (see 2.81) of the transaction certain arrangements are in place for control of the buyer to change, or for consideration to be provided from outside of the group, or for the buyer to cease to be a member of the same LBTT group as the seller.

In accordance with LBTT(S)A 2013, Sch 10, para 3, group relief is not available if, at the effective date (see **2.81**) of the transaction, there are 'arrangements' in existence under which at that or a later time, a person has or could obtain control of the buyer but not the seller (LBTT(S)A 2013, Sch 10, para 3).

For example, this condition may be breached if a third party has options to acquire or subscribe for shares of the buyer. However, if the arrangements are part of a scheme of reconstruction which itself will qualify for stamp duty relief under FA 1986, s 75, relief will not be denied (LBTT(S)A 2013, Sch 10, para 9).

Similarly, if the shares in a company are 'pledged' to a lender as security for a debt then relief will not be denied, unless the lender possesses greater rights in respect of the shares or securities which are the subject of the arrangements than it requires to only protect its interest as mortgagee or transferee; or could alone or together with connected persons dictate the terms or timing of the default or the happening of any event which allows it to exercise its rights/obligations against the company. In determining whether parties are connected for this purpose, the lender is not treated as being connected to the company if it is only by the mortgage arrangement (LBTT(S)A 2013, Sch 10, paras 4 and 10A).

Group relief is not available if the transaction is carried out in connection with an arrangement under which (LBTT(S)A 2013, Sch 10, para 5):

- any part of the consideration for the transaction is to be provided or received (directly or indirectly) by someone other than a group member (LBTT(S)A 2013, Sch 10, para 5(a)). In principle, this could lead to the denial of relief where, for example, the buyer borrows funds from a bank to finance the acquisition of the property. In connection with the equivalent provision under SDLT HMRC stated in para 29 of the technical guidance included in Inland Revenue Tax Bulletin Issue 70 (April 2004) that borrowing on normal commercial terms to fund an intra-group transfer would not normally lead to the denial of SDLT group relief. It is not known whether Revenue Scotland will apply the same principles in relation to LBTT group relief as the Revenue Scotland technical guidance is silent on the matter (LBTT3025) ; or
- the seller and buyer are to cease to be members of the same LBTT group by reason of the buyer leaving the group (LBTT(S)A 2013, Sch 10, para 5(b)). It is not generally a problem if there are arrangements under which the seller is to leave the group. It should be noted that there is no exception, as there is for the change of control provision discussed above, if the arrangements are part of a scheme of reconstruction which itself will qualify for stamp duty relief under FA 1986, s 75. This is surprising given that in many acquisitions to which FA 1986, s 75 will apply both a change of control and a de-grouping event covered by para 5(b) will occur. In relation to SDLT HMRC accept that this would make little sense and interpret the legislation as though there was an exception to the de-grouping arrangements if FA 1986, s 75 applies (SDLTM23035). It is suggested that if this point arises on a transaction an opinion (see **8.49**) should be sought from Revenue Scotland on the basis that it makes little sense, from a policy perspective, to deny group relief in these circumstances.

Finally, group relief is not available if the transaction is not carried out for *bona fide* commercial reasons or it forms part of an arrangement with a main purpose of avoiding LBTT (LBTT(S)A 2013, Sch 10, para 8(a) and (b)). See **5.15** below for a discussion of these two separate conditions.

Reconstruction relief

5.13 Reconstruction relief removes any LBTT charge on land transactions in the course of a qualifying reconstruction under which one company, A, acquires all or part of the undertaking of another company, B, under a scheme for the reconstruction of company B (LBTT(S)A 2013, Sch 11, para 2 and 3(a)). The reconstruction qualifies if:

- the consideration for the acquisition of the undertaking includes the issue of non-redeemable shares in A to all of the shareholders of B (LBTT(S) A 2013, Sch 11, para 3(b));
- there is no other consideration, except that A is permitted to assume or discharge liabilities of B (LBTT(S)A 2013, Sch 11, para 4);
- the shareholders of B before the transaction end up owning identical proportions (or as near as is possible) of company A (LBTT(S)A 2013, Sch 11, para 3(c); and
- the acquisition of the undertaking is for *bona fide* commercial reasons, and does not form part of an arrangement with a main purpose of avoiding a liability to LBTT (LBTT(S)A 2013, Sch 11, para 3(d). See **5.15** for a discussion of these conditions.

This relief is the LBTT equivalent of stamp duty relief under FA 1986, s 75 (confusingly headed 'acquisitions: reliefs' in the stamp duty legislation), and the stamp duty case law relating to the term 'undertaking' is likely to be persuasive here too. The HMRC view on this, in relation to SDLT, is set out in SDLTM23201. Broadly, there must be some form of active business originally carried on by B and subsequently continued by A – a mere transfer of assets which are passively held, or subsequently used by A for a different purpose, will not qualify. The Revenue Scotland technical guidance for LBTT is silent on the matter (LBTT3030).

Acquisition relief

5.14 Acquisition relief reduces the rate of LBTT chargeable to 'the prescribed proportion of the tax that would otherwise be chargeable…' but for the availability of this relief (LBTT(S)A 2013, Sch 11, para 6(2)). The 'prescribed proportion' is the proportion prescribed by an order made by the Scottish Ministers (LBTT(S)A 2013, Sch 11, para 6(3)). The proportion prescribed by Scottish Ministers is 12.5% (The LBTT (Prescribed Proportions) (Scotland) Order 2014, SI 2014/350, art 3). The relief is available where a company, A, acquires all or part of the undertaking of another company, B, and the qualifying conditions are met (LBTT(S)A, Sch 11, paras 6 and 7). Where the relief is available the LBTT charge on land transactions entered into in connection with the transfer of the undertaking is reduced to 12.5% of what it otherwise would have been had the relief not been available. The qualifying conditions are:

(1) the consideration given for the acquisition of the undertaking (or part of the undertaking) includes the issue of non-redeemable shares in A to B, or to any or all of the shareholders of B (LBTT(S)A 2013, Sch 11, para 7(b));

(2) the only other consideration (if any) comprises one or both of:

- — payment of cash not exceeding 10% of the nominal value of the non-redeemable shares issued by A; and
- — the assumption or discharge by A of liabilities of B (LBTT(S) A 2013, Sch 11, para 8));

(3) A is not 'associated' with any company which is party to 'arrangements' with B relating to the non-redeemable shares issued by A (LBTT(S) A 2013, Sch 11, para 7(c));

(4) the main activity of the undertaking acquired consists of a trade other than property dealing or development (LBTT(S)A 2013, Sch 11, para 7(d)); and

(5) the acquisition of the undertaking is carried out for *bona fide* commercial reasons and is not part of an arrangement with a main purpose of avoiding LBTT (LBTT(S)A 2013, Sch 11, para 7(e)). See **5.15** below for a discussion of these conditions.

Condition (3) is intended to prevent relief where the parties agree in advance that B will sell the newly issued shares to a member of A's group or another company associated with A, so that as far as B is concerned the sale of the undertaking is effectively for cash. However, the condition can cause difficulties in relatively innocent circumstances, where A and B are themselves associated perhaps because they are held by members of the same family, and shareholder agreements give pre-emption rights where one shareholder wishes to exit. All such transfers require careful detailed analysis to establish whether the relief applies.

Condition (4) means that the relief does not apply to the transfer of a property letting business (as it is not a trade – the term 'trade' is defined as 'includes any venture in the nature of trade' (LBTT(S)A 2013, Sch 11, para 10) which is not particularly helpful) or a property development activity. The relief is, however, potentially useful in relation to the transfer of a trade where property forms a large proportion of the fixed assets – for example, retailing, chain of pubs or a hotel operation.

Anti-avoidance provision

5.15

> **Focus**
>
> - Group relief, reconstruction relief or acquisition relief will not be available if the transaction is not carried out for bona fide commercial reasons or it forms part of an arrangement with a main purpose to avoid a charge to LBTT.

Each relief is additionally subject to the conditions that the transaction: (a) must be for *bona fide* commercial reasons, and (b) must not form part of an 'arrangement' with a main purpose of avoiding the tax. Here 'the tax' means LBTT (LBTT(S)A 2013, s 65) and not any of the other UK taxes, which is the case for the equivalent SDLT provision. Thus even if a transaction is part of an arrangement which has a main purpose of avoiding UK stamp duty, income tax, corporation tax or capital gains tax, this provision should not deny the availability of LBTT group relief. The condition is effectively a general anti-avoidance provision, albeit that it is narrower in scope than its SDLT counterpart. Unfortunately there is no legislative guidance as to its scope, and doubt over this has led to significant uncertainty, in relation to its SDLT equivalent, as to whether, for example, group relief is due. In response to widespread disquiet, HMRC produced a 'white list' of transactions which would not normally be regarded as falling foul of this condition, for the purposes of SDLT. The list can be found at SDLTM23040. However, the list itself is heavily caveated and gives limited comfort in the context of real commercial transactions. In addition a number of the examples in the list will not be relevant to the LBTT provision as they relate to the potential avoidance of taxes other than SDLT, whereas the provision for LBTT purposes only applies if avoidance of LBTT is in point. It will therefore be necessary to consider carefully the reasons for which the land transaction is carried out, and the purposes of any overall arrangement of which the land transaction is part, to assess whether these conditions have been met.

Clawback of relief

5.16

> **Focus**
>
> - Where group relief, reconstruction relief or acquisition relief have been claimed, the relief may be clawed-back if, within three years of the transaction, the buyer ceases to be a member of the same group as the seller (group relief) or control of the acquiring company changes (reconstruction relief or acquisition relief).

Even where a transaction initially qualifies for one of these reliefs, in certain circumstances the relief may be retrospectively withdrawn, leading to the crystallisation of the LBTT charge originally relieved. Because LBTT is a self-assessment tax, it is for the taxpayer to detect and disclose any situation in which a clawback arises. Where one of these reliefs has been claimed, it is therefore important to put in place arrangements to monitor ownership of the property, and of the companies involved in the original claim, for an appropriate period, which is generally three years.

Clawback of group relief

5.17 Group relief is clawed back if the buyer, while it or a 'relevant associated company' still owns the property (or an interest derived from it), which was the subject of the group relief claim, ceases to be a member of the same LBTT group as the seller, either within three years of the effective date (see **2.81**) of the property transfer, or later but under arrangements entered into within that three-year period (LBTT(S)A 2013, Sch 10, paras 13 to 15). A 'relevant associated company' (LBTT(S)A 2013, Sch 10, para 42) is any other member of the LBTT group, of which the buyer is a member, which leaves the LBTT group 'in consequence of' the buyer leaving. This provision prevents an otherwise simple avoidance arrangement, under which the buyer transfers the property (in relation to which group relief has been claimed) to a wholly-owned subsidiary before leaving the seller's group and is then able to claim that it no longer holds any interest in the property which was the subject of the original group relief claim.

Group relief is also clawed back if the relief was only given as a result of LBTT(S)A 2013, Sch 10, para 10A applying to a 'share pledge' arrangement with a lender (see **5.12**) and, within three years of the effective date, this ceases to apply to the arrangements. (LBTT(S)A 2013, Sch 10, paras 13 and 15A).

Where the relief is clawed-back the amount of the LBTT liability is the amount which would have been payable if the chargeable consideration for the transaction had been an amount equal to the market value (as at the 'effective date' (see **2.81**) of the original transaction) of the relevant interest in land plus, if the transaction was the grant of a lease, the actual rent payable (LBTT(S)A 2013, Sch 10, paras 16 and 17). If the interest which the buyer (or a relevant associated company) still holds is less than the interest originally transferred, and in relation to which group relief was claimed, a *pro rata* amount of the relief is clawed-back (LBTT(S)A 2013, Sch 10, paras 18 and 19).

Where the relief is withdrawn the buyer must file a further land transaction return within the 30 day period beginning on the day after the date on which the buyer ceased to be a member of the same group as the seller or paragraph 10A ceased to apply. The further return must include an assessment of the LBTT chargeable, based on the information included in the further return (LBTT(S)A 2013, s 33(1)(d), (2), (3) and (4)(d)).

Example 5.3 – Clawback of group relief

Mamores Ltd (M) owns 100% of the shares of Laggan Ltd (L) and Fort William Ltd (F). On 1 March 2023, L transfers to F ownership of a commercial property worth £800,000, and LBTT group relief is claimed. In September 2023, F grants a capital lease of part of the property to a third party, in return for a premium of £600,000 and a peppercorn rent. It is agreed that the value of the part thus disposed of by F is three-quarters of the value of the whole property. On 24 February 2024, M sells 50% of the shares of F to another third party, in the course of setting up a joint venture. F therefore leaves the M group while still holding an interest in the property with a value of one quarter of the value of the whole property. The LBTT payable is, therefore, one quarter of the LBTT which would have been payable on the original transfer on 1 March

2023, if group relief had not been claimed. The LBTT on the original transfer would have been as follows:

Market Value	*Rate*	*LBTT*
£	%	£
150,000	0	NIL
100,000	1	1,000
550,000	5	27,500
800,000		28,500

The amount chargeable under the clawback is one quarter of this or £7,125.

Note: the LBTT is *not* calculated as if there was a transfer of a property with a value of one quarter of the original; in the present case, such a calculation would give a liability of 1% × £50,000 = £500 – but, sadly, this is not how the clawback operates. However, even if LBTT rates or thresholds have subsequently changed, the clawback is still calculated on the basis of tax rates and tax bands which applied at the time of the original transfer (see LBTT(S) A 2013, Sch 10, paras 16–19) .

Where group relief is withdrawn the buyer must file a further LBTT land transaction return, within the 30 day period beginning on the day after the date on which the de-grouping event took place (ie in this example the return would be due by 26 March 2024, being 30 days after the date upon which M sold 50% of the shares of F to the third party), which includes a self-assessment of the LBTT payable (LBTT(S)A 2013, s33(1)(d), (2), (3) and (4)(d)).

5.18 Group relief is not clawed back where the buyer ceases to be a member of the same LBTT group as the seller in the following circumstances (LBTT(S) A 2013, Sch 10, paras 20–25):

- as a result of the winding up of the seller or a company above the seller in the group (LBTT(S)A 2013, Sch 10, para 20);
- in the course of a reconstruction which itself qualifies for relief from UK stamp duty under FA 1986, s 75, as a result of which the buyer becomes a member of the same LBTT group as the 'acquiring company' (LBTT(S) A 2013, Sch 10, para 21); or
- in the course of a qualifying demutualisation of an insurance company (LBTT(S)A 2013, Sch 10, para 22).

5.19 Group relief is also not clawed back if it is the seller which leaves the group rather than the buyer (LBTT(S)A 2013, Sch 10, paras 26 and 27). This allows a group to remove property which it wishes to keep from a subsidiary which is to be disposed of. However, if there is subsequently a change of control of the buyer within three years of the original transfer, the buyer is at that time treated as leaving the same group as the seller, and clawback applies accordingly (LBTT(S)A 2013, Sch 10, paras 28 and 29). See **5.21** for a discussion of what amounts to a change of control. There are complex anti-avoidance provisions designed to ensure the 'change of control' rules apply as intended, where successive transfers of the property might otherwise lead to doubt as to their application (LBTT(S)A 2013, Sch 10, paras 32–40).

Clawback of reconstruction or acquisition relief

5.20 These reliefs are clawed back if, within three years of the effective date (see **2.81**) of the property transfer, or later under arrangements entered into within that three year period:

- control of the acquiring company changes; and
- the acquiring company or a relevant associated company holds the property, or an interest derived from it, in relation to which the relevant relief was claimed (LBTT(S)A 2013, Sch 11, paras 12–14).

A 'relevant associated company' (LBTT(S)A 2013, Sch 11, para 35) is a company controlled by the acquiring company immediately before the change in control of the acquiring company, control of which changes as a consequence of the change in control of the acquiring company. Where the relief is clawed-back the amount of the liability is the amount which would have been payable if the chargeable consideration for the transaction had been an amount equal to the market value of the relevant interest in land plus, if the transaction was the grant of a lease, the actual rent payable. If only part of the property, or a lesser interest derived from it, is held, an appropriate proportion of the relief is withdrawn based on the relative values of the whole property and the part or interest still held (LBTT(S)A 2013, Sch 11, paras 29–32). The calculation is analogous with that for withdrawal of group relief (see **Example 5.3**).

Where reconstruction relief or acquisition relief is withdrawn the buyer must file a further LBTT land transaction return, within the 30 day period beginning on the day after the date on which the disqualifying event took place, which includes a self-assessment of the LBTT payable (LBTT(S) 2013, s 33(1)(e),(2),(3) and (4)(e)).

Change of control

5.21 A change in control of the buyer (see **5.19** for the circumstances in which a change of control of the buyer is relevant to the clawback of group relief) takes place for the purposes of clawback of group relief if (LBTT(S)A 2013, Sch 10, para 30):

- a person who controls the buyer (alone or with others) ceases to do so;
- a person obtains control of the buyer (alone or with others); or
- the buyer is wound up.

A change in control of the acquiring company, for the purposes of the withdrawal of reconstruction relief and acquisition relief, takes place if the acquiring company becomes controlled (LBTT(S)A 2013, Sch 11, para 34):

- by a different person;
- by a different number of persons; or
- by two or more persons at least one of whom is not the person, or one of the persons, by whom the company was previously controlled.

For these purposes 'control' is to be interpreted in accordance with the Corporation Tax Act 2010, ss 450 and 451. Broadly, a person is treated as controlling a company if he is able to exercise direct or indirect control over the company's affairs through holding the greater part of the company's issued share capital, the greater part of the voting power in the company, so much of the share capital as would entitle him to the greater part of the company's distributable income or such rights as on a winding up would entitle him to the greater part of the company's assets.

However, for the purposes of group relief a person does not control, or obtain control of the buyer if that person is under the control of another person or other persons (LBTT(S)A 2013, Sch 10, para 31).

In many cases, a change of control is easily identified – for example, when a majority shareholder sells the shares of the acquiring company to a third party. However, a change of control may be very difficult to identify or define in some circumstances and, in the case of a publicly traded company, may be subject to the whim of the market. In relation to SDLT, in the 2003 Finance Bill debates, the Government stated that normal market transactions in the shares of traded companies would not be regarded as giving rise to a change in control (see *Hansard*, Standing Committee B, 10 June 2003, col 425). It is not known whether Revenue Scotland will take a similar approach in relation to LBTT as the Revenue Scotland technical guidance is silent on the matter (LBTT3032). However, even if a similar approach is adopted for the purposes of LBTT, this still leaves open the possibility that the transfer of a minority shareholding in the case of an unlisted company may give rise to a change of control, since the company would then be controlled by a different group of people.

5.22 There is no clawback of reconstruction or acquisition relief where control of the acquiring company changes for one of the following reasons:

(1) as a result of transactions in connection with divorce, dissolution of civil partnership etc or the variation of a disposition of property out of a deceased person's estate, as set out in **(5)** and **(7)** at **5.6** (LBTT(S)A 2013, Sch 11, para 15 and 16);

(2) as a result of a transfer of shares which itself qualifies for UK stamp duty group relief under FA 1930, s 42 or share acquisition relief under FA 1986, s 77 (LBTT(S)A 2013, Sch 11, paras 17, 19 and 35); or

(3) purely as a result of a loan creditor becoming or ceasing to be treated as having control of the acquiring company (LBTT(S)A 2013, Sch 11, para 21). This may happen, for example, when a loan creditor gains additional rights if the company defaults on payments under the loan.

There are anti-avoidance provisions to ensure that, where (2) above applies to prevent clawback of reconstruction or acquisition relief, subsequent transactions leading to: (a) the company holding shares in the acquiring company ceasing to be a member of the same group as the 'target company' (see LBTT(S)A 2013, Sch 11, paras 3(a) and 7(a) for the meaning of 'target company'), or (b) a change of control of the company which acquired the acquiring company within the provisions of FA 1986, s 77, and either of these transactions takes place within the original three-year period (or later under arrangements entered into within that period) will lead to clawback of the reconstruction or acquisition relief (LBTT(S)A 2013, Sch 11, paras 22–24 and 25–28).

OTHER MAJOR RELIEFS

Sale and leaseback relief

5.23

> **Focus**
>
> - Provided certain conditions are satisfied, the leaseback element of a sale and leaseback transaction is exempt from the charge to LBTT.

If A transfers ownership of a property to B (or grants a lease to B) (the Sale), and out of the interest transferred B grants a lease (or sub-lease) back to A (the Leaseback), relief from LBTT is available on the Leaseback, provided certain qualifying conditions are satisfied – see **4.90** and **5.24** (LBTT(S)A 2013, Sch 3). The purpose of the relief is to facilitate the transfer of properties from occupiers to investors. Absent the relief, it might be possible for the same effect to be achieved in some cases by A first granting a lease to a group company, claiming group relief on the grant of the lease, then transferring the property, subject to this lease, to B. However, the relief allows a simpler process and resolves doubts as to whether any anti-avoidance provisions might otherwise apply to deny the availability of group relief on the grant of the lease.

The relief itself does not reduce the LBTT charge on the original transfer from A to B. However, if the sale and leaseback agreement requires the leaseback to be granted, and if this requirement reduces the value of the interest originally transferred, LBTT should be charged on that original transfer, only on the reduced value. This is on the basis that the acquisition of the superior interest by B should be treated as the acquisition of that interest encumbered by the new lease. LBTT is charged on the market value of the interest which is the subject of the original transfer as the exchange provisions (see **2.31**) will apply to B's acquisition. HMRC's agreement with this view, in relation to SDLT, is made clear in SDLTM04020. Whilst it is considered that this analysis should equally apply for LBTT, the Revenue Scotland technical guidance does not cover the point, and it is suggested that an opinion (see **8.49**) be sought from Revenue Scotland if the point is relevant to a transaction being undertaken.

Example 5.4 – Sale and leaseback relief – requirement to grant lease back reduces market value of interest originally transferred

Michael owns premises comprising a shop with apartment over, valued at £500,000. He sells the premises to Claire for £200,000 cash. The sale agreement requires Claire to grant a 100-year lease of the apartment back to Michael at a peppercorn rent. No LBTT will arise on the 100-year lease as sale and leaseback relief should be available. Assuming the transaction is at arm's length, it is reasonable to regard £200,000 as representing the current value of the premises subject to the requirement to lease the apartment back, so Claire should have to pay LBTT on that amount. This assumes that Revenue Scotland adopt a similar treatment as detailed in Stamp Taxes Bulletin 2/2011 in relation to SDLT (see **5.23**).

5.24 The relief should still be available even if, for some reason, no LBTT is payable on the original transfer, but A and B must not be members of the same LBTT group (LBTT(S)A 2013, Sch 3, para 3(c)). The transactions must be entered into in consideration of each other, so it would be wise to have this overtly stated in the documents (LBTT(S)A 2013, Sch 3, para 3(a)). The only other consideration permitted for the original transfer is the payment of money (whether in sterling or another currency) and/or the assumption, satisfaction or release of a debt (LBTT(S)A 2013, Sch 3, para 3(b)). Thus, the relief is not available if, for example, in consideration of the first transfer, B agrees to provide A with services (see **4.91**) or perhaps to transfer a different property to A. However, subject to the possible application of the general anti-avoidance rule (see **9.3**), it may be possible to structure such transactions as separate contracts for cash consideration due from A, left outstanding as a debt. The transfer from A to B could possibly then be partly in satisfaction of the debt, which is within the terms of the relief (LBTT(S)A 2013, Sch 3, para 3(b)).

Transfers involving multiple dwellings

5.25

Focus

- Where two or more dwellings are acquired as part of a single transaction, or as part of a number of linked transactions (see 2.79), it may be possible to reduce the LBTT payable by making a claim for multiple dwellings relief.

This relief aims to encourage investment in residential property for letting (LBTT(S)A 2013, Sch 5). The relief may be claimed if the main subject matter of a transaction, or of a number of linked transactions (see **2.79**), comprises interests in more than one dwelling (see **Example 5.5B** below for the meaning of 'dwelling') (LBTT(S)A 2013, Sch 5, paras 4 to 6). The relief may reduce the amount of the LBTT chargeable on the consideration (other than rent) given for the dwellings.

The steps which should be taken to calculate the LBTT due when a claim for multiple dwellings relief is made are set out below.

Tax due in relation to a dwelling (LBTT(S)A 2013, Sch 5, para 13)

The tax due per dwelling is calculated as follows:

Step 1

Determine the total consideration attributable to dwellings for the transaction or, if the transaction is one of a number of linked transactions (see **2.79**), the total consideration attributable to dwellings for all of the transactions.

Step 2

Divide the total consideration attributable to dwellings determined in Step 1 above by the total number of dwellings by reference to which that total consideration was calculated.

Step 3

Calculate the LBTT chargeable in relation to a dwelling based on the following assumptions:

(a) the chargeable consideration is the average consideration per dwelling calculated in Step 2.

(b) the transaction is a residential property transaction (see **2.36**)

(c) the transaction is not linked (see **2.79**) with any other transaction.

The result of this step is the tax due in relation to a dwelling and is referred to as DT below.

Tax due in relation to remaining property (LBTT(S)A 2013, Sch 5, para 14)

Where the transaction, or the linked transactions, involve land transactions which are not attributable to dwellings (here referred to as the 'remaining property') the tax due in relation to the remaining property is calculated as follows:

Step 4

Calculate the amount of the tax that would be due in relation to the land transaction(s) involving both dwellings and 'remaining property', but on the basis that multiple dwellings relief is not available.

Step 5

Divide the chargeable consideration attributable to the 'remaining property' by the total chargeable consideration for both dwellings and 'remaining property'.

Step 6

Multiply the tax chargeable calculated in Step 4 by the fraction arrived at in Step 5.

The result of this step is the tax due in relation to the 'remaining property' and is referred to as RT below.

Calculation of the LBTT chargeable on the transaction(s) based on a claim for multiple dwellings relief (LBTT(S)A 2013, Sch 5, para 10)

The amount of the LBTT chargeable on the transaction or linked transactions is then calculated as follows:

(DT × ND) + RT

DT – the tax due in relation to a dwelling – see Step 3 above.

ND – the number of dwellings that are part of the subject-matter of the transaction(s)

RT – the tax due in relation to the remaining property – see Step 6 above.

The interaction of the 'additional dwellings supplement' and multiple dwellings relief

If the 'additional dwellings supplement' ('ADS') applies to the acquisition of any of the dwellings (see **2.37** et seq) in relation to which a claim for multiple dwellings relief has been made, the calculation of the LBTT payable is slightly different. For such transactions, 'DT' must be calculated separately for each dwelling, applying the ADS or not, as appropriate, to calculate the 'DT' for each dwelling. Thus, if the ADS does not apply to one of the dwellings acquired under the transaction as that dwelling is a replacement of the individual's only or main residence (see **2.44**), 'DT' in relation to that dwelling would be calculated using the normal LBTT rates for a residential property transaction, whereas 'DT' for each of the other dwellings would be calculated using the LBTT rates for a residential property transaction on the basis that the ADS applies (see **2.35**). Once the 'DT' for each of the dwellings has been calculated, rather than multiply 'DT' by the number of dwellings as outlined above (NT × ND), each 'DT' for each dwelling is added together to get the LBTT payable in relation to dwellings. It is likely that in many cases the 'DT' for each dwelling will be the same as either the ADS will apply to each dwelling or the ADS will not apply to any of the dwellings, in which case the LBTT payable on dwellings will be the same irrespective of whether you add each of the 'DTs' together, or multiply 'DT' by the number of dwellings ('ND'). The difference will however arise if the transaction involves both the acquisition of a dwelling to which the ADS does not apply, as it is a replacement of an individual's dwelling, and the acquisition of one or more other dwellings to which the ADS does apply (see LBT10040).

Under the ADS regime, if six or more dwellings are acquired as part of a **single transaction** it is possible to make a claim in the land transaction return to exempt the transaction from the ADS (LBTT(S)A 2013, Sch 2A, paras 9 and

10), such that the transaction will be charged at the LBTT non-residential property rates (see **2.36** and **2.68**). If a claim for multiple dwellings relief (see **5.25** et seq) is made, and a claim has been made to exempt the transaction from the ADS (LBTT(S)A 2013, Sch 2A, paras 9 and 10), the calculation of the tax due in relation to each dwelling, based on the average consideration given for the dwellings, is made using the normal LBTT rates for residential property (LBTT(S)A 2013, Sch 5, para 10A – inserted by LBTT(A)(S)A 2016, s 2(1)) and the ADS does not apply when calculating 'DT' in relation to any of the dwellings acquired (see **2.69** and **Example 2.21**).

LBTT chargeable cannot be less than the 'minimum prescribed amount' (LBTT(S)A 2013, Sch 5, paras 11 and 12)

However, the relief cannot reduce the LBTT chargeable on the dwellings to below the 'minimum prescribed amount', which is a proportion of: (a) the tax that would have been payable on the transaction(s) under which the dwellings were acquired if multiple dwellings relief was not available, less (b) the tax due in relation to any remaining property ie RT in the formula above. The 'minimum prescribed amount' is calculated using a proportion as prescribed by the Scottish Ministers (LBTT(S)A 2013, Sch 5, paras 11 and 12). The proportion prescribed for the purposes of LBTT(S)A 2013, Sch 5, para 11 is 25% (The LBTT (Prescribed Proportions) (Scotland) Order 2014, SI 2014/350, article 2). This means that on a claim for multiple dwellings relief the LBTT chargeable in relation to the dwellings can never be less than 25% of: (a) the LBTT which would have been chargeable on the transaction in the absence of a claim for multiple dwellings relief, less (b) the tax due in relation to any remaining property ie 'RT' in the formula above.

It is important to understand that to determine the 'minimum prescribed amount' you first have to calculate the LBTT which would be chargeable on the transaction (or transactions if there are a number of linked transactions) on the basis that no claim for multiple dwellings relief is made, including in that calculation the chargeable consideration given for both dwellings and any 'remaining property', and then deduct from that amount the tax due in relation any 'remaining property' ('RT' in the formula above), and then take 25% of the result of that calculation. The answer is the 'minimum prescribed amount'. (LBTT(S)A 2013, Sch 5, para 12).

For example, where the transaction(s) involves both dwellings (ie residential property) and non-residential property (ie 'remaining property'), then in calculating the LBTT liability which would arise in the absence of a claim to multiple dwellings relief (referred to in LBTT(S)A 2013, Sch 5, para 12 as 'TT'), the non-residential tax rates and bands will be used (see **2.35**) – however the ADS (if applicable) will also be chargeable on the consideration given for the dwellings. The first step is therefore to calculate 'TT' using the non-residential tax rates and bands and the ADS where applicable, after which the LBTT payable in relation to the 'remaining property', namely 'RT' is deducted. The 'minimum prescribed amount' is then determined by taking 25% of the result of that calculation. The 'minimum prescribed amount' is then compared to the LBTT payable on the dwellings on the basis of a claim for multiple dwellings relief being made (ie DT

× ND – see above), and whichever is the greater represents the LBTT chargeable on the dwellings. The LBTT payable on the transaction will therefore be the greater of: (a) the 'minimum prescribed amount' and (b) the LBTT due on the dwellings (ie DT × ND) (or the sum of each of the DTs if the ADS is payable), plus the LBTT due on the 'remaining property'.

See **Example 5.5A** for the calculation of the LBTT chargeable where only dwellings are acquired.

See **Example 5.5B** for the calculation of the LBTT chargeable where dwellings are acquired with non-residential property, as part of a single transaction.

Where six or more separate dwellings are the subject of a single transaction, the tax rates and bands for non-residential property should be used in calculating the LBTT payable in the absence of a claim for multiple dwellings relief, (ie 'TT'), which is then used to determine the minimum prescribed amount (LBTT(S)A 2013, s 59(8)). As discussed, in such circumstances, it is possible to make a claim to exempt the transaction from the ADS (LBTT(S)A 2013, Sch 2A, paras 9 and 10).

Excluded transactions (LBTT(S)A 2013, Sch 5, para 6)

Multiple dwellings relief is not available if, in relation to the transaction(s), relief could be claimed under LBTT(S)A 2013, Schs 10 and 11 (group relief, reconstruction relief, and acquisition relief) or LBTT(S)A 2013, Sch 13 (charities relief), or if any of those reliefs has been claimed and withdrawn (LBTT(S)A 2013, Sch 5, para 6(b)). Multiple dwellings relief is also not available if the transaction is such that relief could be claimed under LBTT(S) A 2013, Sch 9 (Crofting community right to buy) (LBTT(S)A 2013, Sch 5, para 6(a)).

Withdrawal of relief (LBTT(S)A 2013, Sch 5, paras 16–20)

Multiple dwellings relief is withdrawn if within the period of three years from the effective date (see **2.81**) of the transaction (or, if shorter, the period from the effective date of the transaction until the buyer disposed of the property to an unconnected person) there is any change of circumstance or change of plan ('an event'), and had that event happened before the effective date of the transaction, multiple dwellings relief would not have been available or, the relief would still have been available, but more tax would have been payable (LBTT(S)A 2013, Sch 5, paras 16 and 18). A common example of a change of circumstance occurring within three years of the purchase of a number of dwellings, which would cause the relief to be partially withdrawn, would be where, say, six flats were acquired under the transaction, which within the three year period were then combined into two flats. In these circumstances the LBTT chargeable would have to be recalculated (see **Example 5.6**).

Where the relief is only partially withdrawn, as in the example above where six flats were combined into two flats, the tax chargeable is calculated as though the event had occurred immediately before the effective date (see **2.81**) of the transaction, so that in this example it would be calculated on the basis that only two dwellings were acquired, rather than six dwellings. The tax chargeable is calculated using the tax rates and tax bands in force at the time of the original transaction (LBTT(S)A 2013, Sch 5, paras 19 and 20).

Where the effect of the subsequent change of circumstance or change of plan is that multiple dwellings relief would not have been available at all, then the amount of the tax chargeable is calculated on the basis that the relief was not available (LBTT(S)A 2013, Sch 5, para 17).

Example 5.5A – Claim for multiple dwellings relief

On 31 March 2024 Property Holdings plc (P) acquires ownership of five new houses in Glasgow from Housebuilder plc (H) for a total consideration of £1.1 million. As P is a company and the 'relevant consideration' (see **2.57**) for each dwelling is £40,000 or more, the ADS will apply to the transaction (see **2.65** et seq). P makes a claim for multiple dwellings relief. In the absence of multiple dwellings relief, LBTT would be calculated as follows:

Purchase Price	*Rate*	*LBTT*
£	%	£
145,000	6	8,700
105,000	8	8,400
75,000	11	8,250
425,000	16	68,000
350,000	18	63,000
1,100,000		156,350

Total consideration attributable to dwellings of £1,100,000 divided by the number of dwellings being 5, gives an average price per dwelling of £220,000.

The tax due in relation to a dwelling is calculated as follows:

Purchase Price	*Rate*	*LBTT*
£	%	£
145,000	6	8,700
75,000	8	6,000
220,000		14,700

The LBTT chargeable is therefore £73,500 (£14,700 + £14,700 + £14,700 + £14,700 + £14,700).

However, the LBTT payable following a claim to multiple dwellings relief cannot be less than 25% of the LBTT which would have been payable in the absence of such a claim, being 25% of £156,350, amounting to £39,088. As 'the minimum prescribed amount' of £39,088 is less than the LBTT charge arising on the five houses following a claim to multiple dwellings relief, the total LBTT payable is £73,500.

Example 5.5B – Claim for multiple dwellings relief where the transaction includes a property which is not a dwelling

The relief may also apply if the transaction includes property which does not count as a dwelling (ie any 'remaining property'). Consideration must then be apportioned on a just and reasonable basis between the dwellings and the 'remaining property' (LBTT(S)A 2013, Sch 5, para 15). The relief is applied to the consideration apportioned to the dwellings. As discussed above, LBTT is charged on the consideration apportioned to the 'remaining property' as follows (LBTT(S)A 2013, Sch 5, para 14):

Step 1 Calculate the amount of LBTT that would be payable in respect of the transaction in the absence of the claim to multiple dwellings relief.

Step 2 Divide the consideration attributable to the 'remaining property' by the total chargeable consideration for the transaction.

Step 3 Multiply the amount calculated in Step 1 by the fraction calculated in Step 2. The result is the LBTT due in relation to the 'remaining property'.

As part of the same transaction in **Example 5.5A**, P also purchases three shop units from H. The total consideration is £1.55 million, of which £1.1 million is justly apportioned to the houses and £450,000 to the shops. The LBTT chargeable on dwellings, on the basis of a claim for multiple dwellings relief, before considering 'the minimum prescribed amount' restriction, is £73,500 as calculated in Example **5.5A**. The LBTT chargeable on the consideration apportioned to the shops is calculated using the three step process described above. The LBTT payable in the absence of a claim to multiple dwellings relief is calculated using the non-residential tax bands and rates as the transaction does not consist entirely of residential property – see **2.35**. The LBTT payable would therefore have been:

Purchase Price	*Rate*	*LBTT*
£	%	£
150,000	0	NIL
100,000	1	1,000
1,300,000	5	65,000
1,550,000		66,000

In addition ADS of £66,000 (£1.1 million × 6%) would also have been payable.

The LBTT chargeable on the three shop units is therefore £450,000/£1,550,000 × £66,000, giving an amount of £19,161.

The amount of the LBTT chargeable in relation to the transaction is then calculated in accordance with LBTT(S)A 2013, Sch 5, para 10 as follows:

(Tax due per dwelling of £14,700 (see **Example 5.5A**) X 5 dwellings) + the tax due in relation to the shops of £19,161 = £92,661.

However, the tax chargeable on the dwellings can never be less than the 'minimum prescribed amount' which is 25% of the tax which would have been payable but for a claim for multiple dwellings relief less the LBTT chargeable in relation to the three shop units as calculated above ie (£132,000 – £19,161) × 25% = £28,210.

As the LBTT chargeable on the 5 dwellings (£73,500) is greater than the 'minimum prescribed amount' of £28,210, the tax payable in relation to the transaction is £73,500 plus the tax due in relation to the shops of £19,161, giving total LBTT chargeable of £92,661.

For the purposes of the relief 'dwelling' means a building or part of a building used or suitable for use as a single dwelling or in the process of being constructed or adapted for such use, together with any garden or other grounds to be enjoyed with it (LBTT(S)A 2013, Sch 5, paras 24 to 27). LBTT4010 sets out that there is no statutory size limit for garden and grounds to be considered residential for LBTT purposes, unlike the 'permitted area' for the purposes of Capital Gains Tax. It will instead be a question of fact whether the land (including any building or structure on such land) is considered to be the garden and grounds of the dwelling. In circumstances where there is doubt as to whether grounds should be treated as part of the dwelling, it is suggested that an opinion (see **8.49**) be sought from Revenue Scotland. The relief may also be available in relation to a property which is to be constructed or adapted as a dwelling but where work has not yet commenced – but only if the LBTT arises on 'substantial performance' of a contract (see **2.7**) LBTT(S)A 2013, Sch 5, paras 28 and 29).

In determining what is and what is not a dwelling, LBTT(S)A 2013, s 59(3)–(6) applies so that the list of categories of buildings set out in s 59(3) are dwellings for the purposes of multiple dwellings relief, subject to those categories of buildings taken out of the meaning of a dwelling by s 59(4) – see **2.36** (LBTT(S)A 2013, Sch 5, para 30).

Example 5.5C – Claim for multiple dwellings relief where the ADS does not apply to the acquisition of one of the dwellings

On 31 March 2024, as part of a single transaction, Rob purchases five dwellings for £800,000. He intends to use one of the dwellings acquired as his main residence (on a just and reasonable apportionment basis consideration of £250,000 is apportioned to that dwelling) and to let the other four dwellings (on a just and reasonable apportionment basis consideration of £550,000 is apportioned to these dwellings) on a commercial basis. On the same date Rob sells his current main residence to a third party. Rob makes a claim for multiple dwellings relief.

In the absence of multiple dwellings relief the LBTT liability would be calculated as follows:

Purchase Price	*Rate*	*LBTT*
£	%	£
145,000	0	NIL
105,000	2	2,100
75,000	5	3,750
425,000	10	42,500
50,000	12	6,000
800,000		54,350

In addition, ADS of £33,000 (£550,000 × 6%) would have been payable on the four dwellings acquired that are not replacements for Rob's main residence. The total LBTT liability would therefore have been £87,350 (£54,350 + £33,000).

However, if Rob makes a claim for multiple dwellings relief the LBTT liability would be calculated as set out below.

Total consideration attributable to dwellings of £800,000 divided by the number of dwellings being five, gives an average price per dwelling of £160,000.

The tax due in relation to a dwelling to which the ADS applies is calculated as follows:

Purchase Price	*Rate*	*LBTT*
£	%	£
145,000	6	8,700
15,000	8	1,200
160,000		9,900

The tax due in relation to the dwelling to which the ADS does not apply is calculated as follows:

Purchase Price	*Rate*	*LBTT*
£	%	£
145,000	0	NIL
15,000	2	300
160,000		300

The LBTT liability is therefore £39,900 (£9,900 + £9,900 + £9,900 + £9,900 + £300).

However, the LBTT payable following a claim to multiple dwellings relief cannot be less than 25% of the LBTT which would have been payable in the absence of such a claim, being 25% of £87,350, amounting to £21,837. As 'the minimum prescribed amount' of £21,837 is less than the LBTT charge arising on the five houses following a claim to multiple dwellings relief, the total LBTT payable is £39,900.

Rob must therefore file a land transaction return, and pay the LBTT due of £39,90, by 30 April 2024.

Example 5.6 – Multiple dwellings relief – partial withdrawal of the relief

On 31 March 2024 Angus pays Fraser £800,000 for a building in Aberdeen on which work has started to convert it into four flats, on the basis that Angus will finish the conversion work. Angus already owns a property which he uses as his main residence and he plans to let the four flats on a commercial basis. The ADS (see **2.37** et seq) therefore applies to the transaction. Angus pays LBTT of £52,400 being the tax payable on an average consideration per flat of £800,000 divided by four. The LBTT liability is calculated as follows:

LBTT payable on the average consideration per dwelling:

Purchase price	*Rate*	*LBTT*
£	%	£
145,000	6	8,700
55,000	8	4,400
200,000		13,100

The LBTT payable in relation to the consideration given for the dwellings is therefore £52,400 (£13,100 + £13,100 + £13,100 + £13,100).

However, the tax chargeable can never be less than the 'minimum prescribed amount' of 25% of the LBTT which would be payable in the absence of a claim for multiple dwellings relief.

LBTT payable in the absence of a claim for multiple dwellings relief:

Purchase price	*Rate*	*LBTT*
£	%	£
145,000	6	8,700
105,000	8	8,400
75,000	11	8,250
425,000	16	68,000
50,000	18	9,000
800,000		102,350

The 'minimum prescribed amount' is therefore 25% × £102,350 = £25,587.

As the minimum prescribed amount is less than the LBTT payable on the consideration given for the dwellings, the LBTT chargeable is £52,400.

Work progresses slowly and, two years later, Angus decides to revise the design and create just two larger flats. If the original plan had been to create only two flats, the LBTT chargeable would have been £74,700, being the tax payable on an average consideration of £800,000 divided by two. The LBTT liability is calculated as follows:

LBTT payable on the average consideration per dwelling:

Purchase price	*Rate*	*LBTT*
£	%	£
145,000	6	8,700
105,000	8	8,400
75,000	11	8,250
75,000	16	12,000
400,000		37,350

The LBTT payable in respect of the consideration given for the dwellings is therefore £74,700 (£37,350 + £37,350).

The 'minimum prescribed amount' remains as calculated above at £25,587, and therefore as the LBTT payable on the consideration given for dwellings of £74,700 exceeds this amount, that is the amount of the LBTT chargeable.

Within 30 days of Angus deciding to create only two flats, he must make a further LBTT return and pay the additional tax of £22,300 (£74,700 – £52,400) (LBTT(S)A 2013, s 33(1)(b) and (2), (3) and (4)(b)) .

Charities relief

5.26

Focus

- Charities relief may be available in full even though the whole of the property may not be acquired for charitable purposes, however in those circumstances the rules providing for the withdrawal of the relief are then different.

There are two circumstances in which an acquisition by a charity or charitable trust may be relieved from charge, and these are as follows (LBTT(S)A 2013, Sch 13, paras 1–3):

(1) Relief is available if the whole of the property acquired is to be held by the buyer for 'qualifying charitable purposes'. This means either furtherance of the charities' own charitable purposes (or the charitable purposes of another charity) or as an investment to produce profits to be used for those charitable purposes.

(2) Alternatively, full relief is still available if less than all, but more than 50% by value, of the property acquired is to be held for qualifying charitable purposes, but in such circumstances the rules around the withdrawal of the relief are then different – **see 5.27**.

However, relief is not available in either of circumstances (1) or (2) above if the transaction was entered into for the purpose of avoiding a liability to LBTT.

Revenue Scotland originally took the view that 'qualifying charitable purposes' did not include co-investment in land and buildings by a charity, with another party that was not a charity. Their technical guidance stated that where a charity acquired land and buildings jointly, with a non-charity, it was not possible for the charity to claim charities relief in respect of the interest in the land and buildings it acquired. This was at odds with the decision in the SDLT case of *The Pollen Estate Trustee Company Ltd/Kings College London and HMRC* [2013] EWCA Civ 753 in which it was held that a land transaction should be exempt from SDLT 'to the extent that' the purchaser is a charity and the qualifying conditions are satisfied. It was not clear why this interpretation did not apply for the purposes of LBTT as the LBTT legislation was very similar to the SDLT legislation. Revenue Scotland have now revised their original view and now accept that charities relief can be claimed for the charity's *pro indiviso* share of the land acquired jointly with one or more parties who are not charities (see LBTT3035).

5.27 In either of circumstances (1) and (2) in **5.26** above, the relief is withdrawn (or partially withdrawn) if, either within three years of the acquisition, or later under arrangements entered into within that three-year period, a 'disqualifying event' occurs and the charity still holds the property in relation to which the relief was claimed or an interest derived from it (LBTT(S) A 2013, Sch 13, para 4).

If relief was obtained under circumstance (1) in **5.26** above, 'disqualifying event' means either: (a) the charity ceasing to be established for charitable purposes only, or (b) the charity beginning to hold or use the property, or any interest derived from it, for non-charitable purposes (LBTT(S)A 2013, Sch 13, para 5). If only part of the property is still held when the disqualifying event occurs, or if only part becomes used for non-charitable purposes, an appropriate proportion of the relief is withdrawn (LBTT(S)A 2013, Sch 13, paras 9 and 10).

Alternatively, if relief was obtained under circumstance (2) in **5.26** above, 'disqualifying event' additionally includes: (a) any transfer of all or part of the land by the charity, or (b) the grant of a lease at a premium (consideration other than rent) and at a rent of less than £1,000 per year, unless that transfer or grant is made in furtherance of the charitable purposes of the buyer (LBTT(S) A 2013, Sch 13, paras 6 and 7).

Where the relief is withdrawn in full, the amount of the tax chargeable is the amount that would have been chargeable in relation to the original transaction, on the basis that charities relief was not available (LBTT(S)A 2013, Sch 13, para 8).

If, at the time the disqualifying event occurs, the charity only holds an interest derived from the interest originally acquired the relief is only partially withdrawn. In such circumstances the amount of the tax chargeable is an 'appropriate proportion' of the tax which would have been chargeable had charities relief not been available. The appropriate proportion is arrived at by having regard to the proportion of the property still held by the buyer compared to what was originally acquired, and the extent to which the property interest still held becomes used or held for purposes other than qualifying charitable purposes (LBTT(S)A 2013, Sch 13, paras 9 and 10).

Where the relief is withdrawn the charity must file a further land transaction return within the 30 day period beginning on the day after the date on which the disqualifying event took place. The further return must include an assessment of the LBTT chargeable, based on the information included in the further return (LBTT(S)A 2013, s 33(1)(f), (2), (3) and (4)(f)).

5.28 For the purposes of the relief a 'charity' means a body registered in the Scottish Charity Register held by the Office of the Scottish Charity Regulator (OSCR: www.oscr.org.uk) or a body satisfying each of the following conditions (LBTT(S)A 2013, Sch 13, para 15):

- the body is established under the law of a 'relevant territory' being England and Wales, Northern Ireland, a member state of the European Union, or any other territory specified in regulations made by the Scottish Ministers. The territories of The Republic of Iceland, The Kingdom of Norway and the Principality of Lichtenstein have been specified as relevant territories for the purposes of the relief (The Land and Buildings Transaction Tax (Definition of Charity) (Relevant Territories) (Scotland) Regulations 2014, SI 2014/352, reg 2).
- the body is managed or controlled wholly or mainly outside of Scotland; and
- the body is registered in a register corresponding to the Scottish Charity Register; or the body's purposes consist only of one or more of the charitable purposes.

For the purposes of the relief 'charitable purposes' has the meaning given by the Charities and Trustee Investments (Scotland) Act 2005 (asp 10), s106, which is a definition section which refers to s7(2) of the same act, which lists sixteen purposes, including: (a) the prevention or relief of poverty, (b) the advancement of education, (c) the advancement of religion, (d) the advancement of health and so on.

These rules are designed to prevent abuses of charitable status.

The relief also applies to a charitable trust which is defined as a trust in relation to which all of the beneficiaries are charities or a unit trust scheme in which all of the unit holders are charities (LBTT(S)A 2013, Sch 13, paras 12–14).

Example 5.7 – Charities relief – withdrawal of the relief claimed

On 1 April 2024, the Q Charitable Trust buys undeveloped land for £1 million, with the intention of constructing a new operations centre for its own use on three quarters (by area and by value) of the site and selling the other quarter to an unrelated company, R, for a previously negotiated price of £300,000. Because the property is not to be used wholly for charitable purposes, full charities relief of £38,500 is claimed under LBTT(S)A 2013, Sch 13, para 2(a)(ii), as set out under circumstance (2) in **5.26** above. The sale to R falls through, but on 1 July 2024, a slightly different plot is sold to another unrelated buyer, S, for £350,000. It is agreed with Revenue Scotland that the value of the plot sold is one quarter of the value of the whole site. At this point, one quarter of the relief previously granted is withdrawn, and Q must complete a new LBTT land transaction return disclosing the charge and making payment. The LBTT payable is one quarter of the LBTT liability which would have arisen if charities relief had not been available. In the absence of the relief the LBTT liability would have been as follows:

Purchase price	*Rate*	*LBTT*
£	%	£
150,000	0	NIL
100,000	1	1,000
750,000	5	37,500
1,000,000		38,500

The LBTT payable is therefore one quarter of £38,500 which is £9,625.

The tax rates and tax bands used are those that would have applied to the whole original purchase price, *not* the rates which would apply to the value of the plot disposed of alone (LBTT(S)A 2013, Sch 13, para 9).

Note that if Q had intended to use the whole site for its charitable purposes at the time of the acquisition, and thus claimed relief under LBTT(S) A 2013, Sch 13, para 2(a)(i), as set out under circumstance (1) in **5.26** above, but subsequently decided to sell the plot to S, this disposal would not have led to any withdrawal of the relief.

As a result of changes at Q during the development period, the operations centre is larger than needed. On 1 November 2024, Q agrees to grant a 25-year lease of one floor to an unrelated company, T, at a premium of £800,000 and a peppercorn rent. The premium is paid and T occupies on 31 March 2025. It is agreed with Revenue Scotland that the value of the floor leased out is 40% of the value of the whole development. At this point, 40% of the relief originally granted is now withdrawn – that is 40% of £38,500, or £15,400. At this point, Q owns less than 50% of the original site, having sold or leased 65% by value of the original site. This is not a problem as, when the relief was claimed, Q intended to use more than 50% for its charitable purposes. However, given the amount finally disposed of, there may be some risk that Revenue Scotland would challenge the original intention.

Alternative finance reliefs

5.29 A series of reliefs has been introduced in an attempt to ensure that additional LBTT liabilities do not arise on property transactions where funding is structured in such a way as to avoid the payment of interest. The need to avoid interest typically arises from specific beliefs, particularly the acceptance of Shari'ah principles; however, availability of the reliefs depends only on the nature of the transaction and participants, and not on subscription to any particular set of beliefs. The reliefs fall into two groups. The first (LBTT(S)A 2013, Sch 7) relates to the purchase or ownership of property where, in other circumstances, mortgage finance might be obtained; these are dealt with in more detail below. The second (LBTT(S)A 2013, Sch 8) relates to property backed investment bonds. Review of the reliefs available to those involved in the issue and management of such bonds is beyond the scope of this book; it is sufficient to note that a portfolio investor in qualifying bonds, although in fact gaining a direct interest in the underlying property, is deemed not to have such an interest for LBTT purposes (LBTT(S)A 2013, Sch 8, para 4(a)). This does not apply if the investor, together with connected persons, has the right of management and control of the underlying property, for example by virtue of the proportion of bonds held (LBTT(S)A 2013, Sch 8, para 5). Careful fact gathering and analysis may therefore be required where anything more than an obvious minority of bonds is held, and especially where family members or connected companies may hold investments in the same products. This difficulty is acknowledged in the legislation. If connected persons obtain control inadvertently, the favourable tax treatment is not lost, provided the control is not in fact exercised and holdings are reduced to remove that control once the issue has come to light (LBTT(S)A 2013, Sch 8, para 6).

5.30 The reliefs relating to the purchase or ownership of property envisage three forms of transaction.

Land sold to financial institution and leased to person:

In the first (LBTT(S)A 2013, Sch 7, paras 2–6), under arrangements with the ultimate or intended owner ('Owner'), a financial institution ('Bank') purchases ownership of land or a leasehold interest, leases or sub-leases it to the Owner and grants the Owner a right (the 'Option') to require Bank to transfer the ownership of the property, or the leasehold interest, to the Owner. The terms of the lease and Option typically ensure that the Bank receives the same economic return as if it had provided a loan secured on the property. If the relief applies, the lease to the Owner and the final transfer to the Owner under the Option are relieved from LBTT (LBTT(S)A 2013, Sch 7, para 4 and 5). Partial transfers to the Owner under the Option during the course of the arrangement (for example, as a result of the Owner making capital payments) are exempt from LBTT. As a result, the only LBTT payable is on the initial purchase by the Bank, which is equivalent to what would happen if the Owner purchased the property from a third party with the aid of conventional loan finance. However, if the Bank buys the property from the Owner or another bank which itself acquired the property from the Owner under the alternative property financing arrangements described above, that purchase is also relieved from LBTT (LBTT(S)A 2013, Sch 7, para 3). In this situation, no LBTT is payable on the overall transaction, reflecting the position where a property owner obtains a loan secured on property already held.

Land sold to financial institution and person in common:

The second form of transaction (LBTT(S)A 2013, Sch 7, paras 7–12) involves the Bank and the Owner entering into an arrangement under which: (a) the Bank and the Owner purchase ownership of land or a leasehold interest as common owners, (b) the Bank and the Owner enter into an agreement under which the Owner has the right to exclusive occupation of the property, and (c) the Bank grants the Owner an option to require the Bank to transfer ownership of the property or the leasehold interest to the Owner in one or a series of transactions. If the relief applies, the grant of the right of exclusive occupation of the property and the transfer of the property to the Owner under the option, either as a single transaction or in a series of transactions, are relieved from LBTT (LBTT(S)A 2013, Sch 7, para 9 and 10). Again, if the purchase by the Bank and the Owner as common owners is itself from the Owner, or another bank which itself acquired the property from the Owner under the alternative property financing arrangement described above, that transaction is also eligible for relief (LBTT(S)A 2013, Sch 7, para 8).

Land sold to financial institution and re-sold to person:

The third form of transaction (LBTT(S)A 2013, Sch 7, paras 13–15) envisages purchase of the property by the Bank and onward sale to the Owner, with the Owner granting the bank a standard security over the property. The onward sale of the property is typically made on instalment terms designed to replicate the economics of a repayment of principal and interest on a loan. If the relief applies, the onward sale to the Owner is relieved from LBTT (LBTT(S)A 2013, Sch 7, para 15). Again, if the purchase by the Bank is itself from the Owner, or another bank which itself acquired the property from the Owner under the alternative property financing arrangement described above, that transaction is also eligible for relief (LBTT(S)A 2013, Sch 7 para 14).

Relief not available:

However, relief under LBTT(S)A 2013, Sch 7, paras 2–12 is denied if, at the time of the transaction, there are arrangements for a person to acquire control of the Bank (LBTT(S)A 2013, Sch 7, paras 17–20). This is an anti-avoidance provision, to counter the possibility of a bank setting up a subsidiary to enter into the transaction, with every intention of then selling the subsidiary to the erstwhile purchaser of the property. A further anti-avoidance provision (LBTT(S)A 2013, Sch 7, para 16) seeks to prevent the combination of these reliefs with group relief, reconstruction relief and acquisition relief described above, to obtain an overall tax advantage.

A Financial Institution is as defined in ITA 2007, s 564B (LBTT(S)A 2013, Sch 7, para 25), but excludes a person authorised by a licence under Part 3 of the Consumer Credit Act 1974 to carry on a consumer credit business or consumer hire business within the meaning of that Act.

5.31 The interest held by the Bank is an exempt interest (LBTT(S)A 2013, Sch 7, para 21 – see **2.14**). This means that any transfer to another financial institution (for example, if the Bank sells its loan book) will not give rise to an LBTT charge.

Relief for first-time buyers

5.31A A relief is available, for transactions with an 'effective date' (see **2.81**) on or after 30 June 2018 (provided the contract (missives) was entered into on or after 9 February 2018), where a 'first-time buyer' (see **5.31E**) purchases their first home, which they intend to occupy as their only or main residence. If the relief is available, the rate of LBTT on the first £175,000 of the chargeable consideration is 0%. First-time buyers acquiring a property for more than £175,000 can also claim the relief which will result in the first £175,000 of the chargeable consideration being taxed at a rate of 0%, with the normal rates of LBTT (see **2.35**) applying to the consideration in excess of £175,000. Consequently, all first-time buyers who acquire a property for chargeable consideration in excess of £145,000 can reduce their tax liability by claiming the relief and the maximum reduction in LBTT payable will be £600 (£175,000 – £145,000 × 2%). The legislation dealing with the relief can be found in LBTT(S)A 2013, Sch 4A (introduced by the Land and Buildings Transaction Tax (First-Time Buyer Relief) (Scotland) Order 2018). The relief must be claimed in a land transaction return, or in an amendment to a land transaction return, by entering Relief Code 27 in the 'Type of relief' field after which the amount of the relief being claimed should be entered in the 'Amount of relief' field.

Revenue Scotland has updated its technical guidance, systems and processes to allow the newly introduced relief to be claimed. The technical guidance can be found at LBTT3048 and includes a number of worked examples. The online tax calculator has also been updated to help calculate the amount of LBTT due to be paid when a claim is being made for the new relief.

Example 5.7A

Rory who, until now, has lived in his parent's house, agrees to acquire ownership of a house in Paisley for a consideration of £180,000. As this is the first house which Rory has ever purchased he is able to claim the first-time buyer's relief and the LBTT payable is calculated as follows:

Chargeable Consideration	*Rate*	*LBTT*
	%	£
On the first £175,000 of the purchase price	0	Nil
On the remaining £5,000	2	100
Total LBTT payable		100

If the relief for first-time buyers had not been available, the LBTT payable would have amounted to £700 (see calculation below) and, therefore, in this example, claiming the relief reduces the LBTT liability by £600.

Chargeable Consideration	*Rate*	*SDLT*
	%	£
First £145,000	0	Nil
Next £35,000	2	700
Total LBTT payable		700

5.31B As with all LBTT reliefs, a number of conditions must be satisfied if the relief for first-time buyers is to be available. The relief will be available in the following circumstances:

(a) the transaction is an acquisition of a 'major interest in land' (see **5.31C**);

(b) the land acquired under the transaction consists entirely of 'residential property' (see **5.31D**) and includes a 'dwelling';

(c) the transaction is not one of a number of 'linked transactions' (see **2.79**) unless the main subject matter of the other linked transactions is the acquisition of gardens or grounds of the dwelling in relation to which the claim is made, or the acquisition of land that subsists for the benefit of that dwelling;

(d) the buyer, or if there is more than one buyer, each of the buyers, is a first-time buyer intending to occupy the dwelling as their only or main residence;

(e) the 'effective date' (see **2.81**) of the transaction is on or after 30 June 2018 and the contract (missives) is entered into on or after 9 February 2018; and

(f) the transaction is not one to which the Additional Dwelling Supplement applies (see **2.37** et seq).

These conditions are considered in more detail below.

5.31C

(1) The acquisition of a 'major interest in land' (LBTT(S)A 2013, Sch 4A, para 1(1)(a))

The transaction must be the acquisition of a 'major interest in land' (see **2.9**). The term 'major interest in land' covers both the acquisition of the ownership of land and the acquisition of a tenant's interest in land subject to a lease (LBTT(S) A 2013, s 60). For the purposes of the first-time buyer relief, the term 'major interest in land' does not include the tenant's interest in a private residential tenancy regulated by statute under the Rent (Scotland) Act 1984, the Housing (Scotland) Act 1988 or the Private Housing (Tenancies) (Scotland) Act 2016.

However, as the grant of a lease over 'residential property', and the assignation of an existing lease over 'residential property' are exempt transactions (LBTT(S) (A) 2013, Sch 1, paras 3(1)(a) and (2) – see **5.6**) in practice a claim for the relief will only be relevant to the acquisition of the ownership of land. The inclusion of leases over 'residential property' within the definition of 'major interest in land', for the purposes of the first-time buyer relief, is however required as ownership of such a lease, by the buyer of a dwelling, will mean that the buyer will not be a first-time buyer (see **5.31F**) for the purposes of the relief.

5.31D

(2) The land acquired under the transaction must consist entirely of 'residential property' (see 2.36) and must include a 'dwelling' (LBTT(S) A 2013, Sch 4A, para 1(1)(b))

The first part of this condition is that the land acquired must consist entirely of 'residential property' (see **2.36**). Residential property means a building that is used or suitable for use as a dwelling (or in the process of being constructed or adapted for such use) and includes associated gardens grounds outbuildings and other rights which subsist for the benefit of the property (LBTT(S) A 2013, s 59(1)). The use of the property at the 'effective date' (see **2.81**) of the transaction is determinate, and trumps any previous or intended future use. Non-residential property is any property which is not residential property (LBTT(S)A 2013, s 59(2)).

Consequently, if the transaction includes the acquisition of any non-residential property, or mixed-use property, first-time buyer relief will not be available.

The second part of the condition is that the 'residential property' acquired under the transaction must include a 'dwelling'. What counts as a dwelling for the purposes of the relief is set out in LBTT(S)A 2013, Sch 4A, para 7(2). A dwelling means a building, or part of a building, which is suitable for use as a single dwelling, or is in the process of being constructed or adapted for use as a single dwelling (LBTT(S)A 2013, Sch 5, para 25). It also includes land that is, or is to be, occupied or enjoyed with the dwelling as gardens, grounds, outbuildings or other structures, and land which subsists for the benefit of the dwelling (LBTT(S)A 2013, Sch 5, paras 26 and 27). There is no definition of the term 'dwelling' in the legislation which must therefore take its ordinary meaning, that is a building which provides those who use it with the facilities required for everyday private domestic existence. A cleared site with no building on it would not come within the meaning of a 'dwelling' even if it had planning permission for the construction of residential property. However, a site with a building suitable for use as a single dwelling would be counted as a dwelling even if the building is to be demolished or refurbished. Holiday homes & lets, including those which cannot be used all year round, are considered as dwellings. Caravans, mobile homes or houseboats will not normally be dwellings unless they have become sufficiently fixed to the land that they have become part of the land (LBTT10018).

An off-plan purchase will count as the acquisition of a dwelling for the purposes of the first-time buyer relief provided (LBTT(S)A 2013, Sch 5, para 28):

(a) contracts have been exchanged for the purchase of a building, or part of a building, which is to be constructed or adapted for use as a single dwelling;

(b) the contract is 'substantially performed' (see **2.81**); and

(c) at the time the contract is 'substantially performed' (see **2.81**) the construction or adaption of the building has not yet begun.

The legislation provides a list of certain types of properties which are included within the definition of 'residential property' for LBTT purposes (see **2.36**) and which are also included within the definition of 'dwelling' for the purposes of the first-time buyer relief (LBTT(S)A 2013, Sch 5, para 30). The types of properties included are those used to provide residential accommodation for school pupils, purpose-built student accommodation, purpose-built accommodation for members of the armed forces and an institution that is the sole or main residence of at least 90% of its residents and does not fall within any of the purposes within LBTT(S)A 2013, s 59(4): see **2.36**.

5.31E

(3) Linked Transactions (LBTT(S)A 2013, Sch 4A, paras 1(1)(d) and 1(2))

If the purchase of the dwelling is 'linked' (see **2.79**) to another transaction, the relief is not available unless the linked transaction relates solely to the acquisition of land which is, or is to be, occupied or enjoyed as the garden or grounds of the acquired dwelling or to the acquisition of land which subsists for the benefit of the dwelling being acquired.

A subsequent 'linked transaction' (see **2.79**) may mean that a transaction (or transactions) which originally qualified for the first-time buyer relief no longer qualifies and, in these circumstances, the relief is withdrawn (LBTT(S)A 2013, Sch 4A, para1(3)). This would happen where, following the relief having been claimed, there is a subsequent 'linked transaction' (see **2.79**) which does not involve solely the acquisition of land which is, or is to be, occupied or enjoyed as the garden or grounds of the acquired dwelling or the acquisition of land which subsists for the benefit of the dwelling being acquired.

Where the First-Time Buyer's Relief is withdrawn the taxpayer must file a further land transaction return with Revenue Scotland and pay the additional LBTT due as a result of the withdrawal of the relief (see **8.15** et seq). The further LBTT return must be filed within 30 days of the date of the subsequent linked transaction and must include an assessment of the LBTT payable based on the tax rates and bands which applied at the 'effective date' (see **2.81**) of the transaction in relation to which First-Time Buyers Relief was claimed. A land transaction return may also have to filed in relation to the subsequent 'linked transaction' itself.

A subsequent 'linked transaction' which relates solely to the acquisition of land which is, or is to be, occupied or enjoyed as the garden or grounds of the acquired dwelling, or to the acquisition of land which subsists for the benefit of the dwelling being acquired, will not cause the first-time buyers relief to be withdrawn but may result in additional LBTT becoming payable on the original transaction, as the amount payable on the aggregate consideration for all 'linked transactions' is apportioned between the transactions based on the 'chargeable consideration' for each transaction (see **Example 5.7B**). In these circumstances a further return would need to be filed in relation to the original transaction with the amended LBTT liability being calculated based on the increase in the chargeable consideration.

5.31F

(4) The buyer or, if there is more than one buyer, each of the buyers, must be a first-time buyer intending to occupy the dwelling as their only or main residence (LBTT(S)A 2013, Sch 4A, paras 1(1)(c) and 2).

The relief is only available if the buyer, or if there is more than one buyer, each of the buyers, is a 'first-time buyer' and the meaning of the term 'first-time buyer' can be found at LBTT(S)A 2013, Sch 4A, para 2.

To be a 'first-time buyer' a person must not have previously been a buyer in relation to the acquisition of a 'major interest in land' (see **5.31C**) which consisted of 'residential property' (see **5.31D**) including a dwelling (see **5.31D**), nor can the person have acquired an interest in a dwelling situated outside of Scotland that is equivalent to the interest of a buyer of a 'major interest in land'.

The 'major interest in land' can be anywhere in the world. At LBTT3048 Revenue Scotland indicate that 'All forms of ownership in the legal systems of the rest of the UK which are equivalent to ownership in Scotland are treated as ownership for the purposes of this relief.' They go on to state 'For instance, a dwelling for which an individual holds a tenant's interest under certain types of lease in the rest of the UK would count towards dwellings owned by an individual'.

Any dwellings which a person has acquired by way of gift or inheritance are also taken into account in determining whether that person is, or is not, a first-time buyer.

Where a person is or was the beneficiary of a 'bare trust' (see **7.3**) in which the trust property includes, or has included, a 'major interest' (see **5.31C**) in a dwelling, the beneficiary is treated as being, or having been, the buyer of the dwelling (LBTT(S)A 2013, Sch 4A, para 5(1)(a) and (2)). This means that such a beneficiary cannot claim first-time buyer's relief.

Similarly, where a person is or was the beneficiary of a 'settlement' (see **7.3**) under which they were entitled to occupy the dwelling for life, or were entitled to the income (whether net or gross) in respect of the dwelling, in which the trust property includes, or has included, a 'major interest' (see **5.31C**) in a dwelling, the beneficiary is treated as being, or having been, the buyer of the dwelling (LBTT(S)A 2013, Sch 4A, para 5(1)(b), (2) and (3)). This means that such a beneficiary cannot claim first-time buyer's relief.

Where a person has, or has had, a 'major interest' (see **5.31C**) in a dwelling as a trustee or a personal representative of another, that person is to be treated as not being, or having been, the buyer of the interest in the dwelling (LBTT(S) A 2013, Sch 4A, para 6). Such an interest will not therefore prevent that person from claiming first-time buyer's relief.

All of the buyers must intend to occupy the dwelling as their only or main residence. There is no definition of only or main residence in the legislation. The Revenue Scotland guidance at LBTT3048 states: 'There should normally be little difficulty in determining if someone intends to occupy the dwelling as their only or main residence.' They go on to state:

> 'The buyer does not need to occupy the dwelling immediately on purchase. For example, if structural repairs or renovation work are required then it may be that the buyer moves into temporary accommodation until they are complete. In such instances, there must be a clear intention to occupy the dwelling as the buyer's only or main residence after the works are completed and consideration must be given to the full facts and circumstances of the case.'

Finally, Revenue Scotland state:

> 'Relief cannot be claimed where evidence clearly shows that either another dwelling will continue to be the buyer's main residence or that the newly purchased dwelling has been acquired for some other purpose (such as it being acquired using a buy-to-let mortgage).'

Example 5.7B

The facts are as in Example 5.7A however as part of the original contract Rory had agreed to pay the seller an additional £80,000 for the ownership of the grounds forming part of the dwelling being acquired. The acquisition of the grounds does not complete until after the land transaction return in relation to the acquisition of the dwelling has been submitted to Revenue Scotland. The original acquisition of the dwelling and the subsequent acquisition of the grounds will be 'linked transactions' (see **2.79**) and the LBTT liability, claiming First-Time Buyer's Relief, is calculated as follows:

Chargeable consideration	*Rate*	*LBTT*
	%	£
On the first £175,000 of the purchase price	0	Nil
On the next £75,000	2	1,500
On the balance of £10,000	5	500
Total LBTT payable		2,000

The LBTT payable in relation to the acquisition of the grounds is therefore £615 (£80,000/£260,000 × £2,000).

Rory must also file an amended land transaction return in relation to the original purchase of the dwelling with the LBTT liability calculated at £1,385 (£180,000/£260,000 × £2,000) and pay the additional LBTT due of £1,285 (£1,385 – £100).

5.31G

(5) The contract (missives) must have been entered into on or after 9 February 2018 and the 'effective date' (see 2.81) of the chargeable transaction under which the dwelling is acquired must be on or after 30 June 2018

This means that if the contract (missives) to acquire the dwelling was entered into prior to 30 June 2018, that contract must not have been 'substantially performed' (see **2.81**), nor completed, before 30 June 2018, otherwise the relief will not be available.

5.31H

(6) The transaction must not be one to which the 'additional dwellings supplement' (see 2.37 et seq) applies.

This could occur, for example, where an individual acquires his or her first home in their own name but the individual's spouse owns a property that the couple previously used as their main residence but is now to be let out.

5.31I The relief for first-time buyers must be claimed in a land transaction return or an amendment to that return (LBTT(S)A 2013, s 27(1) and (2) – 'Schedule 4A (first-time buyer relief)' added by art 3 of the Land and Buildings Transaction Tax (First-Time Buyer Relief) (Scotland) Order 2018). The relief is claimed by entering Relief Code 27 in the 'Type of relief' field after which the amount of the relief being claimed should be entered in the 'Amount of relief' field.

5.31J If a single dwelling is acquired under an 'alternative finance arrangement' (see **5.29** et seq) entered into between an individual and a financial institution, a claim can be made for first-time buyer relief if the relevant conditions are satisfied (LBTT(S)A 2013, Sch 4A, para 4). In such circumstances the individual who is entitled to occupy the property is treated as the buyer in relation to the transaction for the purposes of LBTT(S)A 2013, Sch 4A, paras 1(1)(c) and 2(a) and (b) (requirement that each of the buyers intends to occupy the dwelling as their only or main residence and the definition of the term 'first-time buyer').

SUB-SALE DEVELOPMENT RELIEF

5.32

Background

The LBTT legislation does not include a sub-sale relief equivalent to that within the SDLT regime at FA 2003, s 45 and Sch 2A (see **3.6**). The Scottish Government were clear that they would not introduce a general sub-sale relief, due to the risk that it would be used for the artificial avoidance of LBTT. Equally, however, they recognise that LBTT will be one of the factors taken into account by property developers when assessing the viability of development or redevelopment projects in Scotland. Consequently, on 27 June 2014, the Scottish Government issued a consultation document on a proposed sub-sale development relief.

In that consultation document it was proposed that a targeted relief be introduced, to apply where significant development was to be carried out on the land acquired, but only on the basis that the relief would be claimed up-front in the land transaction return filed by the original buyer and tax would be paid at the time of the submission of that return as though no relief was available. The tax paid up-front would then be reclaimed later if the significant development actually took place within the requisite five year period. However, the view of many of the respondents to the consultation was that requiring payment of the tax up-front was not appropriate, as it was then not a relief in the true sense of the word. Instead, respondents suggested that the relief be granted up-front and clawed back if the significant development did not take place within the designated five year period. The Scottish Government took account of the respondent's views and changed the structure of the relief such that it is claimed up-front and clawed back if the significant development does not take place within five years. There is therefore no requirement that the tax, on the amount of the relief claimed, be paid up-front. The proposed relief does, however, only apply where the second transaction is a sub-sale, and does not apply where it is either an assignation of the existing contract or a novation of the existing contract.

5.33 The Land and Buildings Transaction Tax (Sub-sale Development Relief and Multiple Dwellings Relief) (Scotland) Order 2015, SSI 2015/123 was made on 17 March 2015, applied with effect from 1 April 2015 and introduced a new Sch 10A (Sub-sale development relief) to the LBTT(S)A 2013. The references quoted below are references to that new LBTT(S) 2013, Sch 10A. The Revenue Scotland technical guidance dealing with the relief can be found at LBTT3044.

5.34

Availability of the relief

Sub-sale development relief ('SDR') may be claimed by a buyer ('the First Buyer') under a contract ('the First Contract') for the acquisition of a chargeable interest (see **2.9**), provided the First Contract is to be completed by a conveyance (see **2.9**) and: (a) there is a 'qualifying sub-sale', and (b) each of the conditions set out below is satisfied (LBTT(S)A 2013, Sch 10A, para 2(1)).

The First Contract could, for example, be a contract under which a buyer is to acquire ownership of land and the contract is to be completed by delivery of a disposition. The First Contract cannot, however, be a contract effecting a sub-sale or assignation of rights in relation to another contract (LBTT(S)A 2013, Sch 10A, para 2(2)). This means that the relief is only available in respect of the first sub-sale and cannot be claimed in relation to any subsequent sub-sales.

A sub-sale is a 'qualifying sub-sale' if it is a sub-sale under which the First Buyer contracts to sell the whole or part of the chargeable interest which is the subject of the First Contract to another person ('the Second Buyer') and, as a result, the Second Buyer becomes entitled to call for a conveyance of the whole or part of the chargeable interest which was the subject of the First Contract. In addition, immediately before the First Buyer entered into the sub-sale, the First Buyer must have been entitled to call for a conveyance of the whole or part of that chargeable interest (LBTT(S)A 2013, Sch 10A, para 3).

The following two conditions must both be satisfied for SDR to be available (LBTT(S)A 2013, Sch 10A, para 4):

(1) The substantial performance (see **2.7**) or completion (see **2.9**) of the First contract must take place at the same time as, and in connection with, the substantial performance or completion of the 'qualifying sub-sale'.

    If the Second Buyer enters into an assignation, sub-sale or other transaction relating to the whole or part of the chargeable interest which is the subject of the 'qualifying sub-sale', as a consequence of which a person other than the Second Buyer becomes entitled to call for a conveyance, this is not treated as substantially performing the First Contract for the purposes of determining whether this condition is satisfied (LBTT(S)A 2013, Sch 10A, para 4(2)). Therefore whilst such an action by the Second Buyer will substantially perform the contract effecting the 'qualifying sub-sale', potentially leading to LBTT obligations for the Second Buyer in relation to the 'qualifying sub-sale' (see **2.83**), for the purposes of determining whether this condition is met, and therefore whether the First Buyer can claim SDR, it is treated as though the contract effecting the 'qualifying sub-sale' had not, in fact, been substantially performed.

    See **Example 5.8** for an explanation of what is likely to satisfy the 'at the same time as' requirement in relation to a 'qualifying sub-sale'.

(2) A 'significant development' for commercial purposes must be completed, or partially completed, on the land which is the subject of the 'qualifying sub-sale', within five years from the date on which the First Buyer entered into the 'qualifying sub-sale'.

Sub-sale development relief cannot be claimed if alternative property finance relief (see **5.29** et seq) is being claimed (LBTT(S)A 2013, Sch 10A, para 12).

5.35 In principle, therefore, and by way of example, SDR could be claimed where:

- 'L' (Landowner) agrees to transfer undeveloped land to 'D' (Developer) (the First Contract) and;
- before that contract is substantially performed or completed, 'D' agrees to transfer all or part of the same undeveloped land to Investor 'I' (the 'qualifying sub-sale'), and the 'L' to 'D' contract (the First Contract) is substantially performed and completed at the same time as, and in connection with, the substantial performance and completion of the 'D' to 'I' contract (the 'qualifying sub-sale'); and

- a 'significant development' for commercial purposes is to take place on the land which is the subject of the 'qualifying sub-sale', within five years from the date on which 'D' entered into the 'qualifying sub-sale'.

5.36

Making a claim for SDR

Where the provisions and conditions summarised in **5.34** are satisfied, the First Buyer 'D' (see **5.35**) may claim SDR.

If the whole of the land being transferred under the First Contract is the subject of the sub-sale to 'I', the First Buyer 'D' should be entitled to full relief from LBTT, so that the transaction effected on completion of the First Contract (or deemed to be effected on the substantial performance of the First Contract – see **2.7**) should be exempt from charge (LBTT(S)A 2013, Sch 10A, para 9).

If only part of the land transferring under the First Contract is the subject of the 'qualifying sub-sale', then so much of the chargeable consideration payable under the First Contract as is attributable to that part of the land not subject to the 'qualifying sub-sale' remains chargeable to LBTT (LBTT(S)A 2013, Sch 10A, para 10(1)). The allocation of the chargeable consideration between that part of the land that is not the subject of the 'qualifying sub-sale', and that part of the land that is the subject of the 'qualifying sub-sale', must be done on a just and reasonable basis (LBTT(S)A 2013, Sch 10A, para 10(2)).

Where the First Buyer makes a claim to SDR in relation to the whole, or part, of the land transaction effected on completion, or deemed to be effected on the substantial performance of the First Contract, the legislation states that the land transaction return must include such evidence as Revenue Scotland may specify regarding the 'significant development' for commercial purposes that will be completed within the requisite five year period (LBTT(S)A 2013, Sch 10A, para 11). It is understood that in practice the First Buyer will make the claim in the land transaction return and will not, at that stage, provide evidence regarding the 'significant development'. However, Revenue Scotland may then ask for evidence in support of the claim including development/architectural plans, details of the funding arrangements, building contracts and planning permission applications (LBTT3044).

Definitions

For these purposes 'development' means constructing, on the land which is acquired under the 'qualifying sub-sale', buildings including educational, sports and leisure, residential, retail, office or industrial buildings (but not plant and machinery, agricultural buildings, mining or engineering works – although wind farms are included), and includes the re-development of such buildings where the works carried out are comparable in scale or cost to the construction of such buildings (LBTT(S)A 2013, Sch 10A, para 7(a) and (b)). As the legislation uses the word 'including', the list of qualifying buildings above is not exhaustive and the construction of buildings used for other purposes may therefore come within the meaning of 'development', but only if they are similar in nature to those listed above.

In LBTT3044 Revenue Scotland state that 'The relief is not intended to be available, for example, where an existing building on a site is to be subject to a refurbishment, or where only minor 'development' takes place, relative to the nature, extent and market value of the land that is the subject of the sub-sale arrangement.'

The term 'industrial building' is defined (LBTT(S)A 2013, Sch 10A, para 8) as a building used for the purposes of:

- a trade carried on in a factory, mill or laboratory;
- a dock undertaking;
- a trade of hotel-keeping;
- a trade consisting of the operation or management of an airport.

The term 'a significant development' means a development that is significant having regard to, among other things, the nature and extent of the land which is the subject of the 'qualifying sub-sale' and the market value of that land (LBTT(S)A 2013, Sch 10A, para 7).

If there is uncertainty as to whether a proposed development will come within the meaning of a 'significant development' it should be possible to obtain an opinion (see **8.49**) from Revenue Scotland.

5.37

Chargeable consideration for the 'qualifying sub-sale'

The Second Buyer ('I' in the example in **5.35**) will pay LBTT based on: (a) the consideration given by 'I', or a person connected with 'I', for the 'qualifying sub-sale', plus (b) any part of the consideration to be given for the conveyance of the land under the First Contract as is attributable to the land acquired under the 'qualifying sub-sale' and is to be given, directly or indirectly, by 'I' or a person connected with 'I' (LBTT(S)A 2013, Sch 10A, para 17).

5.38

First Contract not treated as substantially performed

When a contract ('the original contract') for a land transaction is entered into, under which the contract is to be completed by a conveyance, and there is a sub-sale as a result of which a person other than the original buyer becomes entitled to call for that conveyance, the 'original contract' is treated as substantially performed (LBTT(S)A 2013, s14(1)(c) –see **2.83**). However, this rule does not apply in relation to the First Buyer entering into the 'qualifying sub-sale' if SDR is claimed by the First Buyer in relation to the land transaction under the First Contract (LBTT(S)A 2013, Sch 10A, para 16). The legislation actually states that the disapplication of LBTT(S)A 2013, s14(1)(c) applies when SDR 'is given'; however, it is assumed that this should be interpreted as the relief having been claimed, rather than given. This means that, in these circumstances, the entering into of the 'qualifying sub-sale' will not cause the First Contract to be substantially performed.

5.39

Withdrawal of the relief

SDR will be withdrawn in full, or in part, if the 'significant development' is not completed within five years of the date on which the First Buyer entered into the 'qualifying sub-sale' (LBTT(S)A 2013, Sch 10A, paras 13 and 15). It should be noted that the five-year period commences on the date upon which the First and Second Buyers enter into the contract for the sub-sale of the land, which may be well before the development works commence if, for example, planning permission is to be obtained. Consequently, the period available to complete the development may be significantly less than five years. A further difficulty is that the availability of the relief to the First Buyer is dependent upon the Second Buyer completing the development within the five-year period, meaning that it may well be out-with the control of the First Buyer, unless the First Buyer is able to negotiate contractual protection if the development is not completed within the agreed timetable, or the First Buyer is itself carrying out the development. Where the relief is withdrawn in full, the LBTT chargeable is the amount which would have been chargeable had the relief not been available (LBTT(S)A 2013, Sch 10A, para 14).

Relief is only partially withdrawn where, even though the 'significant development' is not completed within the requisite five-year period, some development of the land has taken place during that five year period. In these circumstances the amount of the LBTT payable is an appropriate proportion of the tax that would have been chargeable had no claim for SDR been made. The appropriate proportion is that which is just and reasonable having regard to, among other things, the extent to which the 'significant development', which was originally proposed, has actually taken place (LBTT(S)A 2013, Sch 10A, para 15).

Where the relief is withdrawn in full, or in part, notification must be given to Revenue Scotland by the First Buyer ('D' in the example in **5.35**) filing a further land transaction return within 30 days from the day which is the fifth anniversary of the First Buyer entering into the 'qualifying sub-sale'. The return must include an assessment of the amount of the tax chargeable (LBTT(S) A 2013, s 33(1)(da), (2), (3) and (4)(da)).

Example 5.8 – Sub-sale development relief ('SDR')

On 1 May 2023 Paisley Developments Ltd ('PD Ltd') enters into an agreement to acquire undeveloped land from Canal Property Holdings Ltd ('CPH Ltd') with a view to obtaining planning permission to develop a new shopping centre on the land. The agreed purchase price of the land is £10,000,000. PD Ltd then markets the site to potential investors and eventually, on 1 February 2024, enters into an agreement with Land Investments Ltd ('LI Ltd'), under which LI Ltd will purchase the undeveloped land from PD Ltd for a purchase price of £10,100,000. As a separate matter, PD Ltd and LI Ltd enter into a Development Agreement under which PD Ltd will build the shopping centre for LI Ltd and will hope to make a development profit.

When LI Ltd enters into the contract with PD Ltd for the acquisition of the undeveloped land, LI Ltd will become entitled to call for a conveyance of the undeveloped land, which would normally cause the contract between CPH Ltd and PD Ltd to be substantially performed (see **2.83** et seq) by virtue of LBTT(S)A 2013, s14(1)(c). However, on the basis that SDR is available and is to be claimed by PD Ltd, then LBTT(S)A, s14(1)(c) should be dis-applied by LBTT(S)A 2013, Sch 10A, para 16, so that the contract between CPH Ltd and PD Ltd should not be treated as substantially performed on 1 February 2024.

Up until 31 March 2024 nothing has been done to substantially perform either the contract between CPH Ltd and PD Ltd, or the contract between PD Ltd and LI Ltd, so that no LBTT obligations have arisen in relation to either contract. However, on that date, the contract between CPH Ltd and PD Ltd is substantially performed and completed with PD Ltd making the £10,000,000 payment for the acquisition of the undeveloped land. Immediately afterwards, the contract between PD Ltd and LI Ltd is also substantially performed and completed, with LI Ltd making the £10,100,000 payment for the acquisition of the undeveloped land.

With reference to the circumstances outlined in **5.35,** the contract between CPH Ltd and PD Ltd, for the acquisition of the undeveloped land, will be the First Contract. Before that contract was substantially performed or completed, LI Ltd entered into a contract with PD Ltd to acquire the undeveloped land that was the subject of the First Contract. The contract between LI Ltd and PD Ltd will be the 'qualifying sub-sale'. As the qualifying 'sub-sale' is substantially performed and completed immediately after the substantial performance and completion of the First Contract, with no intervening event, Revenue Scotland should accept that the substantial performance and completion of the First Contract took place at the same time as, and in connection with, the substantial performance and completion of the 'qualifying sub-sale'. For the purposes of SDLT sub-sale relief HMRC state that the 'at the same time as' requirement should be interpreted in accordance with normal conveyancing practice, with no event intervening between completion of the original contract and completion of the secondary contract (SDLTM01080). It seems likely that Revenue Scotland should take a similar approach although their technical guidance does not deal with the point (LBTT3044).

The construction of the shopping centre should come within the meaning of 'development' for the purposes of the relief, as retail buildings are to be constructed on the land, and it should constitute a 'significant development', as undeveloped land was acquired and a new shopping centre is to be constructed on the land.

The conditions which must be satisfied to allow PD Ltd to make a claim for SDR should therefore be met.

By 30 April 2024 PD Ltd should file a land transaction return claiming SDR in relation to its acquisition of the undeveloped land for £10,000,000. Whilst the legislation requires that the return should include such evidence as Revenue Scotland may require regarding the 'significant development' that is to take place on the land within the five years from the date on which PD Ltd entered into the 'qualifying sub-sale', ie by 31 January 2029 (LBTT(S)A 2013, Sch 10A, para 11), it is understood that, in practice, PD Ltd should make the claim in the land transaction return but should not, at that stage, provide evidence regarding the 'significant development'. Revenue Scotland may then ask PD Ltd to provide evidence in support of the claim, including development/architectural plans, details of the funding arrangements, building contracts and planning permission applications (LBTT3044). No LBTT will be payable by PD Ltd at the time of filing the land transaction return, as its acquisition of the undeveloped land is exempt from charge.

The SDR will be withdrawn in full if no part of the 'significant development' is completed by 31 January 2029, or withdrawn in part if only some, but not the whole, of the 'significant development' has taken place.

LI Ltd must also file a land transaction return by 30 April 2024 in relation to its acquisition of the undeveloped land and must pay the LBTT due of £493,500, based on chargeable consideration of £10,100,000.

GREEN FREEPORTS RELIEF

5.39A

Background

In early 2022, discussions between UK and Scottish Government officials led to an agreement to deliver two new freeports in Scotland – tailoring the UK Government's freeport program to a Scottish context.

Freeports were re-introduced into the UK by the 2021 budget. Eight freeports were created in England as a post-Brexit measure to 'level up' parts of the country which, it was felt, had been historically 'left behind' in Government funding. These freeports are areas, normally based around seaports, airports or railports which provide resident businesses with beneficial economic regulations – such as reduced customs tariffs and excise duties, enhanced capital allowances, and relief from business rates and SDLT.

The Scottish Government originally rejected the UK approach to freeports and drafted its own 'Greenport' plans, which would have required businesses to subscribe to real living wage, and net zero, policies. The UK Government effectively blocked the Greenport proposals, as the Scottish Government does not have devolved powers over customs tariffs.

The proposals were revived in 2022, and retitled 'green freeports' to reflect the Scottish Government's desire for a 'strong and visible 'green' element to the freeports offer in Scotland'. An agreement was reached for the funding of two green freeports in Scotland. Five green freeport bids were received and, on 13 January 2023, it was announced that the two green freeports would be located in 'Inverness and Cromarty Firth' and 'Forth'.

5.39B The Land and Buildings Transaction Tax (Green Freeports Relief) (Scotland) Order 2023, SSI 2023/280, was made on 28 September 2023, applied with effect from 1 October 2023 and introduced a new Sch 16D (Green freeports relief) to the LBTT(S)A 2013. The references quoted below are references to that new LBTT(S) 2013, Sch 16D. The Revenue Scotland technical guidance dealing with the relief can be found at LBTT3049.

5.39C

Availability of the relief

Within each green freeport, there are a number of designated tax sites. For the Inverness and Cromarty green freeport, these are:

- Deephaven;
- Invergordon; and
- Nigg.

These tax sites were designated in The Designation of Special Tax Sites (Inverness and Cromarty Firth Green Freeport) Regulations 2024 (SI 2024/380), which came into force on 8 April 2024.

The designation of the tax sites for the Forth green freeport is yet to be confirmed, but are proposed to be Grangemouth, Rosyth and Leith.

LBTT green freeports relief is a full or partial relief from LBTT for eligible transactions relating to land in these green freeport tax sites only.

The relief is available from the later of 1 October 2023 and the designation of the relevant tax site, until 30 September 2034.

5.39D Land is 'qualifying green freeport land' to the extent that, on the effective date (see **2.81**), it is situated in a green freeport tax site and the buyer intends it to be used exclusively in a qualifying manner (LBTT(S)A 2013, Sch 16D, para 6(1)).

The land is used in a qualifying manner where it is used in one of the following ways:

- it is used by the buyer or a connected person in the course of a commercial trade or profession;
- it is developed or redeveloped by the buyer or a connected person (as defined in CTA 2010, s.1122) for use (by any person) in the course of a commercial trade or profession;
- it is exploited by the buyer or a connected person (as defined in CTA 2010, s.1122), in the course of a commercial trade or profession, as a source of rents or other receipts (other than rent in respect of electric lines, gas or oil pipelines, wind turbines or mobile telephone masts). (LBTT(S) A 2013, Sch 16D, para 7(1)).

A commercial trade or profession includes a property rental business, but land is not used in a qualifying manner to the extent that it is used as a dwelling (including gardens and grounds), (re)developed to become residential property, rented out as a dwelling or held as land stock for resale without development (LBTT(S)A 2013, Sch 16D, para 7(2)).

There is no statutory definition of 'development' and Revenue Scotland interpret this as, the physical adaptation for a new use.

Whether development of land has taken place is a question of fact. Consideration of this will be given on a case-by-case basis by Revenue Scotland (LBTT3049). LBTT3049 also sets out some of the factors which Revenue Scotland will use in making this assessment. For example, seeking planning permission or design work are likely to show an intent to develop a property, but marketing a potential development, in isolation, is not likely to be considered sufficient.

Using land in the course of a commercial trade or profession is extended to include land used for a purpose that is ancillary to the use of other land that is situated in a green freeport tax site and is being used, developed or redeveloped, in the course of a commercial trade or profession (LBTT(S)A 2013, Sch 16D, para 7(3)). The ancillary use must support the use of land in a designated tax site land, such as a warehouse access road or a car park (LBTT3049).

5.39E If less than 10% of the consideration attributable to the land located in a green freeport tax site is attributable to land used in a qualifying manner (see **5.39D**), then none of the chargeable consideration is treated as being attributable to qualifying green freeport land and therefore no relief is available. If at least 90% of the relevant land is used in a qualifying manner then all of the chargeable consideration is treated as being attributable to qualifying green freeport land.

Where at least 90% of the total chargeable consideration (see **2.17**) for the transaction is attributable to qualifying green freeport land (see **5.39D** and above) and the effective date of the transaction is between 1 October 2023 and 30 September 2028, the transaction is exempt from LBTT. Where the proportion of the chargeable consideration attributable to qualifying green freeport land is between 10% and 90%, the LBTT liability is reduced by that same proportion (LBTT(S)A 2013, Sch 16D, paras 2 and 3).

Chargeable consideration is apportioned on a just and reasonable basis, where required.

Example 5.8A – Green freeports relief ('GFR')

Highland Imports Ltd (HI) acquires 30 acres of land for £2,500,000, on 31 March 2024.

25 of the 30 acres are within a green freeport tax site. The intention is to use 23 of the 25 acres for HI's trade. The other two acres contain industrial buildings, which HI intends to redevelop into residential flats.

A valuation is obtained, showing the following apportionment of the consideration to the various areas:

(1) 23 acres (trade use) – £1,541,000

(2) 2 acres (residential development) – £134,000

(3) 5 acres (outside green freeport) – £825,000

Land worth £1,675,000 (£1,541,000 + £134,000) is located within the green freeport tax site. However, land which is being redeveloped into dwellings is not being used in a 'qualifying manner'. As such, 92% (£134,000 / £1,675,000) is attributable to land used in a qualifying manner. As this is at least 90%, all of the consideration of £1,675,000 that relates to land within the green freeport tax site is treated as being attributable to qualifying green freeport land.

The total chargeable consideration for the transaction is £2,500,000. Of this, 67% (£1,675,000) has been calculated above as being attributable to qualifying green freeport land. As this is at least 10%, but less than 90%, the LBTT chargeable in relation to the transaction will be reduced by 67%.

HI's LBTT liability, including GFR, is calculated as follows:

Purchase Price	*Rate*	*LBTT*
£	%	£
150,000	0	-
100,000	1	1,000
2,250,000	5	112,500
2,500,000		113,500
Less: GFR (67% × £113,500)		(76,054)
LBTT liability		37,455

The LBTT payable by 30 April 2024 is therefore £37,455.

5.39F

Claiming the relief

Green freeport relief must be claimed in the original LBTT return, or by making an amendment to the LBTT return within the permitted 12-month period (LBTT(S)A 2013, s.27(2)).

5.39G

Withdrawal of relief

Green freeports relief can be withdrawn, in whole or in part, during the period which is the shorter of:

(1) Three years from the effective date (see **2.81**) of the transaction; and

(2) The period beginning with the effective date of the transaction and ending when neither the buyer nor a connected person holds a chargeable

interest in the qualifying green freeport land (see **5.39D**) (LBTT(S) A 2013, Sch 16D, para 9).

5.39H The relief is withdrawn where the qualifying green freeport land (see **5.39D**) ceases to be used in a qualifying manner (LBTT(S)A 2013, Sch 16D, para 8(1)).

However, where there has been a change of circumstances that is both unforeseen and beyond the buyer's control and it is not reasonable to expect the qualifying green freeport land to be used exclusively in a qualifying manner at that time, relief is not withdrawn (LBTT(S)A 2013, Sch 16D, para 8(2)).

Similarly, where the land has not yet begun to be used in a qualifying manner or has ceased to be used in a qualifying manner, relief is not withdrawn if reasonable steps are being taken to ensure that it is used in that manner. Where land has ceased to be used in a qualifying manner, relief is also not withdrawn where reasonable steps are being taken to dispose of all chargeable interests in that land (or that part of the land) that are held by the buyer and connected persons (as defined in CTA 2010, s.1122) in a timely manner (LBTT(S)A 2013, Sch 16D, paras 8(3) and 8(4)). There is no definition or guidance given on the meaning of 'reasonable steps' and 'timely manner'.

Merely disposing of some or all of the qualifying green freeport land will not give rise to a withdrawal of relief (LBTT(S)A 2013, Sch 16D, para 10).

5.39I Where relief is withdrawn, the tax payable is the amount that would have been chargeable but for the relief, ie using the original tax rates and thresholds with no relief.

The buyer must submit a further LBTT return, reflecting the withdrawal of any of relief, within 30 days of the relevant event giving rise to the withdrawal (LBTT(S)A 2013, s.33).

5.39J The withdrawal provisions appear to create some situations where a change of use within three years of the effective date would be treated more harshly than if the subsequent use had been the intention when the land was originally acquired.

To illustrate, Revenue Scotland's example from LBTT3049 is replicated below.

> 'A buyer acquires 30 acres of land for £3,000,000.
>
> Only 24 acres (80%) are within the designated Green Freeport tax site. The intention is to use all 24 acres in a qualifying manner.
>
> The remaining 6 acres are outside the Green Freeport tax site and will not be used in a qualifying manner.
>
> However, the valuation on a just and reasonable basis in this case for the 24 acres is £2,850,000. This is 95% of the total chargeable consideration of £3,000,000. A valuation is available to evidence this.
>
> As 95% of the chargeable consideration meets qualifying conditions full relief is available.

Within a year the buyer changes the use for 4 of the 24 acres to residential.

The buyer must make a further return within 30 days of this change for **the full 30 acres without relief** [emphasis added], paying any tax due.'

This indicates that a change of use, within the three years of the effective date of acquisition, of four of the 24 acres within the designed green freeport tax site would result in all of the tax relief being withdrawn.

However, if the buyer's original intention had been to use only 20 of the 30 acres for a qualifying purpose then (per LBTT(S)A 2013, Sch 16D, para 6(1)) 66.7% (assuming that each acre of land carries the same value) of the transaction land would be 'qualifying green freeport land', being land which is situated in a green freeport site and is to be used exclusively in a qualifying manner. As the proportion of the total chargeable consideration which relates to qualifying green freeport land is at least 10% but less than 90%, partial relief (being 66.7% of the LBTT liability) should have been available (as in the 'partial relief' example given in LBTT3049).

It is the author's view that it is unfair that the legislation appears to penalise a subsequent change of use more harshly than if the same position had been the case at the original effective date.

5.39K

Green freeports and leases

Where the qualifying conditions above are met, relief is available in respect of leases in the same way as for purchased land. The relief period comes to an end at the end of the lease term, or any earlier cessation of qualifying use.

Where the lease was granted before 1 October 2023, no green freeport relief would have been available. Any assignation of the lease during the relief period but out with the normal 12-month amendment period would not qualify for relief.

Where full relief is claimed, there is no requirement for a three-yearly review of the LBTT chargeable to be carried out. Where a lease benefitting from relief is later assigned and relief remains applicable an assignation return is not required. Where a lease in respect of which relief is claimed is later assigned, the first assignation of the lease that does not qualify for any relief and is not assigned to a bare trustee of the assignor will be treated as if it were the grant of a new lease (see **4.35** et seq)

Where only partial relief is claimed, there is a requirement for a three-yearly review and associated returns to be made (see **4.17** et seq). Assignation returns will also be required (see **4.26** et seq). On an assignation, the new tenant would not be able to claim any further relief through a review return as a relief can only be claimed through an original return or amendment to that return within the 12-month amendment period.

If relief is withdrawn during the applicable period (see **5.39G**), a further LBTT return, reflecting the withdrawal of any of relief, is due within 30 days of the relevant event giving rise to the withdrawal (LBTT(S)A 2013, s.33(1)(g)). The lease would then be subject to the normal lease review return process (see **4.17** et seq), using the date of the event giving rise to the withdrawal.

Where a lease becomes notifiable during the relief period, due to a variation in term or rent, a return will be required (see **4.45** et seq). Green freeport relief can be claimed in such cases, where the qualifying conditions are met.

5.39L

Alternative finance arrangements

Where there are alternative property finance arrangements (see **5.29** et seq), the availability and withdrawal of relief is assessed by reference to the person, other than the financial institution, who entered into the arrangements (LBTT(S) A 2013, Sch 16D, para 11).

SPECIALISED RELIEFS

Arrangements involving public or educational bodies

5.40 This is a calculation provision which looks like a hybrid exemption/relief. The provision in LBTT(S)A 2013, Sch 2, para 17 is imported from the SDLT legislation, and the original intention was to provide a relief in relation to PFI type transactions, which in Scotland would have included Public Private Partnership (PPP) transactions. However, the relief does not necessarily apply to all PPP-type transactions, nor does it necessarily remove all liability. It merely excludes certain amounts from the calculation of chargeable consideration where arrangements are entered into under which (LBTT(S)A 2013, Sch 2, para 17(1)):

- there is a transfer of the ownership of land (or the grant or assignation of a lease) from a 'qualifying body' (A) to a non-qualifying body (B); and
- in consideration (whether in whole or in part) there is a lease back of that land (or substantially the whole of the land) to A; and
- an agreement for B to provide services to, or carry out works for, A, to be paid for at least in part in money.

Although not a requirement there may also be a transfer of 'surplus land' from A to B.

5.41 'Qualifying bodies' include public bodies within LBTT(S)A 2013, Sch 16, para 4 (broadly, the Scottish Ministers, a Minister of the Crown, the Scottish Parliamentary Corporate Body, a local authority, health authorities and other statutory bodies, but the list in para 4 should be checked in any individual case). They also include any post-16 education body within the meaning of the Further and Higher Education (Scotland) Act 2005, s 35(1) (asp 6) (see the Land and Buildings Transaction Tax (Qualifying Public or Educational Bodies)

(Scotland) Amendment Order 2014, SI 2014/351) and grant-aided schools (within the meaning of the Education (Scotland) Act 1980 (c44), s 135(1)).

5.42 Where the relief applies, the chargeable consideration for the initial transfer of land does not include the value of the lease-back or the carrying out of works or provision of services by B (LBTT(S)A 2013, Sch 2, para 17(4)). The chargeable consideration for the lease-back does not include the initial transfer of land, any transfer of other (surplus) land from A to B, or the payment of money by A to B for the building works or other services provided (LBTT(S)A 2013, Sch 2, para 17(5)). If the conditions for the relief are satisfied, the LBTT exchange provisions (see **2.31**) do not apply to the transaction (LBTT(S)A 2013, Sch 2, para 5(8)). This means that B does not have to pay LBTT based on the market value of the interest in land it acquires, and only pays LBTT based on any actual consideration given for the acquisition. Depending upon how the transactions are structured it may mean that there is no chargeable consideration for any of the land transfers; however, PPP-type transactions are often more complex than the relief appears to envisage, and each transaction must be analysed carefully to establish whether the precise conditions have been met for all consideration to be excluded from charge.

Example 5.9 – Arrangement involving a public or educational body

Anytown Authority (A) needs a new building for council offices and a public library. This is to be built on a site mostly owned by A. Buildit plc (B) owns a small piece of land adjacent to this site, which is needed for access. It is agreed that:

(1) B will transfer the freehold of the small piece of land to A;

(2) A will grant B a 25-year lease of the whole site at a peppercorn rent;

(3) B will construct the building to A's specification;

(4) B will lease the building back to A for 25 years less one day, on the basis that B will manage the building (cleaning, maintenance, security etc);

(5) A will pay B a fee each year for the provision of the building and services; and

(6) in addition, A will transfer to B the freehold of an old library site, on which B hopes to develop luxury apartments for sale.

Relief from LBTT should be available under LBTT(S)A 2013, Sch 2, para 17 which means that items (3) and (4) do not count as chargeable consideration for the grant of the 25-year lease at (2). Items (2), (5) and (6) do not count as chargeable consideration for the grant of the lease at (4). However, the transfer at (1) is not within the relieving provisions and is potentially subject to LBTT. If A is not able to claim any other relief or exemption, it will be necessary to establish how much of the value of (2), (5) and (6) should be attributed as consideration for the transfer at (1), and LBTT will be charged on this. The natural assumption will be that the consideration is the same as the market value of the small piece of land, unless analysis of the figures suggests otherwise.

Certain acquisitions by registered social landlords

5.43 A land transaction in which a registered social landlord (RSL) is the buyer is exempt from the charge to LBTT if one or more of the qualifying conditions detailed below is satisfied (LBTT(S)A 2013, Sch 6, para 1). For these purposes an RSL means a body registered in the register maintained under s 20(1) of the Housing (Scotland) Act 2010 (asp 17) (LBTT(S)A 2013, s 65). The qualifying conditions are as follows:

- the RSL is controlled by its tenants, meaning that the majority of its directors (where the RSL is a company), or the majority of its members (where the RSL is a body corporate managed by its members), or the majority of its trustees (where the RSL is a trust) or the majority of its management committee members (where the RSL is neither a company, a body corporate managed by its members or a trust) are tenants who occupy properties owned or managed by the RSL (LBTT(S)A 2013, Sch 6, para 2(a), 3 and 4); or
- the seller is an RSL, the Scottish Ministers or a local authority (LBTT(S)A 2013, Sch 6, para 2(b); or
- the transaction is partly or wholly funded with a grant or other financial assistance from the National Lottery or under the Housing (Scotland) Act 1988, s 2 (general functions of the Scottish Ministers).

House trader reliefs

5.44 Full relief from LBTT is available for certain acquisitions of residential property (see **2.36**) from individuals who are buying another property. The acquisition may be made by a house-building company from which the individual is buying a new dwelling (LBTT(S)A 2013, Sch 4, paras 2–4), or by a property trader whose business includes buying such properties from individuals who are acquiring new dwellings from house-building companies (LBTT(S)A 2013, Sch 4, paras 5–8). Relief is also available for the acquisition by such a property trader, whether or not the replacement home is new, if arrangements to sell the old home have broken down (LBTT(S)A 2013, Sch 4, paras 9–12). The aims of the relief are to improve liquidity in the housing market. Conditions apply to ensure the old property was used as the individual's only or main residence, and to guard against exploitation by property traders who may buy property with the intention of refurbishing or redeveloping for onward sale. Thus the reliefs which apply where the purchaser is a property trader are withdrawn if the property trader: (a) spends more than the permitted amount on refurbishment of the old dwelling (for details of the permitted amount see LBTT(S)A 2013, Sch 4, para 28), or (b) grants a lease or licence of the old dwelling (excluding a lease or licence to the individual whose dwelling was acquired of no more than six months), or (c) permits any of its directors, partners or employees (or any person connected with such individuals) to occupy the old dwelling (LBTT(S)A 2013, Sch 4, paras 13–17).

Incorporation of limited liability partnership

5.45 Relief is available where partnership property is transferred to a limited liability partnership (LLP) from some other form of partnership (for example a general partnership or a limited partnership) or from the partners, on incorporation of the LLP (LBTT(S)A 2013, Sch 12). The relief only applies to a straightforward change of form from another kind of partnership, with no change in partners or their relative interests in the partnership. To qualify, the transfer must happen within 12 months of the date of incorporation of the LLP. For these purposes an LLP means a limited liability partnership formed under the Limited Liability Partnerships Act 2000 (c.12) or the Limited Liability Partnerships Act (Northern Ireland) 2002 (c.12(N.I.).

In the absence of the relief, LBTT would be charged on the basis of the special LBTT partnership provisions in LBTT(S)A 2013, Sch 17, Parts 4 and 5 (see **6.13** et seq) and, assuming that there is no change in partners or their relative interests in the partnership, the expectation would be that no material tax liability would arise. However, where a claim is made for relief under LBTT(S)A 2013, Sch 12, para 1, and the requisite conditions are satisfied, Sch 12 relief should take priority over the partnership provisions in Sch 17.

Public bodies' relief

5.46 A land transaction in relation to which both the buyer and seller are 'public bodies', and which is entered into in connection with a 'reorganisation' which is effected under an enactment, is exempt from the charge to LBTT (LBTT(S)A 2013, Sch 16, para 1). For this purpose 'public bodies' are defined in LBTT(S)A 2013, Sch 16, para 4 and include, the Scottish Ministers, a Minister of the Crown, the Scottish Parliamentary Corporate Body, a local authority and others. It also includes a company which is a wholly-owned subsidiary of such a public body and a wholly-owned subsidiary of that company (LBTT(S)A 2013, Sch 16, para 5).

A reorganisation is defined in LBTT(S)A 2013, Sch 16, para 3 and includes: (a) the establishment, reform or abolition of one or more public bodies, (b) the creation, alteration or abolition of functions discharged by one or more public bodies, or (c) the transfer of functions from one public body to another.

This is clearly a very specialised relief and it may be rare in practice for practitioners to have to refer to it, however it is covered here for completeness.

Other specialised reliefs

Crofting community right to buy relief

5.47 A chargeable transaction which is entered into in pursuance of the crofting community right to buy (ie a right exercisable by a crofting community body under Part 3 of the Land Reform (Scotland) Act 2003 (asp2)) and under which two or more crofts are being acquired is exempt from charge (LBTT(S)

A 2013 Sch 9, para 1). LBTT(S)A 2013, Sch 9 originally provided that the tax chargeable on the transaction was restricted to a proportion of the tax which would be payable if no relief was available, with the proportion to be set by an order of the Scottish Ministers. However, given that the average price of a croft was not likely to exceed the nil rate band of £135,000 (which was subsequently increased to £145,000) the Scottish Government came to the conclusion that there was no need to prescribe a minimum proportion for the purposes of this relief and instead, they provided that a transaction falling within the terms of the relief is exempt from the charge to LBTT. (The Land and Buildings Transaction Tax (Addition and Modification of Reliefs) (Scotland) Order 2015, SSI 2015/93, art 2(4)).

Relief for certain compulsory purchases

5.48 The acquisition of a chargeable interest by a local authority that has made a compulsory purchase order in respect of that chargeable interest to facilitate the undertaking or achievement of an activity or purpose mentioned in the Town and Country Planning (Scotland) Act 1997 (c.8), s 189, by a person other than the local authority (typically a property developer), is exempt from the charge to LBTT (LBTT(S)A 2013, Sch 14, paras 1 and 2). The relief is available irrespective of whether the land is acquired compulsorily or under an agreement with the seller (LBTT(S)A 2013, Sch 14, para 3). The relief is not available if the developer is the local authority itself. The objective of the relief is to avoid a double charge to LBTT, the first charge being on the acquisition by the local authority and the second on the acquisition by the developer. Thus if the relief is available no charge arises on the local authority.

Relief for certain acquisitions by local authorities

5.48A A land transaction in which a local authority is the buyer is exempt from the charge to LBTT (and therefore any associated ADS) if one or more of the qualifying conditions detailed below is satisfied (LBTT(S)A 2013, Sch 6A, para 1). This relief was introduced by the Land and Buildings Transaction Tax (Miscellaneous Amendments) (Scotland) Order 2024, SI 2024/104, and has effect from 1 April 2024.

The qualifying conditions are as follows:

- the transaction is entered into in pursuance of powers conferred by section 2 of the Housing (Scotland) Act 1987 (powers of local authority to provide housing accommodation) (LBTT(S)A 2013, Sch 6A, para 2(a)); or
- the transaction is funded with the assistance of a grant or other financial assistance under section 2 of the Housing (Scotland) Act 1988 (general functions of Scottish Homes).

Relief for compliance with planning obligations

5.49 A land transaction entered into to comply with a planning obligation (ie an agreement under the Town and Country Planning (Scotland) Act

1997(c.8), s 75) or a modification of a planning obligation (ie a modification as mentioned in the Town and Country Planning (Scotland) Act 1997 (c.8) s 75A and 75B) is exempt from the charge to LBTT provided each of the following conditions are satisfied (LBTT(S)A 2013, Sch 15, paras 1 and 2):

- the planning obligation or modification is enforceable against the seller;
- the buyer is a 'public body'; and
- the effective date (see **2.81**) of the transaction is within the five year period commencing on the date on which the planning obligation was entered into or modified.

The meaning of public body for this purpose is set out at LBTT(S)A 2013, Sch 15, para 5 and includes a local authority, a health board and a special health board established under the National Health Service (Scotland) Act 1978 (c.29), s 2(1)(a) and (b), the common services agency established under the National Health Service (Scotland) Act 1978 (c.29), s 10(1), Healthcare Improvement Scotland established under s 10A of that Act and any other body that is a planning authority for any of the purposes of the planning Acts within the meaning of the Town and Country Planning (Scotland) Act 1997 (c.8).

Other reliefs

5.50 The Land and Buildings Transaction Tax (Addition and Modification of Reliefs) (Scotland) Order 2015, SSI 2015/93, added the following reliefs:

- Friendly societies relief (LBTT(S)A 2013, Sch 13A).
- Building societies relief (LBTT(S)A 2013, Sch 13B).
- Visiting forces and international military headquarters reliefs (LBTT(S)A 2013, Sch 16A).
- Relief for property accepted in satisfaction of tax (LBTT(S)A 2013, Sch 16B).
- Lighthouses relief (LBTT(S)A 2013, Sch 16C).

These are very specialised reliefs and are mentioned for completeness only, as a detailed consideration of their terms is outside the scope of this book.

Chapter 6

LBTT and Partnerships

SIGNPOSTS

- Overview of Land Buildings Transaction Tax (Scotland) Act 2013, Sch 17 which contains the detailed rules regarding land transactions entered into by partnerships.
- Outline of the general principles applying to partnerships under LBTT and the treatment of land transactions between a partnership and a person unconnected to the partnership.
- Consideration (with examples) of the detailed rules applying to the following transaction types:
  - — transfer of a chargeable interest by a partner, or a person connected with a partner, to a partnership;
  - — transfer of a chargeable interest out of a partnership to a partner or a person connected with a partner;
  - — transfer of a chargeable interest from one partnership to another partnership where there are connections between the partners of the two partnerships;
  - — transfer of an interest in a 'property-investment partnership' (PIP);
  - — transfer of an interest in a partnership which is not a PIP pursuant to earlier arrangements (anti-avoidance provision).
- Application of LBTT reliefs to land transactions involving partnerships.

6.1 The legislation dealing with partnerships is in the Land Buildings Transaction Tax (Scotland) Act 2013, Sch 17. In this chapter, references to paragraph numbers without further identification are references to paragraphs of Sch 17. Part 1 of Sch 17 provides an overview of the provisions relating to partnerships. Part 2 (paras 2–6) and Part 3 (paras 7–10) set out general provisions, including confirmation of the treatment of an ordinary acquisition of a chargeable interest by a partnership from an unconnected seller. Part 4 (paras 11–18) and Part 5 (paras 19–28) contain the detailed rules applying LBTT to transactions involving all other transfers of chargeable interests to, and from, partnerships. Part 6 (para 29) includes provisions applying Parts 3–5 to leases,

Part 7 (paras 30–35) deals with transactions in relation to 'property-investment partnerships', Part 8 (paras 36–41) covers the application of exemptions and reliefs to certain transactions involving partnerships, and finally Part 9 (paras 42–50) defines various expressions used within Sch 17.

6.2 The UK tax system has always had difficulty working out how to deal with partnerships, particularly whether to treat them as separate entities distinct from their members or as mere aggregations of separately taxed members. LBTT continues that uncertainty. This is particularly ironic given that a partnership established in Scotland has a separate legal personality distinct from its members whereas Part 2 of Sch 17 specifically provides that this separate legal personality is to be ignored, and that a chargeable interest held by a partnership is treated as held by the partners, and a land transaction entered into by a partnership is treated as having been entered into by the partners themselves – para 3.

6.3 The LBTT legislation on partnerships is virtually identical to the SDLT provisions on partnerships, and given that the SDLT provisions are notoriously complex and prone to producing anomalous results, it is disappointing that there has been no overhaul of the legislation for LBTT purposes which was, after all, a new tax.

Focus

- The LBTT provisions on partnerships apply not only to the three types of UK-based partnerships (general partnership, limited partnership and limited liability partnership) but also to partnerships formed under the laws of countries outside of the UK, which have similar characteristics to those UK based partnerships.

6.4 Three types of UK-based partnership are recognised – para 2:

- a (general) partnership within the Partnership Act 1890;
- a limited partnership (LP) registered under the Limited Partnerships Act 1907; and
- a limited liability partnership (LLP) formed under the Limited Liability Partnerships Act 2000 or the Northern Ireland equivalent.

The LBTT rules seek to treat all three types of partnership in the same way; they also apply the same treatment to any 'firm or entity of a similar character' to either of these three types of partnership, formed under the laws of another country outside of the UK (para 2(d)). Difficulties can arise because the three types of partnership listed above and many equivalent overseas entities have quite different legal and commercial characteristics. As a result, the LBTT treatment of a particular transaction may be logical in one case (say, involving an English general partnership) but less so in another (say, involving a Scottish LP or an LLP). These differences were a factor in the use of partnerships to mitigate SDLT liabilities, and many of the special rules within the SDLT regime, which have now been imported into the LBTT legislation, were originally intended to combat perceived avoidance. Particular issues arise from the fact that UK LLPs (together with many overseas equivalents) are bodies corporate for the purposes of general law and many other tax purposes, but are treated as 'transparent' as regards ownership of land for LBTT purposes (see, for example, **5.11**). In addition, Scottish general and limited partnerships are not bodies corporate but are treated as being 'opaque' as far as ownership of shares is concerned (see **6.40**).

GENERAL PRINCIPLES AND ORDINARY TRANSACTIONS

General principles

6.5 Property held by or on behalf of a partnership is treated as held by or on behalf of the partners (and not the partnership); a land transaction entered into for the purposes of a partnership is treated as entered into by or on behalf of the partners (and not the partnership); this is so even if the partnership is regarded as a body corporate or other legal entity for other purposes, such as the ability to enter into contracts and to own property in its own right (para 3).

Where a partnership (ie the partners) enter into an ordinary partnership transaction as buyer (ie the seller under the transaction is completely at arm's length to the partnership – see **6.8**) anything which the buyer is required or authorised to do under LBTT(S)A 2013 must be done by the 'responsible partners' (para 8(1)). In relation to such a transaction the responsible partners are as follows (para 8(2)):

(a) the partners at the effective date (see **2.81**) of the transaction; and

(b) any person who becomes a partner after that date.

This means that the 'responsible partners' must complete and file the land transaction return in relation to any notifiable transaction, must pay any LBTT due, and must respond to any enquiry from Revenue Scotland etc.

However, the majority of the partners may nominate a 'representative partner' (or partners), which then means that the LBTT compliance in relation to a transaction may be done by the 'representative partner' (or partners) rather than the 'responsible partners'. This includes making the declaration that the land transaction return is complete and correct, as required by LBTT(S)A 2013, s 36. The nomination, or any revocation of a nomination, must be notified to Revenue Scotland (para 9).

The 'responsible partners' are jointly and severally liable for any LBTT due in respect of the transaction (para 10(1)), however no tax may be recovered from any person who did not become a partner until after the effective date of the transaction in respect of which the tax is payable (para 10(2)).

6.6 If there is a change in the membership of a partnership, it is nonetheless treated as the same continuing partnership, provided at least one member before the change remains a member afterwards (para 5). Thus, despite the assertions in the previous paragraph that a partnership is treated as 'transparent' for LBTT purposes (ie it is the partners and not the partnership which enter into a land transaction), there are still times when a partnership is treated as a separate entity.

References in Sch 17 to a 'transfer of a chargeable interest' include (para 45):

(a) the creation of a chargeable interest, for example, the grant of a lease;

(b) the renunciation or release of a chargeable interest; and

(c) the variation of a chargeable interest.

Partnership share

> **Focus**
>
> - It can be crucial to understand the concept of 'partnership share' in determining the chargeable consideration for many transactions involving partnerships. In some cases it determines whether a chargeable transaction has occurred.

6.7 In order to calculate the chargeable consideration for many partnership transactions, or even in some cases to determine whether a chargeable transaction has occurred, it is necessary to know the shares which the different partners have in the partnership. For most LBTT purposes, a partner's share in a partnership is defined as the proportion in which he is entitled to share in the income profits of the partnership at the effective date (see **2.81**) of the transaction (para 44). When property is transferred out of a partnership, a more complicated definition applies, although in many cases it produces the same result (see **6.23**). Entitlement to capital, or to capital profits, does not enter into the calculation. The definition causes practical difficulties as partnerships often decide the precise sharing of profits after the year end, once total profits, and the contribution of each partner to them, are known. In such cases, it may be necessary to complete an LBTT return and pay tax based on estimated shares, then amend the return once profit shares are finally settled. Since profit shares do not normally vary from day to day, it is considered that the reference to the 'effective date' should be taken to mean the accounting period in which the effective date falls.

Ordinary transactions

6.8 If a partnership (or a partner on behalf of a partnership) enters into a land transaction with a person who is completely at arm's length, that transaction is treated in the same way as an equivalent transaction not involving a partnership. The only modification is that the partners have responsibility for any compliance matters and are jointly and severally liable for any LBTT payable (paras 8 and 10). A person is completely at arm's length if he is neither a partner (whether current, joining or departing) nor connected with a partner. Connected for these purposes is as defined by Corporation Tax Act 2010 (CTA 2010), s 1122, although the automatic connection of partners with each other is omitted (para 49(a)). It follows that, for such an arm's length transaction, LBTT is generally chargeable by reference to the value of the actual consideration given for the chargeable interest, and it is only necessary to consider the market value of the property itself where it would also have to be considered for a non-partnership transaction (eg for exchanges of property interests – see **2.31**).

SPECIAL PROVISIONS

6.9 As discussed in **6.8** the application of the LBTT rules to arm's length transactions is relatively straightforward. Complications arise when there is a connection between the partnership and the other party, ie where the other party is a partner (current, departing or joining) or is connected with a partner (current or joining). In such circumstances it is necessary to consider separately the implications of the partnership acquiring or disposing of property. It is also necessary to consider the implications of changes in the membership or relative interests of the members in a partnership which holds chargeable interests (see **2.12**); in certain cases, such changes are deemed to give rise to a corresponding transfer of chargeable interests between partners.

6.10 In general, when partnership transactions are subject to the 'special provisions', LBTT is charged by reference to the market value of the chargeable interest in question and the proportion of the chargeable interest which is deemed to be transferred. Actual consideration (other than any change in partnership share – see **6.7**) is irrelevant in these cases. However, there are many anti-avoidance rules; in some circumstances, amounts which are commercially equivalent to consideration may trigger these (see **6.17**).

The exemption for transactions in relation to which there is no chargeable consideration in LBTT(S)A 2013, Sch 1, para 1 (see **5.6**) does not apply to the following transactions (para 37(1)):

- the transfer of a chargeable interest to a partnership by an existing partner, or by a person who becomes a partner as a consequence of the transfer, or by a person connected with an existing partner, or by a person connected with a person who becomes a partner as a result of the transfer (see **6.13** et seq);
- the transfer of a chargeable interest from a partnership to a person who is or has been one of the partners, or to a person connected with a person who is or has been one of the partners (see **6.19** et seq);
- the transfer of an interest in a partnership under an arrangement in place at the time of the land transfer to the partnership (see **6.27** et seq);
- the transfer of an interest in a 'property investment partnership' (see **6.30** et seq).

This means that, for example, where a partner transfers an interest in land, which is situated in Scotland, to a partnership in which he is a partner, as a contribution to partnership capital, LBTT will be charged on that proportion of the market value of the interest in land which is treated as being transferred to the other partners in the partnership, even though the partnership gives no chargeable consideration.

6.11 The legislation sets out formulae which must be applied to the market value of the property in question to determine the deemed chargeable consideration for the transaction. The formulae appear complex, but are generally seeking to achieve a relatively simple overall effect, which is to ensure that tax is charged on the economic transfer of value which takes place.

Example 6.1 –Simple Partnership Case

Stuart and Andrew are in a general partnership, sharing income profits equally. They agree to admit Pamela as an equal partner (so each partner has a one-third share in profits, losses and assets) in return for Pamela agreeing, *inter alia*, to contribute freehold premises to the partnership. None of the partners are connected with each other apart from being partners in the partnership. In the absence of any other complicating factors, LBTT is chargeable by reference to two-thirds of the market value of the property contributed by Pamela. This is the proportion which has economically changed hands by transfer to the other partners; Pamela still has a one-third interest in the property through her membership of the partnership, so no LBTT is charged on that proportion.

6.12 Inevitably, real transactions do include complicating factors, and in relation to SDLT HMRC were keen to minimise avoidance. Therefore, the basic formulae are supplemented by definitions and rules for special cases which must be taken into account. These rules have been incorporated into the LBTT legislation. It would not be safe to assume that the simple apportionment set out above gives the correct LBTT charge, without checking the specific facts of the case against the detailed rules. Many changes were made to the SDLT rules in an attempt to combat perceived avoidance, especially attempts to combine the partnership rules with reliefs and other special provisions to mitigate SDLT costs. These changes have also been incorporated into the LBTT provisions without any significant revision.

Acquisition by a partnership

6.13

Focus

- Where a partner (current or joining), or a person connected with a partner, or a person connected with a person who becomes a partner as a consequence of the transfer, transfers a chargeable interest to a partnership, the aim of the legislation is to charge LBTT on that part of the market value of the chargeable interest which is effectively transferred to the other partners, who are not individuals 'connected' with the transferor.

Under paras 12 and 13, when a chargeable interest is acquired by a partnership from a partner, or from a person who becomes a partner as a result of the acquisition, or from a person who is connected with either, LBTT is charged on deemed consideration equal to:

$MV \times (100 - SLP)\%$

where MV is the market value of the chargeable interest at the effective date (see **2.81**) of the transfer, and SLP is the 'sum of the lower proportions'. A five-step calculation is required to determine the SLP, set out in the legislation (para 14) as follows:

(1) Identify the 'relevant owner(s)'. These are persons who have an interest in the property immediately before it is transferred to the partnership and are partners or connected with partners immediately after the property is transferred (para 15) .

(2) For each relevant owner, identify the 'corresponding partner(s)'. These are persons who are partners immediately after the transfer and who are relevant owners (see (1) above) or are individuals connected with relevant owners (para 16). For these purposes, a company may be regarded as an individual connected with a relevant owner only if it holds property as trustee and is only connected with the relevant owner by virtue of CTA 2010, s 1122(6) (trustee connected with settlor etc) (para 16(2)).

(3) For each relevant owner, take the proportion of the property to which he is entitled immediately before the transfer and apportion it between any one or more of his corresponding partners. Where a relevant owner has more than one corresponding partner, the apportionment may be performed in whatever manner gives the best result.

(4) Find the 'lower proportion' for each person who is a corresponding partner in relation to one or more relevant owners. The lower proportion is the lower of:

    (a) the proportion apportioned to him under (3) above, and

    (b) his partnership share (see **6.7**) immediately after the transfer of the chargeable interest.

(5) Add together the lower proportions for each partner who is a corresponding partner. This is the SLP.

Example 6.2 – Calculating the sum of the lower proportions

Allan, Brian and Caroline are in partnership, sharing income profits 40%, 40% and 20% respectively. Brian and Caroline are brother and sister. Apart from the partnership, Allan is not related to or connected with Brian or Caroline. The partners agree to buy a building from Danielle, who is Brian and Caroline's sister, for £500,000. The calculation steps are as follows:

(1) The only relevant owner is Danielle, because she owns 100% of the property before the transfer.

(2) Brian and Caroline are corresponding partners because they are individuals connected with the only relevant owner, their sister Danielle.

(3) Danielle was entitled to 100% of the property before the transfer. We choose to apportion this 50% to each corresponding partner, Brian and Caroline.

(4) For Brian, his partnership share immediately after the transaction is 40%, and the proportion apportioned to him under (3) is 50%, so his lower proportion is 40%; for Caroline, her partnership share immediately after the transaction is 20%, and the proportion apportioned to her under (3) above is 50%, so her lower proportion is 20%.

(5) The sum of the lower proportions is 40% (Brian) plus 20% (Caroline), which is 60%.

The chargeable consideration for LBTT purposes is therefore MV × (100 – 60)%, or 40% of the market value, ie £200,000. In this relatively simple case, it can be seen that this represents the proportion of the property effectively transferred to Allan, the partner who is not connected with the original owner of the property.

6.14 The responsibility for the LBTT compliance in relation to the transfer of a chargeable interest to a partnership, by a partner (existing or joining) or a person connected with a partner (existing or joining), is as described in **6.5** except that the responsible partners (para 13(2)) are as follows:

(a) the partners immediately before the transfer who remain partners immediately after the transfer; and

(b) any person becoming a partner as a result of, or in connection with, the transfer to the partnership.

In most cases before the transfer, the property will be owned by one person, so there will be only one relevant owner. If two or more persons own a property as joint owners, they are treated as owning as common owners, in equal shares (para 15(2)).

Connected companies

6.15 The restriction to individuals connected with relevant owners in step (2) in **6.13** is designed to prevent the use of a partnership arrangement to transfer property to a connected company without suffering LBTT on the full market value of the property. Other anti-avoidance rules are dealt with at **6.17** and **6.27**.

Example 6.3 – Partnership including connected company

Mark sets up a company, MJAR Ltd, in which he is the sole shareholder. Mark and MJAR Ltd form a limited partnership in which Mark is the limited partner with a 1% share and MJAR Ltd is the general partner with a 99% share. Mark transfers a valuable property to the partnership. The steps to calculate the proportion of market value on which LBTT is charged are as follows:

(1) Mark is the only relevant owner with 100%.

(2) Mark is also the only corresponding partner. MJAR Ltd cannot be a corresponding partner, as it is not an individual.

(3) Therefore, Mark's 100% ownership before the transfer must be apportioned 100% to Mark as corresponding partner after the transfer.

(4) Mark's partnership share immediately after the transfer is only 1%, so his lower proportion is 1%; MJAR Ltd is not a corresponding partner, so it does not figure in the calculation.

(5) The SLP is therefore 1%, and LBTT is chargeable on the 99% of the market value effectively transferred to MJAR Ltd.

Lease at rent and other transactions

6.16 The same principle applies where the acquisition takes the form of the grant of a lease at rent to the partnership from a partner (current or joining) or a person connected with a partner (current or joining). In that case, the relevant chargeable proportion (which is 100-SLP% where SLP is the sum of the lower proportions as calculated above) is applied to each year's rent (para 29(3)). The resulting apportioned rent figures are then used to calculate the LBTT on the net present value (NPV) of the rent in the normal way (see **4.13**). The same principle also applies where there is a variation of a lease (or other chargeable interest) which, on normal principles, is regarded as an acquisition of a chargeable interest by the partnership from a partner or person connected with a partner. For details of the circumstances in which the variation of a lease is treated as the acquisition of a chargeable interest see **4.41**.

Example 6.4 – Lease at rent, partnership shares vary

Twin sisters Lilly and Netta carry on a market research business in partnership with Stan, with whom they are not otherwise connected. Partnership profit-sharing ratios are adjusted at the end of each year in accordance with the partnership deed, using a formula which takes account of matters such as business won, hours worked etc. Lilly grants a 20-year lease of non-residential property to the partnership at a time when the profit sharing ratios are 25% to Lilly, 40% to Netta and 35% to Stan. The lease is for a rent of £25,000 per annum (thought to be market rent) and no premium, with a market rent review at the end of every fifth year. The partnership has the option to surrender the lease at each rent review date. The calculation steps are as follows:

(1) Lilly is the only relevant owner, owning 100% of the property before the grant of the lease.

(2) Lilly and Netta are corresponding partners, as they are the relevant owner or an individual connected with the relevant owner.

(3) Lilly's 100% ownership of the property before the grant of the lease is apportioned between Lilly and Netta – we choose to apportion 50% to each.

(4) Lilly's partnership share immediately after the grant of the lease is 25%, and Netta's is 40%. In each case, this is less than the apportioned ownership under (3), so in each case the partnership share is the lower proportion.

(5) Therefore the SLP is 25% + 40% = 65%, and the NPV of the remaining 35% (ie the relevant chargeable proportion) of the rent, ie £8,750 per annum, is subject to LBTT. In this particular case, the NPV of the rent is £124,358 which is less than £150,000 (see **4.13**), so no LBTT will be payable, but it will be necessary to submit an LBTT return (see **4.11**).

It is assumed that the lease granted to the partnership has no capital value on the basis that the annual rent of £25,000 per annum is considered to be a market rate rent. However, if the rent had been less than a market rate, so that the lease did have a capital value, then 35% of that capital value would have been chargeable to LBTT based on the calculation set out in **6.13**.

Two years later, the partners agree to vary certain terms within the lease, and it is also agreed that a market rate rent for a lease with such varied terms is £35,000 per annum. They therefore agree to vary the lease to increase the rent to this sum with effect from the start of the third year. At that time, the profit-sharing ratios are Lilly 30%, Netta 30% and Stan 40%. Carrying out the SLP calculation shows that the NPV of 40% (ie the relevant chargeable proportion) of this rent, or £14,000 per annum, is subject to LBTT. This means that when the three year review (see **4.21**) of the LBTT chargeable on the lease is carried out in one years' time the rent subject to LBTT will be £8,750 for years one and two, and then £14,000 for the remaining eighteen years. As a result, the revised NPV of the rent is £189,000 and LBTT of £390 will be payable at the same time as the further land transaction return is filed and that return is due to be filed within 30 days of the third anniversary of the grant of the lease as a result of this rent increase.

Withdrawal of money after acquisition of property

6.17

Focus

- Where a partner (existing or joining), or a person connected with a partner (existing or joining), has transferred a chargeable interest to

> a partnership, a subsequent withdrawal of money or money's worth, which is not income profit, by the transferor partner (or a partner connected with the transferor), or the repayment of a loan due by the partnership to the transferor partner (or a transferor connected with the partner), within three years of the land transaction, may trigger an LBTT liability.

The transfer of property from a partner (existing or joining) or person connected with a partner (existing or joining) to a partnership marks the start of a three-year period within which certain other events can lead to a further LBTT charge (para 18). If, during that period, the partner concerned withdraws from the partnership money or money's worth which does not represent income profit, but:

- is capital withdrawn from the partners' capital account; or
- arises from the partner reducing his interest in the partnership or ceasing to be a partner,

the withdrawal is treated as a chargeable land transaction (para 18(2)(a) and (4)). Where the original transfer was from a person connected with a partner (existing or joining), withdrawal of value by either the partner or a person connected with the partner is treated as a chargeable transaction (para 18(3)). However, presumably, the connected person would also have to be a partner to be able to legitimately withdraw capital, reduce his interest in the partnership etc.

If the partner (or, where the original transfer was from a person connected with a partner, the partner or a person connected with the partner) has made a loan to the partnership, the repayment of any of the loan, or a withdrawal of any amount by that person which does not represent income profit of the partnership, is also treated as a chargeable land transaction (para 18(2)(b) and (4)).

In either case, the chargeable consideration is the smaller of (para 18(7) and (8)):

- the amount of the money or money's worth withdrawn from or the loan repaid by the partnership; and
- the market value of the land at the date of the original land transfer, reduced by any amount which has already been charged to LBTT.

Where the charge arises because the partner, or a person connected with the partner, has made a loan to the partnership, and has then withdrawn an amount which does not represent income profit of the partnership, the chargeable consideration for the deemed land transaction cannot exceed the amount of the loan (para 18(7)(c)).

If the withdrawal of money or money's worth is also subject to LBTT as a transfer of an interest in a 'property-investment partnership' (see **6.30**), the

LBTT charged under the 'withdrawal of money' provision is reduced by the amount of any LBTT charge under the 'transfer of interest in 'property-investment partnership'' provision (para 18(9)). If a 'para 35 election' (see **6.38**) has been made in respect of the transfer of a chargeable interest to a partnership, no LBTT arises on a subsequent withdrawal of value (para 35(1)).

Example 6.5 – Repayment of loan after transfer

Using the facts as in **Example 6.2**, the partnership does not have enough ready cash to pay the whole price of the building purchased from Danielle, so it is agreed that £350,000 will be left outstanding as a loan from Danielle to the partnership, with interest being charged at 2% above the Bank of England base rate, payable monthly in arrears. The loan arrangement has no effect on the LBTT charge on the initial transfer of the property to the partnership. One year later, after a purge on debtors, the partnership has enough cash and pays off the loan. The loan repayment is taken to be a land transaction, and LBTT is chargeable on the partnership. However, LBTT was paid on £200,000 when the property, with a value of £500,000, was transferred to the partnership. The chargeable consideration for the deemed land transaction cannot exceed the part of that market value which has not yet been taxed (para 18(8)). So, LBTT is chargeable on £300,000 (£500,000 – £200,000), and not on the full £350,000 loan repayment. Note that this limitation is assessed by considering the market value of the property when it was transferred, and not the value at the time of the loan repayment or other withdrawal of value.

Had the partnership borrowed from a bank at the outset and paid Danielle in full, the LBTT charge on the original land transfer would still have been based on £200,000, but the subsequent repayment of the bank debt would not have given rise to an LBTT charge. It is difficult to see any policy reason for this discrimination, which therefore looks rather like a poorly directed anti-avoidance provision which has been imported from the SDLT legislation into LBTT.

Transfer to a property-investment partnership may also involve the transfer of a partnership interest

6.18

Focus

- Where a new or existing partner transfers a chargeable interest to a partnership, which is a 'property-investment partnership' (PIP), there is potentially an LBTT charge for both the partners (acquisition of the chargeable interest by the partnership) and by the new partner or existing partner who has increased his partnership share (transfer of an interest in a PIP).

The charge on the partnership when a new or existing partner (or someone connected with a partner) transfers a chargeable interest to the partnership does not depend on the amount or form of consideration given by the partnership. As suggested in **Example 6.1**, the consideration could take the form of admitting a new partner or increasing a partner's share. This acquisition of, or increase in, partnership share will be regarded as a transfer of an interest in a partnership (para 48). If the partnership is a property-investment partnership (PIP), this transfer will be separately subject to LBTT (see **6.30**), chargeable on the new partner or the partner whose share has increased. This is in addition to the charge on the partnership arising from the acquisition of the property. The transaction is an exchange (see **2.31**). This fact should not affect the calculation of LBTT because, both in transactions between a partnership and its partners (or persons connected with them) and in an exchange, LBTT is normally calculated by reference to the market value of the chargeable interests acquired (albeit indirectly, where a partnership interest is acquired) rather than the consideration given. As noted below (see **6.34** and **6.36**), the newly transferred property is not taken into account in determining the LBTT charge on the transfer of the partnership interest, so there is no double charge.

Example 6.6 – Admission of partner, transfer of property

X Ltd and Y Ltd are limited partners in Propco LP, a limited partnership which owns shopping centres as investments and is clearly a PIP. The general partner is a Jersey-registered company with a negligible partnership share. X Ltd has a 40% partnership share, and Y Ltd has 60%. The shopping centres are located in Scotland and are worth £100 million. It is agreed that Z Ltd will be admitted as a limited partner with a partnership share of 30%, so that X Ltd's share drops to 28% and Y Ltd's to 42%. By way of payment, Z will transfer a further shopping centre also located in Scotland to Propco LP, with a value of £45 million. Apart from membership of Propco LP, there are no other connections between X, Y and Z.

- **Transfer of property to Propco LP**: The calculation set out at **6.13** shows that Propco LP is liable for LBTT on 70% of the £45 million value of the property brought to the partnership by Z Ltd.

- **Transfer of partnership share to Z Ltd**: Z Ltd is deemed to have acquired an interest in the 'relevant partnership property' owned by Propco LP before Z Ltd joined. The consideration is the market value of the 'relevant partnership property' multiplied by the partnership interest acquired, ie 30%. Whether the shopping centres already owned by Propco LP are 'relevant partnership property' will depend on their history, and the question of whether the transfer to Z Ltd is a 'Type A' or 'Type B' transfer (see **6.33** and **6.35**).

Disposal by a partnership

6.19

> **Focus**
>
> - Where a partnership transfers a chargeable interest to a partner (or a person who has been a partner), or a person connected with a partner (or a person connected with a person who has been a partner), the aim is to charge LBTT on that part of the market value of the chargeable interest which is effectively transferred by the other partners in the partnership, who are not individuals connected with the transferee.

A disposal of a chargeable interest should not directly give rise to any LBTT obligations for the partnership; it is for the buyer to deal with any LBTT obligations. If the disposal is to an unrelated third party, the buyer will be liable for LBTT in the normal way, based on the consideration given. However, if the disposal is to a partner (or a person who has been a partner) or a person connected with a partner (or a person connected with a person who has been a partner), special rules come into play (Part 5, paras 20–28). These are similar to those outlined in the previous paragraphs; their purpose is to ensure the buyer pays LBTT only on the proportion of the market value of the property which he and/or connected individual partners did not already own indirectly through membership of the partnership. As in the previous paragraphs, LBTT is charged on deemed consideration equal to:

$MV \times (100 - SLP)\%$

where MV is the market value of the chargeable interest at the effective date (see **2.81**) of the transfer, and the SLP is the 'sum of the lower proportions'. Again, a five-step calculation is required to determine SLP, set out in the legislation (para 22) as follows:

(1) Identify the 'relevant owner(s)'. These are persons who have an interest in the property immediately after it is transferred out of the partnership and are partners or connected with partners immediately before the property is transferred (para 23).

(2) For each relevant owner, identify the 'corresponding partner(s)'. These are persons who are partners immediately before the transfer and who are relevant owners or are individuals connected with relevant owners (para 24(1)). For these purposes, a company may be regarded as an individual connected with a relevant owner *only* if it holds property as trustee and is connected with the relevant owner only by virtue of CTA 2010, s 1122(6) (trustee connected with settlor etc) (para 24(2)).

(3) For each relevant owner, take the proportion of the property to which he is entitled immediately after the transfer and apportion it between any one or more of his corresponding partners. Where a relevant owner

has more than one corresponding partner, the apportionment may be performed in whatever manner gives the best result.

(4) Find the 'lower proportion' for each person who is a corresponding partner in relation to one or more relevant owners. The lower proportion is the lower of:

(a) the proportion apportioned to him under (3) above, and

(b) his partnership share (see **6.23** for the steps to be carried out to determine a corresponding partner's partnership share for the purposes of this Step (4)) immediately before the transfer.

(5) Add together the lower proportions for each partner who is a corresponding partner. This is the SLP.

Example 6.7 – Transfer of property to partner

Allan, Brian and Caroline are still (see **Example 6.2**) in partnership, sharing income profits 40%, 40% and 20% respectively. Brian and Caroline are siblings, Allan is not related to them. Brian decides to withdraw from the partnership and it is agreed he will take one of the properties in satisfaction of his entitlement to partnership capital. The calculation of Brian's LBTT liability is as follows:

(1) The only relevant owner is Brian, because he owns 100% of the property after the transfer.

(2) Brian and Caroline are corresponding partners because they are, or are connected with, the only relevant owner, Brian.

(3) Brian is entitled to 100% of the property after the transfer. We choose to apportion this 50% to each corresponding partner, Brian and Caroline.

(4) For Brian, his partnership share immediately before the transaction is 40%, and the proportion apportioned to him under (3) is 50%, so his lower proportion is 40%; for Caroline, her partnership share immediately before the transaction is 20%, and the proportion apportioned to her under (3) above is 50%, so her lower proportion is 20%.

(5) The sum of the lower proportions is 40% (Brian) plus 20% (Caroline), which is 60%.

The chargeable consideration for LBTT purposes is therefore MV × (100 – 60)%, or 40% of the market value. In this simple case, it can be seen that this represents the proportion of the property effectively transferred from the partner who is not connected with the final owner of the property. Again, the same principles apply in relation to rent if the 'transfer' is the grant of a lease at rent by the partnership. This analysis is subject to any impact which the special rules in relation to calculating a partner's 'partnership share' may have – see **6.23**.

Example 6.8 – Incorporation of a partnership where the partners are individuals connected with each other

Pamela, Caroline and John are in partnership sharing income profits equally and all three are siblings. The partnership holds a number of commercial properties for investment purposes and a decision is taken to incorporate the property investment business into PCJ Ltd, the shares in which will be held equally between the three partners.

The calculation of PCJ Ltd's LBTT liability is as follows:

(1) The only relevant owner is PCJ Ltd as it will own 100% of the properties after the business transfer.

(2) Pamela, Caroline and John are corresponding partners because they are connected with PCJ Ltd (the only relevant owner) as each, together with their siblings, will have control of PCJ Ltd.

(3) PCJ Ltd is entitled to 100% of the property after the transfer. We choose to apportion this 33.333%, to each of the corresponding partners Pamela, Caroline and John.

(4) For each of Pamela, Caroline and John, their partnership share immediately before the transaction is 33.333% and the proportion allocated to them under (3) above is 33.333%, so the lower proportion for each partner is 33.333%.

(5) The sum of the lower proportions is 33.333% (Pamela) plus 33.333% (Caroline) plus 33.333% (John), which is 100%

The chargeable consideration for LBTT purposes is therefore MV × (100 – 100)% amounting to nil. It can therefore be seen that where a partnership is incorporated, the partners are individuals who are connected with each other and the partners control the company, no LBTT charge should arise due to the application of the special partnership rules described at **6.19**.

This analysis is subject to any impact which the rules in relation to calculating a partner's 'partnership share' may have – see **6.23**.

6.20 In most cases after the transfer, the property will be owned by one person, so there will be only one relevant owner. If the transfer is to two or more persons as joint owners, they are treated as owning as common owners in equal shares (para 23(2)).

Transfers between partnerships

6.21 The possibility is recognised that a property may be transferred from one partnership to another and that there may be connections or commonality between the partners. In that case, it is necessary to perform calculations of the chargeable consideration twice: once as set out at **6.13** (transfer to a partnership from connected owner); and once as explained at **6.19** (transfer from a partnership to a connected owner). The chargeable consideration is then to be taken as the higher of the two amounts thus calculated (para 27).

6.22 However, it is considered that the following conditions must be satisfied if para 27 is to apply:

(1) There must be a transfer of a chargeable interest from one partnership (the 'transferor partnership') to another partnership (the 'transferee partnership'). This means that the partnerships are treated as opaque for the purposes of the legislation and para 3 (which treats any chargeable interest held by a partnership as being held by the partners, and any land transaction entered into by the partnership as having been entered into by the partners), cannot apply.

(2) Both paras 12 to 16 (see **6.13**) and paras 20 to 26 (see **6.19**) must apply to the transfer of the chargeable interest. For paras 12 to 16 to apply the transfer must be made by a partner of the transferee partnership, or a person who becomes a partner in the transferee partnership in return for the transfer or, in either case, a person connected with that person. For paras 20 to 26 to apply the transfer must be to a person who is or has been a partner in the transferor partnership or to a person connected with a person who is or has been one of the partners in the transferor partnership. For these requirements to be satisfied the partnerships would have to be treated as transparent either under general law or as a result of the application of para 3 (see above for the impact of para 3). Consequently, if it is accepted that para 3 does not apply to para 27 (it is not known whether Revenue Scotland accept this point) then the partnerships would have to be treated as transparent under general law, which would mean that neither the transferor partnership nor the transferee partnership could be a partnership with separate legal personality such as an LLP, Scottish partnership or a non-UK partnership which had separate legal personality.

It is considered that the better view is that para 3 does not apply for the purposes of para 27 and therefore that para 27 only applies where the transferor partnership and the transferee partnership are partnerships which under general law do not have separate legal personality such as, an English general partnership, an English limited partnership, etc. However, given the complexity of the analysis, it is suggested that consideration should be given to seeking an opinion (see **8.49**) from Revenue Scotland if there is doubt as to whether para 27 applies to a transaction.

Partnership share – special rules

6.23

Focus

- Where a partnership transfers a chargeable interest to a partner (or a person who has been a partner), or a person connected with a partner (or a person connected with a person who has been a partner), there are complex rules for determining the partnership share of any relevant partner, and these rules can have a significant impact on the calculation of the chargeable consideration for the transaction.

As noted at **6.7**, for most LBTT purposes, partnership share is defined as the proportion in which the partner is entitled to share in the income profits of the partnership (para 44). A more complex analysis and calculation are required to determine the partnership share of any relevant partner, when this is required for step (4) (see **6.19**) in the SLP calculation on transfer of a chargeable interest out of a partnership (para 22). In a straightforward case, if LBTT (based on market value or arm's length consideration) has been paid on all properties acquired by the partnership and, where necessary, on transfers of partnership interests, the share of any partner should simply be the proportion in which he is entitled to share in income profits. However, to be certain of having the right numbers, it is necessary to work through the following steps (paras 25 and 26):

(1) Confirm whether any LBTT payable in respect of the transfer of the chargeable interest, which is now the subject of the transfer out of the partnership (or where the transaction is the grant of a new lease, the chargeable interest out of which the lease is granted), was paid on its earlier transfer to the partnership. If any LBTT payable was not in fact paid on the transfer to the partnership, the partnership share attributable to any of the partners, for the purposes of step (4) in the SLP calculation, is zero (para 25(2)). The purpose of this provision is not clear. If LBTT was payable on the transfer of the chargeable interest to the partnership, but has not been paid, then the remedy should be to collect the tax and not to penalise a subsequent transfer of the chargeable interest out of the partnership.

    If the chargeable interest was acquired by the partnership under a transaction which was not chargeable to LBTT because, for example, the effective date (see **2.81**) of the transaction was before 1 April 2015 (so that the transaction was within the SDLT regime), then this rule should have no application and the partnership share attributable to the partners should not be reduced to zero. This is because in these circumstance no LBTT would have been payable in respect of the transfer of the chargeable interest to the partnership as it was not a transaction liable to LBTT. This in turn means that where the partnership acquired the chargeable interest before 1 April 2015 but, for whatever reason, no SDLT was paid on that acquisition, there should be no reduction of a partner's 'partnership share' under this rule.

(2) Where the partner ceases to be a partner in the partnership before the effective date (see **2.81**) of the transfer of the chargeable interest to the partnership, which is now the subject of the transfer out of the partnership (or where the transaction is the grant of a new lease, the chargeable interest out of which the lease is granted), the partnership share attributable to the partner is zero (para 25(3)). Again the purpose of

this provision is not clear. This rule would only seem to be relevant where a person was a partner in the partnership, ceased to be a partner prior to the partnership acquiring the chargeable interest which is now the subject of the transfer out of the partnership (or the chargeable interest out of which a new lease is granted), but then became a partner again before that chargeable interest is transferred out of the partnership. It is understood that Revenue Scotland's view on this point is that to get the benefit of the reduction of the chargeable consideration for the transfer of the chargeable interest out of the partnership, the partner must still be a member of the partnership immediately before the land transaction takes place. This seems self-evident, since if the person was no longer a partner immediately before the land transfer out of the partnership that person would not be a 'corresponding partner' (para 24(1)) and no reduction to the chargeable consideration for the transaction would be obtained.

(3) Assuming that the partnership share is not zero under steps (1) and (2), find the partner's actual partnership share on the 'relevant date' (para 26). The 'relevant date' is:

   (a) if the partner was a partner on the effective date (see **2.81**) of the transfer of the chargeable interest, which is now the subject of the transfer out of the partnership (or the chargeable interest out of which a new lease is now granted), to the partnership, that is the relevant date;

   (b) if the partner became a partner after that date, the date he became a partner is the relevant date.

   Find the partner's actual partnership share on the relevant date (see **6.7**).

(4) Add to the partnership share determined under (3) any increases in the partner's partnership share which occurred in the period starting on the day after the 'relevant date' (as determined in (3) above) and ending immediately before the transfer of the chargeable interest out of the partnership (or the grant of a new lease out of the chargeable interest held by the partnership). However, any such increase in the partner's partnership share in that period is only added if any LBTT payable, as a consequence of the transfer of the interest in the partnership which gave rise to the increased partnership share, has been paid (para 26(1)).

(5) Deduct from the result of (4) any decreases in the partner's partnership share during the period from the day after the 'relevant date' (as determined in (3) above) to the day immediately before the date on which the chargeable interest is transferred out of the partnership (or the grant of a new lease out of the chargeable interest held by the partnership).

These special rules (paras 25 and 26) apply even if the 'relevant date' (see Step (3) above) is prior to 1 April 2015 (the LBTT commencement date), however any references to obligations to pay LBTT in relation to land transactions with an effective date before 1 April 2015 are to be ignored (The Land and Buildings Transaction Tax (Transitional Provisions) (Scotland) Order 2014, SI 2014/377, article 9).

The result, having gone through steps (1) to (5) above, is the partner's partnership share for the purposes of Step (4) in the SLP calculation for the purposes of para 22.

It can, therefore, be seen that in certain circumstances a complex calculation may have to be carried out to determine what should be a simple matter of a partner's partnership share.

Transfer from a corporate partnership

6.24

> **Focus**
>
> - If a chargeable interest is transferred out of a partnership whose members are all bodies corporate and the transferee is a partner with a partnership share of 75% or more, LBTT is charged on the full market value of the chargeable interest.

The rules are modified if a property is transferred from a partnership whose members are entirely bodies corporate and the SLP is 75% or more (para 28). In this case, no reduction is given for the SLP, and the consideration is deemed to be equal to the market value of the property (and, if the transfer is the grant of a lease at rent, the full NPV of the rent is subject to LBTT). This situation can only occur when the transferee is a partner with a 75% or higher partnership share. In this situation, the only way to reduce the LBTT charge is to claim group relief on the transfer (see **6.40**).

Transfer of an interest in a partnership

6.25 Whether a true transfer of an interest in a partnership is possible depends on the law governing the partnership, and the terms of the partnership deed or other agreements governing such matters. In some cases, it may be possible to achieve an effect equivalent to a transfer, only by one partner withdrawing capital or in some other way relinquishing some or all of his entitlement as partner, while another person becomes a partner, introduces new capital or increases his entitlement in some other way. For most transactions, the legislation makes these distinctions irrelevant, defining a transfer of an interest in a partnership as any occasion on which a person acquires or increases a partnership share (para 48). This is regarded as a transfer of a partnership interest to the person acquiring or increasing his partnership share and from the other partners. This is a very wide definition, covering not only situations where a person makes payments to other partners to acquire or increase his partnership share, but also where a person introduces capital on admission to the partnership, such that the actual value of the other partners' interests remains unchanged.

6.26 A potential charge to LBTT only arises on transfers of interests in 'property-investment partnerships' (PIPs) – see **6.29**. As a result, a transfer of an interest in a partnership which is not a PIP will not give rise to LBTT obligations, unless caught by the anti-avoidance provision (see **6.27**). This means that a transfer of an interest in an ordinary trading partnership, which happens to own its premises, will not be chargeable to LBTT. This is fortunate as, for example, profit-sharing ratios within large professional partnerships owning property in Scotland may change several times each year, and complex LBTT calculations would therefore have been required had such changes been within the LBTT regime.

Transfer pursuant to earlier arrangements

Focus

- If there is an arrangement for a partner (existing or joining), or person connected with a partner (existing or joining), to transfer a chargeable interest to a partnership, which is not a 'property-investment partnership', and for an interest in that partnership to subsequently be transferred, a liability to LBTT may arise on the transfer of the partnership interest. This is an anti-avoidance provision to prevent a partnership structure being used to transfer an interest in a property free from a charge to LBTT.

6.27 If:

- a chargeable interest is transferred to a partnership from a partner, a person who becomes a partner in return for the transfer or a person connected with a partner or a person connected with a person who has become a partner in return for the transfer;
- that partner, person who became a partner, or the partner connected to the person who made the transfer, then transfers any or all of his partnership interest under arrangements which were in existence at the time of the land transfer to the partnership; and
- the transfer of the partnership interest would not otherwise be a chargeable transaction (ie it is not a property-investment partnership – see **6.29**),

the transfer of the partnership interest is a chargeable land transaction (para 17(1) and (2)). The partners are treated as the buyers under this deemed transaction (para 17(3)), and the chargeable consideration is the market value of the land at the date of its transfer to the partnership multiplied by the proportionate share in the partnership transferred under the arrangements (para 17(4) and (5)). The transfer of the partnership share and the transfer of the chargeable interest to the partnership are linked transactions (see **2.79**), meaning that the chargeable consideration for both transactions will be aggregated in determining the LBTT payable (para 17(6)). However, this treatment does not apply if an election is made in respect of the land transfer to the partnership under para 35 (see **6.38**).

As in other cases (see **5.12**), arrangements are defined as including any scheme, agreement or understanding, whether or not legally enforceable (para 50).

Please see **2.111** if the transaction transferring the land to the partnership had an effective date (see **2.81**) before 1 April 2015, so that it was within the SDLT regime, but the effective date of the subsequent transfer of the interest in the partnership is on or after 1 April 2015.

6.28 The practical implication of para 17 is that, if a partner transfers a chargeable interest to a partnership which is not a PIP, and shortly after transfers his partnership interest, Revenue Scotland may question whether the transactions are part of a single arrangement. The deemed land transaction arising as a result of such a transfer of an interest in a partnership is notifiable (by completion of a land transaction return) only if the aggregate chargeable consideration for the transfer of the property to the partnership and the transfer of the partnership interest (as these two transactions are treated as being linked) is sufficient for tax to be payable (para 41).

The responsibility for the LBTT compliance in relation to the transfer of the interest in the partnership (the partners are the buyers) is as described in **6.5** except that the responsible partners (para 17(7)) are as follows:

(a) the partners immediately before the transfer of the interest in the partnership who remain partners after the transfer; and

(b) any person becoming a partner as a result of, or in connection with, the transfer of the partnership interest.

Property-investment partnerships

6.29 A property-investment partnership (PIP) is defined as a partnership whose sole or main activity is investing or dealing in chargeable interests, whether or not the activity includes the carrying out of construction activities on the land (para 31(1)). The term 'construction operations' is defined in FA 2004, s 74. For the purposes of the definition of a PIP only 'chargeable interests' includes any land interest which would be a 'chargeable interest' apart from the fact that the land is located outside of Scotland (para 31(2)). This means that you have to consider all of the investing and dealing activities of a partnership in relation to land, irrespective of where that land is located, to determine whether it is a PIP. Consequently, a partnership which invests in property in order to receive rent, or buys and sells property in order to make a profit (whether as a trade or an investment activity), is a PIP if this is its sole or main activity.

The definition of a PIP states that it does not matter whether the activity of the partnership includes the carrying out of 'construction works' on the land which is being held as an investment or being bought and sold. Therefore a partnership whose main activity is investing in or dealing in land will not be excluded from being a PIP merely because it carries out some construction work before any profit is realised. However, as part of the Standing Committee debates on the amendment to the Finance Bill 2003, Sch 7, to restrict the availability of SDLT acquisition relief to companies whose main activity is the carrying on of a trade that does not consist wholly or mainly of dealing in chargeable interests the Economic Secretary to the Treasury stated:

> 'I understand that there have been worries that the concept of dealing in chargeable interests is uncertain, a point made by the hon. Gentleman. It is unclear, for example, whether a property developer or house builder will be caught. While it is ultimately a question of fact what trade a company is carrying on, I can reassure the Committee that property developers and house builders who derive most of their profits from their work, rather than from buying and selling would not be caught by the measure (FA 2003, para 8(5A), Sch 7). Companies that want reassurance about that in relation to their specific trade can approach HMRC to seek clarification'.

On this basis, and in relation to SDLT, it is understood that HMRC accept that a partnership which generates most of its profits from property development should not be treated as a PIP. It would seem that Revenue Scotland may adopt a similar interpretation in relation to LBTT. At LBTT7011 in the LBTT legislation guidance it is stated that: 'The provisions about PIPs in Part 7 of Schedule 17 to the LBTT(S)A 2013 concern a very narrow class of partnerships, namely those whose sole or main activity is investing in or dealing in property. In other words they are firms speculating in property rather than house building firms.' The guidance therefore confirms that Revenue Scotland accept that a partnership whose sole or main business is generating profit from building and selling houses is not a PIP. It is thought that Revenue Scotland should also accept that a partnership whose sole or main business is generating profits from property development is not a PIP.

If a partnership carries on more than one activity, some of which do not consist of investing or dealing in chargeable interests, it will be necessary to determine which is the main activity. In many cases, this may be obvious, but it may be difficult in borderline cases, where the partnership perhaps devotes similar effort to two activities, only one of which is caught, and derives similar levels of profit from them. In such a case, it may be necessary to carry out detailed analysis of time spent on the different activities, capital employed in each and income/profits derived from each, in order to form a defensible view. Unfortunately, there is no room for compromise or apportionment – the partnership must be classified as wholly a PIP or not a PIP. If a partnership is a PIP, all property held which is situated in Scotland must be considered as potential 'relevant partnership property' (as defined below); there is no exemption for any property which may be held for the purposes of a minority 'non-PIP' purpose.

Transfer of an interest in a PIP

Focus

- A transfer of an interest in a 'property-investment partnership' ('PIP') is potentially chargeable to LBTT, and the quantum of the chargeable consideration may depend on whether the transfer is a 'Type A Transfer' (see **6.33**) or a 'Type B Transfer' (see **6.35**).

6.30 A transfer of an interest in a PIP is treated as a chargeable land transaction if the 'relevant partnership property' (see **6.31**) includes a chargeable interest (para 32(1) and (2)). The buyer is the person who acquires an increased partnership share or who becomes a partner as a consequence of the transfer of the partnership interest (para 32(3)).The consideration for the chargeable transaction is a proportion of the market value of the relevant partnership property; the proportion is the proportion by which the buyer's partnership share increases (paras 32(4) and (5)). Where the transfer of an interest in a PIP is one side of an exchange with an existing partner (ie the existing partner is transferring a chargeable interest to the partnership as consideration for the transfer of the interest in the PIP), the interest in the PIP is deemed to be a major interest in land if any of the relevant partnership property is a major interest (para 34(1)) – this then confirms the need to calculate LBTT by reference to the market values of the relevant partnership property (see **2.31**).

Example 6.9 – Retirement of a partner, linked transactions

DEF Partnership is a PIP with three partners D, E and F, each with a one-third partnership share. There is no connection between the partners other than the fact that they are partners in the DEF partnership. F decides to withdraw; as a result, the shares of D and E each increase to 50%. The relevant partnership property (see **6.31**) has a value of £1.2 million. Each of D and E is treated as the buyer under a chargeable transaction with consideration of one sixth of £1.2 million, or £200,000 (one sixth being the proportion by which their respective partnership shares increase). The two acquisitions should be linked (see **2.79**) as they form a series of transactions or a composite transaction between the same seller F (or D, E and F jointly as partners in The DEF Partnership) and buyers D and E, and D and E should be connected with each other within the terms of CTA 2010, s 1122. This is on the basis that the automatic connection of partners in CTA 2010, s 1122(7)(a) applies for the purposes of the linked transactions legislation (LBTT(S)A 2013, s 58). LBTT should therefore be charged based on the aggregate chargeable consideration for the linked transactions being £400,000.

Relevant partnership property

6.31 There are two definitions of relevant partnership property, depending on whether the transfer of the interest in the PIP is classified as Type A or Type B (see **6.33–6.35**). The intention of the legislation is to ensure that LBTT is paid where a partnership structure is used to transfer economic ownership of property between partners for consideration. However, it seeks to avoid difficulties for partnership structures used in widely held property investment schemes or where transfers occur for no consideration (for example, normal periodic adjustments of partner profit-sharing ratios). This does mean that it is necessary to work through the definitions in any particular case. It would not be safe to decide that no LBTT charge arises purely on the basis of the general intention of the legislation. It is important to note that the distinction between Type A and Type B transfers is relevant only for deciding whether the partnership holds relevant partnership property and, if yes, its value. Both types of transfer are potentially subject to LBTT. However, in many Type B transfers, there will be no relevant partnership property and so no LBTT liability.

Market rent leases

6.32 Leases which satisfy certain very stringent conditions are referred to as 'market rent leases' and are always excluded from relevant partnership property (para 33). Therefore, if a partnership only holds leases of this kind, no transfer (whether Type A or Type B) will be a chargeable transaction. In practice, such partnerships are likely to be rare. To qualify as a market rent lease, a lease must have been granted for a market rent only (ie no premium and no arrangements for any future premium) (para 33(2) and (3)). Furthermore, either it must be for a term not exceeding five years or, if for a longer term, it must provide for market rent reviews at no longer than five yearly intervals (para 33(4)). Note that the rent review must provide for adjustment to a market rent, which means it must be possible for the rent to fall if market rents have declined. Many rent review clauses provide for upward-only reviews, and such a lease cannot qualify as a market rent lease, even though the inability of the rent to fall may have no practical effect. An anti-avoidance condition requires that there should not have been any amendment to the lease since it was granted which itself leads to the rent being less than a market rent immediately after the amendment (para 33(5)).

Example 6.10 – Market rent leases, anti-avoidance rule

Partner X has a 99% share in the XY partnership which is a PIP. X grants a 175-year lease of a commercial property to the partnership at a market rent, with five yearly market rent reviews. The partnership pays LBTT on the 1% of the NPV of rent, representing the 1% effectively transferred to Partner Y. X then agrees to reduce the rent to a peppercorn. This is deemed to be the acquisition of a chargeable interest by the partnership (see **4.42**), and the partnership pays LBTT on the 1% of the market value of the variation (in practice, the value of the variation is probably close to the market value of the ownership of the property). The partnership now owns virtually the whole economic value of the property. X then transfers 98% of his partnership share to Y, for consideration. When it was granted, the lease was a market rent lease. But for the prohibition on subsequent amendments (para 33(5)), it might still count as a market rent lease when the partnership share is transferred. The anti-avoidance condition ensures that the lease is not a 'market rent lease' for the purposes of para 33 and consequently the lease is not excluded from relevant partnership property. The value of the lease is, therefore, taken into account in determining any LBTT payable on the transfer of the partnership interest.

Type A transfers

6.33 Two situations give rise to a Type A transfer (para 32(8)). The first occurs when the whole or part of a partner's interest as partner is transferred to another person (whether or not an existing partner) in return for consideration in money or money's worth (para 32(8)(a)). For the legislation to make sense, this must mean consideration given to the partner whose interest reduces (or to someone else at that partner's behest). The mere contribution of capital to the partnership by the person who gains partnership share does not amount to the giving of consideration for these purposes. The second situation occurs when a new partner joins and the partnership share of an existing partner is reduced, or he ceases to be a partner, and the existing partner withdraws money or money's worth from the partnership. However, this is not a Type A transfer if the withdrawal of money or money's worth comes from resources available to the partnership prior to the transfer (para 32(8)(b)).

Example 6.11 – A Type A transfer of an interest in a property investment partnership

The PQR partnership is a PIP with three partners, P, Q and R, sharing profits equally. Apart from being partners in the PQR partnership the partners are not connected. The partnership holds chargeable interests worth £1 million, other assets worth £150,000 and cash on deposit of £200,000. P decides to retire. At the same time, the other partners decide to admit S (who has no connection to the other partners) as a new partner with a 20% share. S introduces capital of £240,000 for this share. The partnership uses £200,000 of this cash and the £200,000 previously on deposit to pay out P's capital. This is a Type A transfer as S has become a partner, the partnership share of P is reduced to nil and P withdraws money from the partnership which is out of resources not available to the partnership prior to the transfer of the interest in the partnership (ie the £200,000 of the cash contributed by S to the partnership on his becoming a partner).

See **Example 6.12** for a calculation of the chargeable consideration in relation to the transfer of the interest in the partnership.

6.34 If the transfer of an interest in a partnership is Type A, all chargeable interests held by the partnership are regarded as relevant partnership property, apart from market rent leases (see **6.32**) and any property transferred to the partnership in connection with the transfer of the partnership interest (para 32(6)). Also excluded from relevant partnership property is any chargeable interest that is not attributable economically to the interest in the partnership which is transferred (para 32(6)(c)). This is intended to cover a situation where different partners have different rights as to profits and proceeds in relation to properties held by the partnership, and the partnership interest transferred does not transfer any such rights in relation to one or more properties held by the partnership. Such properties would not be economically attributable to the partnership interest that is transferred and would therefore be excluded from relevant partnership property in relation to that transfer.

Example 6.12 – Type A transfer of an interest in a property investment partnership –relevant partnership property

The assets held by the PQR partnership (see **Example 6.11**) consist of: various plots of owned building land situated in Scotland and purchased from third parties at various times and currently valued at £750,000; a long leasehold office transferred from P in 2016 and valued at £200,000; a warehouse leased from a third party; and sundry loose furniture and stock-in-trade valued at £150,000. Both the offices and the warehouse are situated in Scotland. The warehouse lease is at rent, subject to five yearly market rent reviews and qualifies as a market rent lease (see **6.32**). However, local rents have increased dramatically since the last rent review 18 months ago. Because this lease has the benefit of three and a half years at the current rent, now substantially below current market levels, it is considered to have a value of £50,000.

The land which is owned and the long leasehold offices, total value £950,000, are relevant partnership property for a Type A transfer. However, the warehouse lease is not relevant partnership property, as it is a market rent lease (see **6.32**), and may be ignored. The total partnership share transferred is 33.3%, being the share relinquished by the retiring partner: 20% of this goes to the new partner S for deemed consideration of £190,000 (20% of £950,000); and 6.67% goes to each of the continuing partners Q and R for deemed consideration of £63,333 each.

These are three separate transfers, so the question arises as to whether they are 'linked' (see **2.79**). If they are not linked, S will pay LBTT of £400, being 1% of £40,000 (£190,000 – £150,000); Q and R will pay no LBTT, because the consideration deemed to be given by each is below the threshold. If the transfers are linked, the aggregate consideration will be £316,666, so each partner will pay LBTT as follows:

Chargeable consideration	*Rate %*	*LBTT payable*
£		£
150,000	0	Nil
100,000	1	100
66,666	5	3,333
316,666		3,433

LBTT payable:

		£
S	190,000/316,666 × £3,433	2,060.00
Q	63,333/316,666 × £3,433	686.50
R	63,333/316,666 × £3,433	686.50
		3,433.00

It is considered that the transactions should be linked as S, Q and R are connected with each other for the purposes of the linked transaction legislation as they are partners in the partnership (CTA 2010, s 1122(7)). This is on the basis that CTA 2010, s 1122(7) applies for the purposes of the linked transaction legislation. Therefore S should pay LBTT of £2,060.00 and Q and R should each pay LBTT of £686.50.

Type B transfers

6.35 Any transfer of an interest in a PIP which is not a Type A transfer is a Type B transfer (para 32(9)). This includes:

- a transfer which is the result of an adjustment of profit-sharing ratios between the partners, with no partner paying any other for the transfer and no new partner being introduced; or
- a transfer which is the result of a partner (X) reducing his share or exiting the partnership, where no payments are made by any other partner and either no new partner is admitted, or, if a new partner is admitted, any amount withdrawn from the partnership by X is paid out of resources which were available to the partnership before the transfer. It is considered that 'resources' here include previously arranged loan facilities.

Example 6.13 – A Type B transfer

The XYZ partnership is a PIP with three partners, X, Y and Z, sharing profits equally. The partnership holds chargeable interests worth £1 million and cash on deposit of £200,000. X decides to retire. It is agreed that X will take £400,000 cash in settlement of his partnership capital and accumulated profits. The partnership borrows £200,000 from its bank to fund this cash payment. Since no new partner has been admitted and no existing partner has paid anything for his increased partnership share, this is not a Type A transfer, so it must be a Type B transfer. Care is needed here. If Y or Z gives any additional security to the bank in relation to the borrowing, this could be interpreted as giving consideration for the additional partnership share acquired on the withdrawal of X, making it a Type A transfer. Treatment as a Type B transfer will be more secure if the borrowing from the bank is arranged before X decides to retire.

Relevant partnership property for Type B transfers

6.36 The following property is excluded from relevant partnership property in a Type B transfer (para 32(7)):

- any chargeable interest transferred to the partnership in connection with the transfer of the partnership interest. For example, if an incoming partner 'pays' his contribution to capital by transferring a property to the partnership, that property is not relevant partnership property. It is reasonable to exclude this from any LBTT calculation on the transfer of the partnership share, since there will be a separate LBTT calculation/ charge in respect of this property transfer in relation to which the partnership (ie the partners) will be the buyer (see **6.13**);
- any market rent lease (see **6.32**);
- any chargeable interest not economically attributable to the partnership interest transferred. For example, it may be that other partners have sole rights to profits and proceeds of a property, so that the partner receiving the partnership share gains no interest in that particular property – although this is an arrangement more commonly seen in relation to the premises of professional and trading partnerships than the assets of PIPs;
- any chargeable interest in respect of whose transfer an election has been made under para 35 (see **6.38**); and
- any other chargeable interest which was not acquired from a partner (existing or newly admitted) or from someone connected with such a partner (see **6.13**).

The net result of these exclusions is that relevant partnership property for a Type B transfer consists only of property transferred to the partnership from a partner (existing or newly admitted) or a person connected with such a partner, in respect of which no election has been made under para 35, which is not a market rent lease, and which is not held solely for the benefit of partners other than the recipient of the transfer of the partnership interest ie any chargeable interest not economically attributable to the partnership interest transferred.

Notifying liability

6.37 A land transaction consisting of the transfer of an interest in a PIP is notifiable just like any other land transaction by completion of an LBTT return, but only if the deemed consideration, together with that for any linked transactions, is sufficient to give rise to an LBTT liability (para 41(1)). This contrasts with many other land transactions, where notification is needed even when no LBTT liability arises. The consideration exceeds the nil rate tax band if the chargeable consideration, or if the transfer of the interest in the partnership is linked (see **2.79**) with any other land transactions, the total chargeable consideration for all of the linked transactions, exceeds the nil rate tax band applicable to the transaction (para 41(2)).

Paragraph 35 election

6.38

> **Focus**
>
> - A paragraph 35 election is only likely to be attractive where the increase in the LBTT payable as a result of making the election is not significant and it is anticipated that there may be future 'Type B Transfers' of a partnership interest.

Normally, when a property is transferred to a partnership from one or more partners (existing or joining), or persons connected with such partners, LBTT is not charged on the full market value, as explained at **6.13**. However, it is possible for a PIP to make an election under para 35 to disapply that rule and have LBTT charged on the full market value of the property (para 35(1) and (2)). The property is thereafter effectively treated as if it had been acquired from an unconnected third party. The election must be made in the LBTT return for the transaction or in an amendment of that return and, once made, is irrevocable (para 35(3) and (4)).

If the election is made, it will normally increase the amount of LBTT payable immediately, since there will be no reduction in deemed consideration for the part of the property effectively remaining in the ownership of the transferor or his corresponding partner(s). This is not likely to be an attractive option in many cases, but may be worthwhile where the extra LBTT is not significant and it is anticipated that there will in the future be Type B transfers of partnership interests. The election will then exclude the property from the calculation of LBTT on such transfers (see **6.36**).

Reliefs

6.39 For the avoidance of doubt, LBTT(S)A 2013, Sch 1, para 1 (exemption for transfer for no chargeable consideration) is specifically disapplied to transactions involving partnerships (para 37(1)), other than an ordinary transaction (see **6.8**). Apart from that, other reliefs and exemptions do generally apply (para 37(2)).

> **Focus**
>
> - Group relief may be available where a company transfers a chargeable interest to a partnership, and one or more of the partners are in the same LBTT group. However, if the partner ceases to be a member of the same LBTT group as the seller within three years the relief may be withdrawn.

- Group relief may also be available where a partnership transfers a chargeable interest to a company, and **all** of the partners are in the same LBTT group as the buying company.

6.40 Although group relief under LBTT(S)A 2013, Sch 10 may apply to transfers involving partnerships, careful analysis of the various relationships will be required. All partnerships are regarded as 'transparent' as far as ownership of chargeable interests is concerned (para 3). However, some kinds of partnership are unlikely to be treated as 'transparent' as far as ownership of shares, for the purposes of establishing an LBTT group, is concerned.

(1) English general and limited partnerships do not have separate legal personality and are therefore regarded as transparent in relation to share ownership. As a result if all partners in such a partnership are members of an LBTT group, any company at least 75% owned by the partnership will also be a member of the group for LBTT purposes. Transfers of chargeable interests between the partners, the partnership and companies owned by the partnership (satisfying the normal 75% ownership test) will potentially qualify for group relief.

(2) All Scottish partnerships and all UK LLPs have separate legal personality and are therefore not transparent in relation to share ownership. Consequently, a company owned by such a partnership cannot be in an LBTT group with the partners. Transfer of a chargeable interest between one or more partners and a company owned by the partnership cannot qualify for group relief. Furthermore, because chargeable interests held by such a partnership are treated as owned by the partners, transfers between the partnership and a company which it owns cannot qualify for group relief.

(3) Scottish general and limited partnerships are not bodies corporate and so cannot function as the parent of a group (LBTT(S)A 2013, s 65 and Sch 10, para 2). Therefore two companies, each directly owned by such a partnership, are not grouped with each other and a transfer of a chargeable interest between them cannot qualify for group relief. In contrast a UK LLP is a body corporate and can function as the parent of an LBTT group. A transfer of a chargeable interest between companies directly or indirectly owned by an LLP may qualify for group relief, subject to satisfying the normal 75% ownership tests. It remains the case however that a transfer directly between the LLP and a company which it owns cannot qualify as explained at (2) above.

HMRC set out their views on these matters at www.hmrc.gov.uk/so/group-rel-sdlt-sd.htm in relation to SDLT. Revenue Scotland appear to take a similar view in the LBTT legislation guidance at LBTT7012. It is considered that an opinion (see **8.49**) should be sought from Revenue Scotland in any case where it is necessary to understand the treatment of a partnership (ie transparent or opaque), within a corporate structure, to establish whether a group relationship exists.

6.41 A transfer of property to or from a partnership may qualify for a relief (see **Chapter 5**) from LBTT in just the same way as a transfer to or from another entity.

The wording of the group relief provisions is modified to ensure that:

(1) the relief is available where a chargeable interest is transferred to a partnership by: (a) a company which is a partner in the partnership, or (b) a company which becomes a partner in the partnership as a consequence of the transfer, or (c) a company connected to a company which is a partner in the partnership, or connected to a company which becomes a partner as a consequence of the transfer, and the transferor company and one or more of the corporate partners are members of the same LBTT group (para 38(1)(a)). Group relief is granted by reference to the partnership share (see **6.7**) to which the partner(s) which is (are) in the same LBTT group as the transferor company are entitled (para 39);

(2) a transfer of an interest in a partnership pursuant to earlier arrangements (see **6.27**), and a deemed chargeable transaction arising under para 18 (withdrawal of money etc. from a partnership after transfer of chargeable interest – see **6.17**), between members of the same LBTT group (all of the partners in the partnership would have to be members of the same LBTT group as the company which is the seller, since all of the partners in the partnership are treated as the buyers under both scenarios – see paras 17(3) and 18(5)) qualifies for group relief (para 38(1)(a) and (b)); and

(3) group relief is clawed back if a company which was a partner in the partnership at the effective date (see **2.81**) of the transaction transferring the chargeable interest to the partnership (or the effective date of the transaction to which para 17 or para 18 apply) ceases to be in the same LBTT group as the transferor company within three years of the effective date of the transfer of the property to the partnership, or pursuant to an arrangement made within that three year period, at a time when the partnership still holds the property or an interest derived from it (paras 38(2) and 39(3)(b)).

There are no special provisions modifying the availability of group relief where a chargeable interest is transferred out of a partnership to a company(ies), where the partners in the partnership and the transferee company(ies) are members of the same LBTT group. However, it is considered that provided all of the partners in the partnership are members of the same LBTT group as the company(ies) which is the buyer then group relief should, in principle, be available.

6.42 A transfer of an interest in a partnership that is a chargeable transaction under either para 17 (see **6.27**) or para 32 (see **6.30**) may qualify for a relief if a direct transfer of the relevant chargeable interests held by the partnership would have qualified (para 37(2)). The wording of the relief for charities is modified to ensure that it applies only if all of the chargeable interests held by the partnership immediately after the transfer are held for charitable purposes

– that is, there is no partial relief if the partnership holds some properties for charitable purposes and some not (para 40(3)).

SUNDRY PROVISIONS

6.43 UK stamp duty continues to apply to a document which transfers an interest in a partnership, if that partnership holds stock or marketable securities (FA 2003, Sch 15, ss 31–33).

The acquisition of a partnership interest is only subject to LBTT as set out at **6.13**, **6.27** and **6.30** (para 4). If an interest in a partnership is acquired in some other way, it is not subject to LBTT.

Example 6.14 – Non-chargeable acquisition of partnership interest

Reid and Wright LLP ('RW LLP') is a business advisory partnership with 53 partners, employing 371 staff working out of 11 offices. RW LLP has various interests in its office buildings, and a portfolio of business premises which it lets out, but rental income forms only 20% to 30% of its income, the balance coming from advisory and consulting activities. It is therefore considered that RW LLP is not a PIP. The partners decide to admit three new partners, two from the existing workforce and one by direct appointment from outside. Each partner contributes £20,000 partnership capital (funded, in the case of the existing staff, by a corresponding loan from the partnership, to be repaid out of profit share) and has an initial profit share of 0.25%.

On the general definition, this amounts to three transfers of partnership interest to the new partners (para 48). However, as RW LLP is not a PIP, and the transfers are not in connection with the transfer to the partnership of chargeable interests in land located in Scotland, nor are they 'pursuant to earlier arrangements' involving transfers of chargeable interests to the partnership, the transfers of partnership interests are not within the charge to LBTT.

Partnership property

6.44 Partnership property is any interest in, or right over, land held by or on behalf of a partnership, or the members of a partnership, for the purposes of the partnership business (para 43). In LBTT7003 of the LBTT legislation guidance it is stated that:

> 'Partnership property is an interest or right held by or behalf of a partnership, or the members of a partnership, for the purposes of the partnership business. Amongst other things this reflects the practice in Scotland that title to partnership property is not held in the name of the firm itself. Section 70 of the Abolition of Feudal Tenure etc. (Scotland) Act 2000 allows Scottish firms to hold title in their own name but the

practice of title being otherwise held remains more common, eg title held in the name of a trust for the firm or in the name of one of the partners.'

The important point therefore appears to be that the property must be held for the purposes of the partnership's business, either by the partnership itself or by some other person on behalf of the partnership.

Based on the guidance in the HMRC Business Income Manual BIM72058, in relation to SDLT, mere use of land and buildings by the partnership should not mean they become partnership property. In such circumstances the intention of the parties will be important ie was it the intention of the parties that the land and buildings be partnership property? Were the land and buildings held for the purposes of the partnership's business (in which case they should be partnership property) or were they, for example, simply let to the partnership (in which case they should not be partnership property although the lease itself would be partnership property)? However, if the land and buildings have been acquired with the partnership's money they are likely to be partnership property.

It is important to understand what is and is not partnership property as there is only a transfer of a chargeable interest to a partnership where the chargeable interest becomes partnership property (para 46). Equally, there is only a transfer of a chargeable interest from a partnership where a chargeable interest ceases to be partnership property, or a chargeable interest is created out of partnership property (for example a lease created out of the ownership of land) and the interest which is created is not partnership property (para 47(a) and (b)).

Chapter 7

LBTT and Trusts

SIGNPOSTS

- Outline of how LBTT operates in relation to the two types of trust recognised for LBTT purposes being a 'bare trust' and a 'settlement'.
- Details of the person responsible for satisfying the LBTT obligations when the buyer is a trustee.

7.1 The legislation in relation to trusts is found in the Land and Buildings Transaction Tax (Scotland) Act 2013, Sch 18. In this chapter references to paragraphs without further identification are references to Sch 18. Part 1 of Sch 18 provides an overview of the provisions in relation to trusts, Part 2 makes provision for the application of LBTT to trusts and beneficiaries generally, Part 3 deals with transactions involving 'bare trusts', Part 4 deals with transactions involving trusts which are 'settlements', Part 5 makes provision for the payment of LBTT and the making of land transaction returns and Part 6 sets out a number of definitions used in Sch 18.

7.2 Rather bizarrely for what is, after all, a Scottish tax, in relation to certain trusts the legislation adopts the law of England and Wales. Consequently, where property is held in trust under the law of Scotland, or under the law of a country or territory outside of the UK, on terms such that if the trust had effect under the law of England and Wales, the beneficiary would be treated as having an equitable interest in the property held by the trust, the beneficiary is to be treated as having such a beneficial interest (paras 2 and 3). This is despite the fact that no such beneficial interest is recognised by the law of Scotland or the relevant country or territory outside of the UK. In addition, the acquisition of the interest of a beneficiary under such a trust is to be treated for LBTT purposes as involving the acquisition of an interest in the underlying trust property (para 4). Consequently, if that underlying trust property includes a chargeable interest (see **2.9**), the acquisition of the interest of a beneficiary will be a land transaction, potentially giving rise to LBTT obligations.

BARE TRUSTS AND SETTLEMENTS

7.3 The legislation recognises two types of trust being a 'bare trust' and a 'settlement'. A 'bare trust' is a trust under which the trustee holds the property for a person who is 'absolutely entitled' as against the trustee, or holds the property for two or more persons who are so entitled against the trustee, and includes a person holding property as nominee for another person (para 19). For these purposes 'absolutely entitled' refers to the position where the person has the exclusive right, subject only to satisfying any outstanding charge, lien or other right of the trustee, to use the property for payment of duty, taxes, costs or other outgoings or to direct how the property is to be dealt with (para 20).

A trust that is not a 'bare trust' is a 'settlement' for LBTT purposes (para 21). Examples of 'settlements' would be 'interest in possession trusts' (where the beneficiary has entitlement to the income of a trust but generally no entitlement to the capital), 'discretionary trusts' (where the use of the capital and income of the trust is at the discretion of the trustees) and 'trusts for accumulation and maintenance' etc.

TRANSACTIONS INVOLVING BARE TRUSTS

7.4 Where a person acquires a chargeable interest, or an interest in a partnership, as bare trustee it is treated, for LBTT purposes, as though the chargeable interest or partnership interest were acquired by the beneficiary and as though the acts of the trustee were the acts of the beneficiary (para 5). However, this treatment does not apply to the grant of a lease to, or by, a bare trustee (para 7 – see **7.5**). Even though the beneficiary of a bare trust is treated as the buyer for LBTT purposes (other than in relation to the grant of a lease) any tax due by the beneficiary may be recovered from the trustee (para 6).

7.5 Where a lease is granted to a person as bare trustee, the trustee is treated for LBTT purposes as the buyer of the whole of the interest acquired in the lease (para 8). Similarly, where a bare trustee grants a lease to another person the trustee is treated for LBTT purposes as the seller of the whole of the interest in the lease which has been disposed of (para 9). These provisions were introduced into the SDLT legislation to try to combat transactions seeking to avoid a tax charge by, for example, a person granting a lease to his nominee which, absent this legislation, would be a nothing for SDLT purposes. The anti-avoidance provisions have been imported into the LBTT legislation even though, under Scots law, it may not be possible for a person to grant a lease to a person acting as his nominee, as it is a basic principle of the law of contract in Scotland that a person cannot contract with themselves.

TRANSACTIONS INVOLVING TRUSTS OTHER THAN BARE TRUSTS

7.6 Where the trustees of a 'settlement' (ie a trust which is not a bare trust) acquire a chargeable interest or an interest in a partnership, the trustees are treated for LBTT purposes as buyers of the whole of the interest acquired, including the beneficial interest (para 10).

PAYMENT OF LBTT AND FILING OF LAND TRANSACTION RETURNS

7.7 Where the trustees of a 'settlement' are liable to pay LBTT the payment may be recovered (but only once) from any one or more of the 'responsible trustees', who may also file the land transaction return in relation to the transaction (paras 15 and 16). The declaration that the land transaction return is, to the buyer's knowledge, correct and complete, must be made by the trustees making the return (para 17). For these purposes the 'responsible trustees' for a land transaction are the persons who are trustees at the effective date (see **2.81**) of the transaction and any person who subsequently becomes a trustee (para 18). This means that LBTT can be recovered from a trustee who was not a trustee at the time of the transaction, but subsequently became a trustee.

7.8 Where a lease is granted to a person as bare trustee, the trustee is the buyer and therefore has the obligation to notify the transaction (see **4.11** and **4.12**) and to pay any LBTT liability. In relation to any other chargeable transactions entered into by a person as bare trustee, the beneficiary is the buyer and therefore it is the beneficiary who has the obligation to notify the transaction and pay any LBTT liability.

OTHER MATTERS

7.9 Where a chargeable interest is acquired as a result of the trustee exercising a power of appointment or exercising the discretion vested in him, any consideration given for the person in whose favour the appointment is made, or the discretion was exercised, is treated for LBTT purposes as the consideration given for the acquisition of the chargeable interest (para 12).

Where the trustees of a 'settlement' reallocate trust property such that a beneficiary acquires an interest in certain trust property and ceases to have an interest in other trust property, the giving of consent to this reallocation by the beneficiary does not count as chargeable consideration for the acquisition of any chargeable interest included in such trust property (paras 13 and 14).

Chapter 8

LBTT Administration and Compliance

SIGNPOSTS

- Sets out what must be notified to Revenue Scotland, on whom the responsibility for notification and payment of LBTT falls, and the processes involved.
- Outline of the deadlines which must be met, the costs arising if those deadlines are not met, and the occasions on which the payment of LBTT may validly be postponed.
- Explains how to claim repayment if the payment of LBTT proves excessive.
- Reviews the powers which Revenue Scotland have to enquire into and amend returns, assess unpaid or underpaid LBTT and seek penalties.
- The relevant legislation is found in the Land and Buildings Transaction Tax (Scotland) Act 2013, ss 29–43 and the Revenue Scotland and Tax Powers Act 2014 (RSTPA 2014) ss 73–251 and Sch 3. Precise references are given in the paragraphs below.
- LBTT is not within the UK regime for disclosure of tax avoidance schemes (DOTAS).

NOTIFICATION

What is notifiable, and by whom?

8.1

Focus

- A transaction may be notifiable even though a relief is available to reduce or eliminate the LBTT liability. A relief must be claimed in a land transaction return.

In general, land transactions (see **2.5**) are notifiable unless the transaction is in relation to an exempt interest (see **2.14**), or the transaction is an exempt transaction (see **5.6**) or one of the exceptions (LBTT(S)A 2013, s 30 (1) and (2)) from notification apply (see **8.2**). If the transaction is a chargeable transaction (see **2.12**), and none of the notification exceptions apply (see **8.2**), the transaction is notifiable even if no LBTT is payable. It is especially important to note that a transaction is not excused from being notified merely because a relief is available to reduce or remove the LBTT liability – reliefs must be claimed in a land transaction return.

Deemed land transactions may also give rise to the obligation to notify. In many cases, a real transaction is deemed to be a land transaction (or to be the acquisition of a chargeable interest, which is automatically a land transaction; see **2.5**). Examples of deemed land transactions include the substantial performance of a contract, which is to be completed by a conveyance, before completion (see **2.7**), or the variation of a lease to reduce the rent or term (see **4.42** and **4.43**). In other cases, actions or events are deemed to amount to transactions which are specifically stated to give rise to an obligation to submit an LBTT return. An example is on final determination of uncertain consideration, if that leads to further LBTT becoming payable or, in the case of rent, if it leads to the grant of the lease becoming notifiable (see **2.18**). The buyer, in certain circumstances, has an obligation to file further land transaction returns under the provisions for a regular review of the LBTT chargeable on a lease (see **4.21**) and on the assignation or termination of certain leases (see **4.26**).

8.2

Focus

- The acquisition of a chargeable interest (ie a land transaction) is notifiable unless it falls within one of the exceptions detailed below.

A land transaction is notifiable unless:

(1) It is an exempt transaction (LBTT(S)A 2013, s 30(1)(a) – see **5.6**).

(2) It is the acquisition of the ownership of land where the chargeable consideration is less than £40,000 or, if it is one of a number of linked transactions (see **2.79**), the aggregate of the chargeable consideration for all of the linked transactions is less than £40,000. The availability of any relief is ignored in determining the amount of the chargeable consideration (LBTT(S)A 2013, s 30(1)(b) and (3)).

(3) It is the acquisition of a chargeable interest which is not a major interest in land (see **2.9**), for example an option, and the chargeable consideration for the transaction or, if it is one of a number of linked transactions (see **2.79**), the aggregate of the chargeable consideration for all of the linked transactions, does not exceed the nil rate tax band applicable to the transaction (LBTT(S)A 2013, s 30(1)(c) and (3)).

(4) The grant of a lease for a period of seven years or more where any chargeable consideration other than rent or, if the grant of the lease is one of a number of linked transactions (see **2.79**), the aggregate of the chargeable consideration other than rent for all of the linked transactions, is less than £40,000 and the annual rent or, if the grant of the lease is one of a number of linked transactions, the aggregate annual rent for all of the linked transactions, is less than £1,000 (LBTT(S)A 2013, s 30(2)(a), (3) and (4)).

(5) The assignation or renunciation of a lease which was originally granted for a period of seven years or more and the chargeable consideration for the assignation or renunciation or, if it is one of a number of linked transactions (see **2.79**), the aggregate of the chargeable consideration for all of the linked transactions, is less than £40,000.

(6) The grant of a lease for a period of less than seven years where the chargeable consideration (both rent and consideration other than rent), or if it is one of a number of linked transactions (see **2.79**), the aggregate of the chargeable consideration (both rent and consideration other than rent) for all of the linked transactions, does not exceed the nil rate tax band applicable to the transaction (LBTT(S)A 2013, s 30(2)(c) and (3)).

(7) The assignation or renunciation of a lease which was originally granted for a period of less than seven years and the chargeable consideration for the assignation or renunciation or, if it is one of a number of linked transactions (see **2.79**), the aggregate of the chargeable consideration for all of the linked transactions, does not exceed the nil rate tax band applicable to the transaction (LBTT(S)A 2013, s 30(2)(d) and (3)).

The notification exceptions detailed in (1)–(7) above do not apply to a deemed land transaction on the 'substantial performance' (see **2.7**) of a contract under which a chargeable interest is to be conveyed by one party to the contract (A) at the direction of the other party to the contract (B), either to (C) who is not party to the contract, or either to C or to B (LBTT(S)A 2013, s 30(5)). Therefore, if such a contract for the acquisition of the ownership of land is substantially performed by B before it is completed, the deemed land transaction which is treated as taking place as a consequence of substantial performance (LBTT(S) A 2013, s 11(3)) is notifiable even if the chargeable consideration is below the normal £40,000 notification threshold.

The notification rules in LBTT(S)A 2013, s 30 are subject to other notification provisions found elsewhere in the legislation (LBTT(S)A 2013, s 30(6)). These are as follows:

- Where a contract, which is to be completed by a conveyance, is 'substantially performed' before it is completed, both the deemed transaction on substantial performance of the contract, and the actual transaction on completion of the contract are notifiable transactions, irrespective of the chargeable consideration (LBTT(S)A 2013, s 30(6) (a) and s 10(3)). In relation to SDLT, HMRC only require a return for the actual transaction, following completion, if additional tax is payable – see SDLTM 50250. However, in LBTT1005 of the LBTT legislation guidance, Revenue Scotland simply state that there may be a requirement to notify the completion transaction without elaborating on the circumstances in which notification would not be required. It is considered that if no additional tax is payable on the completion transaction confirmation should be requested from Revenue Scotland that there is no need to file a land transaction return.

- Where certain items are excluded from being chargeable consideration under LBTT(S)A 2013, Sch 2, para 17(4) and (5) (arrangements involving public or educational bodies) (see **5.40**), those items are included in arriving at the chargeable consideration for the purposes of determining whether the transactions are notifiable by reference to the exceptions in (1) to (7) above (LBTT(S)A 2013, s 30(6)(b) and Sch 2, para 17(6)).
- A further transaction that is exempt from charge under LBTT(S)A 2013, Sch 7, para 10 (Alternative Property Finance: Land sold to financial institution and person in common) is not a notifiable transaction unless it involves the transfer to the person of the whole of the interest acquired by the Bank under the first transaction (see **5.30**) (LBTT(S)A 2013, s 30(6)(c) and Sch 7, para 12).
- A transaction involving a transfer of an interest in a partnership under either LBTT(S)A 2013, Sch 17, para 17 (see **6.27**) or para 32 (see **6.30**) is a notifiable transaction only if the chargeable consideration for the transaction, or if it is one of a number of linked transactions (see **2.79**), the aggregate chargeable consideration for all of the linked transactions, exceeds the nil rate tax band applicable to the transaction (LBTT(S)A 2013, s 30(6)(d) and Sch 17, para 41).

Sometimes, taxpayers may choose to complete returns for transactions which appear to be exempt or are otherwise not notifiable. This would generally be done to guard against future allegations of failure to notify, where exemption is dependent on a treatment of the facts which could be susceptible to challenge.

Transactions which are not notifiable – retention of records

8.3 If a transaction is exempt (see **5.6**) or a notification exception applies (see **8.2**), there is no obligation to notify the transaction to Revenue Scotland (LBTT(S)A 2013, s30(1) and (2)). However, even though there is no obligation to file a land transaction return the Scottish Ministers may, by regulations, make provision for the maintenance of records for the normal five year period, in relation to transactions which were not notifiable. The regulations may require the buyer to keep such records as are necessary to demonstrate that the transaction was not notifiable (RSTPA, s 81). The Revenue Scotland and Tax Powers Act (Record Keeping) Regulations 2015, SSI 2015/130 provide as follows (reg 4):

- The buyer in a land transaction which is not notifiable must keep such records as may be needed to enable the buyer to demonstrate that the transaction is not notifiable.

- The five year retention period specified in RSTPA 2014, s 74(2) applies, with the five year period beginning on the date by which the return would have been required to have been filed, had the transaction been notifiable.
- The records to be preserved include any contract or conveyance and any supporting maps, plans or similar documents.
- The penalties for failure to keep and preserve records apply even though the transaction was not notifiable (see **8.86**).

In any event it would be prudent in practice to retain such records in case a subsequent challenge arises as to whether or not the transaction was in fact an exempt transaction, or whether it fell within one of the notification exceptions, and therefore whether the transaction was notifiable.

Registration of land transactions

Notifiable transactions

8.4 The Keeper of the Registers of Scotland need not accept an application to register a document effecting or evidencing a notifiable transaction unless: (a) a land transaction return has been filed in relation to the transaction, and (b) any tax payable in respect of the transaction has been paid (LBTT(S)A 2013, s 43(1)). Tax is treated as having been paid if 'arrangements satisfactory' to Revenue Scotland have been made for the payment of the tax – see **8.25**.

Transactions which are not notifiable

8.5 The Registers of Scotland application form to register title poses the question as to whether the transaction is a notifiable transaction in terms of LBTT(S)A 2013, s 30 (see **8.10**). If the completed application form indicates that the transaction is not notifiable and, based on the documentation and information supplied this appears to be correct, then the application for registration should be accepted. However, if it appears that the question has been answered incorrectly Registers of Scotland (or Revenue Scotland) may make further enquires to validate the view that the transaction is not notifiable. Equally, if it is clear that the transaction is notifiable Registers of Scotland will reject the application for registration, until a land transaction return has been filed and any LBTT liability settled.

Ownership of land in Scotland does not pass until registration

8.6 The technicalities of conveying land in Scotland are beyond the scope of this book. However, in a Scottish conveyancing transaction the seller receives the money (or other consideration) from the buyer in return for a personal right, and a real right is only created when the deed is registered in the land register. This means that there is likely to be a period of time (however short) between the settlement of the transaction and payment of the consideration, and the registration of the deed in the land register. During that period the buyer is at risk of:

- the seller becoming insolvent; or
- a competing deed over the same land being entered in the register first.

The solution to this 'gap risk period' was the introduction by the Land Registration etc. (Scotland) Act 2012, with effect from 8 December 2014, of the 'advance notice scheme'. Under this scheme an advance notice can be registered in the land register creating a 'protected period' of 35 days from:

- an inhibition registered against the seller in the Register of Inhibitions; and
- a competing deed granted by the seller to a third party being registered before the deed granted to the buyer.

The protected period begins the day after the advance notice is entered in the land register and continues in force for 35 calendar days. It is not possible to extend or renew the protected period and if it expires before settlement and registration of the deed a new advance notice would need to be sought. The advance notice does not have the effect of freezing the register in any way but instead gives preference to the protected deed. Where an advance notice has been registered this could mean in principle that there is not quite the same impetus to register a land transaction (and therefore file any land transaction return and pay any LBTT due); however, in practice, as ownership is not secured until registration takes place, it is likely that the registration application will be made at as early a date as possible.

Responsibility for notifying

8.7

> **Focus**
>
> - It is important to identify the 'buyer' in relation to a chargeable transaction as it is the buyer who is responsible for notifying the transaction and paying the LBTT.

Responsibility for notification and payment of any tax falls on the buyer (LBTT(S)A 2013, ss 28(1) and 29(1)). The identity of this person is usually self-evident, being the person who gains ownership of the land interest. However, there are several provisions identifying the buyer in particular circumstances:

- When property is acquired by a partnership, or transferred to a partnership by a partner (or a person who becomes a partner) or a person connected with a partner, or where value is withdrawn from a partnership after such a property transfer (see **6.8, 6.13** and **6.17**), all of the partners are buyers and have joint and several responsibility for notification. They may nominate one or more representative partners, but this does not remove the responsibilities of individual partners if the nominated partner(s) fails in his or her duties (LBTT(S)A 2013, Sch 17, paras 8-10, para 13(2) and para 17(7)).

- When a lease is varied to reduce the rent, the tenant is the buyer. If it is varied to shorten the term, the landlord is the buyer (LBTT(S)A 2013, Sch 19, paras 29(1) and (3)).
- Where the trustees of a trust, other than a bare trust (see **7.3**), acquire beneficial ownership of a property, they are the buyers (LBTT(S) 2013, Sch 18, para 10). The obligation to make a return may be discharged by any one or more of the trustees who are referred to as the 'relevant trustees' in the legislation (LBTT(S)A 2013, Sch 18, para 16 – see **7.7**). Where trustees (or nominees) acquire a property under a bare trust, the person on behalf of whom the acquisition is made is normally treated as the buyer (LBTT(S)A 2013, Sch 18, para 5 – see **7.4**). However, if the acquisition by the bare trustees takes the form of the grant of a lease to them, they are treated as the buyers of the whole beneficial interest in the lease (LBTT(S)A 2013, Sch 18, para 8 – see **7.5**). This is an anti-avoidance provision which has been taken from the equivalent SDLT legislation.

How to notify

8.8 Notification is by submission of a land transaction return (LTR) to Revenue Scotland. The LTR is due within 30 days from the effective date (see **2.81**) of the transaction (LBTT(S)A 2013, s 29(3) – see **2.6**).

Paper forms

8.9 The facility to file a paper return does exist, but is only available to taxpayers without a solicitor or conveyancer.

An LTR must be in the form and contain the information prescribed by Revenue Scotland (LBTT(S)A 2013, s 35(1)). The paper LBTT return can be obtained by emailing lbtt@revenue.scot. In contrast to SDLT, in relation to which there are a number of forms (SDLT1, 2, 3 and 4 forms) which may have to be filed depending on the nature of the transaction, there is only one LBTT return. If additional space is required for further buyers, sellers or properties an 'Additional Details' form should be completed.

When sending the paper form, Revenue Scotland will also provide guidance for completing the LBTT paper return.

8.10 Paper LTRs should be scanned and emailed to Revenue Scotland. Payment of the LBTT must be made at the same time as the LTR is filed. LBTT is treated as having been paid provided 'arrangements satisfactory' to Revenue Scotland are in place at the time the LTR is filed – see **8.25** (LBTT(S)A 2013, s 40(2) and (4)). The paper LTR, a plan (if one is provided), the Registers of Scotland application form to register title (if relevant) and any document which is capable of being registered under the Land Registration etc. (Scotland) Act 2012 or any other enactment should be sent to Registers of Scotland. No correspondence or other documents should be included. For guidance where it is considered necessary to submit other information or documents to Revenue Scotland, see **8.48**.

The Registers of Scotland application form to register any document effecting a land transaction poses the following questions:

(1) 'Is the transaction to which this application relates a notifiable transaction in terms of section 30 of The Land and Buildings Transaction Tax (Scotland) Act 2013?'

If an LTR is being filed the answer will be 'Yes'.

(2) 'If yes, has a land transaction return been made, and have arrangements satisfactory to the tax authority been made for the payment of any tax payable in respect of the transaction?'

Assuming this question is answered in the affirmative Registers of Scotland should proceed with the registration process.

Electronic returns

8.11 Revenue Scotland offer the facility to complete and submit LTRs via the online portal, once the person making the submission has registered for this purpose. There is guidance on the Revenue Scotland website on how to register for the online portal and how to log into the online portal. From 1 May 2020, all LBTT returns (conveyance, lease, or lease review) submitted by solicitors or conveyancers must be submitted online, using the Scottish Electronic Tax System (SETS).

The online forms are 'intelligent', in that they decide which sections to present for completion in accordance with sections already completed. The software also checks for inconsistencies or omissions and will prevent submission if these are found. It will not, however, check for technical errors, so the fact that submission is allowed does not guarantee that the return is technically correct! The electronic forms are just as restrictive and limited as their paper counterparts in terms of lack of space to provide additional information, so the same difficulties will arise in ensuring adequate disclosure (see **8.48**).

8.12 Once you are logged into the online portal a new LBTT return can be prepared by selecting 'Create LBTT Return' on the 'Dashboard' page. You will then be prompted to select which type of return is required:

- Conveyance or transfer
- Lease
- Three year lease review
- Assignation
- Termination

The online LBTT return is divided into sections, which can be completed in any order. The sections are as follows:

- Contact details for agent
- About the buyer
- About the seller
- About the property
- About the Additional Dwelling Supplement (if ADS is selected in the "about the property" section)
- About the transaction
- About the calculation
- Declaration

The online LBTT return is very flexible in that you can move around the return at any time, save draft returns, edit a draft return or delete a draft return before it has been submitted to Revenue Scotland. It is also possible to preview an LBTT return before it is filed and the return can be printed off while in 'Preview' mode to allow a review to be carried out.

Once the return has been filed electronically, a 'Tax Return Acknowledgement' will be shown. This cannot be viewed later and therefore must be printed at that time, if a copy is required.

The points made at **8.9** regarding completion of the Paper Return generally apply to the online return; however, it is possible to enter as many buyers, sellers or properties in the online return whereas an 'Additional Details' form may have to be used for a paper return.

Where the LTR is filed electronically, the normal practice is for the Registers of Scotland application form (to register the transaction, assuming that the transaction can be registered), to be sent to Registers of Scotland as soon as possible after the transaction has taken place, together with the documents which are capable of being registered under the Land Registration etc. (Scotland) Act 2012 or any other enactment. As set out at **8.10** the application form for registration will ask whether the transaction is notifiable under LBTT(S)A 2013, s 30 and, if it is, whether the LTR has been filed and whether arrangements satisfactory to Revenue Scotland have been made for the payment of any tax due in relation to the transaction (see **8.25**). Assuming both questions are answered in the affirmative, Registers of Scotland should confirm that the LTR has been filed and the tax paid, by checking a data feed from Revenue Scotland and, assuming that confirmation is received, should proceed with registering title.

8.13 Paper returns have to be signed by the buyer(s) or the buyer's agent declaring that the return is, to the best of their knowledge, correct and complete (LBTT(S)A 2013, s 36(1)), but clearly this is not possible for electronic forms. Instead, before an agent is permitted to submit the final return, they must certify in the return that the buyer has declared that the information included within the return is to the best of the buyer's knowledge correct and complete. The only fact which is allowed to be missing from the 'draft' approved by the buyer is the 'relevant date' (LBTT(S)A 2013, s 36(2)(a)). LBTT(S)A 2013, s 36(3) provides that the 'relevant date' for this purpose is:

(1) The 'effective date' (see **2.81**) of the transaction if it is notifiable under LBTT(S)A 2013, s 29(1) (return made in relation to a chargeable transaction which is notifiable).

(2) The date on which the contingency to which the consideration was subject ceased or the consideration was ascertained where the return is made under LBTT(S)A 2013, s 31(1) (return where contingency ceases or consideration ascertained – see **2.18**).

(3) The date on which an event occurred causing a relief to be withdrawn where the return is made under LBTT(S)A 2013, s 33(1) (further return where a relief is withdrawn).

(4) The 'effective date' (see **2.81**) of the later transaction where the return is made under LBTT(S)A 2013, s 34 (return or further return as a consequence of a later linked transaction).

(5) The 'review date' (see **4.21**) where the return is made under LBTT(S)A 2013, Sch 19, para 10 (three-yearly review of the LBTT chargeable on a lease).

(6) The date upon which the lease is assigned or terminated where the return is made under LBTT(S)A 2013, Sch 19, para 11 (review of the LBTT chargeable on a lease when it is assigned or terminated – see **4.26**).

(7) The date upon which the one year period which triggered notification of the transaction ended where the return is made under LBTT(S)A 2013, Sch 19, para 20(3) (notification required following the deemed extension of a lease which continues beyond its fixed term – see **4.77**).

(8) The date upon which the one year period which triggered notification of the transaction ended where the return is made under LBTT(S)A 2013, Sch 19, para 22(2) (notification required following the deemed extension of a lease for an indefinite term – see **4.80**).

(9) The date from which the variation takes effect where the return is made under LBTT(S)A 2013, Sch 19, para 30(2) (notification required where a lease is varied to increase the rent payable or extend the term of the lease – see **4.45**).

This allows the return to be drafted before completion of the transaction, approved by the buyer, and then finalised and submitted immediately on, or shortly after, the 'relevant date'**.** The LTR must also include a declaration by the agent that the 'relevant date' included in the return is, to the best of the agent's knowledge, correct (LBTT(S)A 2013, s 36(2)(b)).

Once the LBTT return has been filed electronically, it will be given a unique transaction reference (commencing 'RS'), which will be displayed on the screen after submission. This reference number must be quoted when making payments in relation to the transaction to which the return relates and also when contacting Revenue Scotland about the transaction.

8.14 When a return is submitted online, and 'arrangements satisfactory' (see **8.25**) to Revenue Scotland have been made for the payment of any LBTT liability, other than an amount of LBTT in relation to which a deferment application has been made (see **8.27**), Registers of Scotland should register title (assuming that the transaction can be registered), on receipt of the registration application form and the documents which are capable of being registered under the Land Registration etc (Scotland) Act 2012 or any other enactment (see **8.4** – LBTT(S)A 2013, s 43).

Further and amended returns

8.15

> **Focus**
>
> - It will be important to understand whether the requirement is to file: (a) a new return for a new transaction (which may be linked (see **2.79**) with the original transaction), or (b) a further return in relation to the original transaction, or (c) an amendment of the original return.

A number of transactions and events, described at various points in this book, give rise to the requirement to submit a further LTR when one has already been submitted for the original transaction, or to submit an amendment to the original LTR.

Example 8.1 – Further return, uncertain consideration

On 1 April 2024 Joe acquires ownership of a pub for an initial consideration of £200,000, to be adjusted upwards based on a formula which takes account of the turnover of the pub in the two years following the effective date (see **2.81**) of the acquisition of the property. An LTR is submitted within 30 days of the effective date of the acquisition, and the chargeable consideration returned is the £200,000. This is on the basis that a reasonable estimate of the additional consideration likely to be payable, based on the forecast turnover of the business, is nil (see **2.18**). At the end of the two year period, it is established that turnover has been significantly higher than originally forecast so that, based on the formula, further consideration of £75,000 is payable. Additional LBTT is therefore payable and a further return is due within 30 days of the amount of the additional consideration payable becoming ascertained (LBTT(S)A 2013, s31(1), (2)(b), (3) and (4)).

Example 8.2 – Further return, clawback of relief

On 1 May 2024 A Ltd purchases a property from group company D Ltd and submits an LTR on which group relief from LBTT is claimed. Two years later, A Ltd, while still owning the property, is sold to a third party. A Ltd must make a further return reporting the withdrawal of group relief within 30 days of whichever step leads to it ceasing to be a member of the same LBTT group as D Ltd (LBTT(S)A 2013, s 33(1)(d), (2), (3) and (4)(d)) – see **5.17** et seq).

Example 8.3 – Amended return, in consequence of a later linked transaction

On 1 June 2024 B Ltd agrees to buy two commercial properties located in Scotland from an unrelated company M Ltd, the consideration payable for the first property is £300,000 and for the second property it is £450,000. The agreement is not substantially performed before completion, however the acquisition of the first property completes on 1 July 2024 as originally planned, but there is an issue over title in relation to the second property, and its acquisition does not complete until 1 September 2024. B Ltd files an LTR by 31 July 2024, paying LBTT based on the acquisition of the first property for £300,000, so that LBTT of £3,500 is paid. This is calculated as follows:

Consideration	*Rate*	*LBTT*
£	%	£
150,000	0	NIL
100,000	1	1,000
50,000	5	2,500
300,000		3,500

On completion of the acquisition of the second property on 1 September 2024, not only must B Ltd file an LTR for the acquisition of the second property by 1 October 2024, it must also file an amended LTR, and pay the additional LBTT due of £6,900, on the acquisition of the first property, as a consequence of that transaction being linked (see **2.79**) with the later acquisition of the second property (LBTT(S)A 2013, s 34).

The LBTT payable is calculated as follows:

Consideration	*Rate*	*LBTT*
£	%	£
150,000	0	NIL
100,000	1	1,000
500,000	5	25,000
750,000		26,000

LBTT payable on first property – £300,000/£750,000 × £26,000 = £10,400

LBTT payable on second property – £450,000/£750,000 × £26,000 = £15,600

The additional LBTT payable on the first property is therefore £6,900 (£10,400 – £3,500).

Example 8.4 – Further returns as a result of the three-yearly review, and the review on termination, of a lease

The facts are as set out in **Example 4.6**. John must file further LBTT returns by each of 31 July 2027, 31 July 2030 and 31 July 2033 as a consequence of the requirement to carry out a three-year review of the LBTT chargeable on a lease (see **4.21**). He must also file a further LBTT return by 30 July 2034 as a result of the requirement to carry out a review of the LBTT chargeable on termination of a lease (see **4.26**).

8.16 It is important to establish whether the required action is:

(1) submission of a new return for a new transaction, which may or may not be linked (see **2.79**) with the original transaction;

(2) submission of a further return for the original transaction, perhaps now modified in the light of subsequent events or facts; or

(3) amendment of the return originally submitted in respect of the original transaction.

In some cases, (1) may be necessary as well as either (2) or (3). Even where an amendment is not required, a buyer may voluntarily amend a return within 12 months of the filing deadline for the original return, for example, in order to claim a relief which was omitted from the original return, or to correct a calculation error which led to the payment of the wrong amount of LBTT (RSTPA 2014, s 83). If an error is discovered by the buyer which led to an underpayment of LBTT, or a false or inflated statement of an exemption or relief or repayment of tax, the error will be treated as arising from the carelessness of the buyer if he fails to amend the return, and this may then give rise to a penalty (RSTPA 2014, s 182(1), (2), (3) and (5) – see **8.67**). A new return for a new transaction is generally made by completion of a new LTR (whether paper or online). If the new transaction is linked with a previous transaction this is required to be noted in the new return. This linking may also lead to the need to amend the return, or to submit a further return, for the original transaction.

How to submit further and amended returns

8.17 In principle, submission of a further return for the original transaction and amendment of the original return are different processes; the legislation specifies which is required in each situation.

A further return is filed in the same manner as an original return and can either be filed using the Revenue Scotland online portal or by completing a paper return (see **8.9** et seq).

8.18 An amendment to a return is to be made by giving notice to Revenue Scotland, and Revenue Scotland may require that the notice is in a particular form and specify the information the notice is to contain (RSTPA 2014, ss 83(1) and 251). An online return can be within the 'All returns' selection from the 'Dashboard' page, and then selecting the 'Amend' option below the relevant return. This should then take you into the LBTT return where amendments can be made to that return. Once the amendments have been made the amended return can be filed electronically. If the 12-month time limit (see below) for making an amended return has already elapsed, it will not be possible to select the 'Amend' option. Any additional LBTT payable should also be paid in the normal way (see **8.25**) at the time of submission of the amended return. Any interest on overdue tax will be calculated and administered separately by Revenue Scotland. If less tax is payable Revenue Scotland should repay the amount overpaid together with interest on overpaid tax if appropriate.

It is possible to amend all details on the LBTT return apart from the 'About the Return' section. If, unusually, that field does have to be amended then a new LBTT return must be made and Revenue Scotland must be contacted. Agents can no longer void a return. They can request a return be disregarded. A request for a return to be disregarded can be made where: (1) the transaction was non-notifiable and a return was made in error; or (2) a duplicate return was submitted in error. All requests for returns to be disregarded must be made in writing and accompanied by the relevant documents/evidence.

8.19 If the original was a paper return, or the online return can no longer be accessed, it can be amended by writing to Revenue Scotland (see the addresses in Appendix A) setting out for each field to be amended, the current entry and the revised entry. The return reference number should be quoted in the letter requesting the amendment. If additional tax is payable a cheque for the amount underpaid should also be sent to Revenue Scotland.

The amendment (whether made online or by letter) must be made before the end of the 12 month period commencing with the 'relevant date' (RSTPA 2014, s 83(2)). The 'relevant date' is the 'filing date' (RSTPA 2014, s 83(3)) and the 'filing date' is the date by which the return which is being amended was due to be filed (RSTPA 2014, s 82).

Correction of errors in returns

8.20 Revenue Scotland may also unilaterally correct minor errors and omissions, in which case notice must be given to the person(s) who submitted the return (RSTPA 2014, s 84). The example given in the legislation of a 'minor error' is an arithmetical mistake or an error of principle (RSTPA 2014, s 84(3)). However, the correction to the land transaction return must be made within 12 months from the date the return was made (RSTPA 2014, s 84(4)). The person(s) to whom notice is given may reject the amendment (RSTPA 2014, s 84(5) and (6)):

- by re-amending the return within the permitted 12-month period from the filing date (see **8.17**); or
- after the end of that 12-month period, by giving notice that the amendment is rejected within three months of the date of issue of Revenue Scotland's notice.

If the error is such that it prevents online processing it may be rejected and will require re-submission after correction by the taxpayer. A major point in favour of online submission is that many errors are highlighted and must be corrected before the return is accepted.

SPECIAL CASES

Linked transactions

8.21 Generally, separate transactions will require separate returns, and it is understood that it is acceptable to report the acquisition of separate properties on separate returns, even if they are acquired under a single transaction or arrangement. Where two or more linked transactions (see **2.79**) have the same effective date (see **2.81**), LBTT(S)A 2013, s 57(2) provides that the buyer(s) may opt to make a single land transaction return as if all of the transactions formed a single notifiable transaction. If there are two or more buyers who will be jointly entitled to the land interest acquired, they must make the return jointly, which means that they have joint and several liability for payment of the LBTT and any interest and penalties which may arise from late submission/payment or errors (LBTT(S)A 2013, s 48).

Multiple properties

8.22 Where linked (see **2.79**) acquisitions are reported on one land transaction return, which is to be filed in paper format, the main (or first) property should be entered on the return itself and all other properties included in an 'Additional Details' form (see **8.9**).

When to notify

8.23 In general, the deadline for submission of a land transaction return in relation to a notifiable transaction is 30 days from the effective date (see **2.81**) of the transaction (LBTT(S)A 2013, s 29(3)). If an amended or further return is required as a result of an action or event (see **8.13** at **(2)**–**(9)**) occurring after the effective date, the return is due within 30 days of that event.

Penalties for late submission

8.24 A land transaction return will be late if it is not filed within 30 days of the effective date (see **2.81**) of the transaction or, if it is an action or event which triggers the filing requirement, within 30 days of the date of that action or event.

(1) If a return is submitted up to three months late, a penalty of £100 is chargeable (RSTPA 2014, s 160), irrespective of whether LBTT is chargeable or whether the LBTT is paid on time.

(2) If the return is more than three months late, and Revenue Scotland decides that a daily penalty should be payable, and gives notice to the buyer specifying the date from which the penalty is payable, then a penalty of £10 per day is charged for the period of 90 days beginning with the date specified in the notice given by Revenue Scotland. The date specified in the notice can be earlier than the date of the notice itself but cannot be earlier than the date which is three months after the date by which the return should have been filed. The maximum penalty payable under this provision is therefore £900 (RSTPA 2014, s 161).

(3) If the failure continues beyond six months from the day after the filing date then the penalty is the greater of: (a) 5% of any LBTT which would have been shown in the land transaction return, and (b) £300 (RSTPA 2014, s 162).

(4) Finally, if the failure continues beyond 12 months the penalty is the greater of: (a) 5% of any LBTT which would have been shown in the land transaction return, and (b) £300 (RSTPA 2014, s 163(3)). However, where the failure to file the land transaction return has continued beyond 12 months from the filing date, and the buyer deliberately withholds information which would allow Revenue Scotland to assess the buyer's liability to LBTT, the penalty is increased to the greater of: (a) 100% of any LBTT which would have been shown in the land transaction return, and (b) £300 (RSTPA 2014, s 163(2)).

The penalties detailed above are cumulative, meaning that the buyer can be liable for each of the penalties described in (1)–(4) above, in relation to the same return, if the failure continues beyond 12 months (RSTPA 2014, s 159(2)). This means, assuming that the buyer has not deliberately withheld information from Revenue Scotland, a failure to file a land transaction return for more than 12 months from the filing date could incur a penalty as follows:

	Fixed penalty	*Tax geared penalty*
Penalty for not filing LTR within 30 days of the effective date (see 2.81) of the transaction	£100	-
Maximum daily penalty if the land transaction return has not been filed within 3 months of the filing date (ie 30 days after the effective date)	£900	-
If the failure continues beyond 6 months	£300 or if greater	5%
If the failure continues beyond 12 months	£300 or if greater	5%

The maximum penalty payable per late return (ie filed more than 12 months after the filing date) would therefore be £1,000 plus 10% of the LBTT payable, unless the total LBTT liability was £6,000 or less, in which case the maximum penalty would be fixed at £1,600.

Item 1 in the table in RSTPA 2014, s 159(1) details all of the returns in relation to which a late filing penalty can be charged and these are as follows:

(1) Return made in relation to a chargeable transaction which is notifiable – LBTT(S)A 2013, s 29(1).

(2) Return where contingency to which consideration is subject ceases or consideration ascertained – LBTT(S)A 2013, s 31(1).

(3) Further return where a relief is withdrawn – LBTT(S)A 2013, s 33(1).

(4) Return or further return as a consequence of a later linked transaction – LBTT(S)A 2013, s 34.

(5) Return following three-yearly review of the LBTT chargeable on a lease – LBTT(S)A 2013, Sch 19, para 10.

(6) Return following review on assignation or termination of a lease – LBTT(S)A 2013, Sch 19, para 11.

(7) Return following deemed extension of a lease which continues beyond its fixed term – LBTT(S)A 2013, Sch 19, para 20(3).

(8) Return following deemed extension of a lease for an indefinite term – LBTT(S)A 2013, Sch 19, para 22(2).

(9) Return where a lease is varied to increase the rent payable or extend the term of the lease – LBTT(S)A 2013, Sch 19, para 30(2).

It should be noted that the aggregate tax geared penalty can never exceed 100% of the buyer's liability to LBTT in relation to the transaction(s) for which no return(s) has been made (RSTPA 2014, s 159(3)).

However, as indicated above if, by failing to make the return the buyer deliberately withholds information which would enable Revenue Scotland to assess the buyer's liability to LBTT, and the LBTT liability exceeds £300, then the penalty would be 100% of the LBTT liability.

Revenue Scotland may reduce the amount of the penalty for failure to file an LTR by the filing date if the buyer discloses information which would otherwise have been included in the return. The amount of the reduction may be impacted by whether the disclosure is prompted or unprompted, and the quality of the disclosure made (RSTPA 2014, s 175).

PAYMENT OF LBTT

Payment methods

8.25 Payment of LBTT must be made at the same time that the land transaction return is filed, and LBTT payable as a consequence of an amendment to a return must be paid at the same time that the amendment is made (LBTT(S)

A 2013, s 40(2) and (3)). For the purposes of LBTT, tax is treated as having been paid provided 'arrangements satisfactory' to Revenue Scotland are made for payment of the tax (LBTT(S)A 2013, s 40(4)). The obligation to make payment is subject to any application to defer the payment of LBTT (see **8.26** et seq) in relation to contingent or uncertain consideration (LBTT(S)A 2013, s 40(5)).

The arrangements satisfactory to Revenue Scotland for the payment of LBTT are direct debit (if the agent is registered), BACS, CHAPS or Faster Payment. When the electronic return passes validation a unique nine-character transaction reference will be allocated which should ensure the payment is matched to the correct return. Instructions will be given by Revenue Scotland if a paper return is being completed. Cheque payments are no longer accepted by Revenue Scotland.

Where payment is made by BACS, CHAPS or Faster Payment, the latest payment date must be shown on the return. If the return is submitted before the effective date (see **2.81**) the latest payment date should be the fifth day after the effective date of the transaction. If the return is submitted on or after the effective date of the transaction the latest payment date, must be the earlier of: (a) the fifth working day after the date on which the return is filed, and (b) the last working day which is, or precedes, the thirtieth calendar day after the effective date of the transaction. A separate payment must be made for each transaction and the latest payment date must be a banking day. BACS/CHAPS payments and Faster Payments should be made to the Revenue Scotland bank account shown below and must quote the unique nine character transaction reference as the payment reference:

Account Name:	Revenue Scotland
Sort Code:	60-70-80
Account Number:	10019456
IBAN:	GB93NWBK60708010019456
SWIFT:	NWBKGB2L
Bank:	National Westminster
Address:	London Corporate Service Centre, CPB Services, 2nd Floor, 280 Bishopsgate, London EC2M 4RB

Registration payments to Registers of Scotland must be paid separately.

If the LTR is submitted close to the filing date, full payment should reach Revenue Scotland by no later than the filing date for the return otherwise interest on overdue tax will be payable (see **8.36**).

Revenue Scotland offers agents the option of paying LBTT by their Direct Debit Scheme. If an agent wishes to pay LBTT by direct debit they should complete a 'Direct Debit instruction form' and send it to Revenue Scotland at the address detailed in Appendix A. The 'Direct Debit consent form' can be found on the Revenue Scotland website.

Each successful tax return submitted online, and each paper return, will be given or will have a unique reference number and this must be quoted when LBTT is paid to enable the payment to be linked to the correct land transaction return. In relation to paper returns, the Revenue Scotland will use the unique reference number to process the cheque sent with the return.

Due date and deferment

8.26

> **Focus**
>
> - It is possible to apply to defer payment of LBTT on chargeable consideration (but not rent) which is either contingent or uncertain and any part of that consideration falls to be paid, or may fall to be paid, more than six months after the effective date (see **2.81**) of the transaction.

LBTT is generally due 30 days from the effective date (see **2.81**) of the transaction – usually the earlier of substantial performance (see **2.7**) of the agreement (assuming the agreement is to be completed by a 'conveyance') and legal completion of a transfer or execution of a lease (see **2.8**). There is no automatic right to defer payment where there are delays in paying consideration, occupying the property or determining the amount of consideration. If, for any reason, the amount of the consideration has not been finally determined when payment of LBTT falls due, payment must be based on a reasonable estimate (see **2.18**). Further LBTT may then be due once the consideration is finally determined, and this must generally be paid within 30 days of that final determination. However, interest will be chargeable on this additional LBTT from the original due date of the main payment, unless deferment has been granted in respect of the additional tax.

8.27 If, at the effective date (see **2.81**) of a transaction:

- the LBTT cannot be finally determined because any amount of consideration is uncertain or contingent; and
- any part of that consideration falls to be paid on one or more future date(s) which fall, or may fall, more than six months after the effective date of the transaction,

the taxpayer may apply to defer payment of LBTT on the consideration which falls to be paid later (LBTT(S)A 2013, s 41(1)). It is not, however, possible to defer payment on any element of the consideration which is not contingent and whose amount is certain or ascertainable at the date the application is made, or on consideration which has already been paid or provided by the date the application is made (LBTT(S)A 2013, s 41(3)). Deferment is only possible if uncertainty about the consideration arises from future events – if the amount of the consideration depends on accounts drawn up to the effective date (see **2.81**) but the consideration is not known at that date because the accounts have not yet been drawn up, it is not dependent on future events and deferment is not possible on these grounds. Deferment is not possible in respect of any LBTT which arises on rent under a lease unless the Scottish Ministers provide to the contrary by order (LBTT(S)A 2013, s41(5)), which they have not currently done, but deferment may be possible in respect of LBTT on a lease premium.

8.28 If deferment is granted by Revenue Scotland, the notification of that fact will set out details of when further payments of LBTT must be made. If the specified payments of LBTT are made by the specified dates, interest will not be charged. If payments are late, interest will be charged only from the specified dates on which they should have been made, as notified to the taxpayer. The fact that deferment can be interest-free is the principal reason for going to the trouble of making an application.

Example 8.5 – Deferment

On 1 January 2024, Pamela agrees to buy a block of flats from Alan for £10 million payable now and up to a further £5 million payable on 1 January 2025. The amount payable on 1 January 2025 will be determined in accordance with a formula where the only variable is the net rents received in the year to 30 June 2024. The agreement is completed without prior substantial performance on 31 March 2024. Alan must pay LBTT on the £10 million consideration no later than 30 April 2024. He may apply to defer payment on the additional consideration because: (a) that consideration falls to be paid more than six months after the effective date of the transaction,; and (b) the amount cannot be determined at the effective date (or later date of application) since it depends on rent receipts for a period ending after that date ie the year to 30 June 2024. However, if the contingent amount had depended on the net rents for the year to 31 March 2024, deferment would not have been possible. Although, at the effective date, that amount might not have been finally worked out, it would in principle be possible to know the amount at that date, so the amount is not 'uncertain' as defined by LBTT(S)A, s 19(3).

Applying for deferment

8.29 An application for deferment must be made no later than the due date for submission of the original return, ie 30 days after the effective date (LBTT(S) A 2013, s 41 and The Land and Buildings Transaction Tax (Administration) (Scotland) Regulations 2014, SI 2014/375, reg 4). It will not be accepted if it is made after that date. It is likely that this deadline will be rigidly enforced, and that Revenue Scotland will encourage early submission of applications, even before the transaction is finalised if possible. Application is made by completing the Deferral Application Form, available at LBTT4016. LBTT4016 of the LBTT legislation guidance requires the following information to be included in the application:

- the transaction reference number (if a return has been submitted);
- the effective date of the transaction;
- the identity of the buyer;
- the buyer's correspondence address;
- the location of the land involved;
- the certain chargeable consideration;
- the amount of consideration for which deferment is sought;
- a reasoned opinion as when this part of the consideration will cease to be contingent or can be ascertained;
- the total chargeable consideration;
- a calculation of the amount of LBTT due on the total chargeable consideration;
- a calculation of the LBTT payable in respect of which the application to defer payment refers. (Please see the example below for guidance on calculating deferred tax);
- the nature of the contingency/uncertain payment(s); and
- as much detail of the times of expected payments as it is possible to give.

8.30 Revenue Scotland are entitled to ask for further information, and are likely to do so if the transaction is unusual or if avoidance is suspected (Land and Buildings Transaction Tax (Administration) (Scotland) Regulations 2014, SI 2014/375, reg 6). If deferment is denied, it is possible to appeal the decision (RSTPA 2014, ss 233(1)(f) and 241(1) – see **8.89** et seq), but in practice this will be worthwhile only where very large sums of LBTT are at stake. Where Revenue Scotland have not yet considered the application or deferment is denied, the tax remains due and payable as if there had been no deferment application (or appeal if relevant), however payment of the tax for which deferment has been applied is postponed until a decision is reached on the application (Land and Buildings Transaction Tax (Administration) Regulations 2014, SI 2014/375, reg 7(2) and (3)). If a deferment application is refused by Revenue Scotland, and there is no appeal under RSTPA 2014, s 241(1), the tax for which deferment was sought is due and payable 30 days after the date on which Revenue Scotland issued the notice of the refusal of the application to the taxpayer (Land and Buildings Transaction Tax (Administration) Regulations 2014, SI 2014/375, reg 7(4).

8.31 An application may be refused by Revenue Scotland if (see the Land and Buildings Transaction Tax (Administration) (Scotland) Regulations 2014, SI 2014/375, reg 9):

- the conditions for making an application specified in LBTT(S)A 2013, s 41(1) are not met, namely that at the effective date (see **2.81**) of the transaction all or part of the chargeable consideration is contingent or uncertain and that chargeable consideration falls, or may fall, to be paid on a date more than six months after the effective date of the transaction;

- the application is not in the form specified by Revenue Scotland under LBTT(S)A 2013, s 41(2)(a) or it does not contain the information required by Revenue Scotland under LBTT(S)A 2013, s 41(2)(b);
- the transaction includes 'artificial tax avoidance arrangements' (as defined in RSTPA 2014, ss 63 and 64 – see **9.3**);
- the application, or information provided in connection with it, is incorrect; or
- any further information requested by Revenue Scotland in relation to the application is not provided within the time Revenue Scotland has 'reasonably' required in its notification to the taxpayer requesting such further information.

8.32 Revenue Scotland must notify the buyer in writing as to whether the application has been accepted or refused (Land and Buildings Transaction Tax (Administration) (Scotland) Regulations 2014, SI 2014/375, reg 8(1)). If the application is accepted the notice must specify (Land and Buildings Transaction Tax (Administration) (Scotland) Regulations 2014, SI 2014/375, reg 8(2)).

- any LBTT payable in accordance with a land transaction return notifying the transaction in relation to which the deferment application was made;
- the nature of any events on the occurrence of which the whole or any part of the consideration to which the deferment application relates will cease to be contingent or become certain (referred to in reg 8 as 'relevant events');
- the dates (if known) on which any 'relevant events' are expected to occur; and
- confirm that LBTT is payable 30 days after the occurrence of a relevant event.

Alternatively, if Revenue Scotland refuse the deferment application the notice must specify (Land and Buildings Transaction Tax (Administration) (Scotland) Regulations 2014, SI 2014/375, reg 8(3)):

- the reasons why the application has been refused; and
- the total amount of LBTT payable as a consequence of the refusal.

8.33 If a deferment application is accepted by Revenue Scotland, and any tax for which deferment is sought has already been paid, such tax will be repaid, together with interest, from the date of payment (Land and Buildings Transaction Tax (Administration) (Scotland) Regulations 2014, SI 2014/375, reg 11(2)). The buyer must file an LTR, or further LTR, within 30 days of the date on which the whole or any part of the consideration to which a deferment relates ceases to be contingent or becomes certain (ie 30 days after the occurrence of a 'relevant event'). Where the contingent or uncertain consideration to which the deferment application applies includes the value of works of construction, improvement or repair of a building etc or the provision of other services (other than the carrying out of such works) the LTR, or further LTR, must be filed: (a) within 30 days after the carrying out of the works or provision of the services is substantially complete; or (b) in accordance with the agreed scheme of payment of tax at intervals of not more than six months (where the carrying out of the works or provision of the services is expected to last for more than six months); or (c) after the final payment has been made under the scheme of payments, within 30 days after the buyer obtains new information the effect of which is that more or less tax is payable than has already been paid (Land and Buildings Transaction Tax (Administration) (Scotland) Regulations 2014, SI 2014/375, reg 11(3)). The tax or additional tax payable as a consequence of filing the LTR must be paid at the time of filing the LTR (Land and Buildings Transaction Tax (Administration) (Scotland) Regulations 2014, SI 2014/375, reg 11(4)). If the effect of the LTR, or further LTR, is that less tax is payable, then the tax overpaid must be repaid with interest from the date of payment of the tax (Land and Buildings Transaction Tax (Administration) (Scotland) Regulations 2014, SI 2014/375, reg 11(5)).

8.34 Where tax has already been paid under LBTT(S)A 2013, s 41(3) – see **8.27** (ie tax paid in relation to chargeable consideration that has already been paid or provided at the time the deferment application is made or tax paid in relation to chargeable consideration which is not contingent and whose amount is ascertainable at the time the deferment application is made) and a deferment application is accepted in respect of other chargeable consideration which has been taken into account in that payment of tax, the provisions of LBTT(S) A 2013, s 31 (Return where contingency ceases or consideration ascertained) and s 32 (Contingency ceases or consideration ascertained: less tax payable) apply – see **2.18** (Land and Buildings Transaction Tax (Administration) (Scotland) Regulations 2014, SI 2014/375, reg 12).

8.35 If a deferment application which Revenue Scotland have accepted contained false or misleading information, or the application failed to disclose any relevant facts or circumstances, the application will have no effect, and the tax will remain due and payable from the original due date. In addition, the acceptance of a deferment application shall cease to have any effect if the facts and circumstances relevant to it materially change (Land and Buildings Transaction Tax (Administration) (Scotland) Regulations 2014, SI 2014/375, reg 13).

Interest on LBTT

8.36

> **Focus**
>
> - LBTT is paid late if it is paid after the 'relevant date' (see below) and interest on overdue tax will then be payable.

Interest on overdue tax and on any late paid penalty

As with other taxes, interest is charged on LBTT which is paid late (RSTPA 2014, s 217(1)), at the rates set by regulation under RSTPA 2014, s 220(1). The Revenue Scotland and Tax Powers Act (Interest on Unpaid Tax and Interest Rates in General) Regulations 2015, SSI 2015/128 provides that the rate of interest on late paid tax should be the Bank of England base rate plus 2.5%. Any change of Bank of England base rate applies from the fourth working day following the date of the meeting at which the change of interest rate was announced (Revenue Scotland and Tax Powers Act (Interest on Unpaid Tax and Interest Rates in General) Regulations 2015, SSI 2015/128 regs 5 and 6). On 3 August 2023, the Bank of England announced an increase in its base rate from 5% per annum to 5.25% per annum. This means that the interest rate on late paid LBTT was 7.5% per annum until 8 August 2023, and from 9 August 2023 it rose to 7.75% per annum. This remains the case at the date of publication.

In most cases, tax is paid late if it is paid after the 'relevant date' (RSTPA 2014, s 217(1)). The relevant date in various situations is as follows (Revenue Scotland and Tax Powers Act (Interest on Unpaid Tax and Interest Rates in General) Regulations 2015, SSI 2015/128, reg 4):

(1) where a relief is withdrawn as a result of a later event (eg group relief withdrawn because the buyer leaves the group within three years), 30 days after the date of the event giving rise to the withdrawal (see for example **5.16** and **5.20**). The reliefs are (a) the reliefs for certain acquisitions of residential property, (b) multiple dwellings relief, (c) relief for alternative finance investment bonds, (d) group relief, (e) sub-sale development relief, (f) reconstruction relief, (g) acquisition relief and (h) charities relief;

(2) where deferment has been granted as set out at **8.29**, the date on which the deferred LBTT payment is due;

(3) where in the case of contingent consideration, the contingency ceases or it becomes clear that it will not occur, or unascertainable consideration becomes ascertained, 30 days after the date on which either of these events occurs (see **2.18**). (Note: This is what is stated in the regulation however there does not seem to be any logic to this provision as it would mean that there would be little incentive to make a deferment application if interest does not run until 30 days after the contingent or uncertain consideration is determined.);

(4) in a case where payment of the tax is not deferred under LBTT(S) A 2013, s 41, the date by which the land transaction return in relation to the transaction had to be filed;

(5) for any other return under LBTT(S)A 2013, the date by which the return had to be filed;

(6) an adjustment under RSTPA 2014, s 66 to counteract a tax advantage arising from a tax avoidance arrangement that is artificial, the filing date for the return or, if there is no return, the filing date of the return that

would have been required to have been made, had the tax avoidance arrangement not been carried out;

(7) an amount, or additional amount of LBTT payable following an amendment of a return by the buyer under RSTPA 2014, s 83 (see **8.17**), the date by which the original return had to be filed;

(8) an amount, or additional amount of LBTT payable following a correction of a return by Revenue Scotland under RSTPA 2014, s 84, the date by which the original return had to be filed;

(9) an amount, or additional amount, payable following an amendment of a return during an enquiry by Revenue Scotland under RSTPA 2014, s 87, the date by which the original return had to be filed;

(10) an amount, or additional amount, payable following the issue of a Revenue Scotland assessment, on completion of an enquiry, under RSTPA 2014, s 93, the date by which the original return had to be filed;

(11) an amount, or additional amount, payable as a result of a determination made by Revenue Scotland under RSTPA 2014, s 95, where no return has been made, the date by which Revenue Scotland believes the return should have been made;

(12) an amount, or additional amount, payable following the issue of a Revenue Scotland assessment under RSTPA 2014, s 98 (discovery assessment – see **8.46** et seq), the date by which the return had to be filed or, if there is no return the date by which the return, should have been filed.

If a penalty is payable in relation to LBTT under the provisions of RSTPA 2014, Part 8 (see **8.55**), and it is not paid by the due date, interest is payable on the amount of the penalty, from the date the penalty was due to be paid to the date of payment (RSTPA 2014, s 218(1)).

Interest to be paid by Revenue Scotland on overpaid tax, or on a penalty or interest which is to be repaid

When LBTT is repaid (or a penalty or interest on overdue tax, or interest on a late paid penalty, is repaid), interest is payable by Revenue Scotland (RSTPA 2014, s 219(1)) at rates set by regulation under RSTPA 2014, s 220(1). The Revenue Scotland and Tax Powers Act (Interest on Unpaid Tax and Interest Rates in General) Regulations 2015, SSI 2015/128, regs 5 and 7 provides that the interest rate on repayments of tax, penalties or interest on overdue tax will be the greater of: (a) 0.5% per annum; and (b) the Bank of England base rate. Any change of Bank of England base rate applies from the fourth working day following the date of the meeting at which the change of interest was announced. The interest is payable for the period from receipt of the tax (or receipt of the penalty or the interest on overdue tax or the interest on a late paid penalty) by Revenue Scotland to the date of repayment. On 3 August 2023, the Bank of England announced an increase in its base rate from 5% per annum to 5.25% per annum. As the interest rate on repayments of tax is the greater of: (a) 0.5% per annum; and (b) the Bank of England base rate, the increase in the base rate caused the interest rate on overpaid LBTT to rise, from 5% to 5.25%. This remains the case at the date of publication.

Example 8.6 – Relevant date by which tax must be paid and the date from which interest on overdue tax begins to run

On 1 May 2024, Mark acquires a commercial property for an initial payment of £2,500,000, but the amount is to be finally determined by reference to performance of the business carried out in the property during the year to 30 June 2024. Any additional amount payable for the property is due to be determined, and paid, by 31 December 2024. On 31 May 2024, Mark pays LBTT on the basis of the purchase price of £2,500,000, and applies to defer the LBTT on any additional amount payable for the property. The deferment application is accepted by Revenue Scotland. On 31 December 2024 the purchase price is finally determined to be £2,725,000, and the additional amount of consideration of £225,000 is paid on that date. The LBTT liability is recomputed, and the additional LBTT is due 30 days after the date on which the purchase price is finally determined ie by 30 January 2025 (LBTT(S)A 2013, s 31(3)). Interest will therefore only be payable if the additional LBTT is not paid by 30 January 2025, being 30 days after the date upon which the consideration was ascertained.

Collection and enforcement

8.37 LBTT is due and payable, whether under a self-assessment (that is, as a result of submission of a land transaction return by the buyer), or under a determination or assessment issued by Revenue Scotland, unless deferment has been granted as outlined at **8.29** et seq or postponement has been agreed/ granted (see **8.41** and **8.53**). Revenue Scotland are empowered to enforce payment of outstanding LBTT by proceedings in the sheriff court or in the Court of Session (RSTPA 2014, s 224).

REVENUE SCOTLAND ENQUIRIES

8.38

Focus

- Revenue Scotland have three years from the date by which the land transaction return was due to be filed (assuming it was filed on time) to enquire into the land transaction return, and to issue a closure notice in relation to that enquiry.

The process for Revenue Scotland to enquire into an LBTT return is similar to that which applies to SDLT and other UK direct tax returns (RSTPA 2014, s 85). It begins by Revenue Scotland giving a notice of enquiry to the buyer before the end of the period during which it is possible for an enquiry notice to be given (see below); it ends when Revenue Scotland gives a 'closure notice' (RSTPA 2014, ss 93 and 94). The closure notice may be given because Revenue Scotland are satisfied that their enquiry is complete (RSTPA 2014, s 93) or because the Tax Tribunal gives a direction to that effect on application by the buyer (RSTPA 2014, s 94). The period in which the notice of the intention to make an enquiry must be given by Revenue Scotland is three years from (RSTPA 2014, s 85(3)):

- the filing date (which is itself 30 days after the effective date (see **2.81**) of the transaction), if the return was filed on time; or
- the actual date of filing if the return was late.

The closure notice must be issued not later than three years after the date by which the LTR had to be filed or, if the return was filed late, three years after the date upon which the LTR was filed (RSTPA 2014, s 93(2) and (7)). This means that Revenue Scotland have a three year period during which they must both launch any enquiry into an LTR and issue a closure notice.

This is a much longer period in which to launch an enquiry than for SDLT in relation to which the enquiry period is nine months from the date by which the LTR must be filed, and will therefore lead to greater uncertainty for taxpayers under LBTT compared to SDLT.

8.39 The enquiry can cover anything contained in the LTR, or required to be contained in the LTR, that relates to: (a) whether the buyer is chargeable to LBTT, or (b) the amount of the LBTT chargeable on the buyer. However, if the notice of enquiry is given as a result of an amendment to the return by the buyer (see **8.17**), and an enquiry into the original return has already been completed, the enquiry is limited to matters to which the amendment relates or to matters that are affected by the amendment (RSTPA 2014, s 86(2) and (3)). In contrast, if no enquiry has been made into the original return then an enquiry into the amended return can extend to all matters included in that return, and not only those relating to or affected by the amendment. Outside the time limits referred to in **8.38**, Revenue Scotland may only pursue a potential underpayment of tax by making a 'discovery assessment' (see **8.46**).

Example 8.7 – Time limits for enquiry into return

On 1 March 2024 (effective date (see **2.81**) and date of completion (see **2.8**)), A Ltd buys a business from B Ltd, an unrelated company. Payment takes the form of A Ltd accepting responsibility for debts of the business amounting to £2 million plus an issue of shares in A Ltd to B Ltd with a market value of £1 million. The business includes a commercial property provisionally valued at £1.5 million. On 20 March 2024, A Ltd submits an LTR on the basis of this valuation, claiming relief under LBTT(S)A 2013, Sch 11, para 6 (Acquisition relief; see **5.14**). The LBTT chargeable on A Ltd is therefore 12.5% of the LBTT which would have been chargeable had acquisition relief not been available

(LBTT(S)A 2013, Sch 11, para 6(2)). On 31 January 2025, A Ltd gives notice to amend the return, decreasing the value attributed to the property to £1.2 million. On 15 January 2026, Revenue Scotland give notice of enquiry into the return. The enquiry period for the original return ends on 31 March 2027 (three years after the filing date), and for the amended return on 31 January 2028, and therefore Revenue Scotland are within the time limit to enquire into the return. As no earlier enquiry had been opened and completed in relation to the original return the enquiry can cover matters included in both the original and the amended return. In this case, it is considered that the enquiry may relate to both the valuation of the property and the availability of acquisition relief. Revenue Scotland must issue a closure notice by 31 January 2028 (three years after the date upon which the amended return was filed).

8.40 As part of an enquiry into an LTR, Revenue Scotland may ask to see documents and information from the buyer, but only where such documents are reasonably required to check the buyer's tax position (ie any LBTT liability he may have to pay etc – see RSTPA 2014, s 120) and it is reasonable for the buyer to be required to provide the information or to produce the document (RSTPA 2014, s 123). In the legislation the demand from Revenue Scotland is referred to as a 'taxpayer notice' (RSTPA 2014, s 123(3)). The buyer may appeal against such a demand (RSTPA 2014, s 233(1)(h)) – see **8.89**). If no appeal is lodged, or after any appeal is settled, initial (£300) and daily penalties (£60 per day for each subsequent day on which the failure continues) may be imposed for failure to produce the outstanding documents and information (RSTPA 2014, ss 195 and 196). In addition to a general right to demand documents and information from the buyer, Revenue Scotland have powers to seek information and documents from third parties, including tax accountants and other advisers (RSTPA 2014, s 124). Exercise of these powers in relation to third parties is subject to the agreement of the buyer or the approval of the Tax Tribunal (RSTPA 2014, s 125). Situations in which these powers may be invoked are beyond the scope of this book. The relevant parties will normally require specialist advice in these cases.

8.41 While an enquiry is in progress, Revenue Scotland may amend the return if they conclude that additional tax is due and amendment is necessary to prevent a loss of tax (RSTPA 2014, s 87(1)). Written notice of the amendment must be given to the buyer. This power is only likely to be used where a *prima facie* underpayment has been established, but the buyer refuses to make an appropriate payment on account, suggesting there may be a risk of eventual default. The buyer may appeal to the Tax Tribunal against the amendment, but only when the enquiry into the return has been completed and may apply to have collection of any additional tax postponed (RSTPA 2014, ss 233(1)(d) and 241(1) and (3)). The buyer must give notice of the appeal to the tribunal within 30 days of the date upon which the buyer was given notice that the enquiry was completed (RSTPA 2014, s 242(2)(a)). Postponement of the payment of the additional LBTT payable as a consequence of the amendment may be agreed by Revenue Scotland, but only where Revenue Scotland is satisfied that there are exceptional circumstances which justify postponement or the question may be determined by the tribunal if the taxpayer and Revenue Scotland cannot reach agreement (RSTPA 2014, s 245 and the Revenue Scotland and Tax Powers Act (Postponement of Tax Pending a Review or Appeal) Regulations 2015, SSI 2015/129, reg 3).

8.42 During the course of an enquiry by Revenue Scotland the buyer may also amend the return, if the normal period allowed for amendment has not yet expired (RSTPA 2014, s 83 – see **8.17**). Voluntary amendment to correct any errors which have come to light may be taken into account in determining any penalty position (see **8.55** et seq).

8.43 Revenue Scotland and the buyer may agree to refer matters to the Tax Tribunal during an enquiry, and more than one notice of referral to the Tribunal may be given in the course of an enquiry (RSTPA 2014, s 88). Subject to the normal rights of appeal through the courts, the decision of the Tribunal is binding on all parties (RSTPA 2014, s 91).

8.44 Normally, enquiries will be closed by Revenue Scotland giving a notice of closure once they are satisfied that the enquiry is complete (RSTPA 2014, s 93). The notice must state the conclusions reached following the enquiry and set out whether in the designated officer's opinion no amendment is required to be made to the LTR, or make the amendments to the return based on the officer's conclusions (RSTPA 2014, s 93(3)). A closure notice must however be given no later than three years after the date by which the LTR had to be filed or, if the return was filed late, three years after the date upon which the LTR was filed (RSTPA 2014, s 93(2)). If no closure notice has been given within that three year period, the enquiry is treated as being completed (RSTPA 2014, s 93(1)(b)). This means that Revenue Scotland have a three year period during which they must both launch any enquiry into an LTR and issue a closure notice. The buyer may appeal to the Tax Tribunal against a closure notice (RSTPA 2014, ss 233 (1) and 241(1)). Alternatively, the buyer may apply to the Tax Tribunal for a direction that the enquiry be closed (RSTPA 2014, s 94)).

FAILURE TO DELIVER A RETURN – REVENUE SCOTLAND DETERMINATIONS

8.45

Focus

- If the buyer does not deliver a land transaction return by the due date or Revenue Scotland believe that a return should have been made, Revenue Scotland can make a determination which is then treated as though it were a land transaction return filed by the buyer.

If a buyer fails to deliver a return by the filing date (RSTPA 2014, s 82), or if Revenue Scotland believe that a return should have been delivered, Revenue Scotland may make a determination of the LBTT which they believe to be unpaid. This is then treated as a self-assessment (that is, as if a land transaction return had been submitted) for the purposes of enforcement, including the right of Revenue Scotland to demand the tax due from the buyer and to recover the tax from the buyer by proceedings in the sheriff court or the Court of Session or by obtaining a summary warrant from a sheriff. It also includes the right to recover any unpaid penalty or interest etc. (RSTPA 2014, ss 95 and 96). The determination must be given to the buyer and must state the date upon which it is issued (RSTPA 2014, s 95(4)). A determination may not be made more than five years after the date by which Revenue Scotland believes the land transaction return should have been filed. (RSTPA 2014, s 95(5)). If the buyer subsequently makes a self-assessment by delivering a return, provided this occurs by whichever is the later of: (a) five years after the date by which the land transaction return should have been filed; and (b) three months after the date of the Revenue Scotland determination, the self-assessment displaces the determination (RSTPA 2014, s 97). This, of course, then allows Revenue Scotland to launch an enquiry into the return. As an alternative, the buyer may appeal to the Tax Tribunal against the determination (RSTPA 2014, ss 233(1), 241 and 242).

DISCOVERY ASSESSMENT

8.46

> **Focus**
>
> - In circumstances where the three year period which Revenue Scotland have to raise an enquiry into a land transaction return has expired, Revenue Scotland may still be entitled to raise an assessment (a 'discovery assessment') to recover LBTT, if the under-assessment is brought about carelessly or deliberately by the buyer.

If a land transaction return has been made (or is deemed to have been made by virtue of a Revenue Scotland determination – see **8.45**) and the period in which an enquiry can be started (see **8.38**) has not yet ended, any possible loss of tax will normally be investigated by launching an enquiry. Once an enquiry has commenced, if Revenue Scotland are concerned that recovery of additional tax is at risk, they may amend the return as described at **8.41**, thereby allowing action to be taken to collect the tax. Once the period in which an enquiry can be launched has ended, or an enquiry has been completed, Revenue Scotland has no automatic right to reopen matters and seek further tax.

8.47 However, if Revenue Scotland (a designated officer) comes to the view honestly and reasonably that LBTT which ought to have been assessed has not been assessed, or an assessment to LBTT has become insufficient or a relief has been claimed that has become excessive, the designated officer may assess any tax which has been discovered to have been underpaid (RSTPA 2014, ss 98 to 105). However a 'discovery' assessment may only be made to recover tax lost as a result of an under-assessment to tax brought about carelessly or deliberately by the buyer, a person acting on behalf of the buyer, or a person who was a partner of the buyer (RSTPA 2014, s 102(1)). In addition, no assessment may be made if the under-assessment to tax is caused by a mistake in the return as to the basis on which the LBTT liability ought to have been calculated, and the basis used was in accordance with the practice generally prevailing at the time the return was made (RSTPA 2014, s 102(2)).

An under-assessment to LBTT is brought about carelessly by a person if the person fails to take reasonable care to avoid bringing about that under-assessment (RSTPA 2014, s 104(2)). In this context 'carelessness' can be likened to the concept of 'negligence'. In the case of *Blythe v Birmingham Waterworks Co* (1856) Baron Alderson said 'Negligence is the omission to do something which a reasonable man, guided upon those considerations which ordinarily regulate the conduct of human affairs, would do, or doing something which a prudent and reasonable man would not do. The defendants might be liable for negligence if, unintentionally, they omitted to do that which a prudent and reasonable person would have done, or did that which a person taking reasonable care would not have done.' The question is therefore not whether the person concerned knew about the situation which brought about the under-assessment, as that would then be a deliberate understatement of the LBTT liability, it is whether a prudent and reasonable person, taking reasonable care, would have done what the person has done. If they would not, then what has been done is likely to be treated as carelessness.

If a person has supplied information to Revenue Scotland and they discover at a later date that the information was inaccurate, then unless they take reasonable steps to inform Revenue Scotland of the inaccuracy, any loss of tax brought about by the inaccuracy will be treated as having been brought about by that person's carelessness (RSTPA 2014, s 104(3) and (4)).

8.48 In circumstances where the LBTT implications of a particular transaction may be complex, or open to alternative interpretations, and to reduce the possibility of Revenue Scotland subsequently raising an assessment, taxpayers and their agents should consider submitting further information to Revenue Scotland at the time of submission of the LTR.

8.49 An alternative course of action would be to obtain a formal opinion from Revenue Scotland either in advance of the transaction taking place or after it has taken place. Revenue Scotland will only provide a formal opinion where there is uncertainty about the interpretation of recent tax legislation and the uncertainty is not covered in the LBTT legislation guidance.

In addition, Revenue Scotland will not provide an opinion in the following circumstances:

- The transaction is speculative in nature nor will they opine on 'what if' type of queries.
- The buyer has not provided all of the necessary information (see **Appendix C**).
- In Revenue Scotland's view there are no genuine points of uncertainty as to how the LBTT legislation applies to the transaction. In these circumstances they will explain why they have reached that view and direct the buyer to the relevant online guidance.
- Revenue Scotland will not provide tax planning advice or approve tax planning products or arrangements.
- The application relates to transactions which, in the opinion of Revenue Scotland, are for the purposes of avoiding tax.
- The request is about the possible application of the General Anti-avoidance Rule (see **9.3**).
- Revenue Scotland is already enquiring into the buyer's tax position in relation to the transaction in which case the officer dealing with the transaction should be contacted.
- The LBTT return is final and cannot be amended.

The checklist of the information to be provided to Revenue Scotland, when making an application for an opinion, is set out in **Appendix C**. In the request for the opinion a certification must be given that the information provided is, to the best of the applicant's knowledge and belief, complete and correct. The application should be sent to lbtt@revenue.scot.

8.50 Revenue Scotland will usually reply to the application for an opinion within 25 working days and straightforward cases should be dealt with more quickly than that. Where more difficult or complicated issues are involved it may take longer for the opinion to be given. In these circumstances Revenue Scotland should acknowledge the application and advise when the opinion will be issued. Sometimes Revenue Scotland may need more information to enable them to conclude on the matter in which case they will request the additional information and suspend dealing with the application until that information is supplied.

An application for an opinion does not impact the time at which any LBTT payable is due for payment, nor does it affect the date by which the land transaction return must be filed. If the buyer has not received the opinion by the date by which the land transaction return must be filed, the return should be filed by the due date, based on the buyer's view of the application of the legislation to the transaction. It should be possible to amend the return, if appropriate, following receipt of the Revenue Scotland opinion, provided the 12-month time period has not expired.

If the buyer disagrees with the opinion the land transaction return can still be filed based on the buyer's LBTT analysis, however it will be highly likely that the return will be the subject of a Revenue Scotland enquiry. In these circumstances the Revenue Scotland guidance indicates that the buyer should draw the particular entry in the LBTT return to Revenue Scotland's attention or, perhaps more likely, write to them separately and explain what has been done.

Provided that the information supplied to Revenue Scotland is accurate and complete, and the transactions are carried out in accordance with the application, the buyer should be able to rely on the opinion.

There is no general right to appeal against a Revenue Scotland opinion except where there is a specific right set out in the legislation to appeal against an action taken by Revenue Scotland, such as the issuing of an assessment (see **8.89**).

8.51 If further information regarding a land transaction is to be sent to Revenue Scotland, the decision as to what further information to submit requires careful thought. Submission of further information may increase the likelihood of the transaction being selected for enquiry. If the treatment originally adopted in the return is clearly correct, any such enquiry will normally be fruitless, but will incur administrative costs. Alternatively, if there is genuine doubt over the treatment of the transaction, it will be important to ensure that the information submitted is sufficiently comprehensive. If Revenue Scotland cannot see the full facts and circumstances to enable them to make their own judgement of the treatment adopted, a discovery assessment may be issued should further information come to their attention later.

8.52 The general time limit for Revenue Scotland to make a discovery assessment is five years from the date by which the LTR should have been filed, which would normally be 30 days after the effective date (see **2.81**) of the transaction (RSTPA 2014, s 103(1)). However, if the LTR was filed after the date by which it should have been filed, then the time limit by which Revenue Scotland must raise a discovery assessment is five years from the date upon which the LTR was actually filed (RSTPA 2014, s 103(6)). This period is extended to 20 years where the under-assessment to tax has been brought about deliberately by the buyer or a 'related person' (RSTPA 2014, s 103(2)). For these purposes a 'related person' means a person acting on the buyer's behalf or a person who was the partner of the buyer (RSTPA 2014, s 103(6)). If the buyer has died, a discovery assessment must be made in the three year period from the date of death and the assessment cannot be in respect of an LTR in relation to which the date by which the LTR was due to be filed was more than five years before the person's death (RSTPA 2014, s 103(4)). If the assessment is to recover an excessive repayment of LBTT (RSTPA 2014, s 99), it may also be made up to 12 months after the repayment is made, even if this is outside the normal five year time limit (RSTPA 2014, s 103(3)).

Revenue Scotland must give the buyer notice that the discovery assessment has been issued and the notice must state: (a) the amount of the LBTT payable, (b) the date on which the notice is issued, (c) the date by which the LBTT, or additional LBTT, chargeable as a result of the assessment must be paid, and (d) the time by which any review (see **8.53**) or appeal (see **8.89**) against the assessment must be requested (RSTPA 2014, s 105(1) and (2)).

8.53 The buyer may request that Revenue Scotland review the decision to make the discovery assessment and may apply to have the payment of any additional tax postponed, which may be agreed by Revenue Scotland but only where Revenue Scotland is satisfied that there are exceptional circumstances which justify postponement (RSTPA 2014, ss 233, 234 and 245 and The Revenue Scotland and Tax Powers Act (Postponement of Tax Pending a Review or Appeal) Regulations 2015, SSI 2015/129, reg 3). The request for the review must be made to Revenue Scotland in writing, specifying the grounds for the review, and must be made within 30 days of being notified of the issue of the discovery assessment (RSTPA 2014, s 235). If a request is made for a review, Revenue Scotland must notify the buyer of its view on the matter to be reviewed and must then carry out the review in accordance with RSTPA 2013, s 238 (RSTPA 2014, s 237(1)). The review will be carried out by an independent officer within Revenue Scotland, but only to the extent Revenue Scotland consider appropriate, taking account of any representations made by the buyer. The review may either uphold Revenue Scotland's view, vary it or cancel it (RSTPA 2014, s 238(5)). Revenue Scotland must notify the buyer of the conclusions reached following the review, giving its reasoning, within 45 days of the date on which Revenue Scotland notified the buyer of its view on the matter (RSTPA 2014, s 239(1)). See **8.89** for more detail regarding the Revenue Scotland review process.

The buyer may appeal against a discovery assessment and may apply to have payment of any additional tax postponed (RSTPA 2004, ss 233, 241, and 242). As in other cases, postponement may be agreed by Revenue Scotland, but only where Revenue Scotland is satisfied that there are exceptional circumstances which justify postponement, or the matter may be determined by the tribunal (RSTPA 2004, s 245 and The Revenue Scotland and Tax Powers Act (Postponement of Tax Pending a Review or Appeal) Regulations 2015, SSI 2015/129, reg 3).

MISTAKE IN RETURN ETC – CLAIM FOR RELIEF BY BUYER

8.54

> **Focus**
>
> - It may be possible to reclaim LBTT overpaid either by amending the original land transaction return if still within the 12-month time limit or by making a claim for relief from an excessive assessment arising from a mistake in a return. There are, however, significant restrictions on making such a claim.

If a mistake is discovered in a return within the period allowed for amendment (usually up to one year after the normal submission deadline), this should be dealt with by amending the return as set out at **8.17**. If this deadline is missed, it may be possible to make a claim for relief from excessive assessment arising from a mistake in a return (RSTPA 2014, s 107(1) and (2)). Claims may only be accepted if made within five years of the date by which the LTR was due to be filed, may not be made by being included in an LTR, and must therefore be made by writing to Revenue Scotland (RSTPA 2014, s 115(1)). There is no provision to extend this period where, for example, the return was made after the normal submission deadline. There are also severe restrictions on the acceptable grounds for making a claim – for example, if there was a mistake in making or failing to make a claim (for example a claim for group relief) or election, it is not possible to correct this by way of a claim under these provisions (RSTPA 2014, s 113(1) and (2)). Similarly, if the taxpayer knew or ought reasonably to have known the grounds for the claim before the normal period for making the claim had expired, relief under these provisions will be refused (RSTPA 2014, s 113(1) and (4)). If the claim is made on behalf of a partnership, all of the partners must nominate someone who was a partner at the time of the relevant transaction to make the claim (RSTPA 2014, s 116). This provision may be to prevent a dissident partner seeking to change the treatment of an old transaction.

RSTPA 2014, Sch 3 applies in relation to the making of a claim for a repayment of overpaid LBTT and provides as follows:

- The claim must be made in such form as may be determined by Revenue Scotland and must contain a declaration that all of the particulars given in relation to the claim are correctly stated to the best of the claimant's information and belief.
- The form of the claim may require:
  - a statement of the amount of the LBTT to be repaid to give effect to the claim;
  - such information as is required to determine whether, and the extent to which, the claim is correct;
  - statements and documents to be provided in support of the claim.
- The claimant must have documentary evidence that the LBTT was paid in the first instance.
- There is a duty to keep and preserve records in support of the claim for three years from the date upon which the claim is made or, if later, the completion of an enquiry by Revenue Scotland into the claim.
- A claim may be amended by notice to Revenue Scotland within 12 months of the day on which the claim was made or, if Revenue Scotland give notice under RSTPA 2014, Sch 3, para 13 that they intend to enquire into the claim, an amendment may be made from the day on which the notice is given through to the day on which the enquiry is completed.
- Revenue Scotland can by notice to the claimant amend any obvious errors or omissions in the claim, such as errors of principle or arithmetical mistakes.

- Revenue Scotland may enquire into a claim if it gives notice before the end of 3 years after the date on which the claim was made. The enquiry will be completed if Revenue Scotland issues a closure notice, or if no closure notice has been issued 3 years after the date on which the claim was made. The claimant may also apply to the tribunal for a direction that Revenue Scotland issue a closure notice.
- As soon as practicable after a claim is made, amended or corrected Revenue Scotland must repay the LBTT to give effect to the claim, unless Revenue Scotland enquire into the claim or amendment, in which case it does not need to give effect to the claim until a closure notice is given or deemed to be given in relation to the enquiry.
- The closure notice must state whether in Revenue Scotland's opinion no amendment of the claim is necessary or, if Revenue Scotland consider the claim is insufficient or excessive, it must amend the claim accordingly.
- If Revenue Scotland has amended the claim on the basis it is insufficient or excessive it must then give effect to that amendment, within 30 days of the issue of the closure notice, by either issuing an assessment for additional tax or by repaying tax.
- The claimant may appeal against a conclusion stated, or amendment made, by the closure notice, and the appeal must be made within 30 days of the closure notice being issued.

Making a claim under these provisions will also remove restrictions on Revenue Scotland's ability to make a discovery assessment (RSTPA 2014, s 117). Therefore, careful analysis will be required before deciding to pursue such a claim.

A claim for relief may also be made where a person believes he has been assessed more than once in respect of the same transaction (RSTPA 2014, s 106). The claim must be made within five years of the date by which the LTR in relation to the transaction was due to be filed and, unlike a claim under RSTPA 2014, s 107, can be made in an LTR (RSTPA 2014, s 115).

PENALTIES, FINES AND OTHER SANCTIONS

Penalties

8.55

Focus

- Penalties may be payable in relation to a failure to comply with LBTT obligations. Some of the penalties are fixed in amount and apply automatically, others are tax geared.

Interest charged when LBTT is paid after the date on which it ought to have been paid does no more than compensate the Scottish Government for loss of the use of the money. As a separate matter, penalties are provided for various failures (RSTPA 2014, ss 76–80 and 157–208 but excluding ss 164–167 and ss 170–173 which relate to Scottish landfill tax). Some are fixed amounts and apply automatically; others are for variable amounts up to a ceiling.

The failures giving rise to a penalty are as follows:

- Failure to file an LTR, or to pay the LBTT liability, by the due date (RSTPA 2014, ss 159–163, ss 168 and 169, and ss 174–181).
- Delivering a document to Revenue Scotland which contains an inaccuracy(ies) (RSTPA 2014, ss 182–194).
- Failure to comply with a Revenue Scotland 'information notice' or obstructing a designated officer from Revenue Scotland in the course of an inspection of business premises (RSTPA 2014, ss 195–208).
- Failure to keep and preserve records as required (RSTPA 2014, ss 76–81).

Penalties for failure to file an LTR by the due date

8.56 The penalties for the late submission of an LTR are considered in detail at **8.24** and in summary are as follows:

(1) Late submission of return (RSTPA 2014, s 160) – up to three months after the due date, £100.

(2) Late submission of return (RSTPA 2014, s 161) – if the return has not been filed within three months, and Revenue Scotland decides, and gives notice to the buyer, that a daily penalty should be payable, a penalty is payable of £10 for each day that the failure continues up to a maximum of 90 days starting with the date specified in the notice given by Revenue Scotland. The date specified in the notice can be before the date on which the notice is given, but cannot be before the date which is three months after the filing date. The maximum penalty payable under this provision is £900 and it is expected that it would be applied for the three-month period beginning three months after the date by which the return should have been filed.

(3) Late submission of return (RSTPA 2014, s 162), if the failure continues beyond six months the penalty is the greater of: (a) 5% of the LBTT liability which would have been included in the return had it been filed, and (b) £300.

(4) Late submission of return (RSTPA 2014, s 163), if the failure continues beyond 12 months or more after the due date, the penalty is the greater of: (a) 5% of the LBTT which would have been shown in the return had it been filed, and (b) £300.

    However where, by not filing the return, the buyer deliberately withholds information which would have enabled Revenue Scotland to assess the buyer's liability to LBTT the penalty under RSTPA 2014, s 163 is increased to the greater of: (a) 100% of the LBTT liability which would have been shown in the return had it been filed, and (b) £300 (RSTPA 2014, s 163(2)).

The penalties set out in (1)–(4) above apply separately to each land transaction return that is late, and the penalties are cumulative in that they can be charged under each of (1), (2), (3) and (4) in relation to the same return (RSTPA 2014, s 159(2)). However, the aggregate of the tax geared penalties charged can never exceed 100% of the LBTT liability brought out by the land transaction return which is late (RSTPA 2014, s 159(3)).

For details of the returns in relation to which a late filing penalty can be charged, see **8.24**.

Revenue Scotland may reduce the amount of the penalty for failure to file an LTR by the filing date if the buyer discloses information which would otherwise have been included in the return. The amount of the reduction may be impacted by whether the disclosure is prompted or unprompted, and the quality of the disclosure made (RSTPA 2014, s 175).

Penalties for failure to pay the LBTT by the due date

8.57 A penalty arises if the LBTT is not paid on or before the date specified in column 4 of the table in RSTPA 2014, s 168(1), and this penalty is in addition to any penalty payable under (1), (2), (3) and (4) in **8.56** above.

The date after which a penalty for late payment of an LBTT liability will be incurred will generally be the date which is 30 days after the date by which the LBTT must be paid. This is referred to as the 'penalty date' (RSTPA 2014, s 168(3)).

Consequently, a penalty for late payment of LBTT will be incurred, if payment is not made within the 30 day period after the date by which it was due, in relation to the following liabilities:

- LBTT payable under LBTT(S)A 2013, s 40 which covers the following:
  - (a) the tax payable in relation to a land transaction return filed under LBTT(S)A 2013, s 29 – a penalty for the late payment of LBTT will be incurred if the tax is not paid within the period of 30 days after the date by which the land transaction return must be filed (see **8.23**) ie payment must be made within the 60 day period after the effective date (see **2.81**) of the land transaction;
  - (b) the tax payable in relation to consideration which ceases to be contingent or becomes ascertained and the buyer makes a land transaction return under LBTT(S)A 2013, s 31 (see **2.18**) – a penalty for the late payment of LBTT will be incurred if the tax is not paid within the period of 60 days from the day after the date on which the consideration ceased to be contingent or became ascertained;
  - (c) the tax payable where a relief is withdrawn and the buyer files a land transaction return under LBTT(S)A 2013, s 33 (see **5.17, 5.20**

and **5.27**) – a penalty for late payment of LBTT will be incurred if the tax is not paid within 60 days from the day after the date on which the 'relevant event' occurred which caused the relief to be withdrawn;

(d) the tax payable where the buyer files a further land transaction return as a result of a later linked transaction under LBTT(S)A 2013, s 34 (see **2.79** and **Example 8.3**) – a penalty for late payment of LBTT will be incurred if the tax is not paid within the period of 60 days after the effective date (see **2.81**) of the later transaction,

(e) leases:

(i) the tax payable in relation to a further return filed by the buyer in respect of a 3-yearly review of the LBTT chargeable on a lease under LBTT(S)A 2013, Sch 19, para 10 – a penalty for late payment of LBTT will be incurred if the tax is not paid within the period of 60 days beginning with the day after the 'review date' (see **4.21**);

(ii) the tax payable in relation to a further return filed by the buyer in respect of a review of the LBTT chargeable on a lease, on the assignment or termination of the lease under LBTT(S)A 2013, Sch 19, para 11 – a penalty for late payment of LBTT will be incurred if tax is not paid within the period of 60 days beginning with the day after the lease is assigned or terminated (see **4.26**);

(iii) the tax chargeable when a lease for a fixed term continues after the end of that term and the buyer is required to file a land transaction under LBTT(S)A 2013, Sch 19, para 20(3) – a penalty for late payment of LBTT will be incurred if tax is not paid within the period of 60 days beginning with the day after the end of the one year period which triggered notification of the lease (see **4.77**);

(iv) the tax payable when a buyer is required to file a land transaction return under LBTT(S)A 2013, Sch 19, para 22(2) in respect of a lease for an indefinite term becoming notifiable – a penalty for late payment of LBTT will be incurred if tax is not paid within the period of 60 days beginning with the day after the expiry of the last notional term of the lease before it becomes notifiable (see **4.16**);

(v) the tax payable when a buyer is required to file a land transaction return under LBTT(S)A 2013, Sch 19, para 30(2) when a lease is varied so as to extend its term or increase the amount of the rent and the effect of the variation is that the lease becomes notifiable – a penalty for late payment of LBTT will be incurred if the tax is not paid within the 60 day period commencing on the day after the variation to the lease takes effect (see **4.45**).

Thus in most cases if the LBTT is paid late, but is paid within the period of 30 days after the date by which payment was due, only interest on overdue tax will be payable (see **8.36**). However, if the LBTT is paid outside of that additional 30 day window a penalty for the late payment of the LBTT will be payable.

8.58 In relation to the following LBTT liabilities, however, the date after which a penalty will be payable (ie the penalty date) will be the date by which the LBTT is due to be paid (ie there is no additional 30 day period before which a penalty is incurred):

- additional LBTT payable as a result of an adjustment under RSTPA 2014, s 66 to counteract a tax advantage arising from an artificial tax avoidance arrangement. The date by which the payment of the LBTT will be due will depend on how the adjustment is made under RSTPA 2014, s 66(4);
- additional LBTT payable as a result of an amendment of an LTR by the buyer within 12 months of the filing date under RSTPA 2014, s 83. The LBTT is due to be paid when the amendment is made – see LBTT(S) A 2013, s 40(3);
- additional LBTT payable as a result of Revenue Scotland issuing a closure notice on completion of an enquiry into an LTR under RSTPA 2014, s 93. The LBTT is due to be paid within the period of 30 days beginning with the day on which the closure notice is given – see RSTPA 2014, s 93(6); and
- additional LBTT payable as a result of Revenue Scotland raising an assessment under RSTPA 2014, s 98 to make good a loss of tax. The LBTT is due to be paid within the period of 30 days beginning with the date on which the assessment is issued – see RSTPA 2014, s 105(3).

8.59 The penalty payable for late payment of LBTT is as follows:

- Tax paid late – buyer liable to a penalty of 5% of the unpaid tax (RSTPA 2014, s 169(2)).
- Tax unpaid more than five months after the penalty date (generally six months after the date by which the LBTT must be paid) – buyer liable to a penalty of 5% of the tax remaining payable (RSTPA 2014, s 169(3)).
- Tax unpaid more than 11 months after the penalty date (generally 12 months after the date by which the LBTT must be paid) – buyer liable to a penalty of 5% of the tax remaining payable (RSTPA 2014, s 169(4)).

The penalties for late payment are cumulative and therefore if all of the tax payable remained outstanding more than 11 months after the 'penalty date', the penalty would be 15% of the tax unpaid (RSTPA 2014, s 168(2)).

Circumstances in which a penalty for a failure to file an LTR, or pay an amount of LBTT, may be reduced or deferred

8.60 Where the buyer incurs a tax geared penalty as a consequence of a failure to file an LTR or because the LBTT was paid late, the amount of that penalty is reduced by any other tax geared penalty he incurs if that other penalty is determined by reference to the same LBTT liability (RSTPA 2014, s 174).

If the buyer satisfies Revenue Scotland (or the tribunal on appeal) that there is a reasonable excuse for the failure to file an LTR or make a payment of LBTT, then no penalty is payable in relation to such failures (RSTPA 2014, s 178). However, the following are not reasonable excuses:

- a lack of funds to pay the LBTT unless as a result of events outside of the buyer's control (RSTPA 2014, s 178(3)(a)); and
- where the buyer has relied on another person to do something, for example an agent, which has not then been done, unless the buyer took reasonable care to avoid the failure (RSTPA 2014, s 178(3)(b)).

Where the buyer did have a reasonable excuse for the failure, but that excuse has come to an end, the buyer is treated as still having that reasonable excuse provided he remedies the failure without unreasonable delay (RSTPA 2014, s 178(3)(c)).

8.61 If the buyer fails to pay an amount of LBTT by the due date, but requests Revenue Scotland to defer payment of the tax, and Revenue Scotland agrees that request, then the buyer is not liable for a penalty for late payment of the tax (RSTPA 2014, s 176(1) and (2)). But if the buyer breaks the agreement with Revenue Scotland, for example he fails to pay the LBTT at the end of the deferral period, then the buyer becomes liable to pay the penalty which would otherwise have been due, from the date of the notice issued by Revenue Scotland that the penalty is due (RSTPA 2014, s 176(3) and (4)).

8.62 Revenue Scotland may reduce a penalty for failure to file an LTR or pay an amount of LBTT if it considers it is right to do so because of 'special circumstances'. For these purposes 'special circumstances' does not include a buyer's ability to pay the penalty, nor the fact that a potential loss of revenue from one taxpayer is balanced by a potential overpayment by another taxpayer (RSTPA 2014, s 177).

Assessment of penalties for failure to file an LTR and for late payment of LBTT

8.63 If the buyer becomes liable to a penalty for the failure to file an LTR and/or for the late payment of LBTT, Revenue Scotland must assess the penalty, notify the buyer and state in the notice the transaction in relation to which the penalty is assessed (RSTPA 2014, s 179(1)).

The penalty must be paid within the period of 30 days beginning with the day on which the penalty notification is given (RSTPA 2014, s 179(2)). If the penalty is not paid by the due date interest for late payment will become payable – see **8.36**.

8.64 Revenue Scotland may make supplementary assessments or replacement assessments in relation to a penalty for failure to file an LTR or to pay an amount of LBTT if it transpires that the LBTT payable, on which the penalty is based, was either underestimated or overestimated (RSTPA 2014, s 179(4) and (5)).

8.65 An assessment of a penalty for a failure to file an LTR must be made on or before the **later** of the following (RSTPA 2014, s 180):

- two years beginning with the date on which the LTR should have been filed and, where it applies;
- 12 months beginning with the end of the appeal period for the assessment of the LBTT which would have been shown in the return, or if there is no such assessment, the date on which the liability to LBTT is ascertained or it is ascertained that the liability is nil.

8.66 An assessment of a penalty for failure to pay an amount of LBTT must be made on or before the **later** of the following (RSTPA 2014, s 180):

- two years beginning with the last date on which payment can be made without paying a penalty (ie the 'penalty date' – see **8.57**) and, where it applies;
- 12 months beginning with the end of the appeal period for the assessment of the LBTT in respect of which the penalty is assessed or, if there is no such assessment, the date on which the LBTT in respect of which the penalty is assessed is ascertained.

The 'appeal period' is the period during which an appeal can be made or, the period during which an appeal which has been made has not been determined or withdrawn (RSTPA 2014, s 180(4)).

Penalties for inaccuracies in an LTR or other document

8.67 A penalty is payable if a document relating to LBTT has been delivered to Revenue Scotland by a person which is inaccurate leading to: (a) an understatement of the LBTT liability, or (b) a false or excessive claim for an exemption or relief, or (c) a false or excessive claim for relief from, or repayment of, tax and the inaccuracy was either a deliberate inaccuracy by the person delivering the document or arose as a result of the carelessness of the person delivering the document (RSTPA 2014, s 182(1)–(3)). An inaccuracy is careless if it is due to a failure by the person delivering the document to take reasonable care (RSTPA 2014, s 182(4)). An inaccuracy in a document which was neither deliberate nor careless on the part of the person delivering the document will however be treated as being caused by that person's carelessness where that person became aware of the inaccuracy and did not take reasonable steps to inform Revenue Scotland of the inaccuracy (RSTPA 2014, s 182(5)). Where a document contains more than one inaccuracy a penalty is payable for each inaccuracy (RSTPA 2014, s 182(6)). In these circumstances the penalty is payable by the person who gave the document to Revenue Scotland (RSTPA 2014, s 182(1)).

8.68 The documents (referred to below as 'Relevant Document') in relation to which a penalty for an inaccuracy might arise are as follows:

- A land transaction return in relation to: (a) a land transaction, (b) where a contingency ceases or consideration is ascertained (see **2.18**), (c) the withdrawal of a relief (for example, group relief – see **5.17**), and (d) a later linked transaction (see **2.79**).
- As regards leases a further (or original) land transaction return in relation to: (a) the three-yearly review (see **4.21**), (b) the review on the assignation or termination of a lease (see **4.26**), (c) a lease continuing beyond its fixed term (see **4.77**), (d) a lease for an indefinite period becoming notifiable (see **4.16**), and (e) the notification of an increase of the rent payable or an extension of the term of the lease (see **4.45**).
- An application to Revenue Scotland to defer payment of tax in the case of contingent or uncertain consideration (see **8.27**).
- An amendment of a land transaction return by the buyer within the 12 month amendment period (see **8.17**).
- A claim by the buyer that LBTT has been assessed more than once in respect of the same matter (see **8.54**) and a claim that LBTT has been overpaid (see **8.54**).

The amount of the penalty for an inaccuracy in a 'Relevant Document'

8.69 The penalty for delivering a Relevant Document to Revenue Scotland containing an inaccuracy is as follows (RSTPA 2014, s 183):

Deliberate inaccuracy	A penalty of 100% of the 'potential lost revenue'
Careless inaccuracy	A penalty of 30% of the 'potential lost revenue'

Generally for these purposes the 'potential lost revenue' is the amount of the LBTT due and payable as a result of correcting the inaccuracy or under-assessment, and also includes the amount of any repayment of LBTT erroneously made by Revenue Scotland as a result of the inaccuracy (RSTPA 2014, s 187).

8.70 Where a 'relevant document' is given by a person ('P') to Revenue Scotland containing a 'relevant inaccuracy' and the inaccuracy was attributable to another person ('T') deliberately supplying false information to P or deliberately withholding information from P, with the intention that the document would contain inaccuracies, a penalty is payable by T. For these purposes a 'relevant inaccuracy' is an inaccuracy which leads to: (a) an understatement of the liability to LBTT, or (b) a false or excessive claim for an exemption or relief, or (c) a false or excessive claim for relief from, or repayment of, tax (RSTPA 2014, s 185(1) and (2)). The penalty is payable by T irrespective of whether a penalty is also payable by P in respect of the same inaccuracy (RSTPA 2014, s 185(3)). The penalty which is payable by T is 100% of the potential lost revenue (see **8.69**).

8.71 A penalty is payable by the buyer if he fails to take reasonable steps to notify Revenue Scotland, within 30 days of the date of the issue of an assessment or determination by Revenue Scotland, that it is an under-assessment or under-determination, in circumstances where the buyer knew, or ought to have known, that it was an under-assessment or under-determination (RSTPA 2014, s 186(1) and (2)).

In deciding what reasonable steps the buyer could have taken, Revenue Scotland must consider: (a) whether the buyer knew, or should have known, about the under-assessment or under-determination and what steps he could have taken to notify Revenue Scotland (RSTPA 2014, s 186(2)).

The penalty for failure on the buyer's part to take the reasonable steps is 30% of the potential lost revenue (RSTPA 2014, s 186(3) – see **8.69**).

Circumstances in which a penalty for an inaccuracy in a document may be reduced

8.72 The penalty for an inaccuracy in a Relevant Document may be reduced where a person discloses to Revenue Scotland: (a) the inaccuracy, or (b) the fact that false information has been supplied, or that information has been withheld, or that an under-assessment has not been disclosed (RSTPA 2014, s 192(1) and (2)). The person making the disclosure must also help Revenue Scotland quantify the inaccuracy and give them access to records to allow Revenue Scotland to confirm that the inaccuracy is fully corrected (RSTPA 2014, s 192(3)). The amount of the reduction of the penalty may reflect whether the disclosure was prompted or unprompted, and the quality of the disclosure made (RSTPA 2014, s 192(4)). The disclosure will be prompted unless it is made at a time when the person making the disclosure has no reason to believe that Revenue Scotland has discovered, or is about to discover, the inaccuracy, the supply of false information, the withholding of information or the under-assessment (RSTPA 2014, s 192(5)).

8.73 Revenue Scotland may also reduce a penalty for an inaccuracy in a Relevant Document if it considers that it is right to so because of 'special circumstances'. For these purposes 'special circumstances' does not include the buyer's ability to pay the penalty nor the fact that a potential loss of revenue from one taxpayer is balanced by the potential overpayment by another taxpayer (RSTPA 2014, s 191).

Assessment of penalties arising from an inaccuracy in a Relevant Document

8.74 If the buyer becomes liable to a penalty as a result of an inaccuracy in a Relevant Document, Revenue Scotland must assess the penalty, notify the buyer and state in the notice the Relevant Document in relation to which the penalty is assessed (RSTPA 2014, s 193(1)). (Note: the legislation actually states that the notice must state the period in respect of which the penalty is assessed. However, as LBTT is not assessed by reference to a period it is assumed that the notice will identify the relevant document.)

The penalty must be paid within the period of 30 days beginning with the day on which the penalty notification is given (RSTPA 2014, s 193(2)). If the penalty is not paid by the due date interest for late payment will become payable – see **8.36**.

8.75 An assessment of a penalty for an inaccuracy in a Relevant Document, charged on either the buyer or the other person who deliberately supplied false information to, or withheld information from, the buyer, must be made on or before the end of the 12 month period beginning with: (a) the end of the appeal period for the decision issued by Revenue Scotland correcting the inaccuracy, or (b) if there is no assessment to the tax arising as a result of the inaccuracy, the date on which the inaccuracy is corrected (RSTPA 2014, s 193(4)).

8.76 An assessment of a penalty for a failure on behalf of the buyer to take reasonable steps to notify Revenue Scotland that an under-assessment or under-determination has been issued must be made on or before the end of the 12-month period beginning with: (a) the end of the appeal period for the assessment of the tax correcting the under-assessment or under-determination, or (b) if there is no such assessment, the date on which the under-assessment or under-determination is corrected (RSTPA 2014, s 193(5)).

For these purposes 'appeal period' means the period during which: (a) an appeal could be brought, or (b) an appeal that has been brought has not been determined or withdrawn (RSTPA 2014, s 193(6)).

8.77 Revenue Scotland may also raise a supplementary assessment of a penalty if an earlier assessment was based on an underestimate of the potential lost revenue – see **8.69** (RSTPA 2014, s 193(7)).

Penalties relating to Revenue Scotland investigations

8.78 A penalty is payable if a person fails to comply with an 'information notice' or deliberately obstructs a member of staff of Revenue Scotland, or a person authorised by such a member of staff, in the course of an inspection of business premises (RSTPA 2014, s 195(1)(a)). An 'information notice' (RSTPA 2014, s 131(1)) includes a notice under RSTPA 2014, s 123 or s 124 requesting the provision of information or a document from the buyer or a third party. It also includes notices under RSTPA 2014, ss 127 and 130 (Power to obtain information and documents about persons whose identity is not known and persons whose identity can be ascertained). In such circumstances the person is liable to a penalty of £300 (RSTPA 2014, s 195(2)). If the failure or obstruction continues after the date on which the £300 penalty is imposed the person is liable to a further penalty not exceeding £60 for each subsequent day on which the failure or obstruction continues (RSTPA 2014, s 196).

8.79 If a daily penalty has been assessed for failure to comply with a notice under RSTPA 2014, s 127 (Power to obtain information and documents about persons whose identity is not known) and the failure continues for more than 30 days beginning with the date on which notification of the assessment of the penalty was issued, and the person has been told that Revenue Scotland may make an application for an increased daily penalty under RSTPA 2014, s 204, then Revenue Scotland may make such an application to the tribunal (RSTPA 2014, s 204(1) and (2)). The tribunal may then impose an increased daily penalty which cannot exceed £1,000 per day (RSTPA 2014, s 204(3) and (4)). In determining the amount of the increased daily penalty the tribunal must have regard to: (a) the likely cost to the person of complying with the notice under RSTPA 2014, s 127, (b) any benefits to the person of not complying with it, and (c) any benefits to anyone else as a result of non-compliance with the notice (RSTPA 2014, s 204(5)). If a person becomes liable to pay an increased daily penalty Revenue Scotland must notify the person liable and the notification must state the date from which the penalty is to apply (RSTPA 2014, s 204(6) and (7)). Any increased daily penalty must be paid before the end of the 30 day period beginning with the date on which notification of the penalty is issued (RSTPA 2014, s 205(1)). If the penalty is not paid by the due date interest for late payment will become payable – see **8.36**.

Imposition of additional penalties

8.80 If the failure or obstruction continues after the £300 penalty has been imposed under RSTPA 2014, s 195, and the designated officer (member of staff of Revenue Scotland) believes that as a result of the failure, the tax the buyer has paid, or is likely to pay, is significantly less than it otherwise would have been, then within 12 months of the 'relevant date' the designated officer may make an application to the Upper Tribunal for an additional penalty to be imposed on the person. The 'relevant date' is the date upon which the person became liable for the penalty for the failure to comply or obstruction, unless it relates to an information notice against which a person may appeal in which case it is the later of:

(a) the date on which the person became liable for the penalty;

(b) the end of the period in which an appeal against the information notice could be made, and

if a notice of appeal has been given, the date on which the appeal is determined or withdrawn.

If the Upper Tribunal decides that an additional penalty should be imposed, then the person is liable for a penalty of an amount decided by the Upper Tribunal. (RSTPA 2014, s 206). The penalty under RSTPA 2014, s 206 must be paid before the end of the 30-day period beginning with the date on which notification of the penalty is issued (RSTPA 2014, s 207).

Provision of inaccurate information or an inaccurate document

8.81 A penalty is payable if in complying with an 'information notice' within the meaning of (RSTPA 2014, s 131(1)) a person provides inaccurate information or produces a document which is inaccurate and: (a) the inaccuracy is careless or deliberate, or (b) the person knows of the inaccuracy at the time the information is provided or document produced and does not inform Revenue

Scotland at that time, or (c) the person discovers the inaccuracy some time later and fails to take reasonable steps to inform Revenue Scotland. The person is liable to a fine not exceeding £3,000 for each inaccuracy in the information provided or document produced (RSTPA 2014, s 197).

Reasonable excuse for failure to comply with an 'information notice'

8.82 A penalty for failure to comply with an information notice or for obstructing a member of staff of Revenue Scotland in the course of an inspection of business premises does not arise if the person satisfies Revenue Scotland (or, on appeal, the tribunal) that there is a reasonable excuse for the failure to comply or the obstruction. For these purposes a lack of funds is not a reasonable excuse unless it is attributable to events outside the buyer's control and, where the buyer relies on another person to do anything, and they failed to do that thing, that is not a reasonable excuse unless the buyer took reasonable care to avoid the failure to comply or obstruction (RSTPA 2014, s 201(1) and (2)). Where the buyer had a reasonable excuse for the failure to comply or obstruction, and the excuse has ceased, the buyer is treated as having continued to have a reasonable excuse provided the failure to comply or obstruction stops, without unreasonable delay after the excuse ceased (RSTPA 2014, s 201(2)(c)).

Penalties must be assessed

8.83 A penalty for a failure to comply or obstruction must be assessed by Revenue Scotland, who must notify the person liable for the penalty (RSTPA 2014, s 202(1)). The assessment for such a penalty must be made within the period of 12 months beginning with the date on which the person became liable for the penalty (RSTPA 2014, s 202(2)), unless it refers to an information notice against which an appeal can be made. Where such an appeal can be made the penalty must be assessed within the 12 months beginning with the latest of the following (RSTPA 2014, s 202(3)):

- the date on which the person became liable to the penalty;
- the end of the period in which an appeal against the information notice could be made; and
- if a notice of appeal is given, the date on which the appeal is determined or withdrawn.

Time limit for making penalties

8.84 A penalty for providing inaccurate information when complying with an information notice must be made within the 12-month period beginning with the date the inaccuracy first came to the attention of Revenue Scotland and within the period of six years beginning with the date on which the person became liable to the penalty (RSTPA 2014, s 202(4)).

Time limit for payment of penalties

8.85 A penalty for a failure to comply with an information notice, or for obstructing a Revenue Scotland staff member in the course of an inspection of business premises or for the provision of inaccurate information when complying with an information notice must be paid (RSTPA 2014, s 203):

- within the 30-day period beginning with the date on which the penalty was notified by Revenue Scotland;
- if a notice of review (see **8.53**) against the penalty is given, within the 30-day period beginning with the date on which the review is concluded;
- if, following a review, mediation is entered into, within the 30-day period beginning with the date on which either party gives notice of withdrawal from mediation;
- if a notice of appeal is given against the penalty, within the 30-day period beginning with the date on which the appeal is determined or withdrawn.

If the penalty is not paid by the due date interest for late payment will become payable – see **8.36**.

Penalties for failure to keep and preserve records as required

8.86 If a person fails to keep and preserve records as required – see **8.92** et seq – a penalty of up to £3,000 is payable (RSTPA 2014, s 76(1)). However, no penalty is payable if Revenue Scotland is satisfied that any facts which it requires to be proved, and would have been proved by the records had they been kept, are proved by other documentary evidence provided to Revenue Scotland (RSTPA 2014, s 76(2)).

8.87 If the buyer satisfies Revenue Scotland (or on appeal the tribunal) that there is a reasonable excuse for the failure to keep and preserve records as required, no penalty arises (RSTPA 2014, s 77(1)). An insufficiency of funds is not a reasonable excuse unless attributable to events outside of the buyer's control (RSTPA 2014, s 77(2)(a)). If the buyer relies on any other person to do anything, and they fail to do that thing, that is not a reasonable excuse unless the buyer took reasonable care to avoid the failure (RSTPA 2014, s 77(2)(b)). Where the buyer had a reasonable excuse for the failure but the excuse has ceased, the buyer is treated as continuing to have the excuse if the failure is remedied without unreasonable delay after the excuse ceased (RSTPA 2014, s 77(2)(c)).

8.88 A penalty for a failure to keep and preserve records must be assessed by Revenue Scotland who must notify the person concerned. The penalty must be assessed within the 12-month period beginning with the date on which the person became liable to the penalty (RSTPA 2014, s 78). The penalty must be paid (RSTPA 2014, s 79):

- within the 30 day period beginning with the date on which the penalty was notified by Revenue Scotland;
- if a notice of review (see **8.53**) against the penalty is given, within the 30-day period beginning with the date on which the review is concluded;

- if, following a review, mediation is entered into, within the 30-day period beginning with the date on which either party gives notice of withdrawal from mediation;
- if a notice of appeal is given against the penalty, within the 30-day period beginning with the date on which the appeal is determined or withdrawn.

APPEALS AND REVIEWS

Independent review by Revenue Scotland

8.89

> **Focus**
>
> - In certain circumstances it is possible to appeal against Revenue Scotland decisions, determinations and assessments.

If the buyer and Revenue Scotland are unable to reach agreement on an appealable decision (see **8.90**), and no appeal has been made by the buyer in relation to the decision, and the buyer has not entered into a settlement agreement with Revenue Scotland, the buyer may request an 'independent review' under RSTPA 2014, s 234(1) (that is, a review by one or more Revenue Scotland officers not involved in the making of the decision, assessment, determination, etc). The request for a review must be made within 30 days of the date on which the buyer was notified of the Revenue Scotland decision or, if the decision relates to the amendment of an LTR by Revenue Scotland during the course of an enquiry into that LTR, within 30 days of the date that notice was given that the enquiry was complete or, where no such notice is given, the date which is three years after the filing of the LTR (or, if the LTR was filed late, three years from the date on which it was filed). Where the appellant and Revenue Scotland have entered into a settlement agreement, but the appellant then withdraws from the agreement, the notice requesting a review must be made within 30 days of the date of withdrawal from the agreement (RSTPA 2014, s 235(1) and (2)).

Within 30 days (or such longer period as is reasonable) following receipt of the request for a review, Revenue Scotland must notify the buyer of its view of the matter in question and then carry out the review (RSTPA 2014, s 237). Revenue Scotland must then notify the buyer, within 45 days of the date upon which it notified him of its view on the matter in question, whether that view is upheld, varied or cancelled (RSTPA 2014, ss 238 and 239). The conclusions of the review are treated as though they were contained in a settlement agreement (see RSTPA 2014, s 246(2)). This means that the conclusions of the review are treated as though the tribunal had determined an appeal in relation to the matter in question, in line with the conclusions of the review unless: (a) the buyer and

Revenue Scotland enter into mediation which is concluded by entering into an actual settlement agreement, or (b) the buyer gives notice of an appeal in relation to the conclusions of the review (RSTPA 2014, s 240). Such an appeal must be made within 30 days of the date on which the conclusions of the review were notified to the buyer by Revenue Scotland (RSTPA 2014, s 242(2)(c)).

Appeals to the First-tier Tax Tribunal

8.90 There are various references in this chapter to appealing against Revenue Scotland decisions, determinations and assessments. Initially, appeals are made to the First-tier Tribunal. A letter of appeal must set out the details necessary to allow the First-tier Tribunal to identify the tax return or transaction and decision involved (including the Revenue Scotland reference) and the grounds of the appeal (RSTPA 2014, s 242(2)(c)).

The following decisions by Revenue Scotland can be appealed to the tribunal (RSTPA 2014, s 233):

(a) a decision under RSTPA 2014, s 66 to counteract a tax advantage arising from a tax avoidance arrangement which is artificial;

(b) a decision which affects whether a person is chargeable to LBTT;

(c) a decision which affects the amount of LBTT to which a person is chargeable;

(d) a decision which affects the amount of LBTT a person is required to pay;

(e) a decision which affects the date by which any amount by way of tax, penalty or interest must be paid;

(f) a decision in relation to a penalty in respect of any of the following:

 (i) failure to keep and preserve records – RSTPA 2014, s 76;

 (ii) unjustified enrichment – reimbursement arrangements – RSTPA 2014, s 112;

 (iii) computer records – RSTPA 2014, s 151;

 (iv) failure to file a land transaction return or pay the LBTT by the due date, an inaccuracy in a taxpayer document, failure to comply with an information notice or obstructing Revenue Scotland in the course of an inspection of business premises, and providing inaccurate information or producing a document which is inaccurate in response to an information notice;

 (v) failure by a third party to comply with a notice – RSTPA 2014, s 231;

 (vi) failure to keep and preserve records in support of a claim for overpaid LBTT – RSTPA 2014, Sch 3, para 5.

(g) subject to certain exceptions (see (RSTPA 2014, s 152) the giving of an information notice by Revenue Scotland;

(h) the giving of a third party notice under RSTPA 2014, s 228 but the only grounds for appeal are that it would be unduly onerous for the third party to comply (RSTPA 2014, s 229(2)).

In contrast, the following decisions of Revenue Scotland cannot be appealed:

(a) the giving of a notice that a tax advantage arising under a tax avoidance arrangement is to be counteracted under RSTPA 2014, s 68;

(b) the making of a Revenue Scotland determination under RSTPA 2014, s 95; and

(c) a decision to enquire into a land transaction return RSTPA 2014, s 85, or to enquire into a claim for overpaid LBTT under RSTPA 2014, Sch 3, para 13.

In general, the appeal to the tribunal must be made within 30 days of the appellant being given notice of the decision, assessment, determination etc (RSTPA 2014, s 242(1)(a)).

8.91 A detailed consideration of the appeals process is beyond the scope of this book and specialist advice should be sought.

RECORD KEEPING

8.92

> **Focus**
>
> - The buyer must retain and preserve records not only for transactions which are chargeable to LBTT but also for exempt transactions, so that it can be demonstrated that the transaction was in fact exempt.

A buyer is required to keep and preserve whatever records may be required to enable the delivery of correct and complete returns (RSTPA 2014, s 74(1)). Such records include original contracts and dispositions, supporting maps, plans and other similar documents, and records of payments, receipts and financial arrangements (RSTPA 2014, s 74(8)). The records must be kept for at least five years from the date on which the LTR is filed or, if the LTR is amended, five years from the day notice of the amendment is given under RSTPA 2014, s 83 or any earlier date that may be specified by Revenue Scotland (RSTPA 2014, s 74(2) and (5)). They must also be kept until any enquiry into the return is completed, and until Revenue Scotland no longer have the right to enquire into the return, if these dates are later than the five-year time limit (RSTPA 2014, s 74(2)). It is acceptable to keep the information from the documents (for example, scanned copies) rather than the documents themselves (RSTPA 2014, s 75).

The records may be maintained in whatever format the buyer wishes, paper or electronic, including, but not limited to, the following:

- Computer hard drive.
- Tablet or smart phone.
- Magnetic tape.
- Flash drive or memory stick.
- Optical media such as CD, DVD, or Blu-Ray.

However, buyers may be concerned about the ability to demonstrate that such information is in accordance with the original document. So, in most cases, the original document is likely to be retained, albeit in a document storage facility, even if the information is also stored electronically.

If a computer system containing retained records is upgraded and the new computer system is not compatible with the old system, the records held on the old system must remain accessible for the time period discussed above.

8.93 The requirement to keep and preserve records applies where a return has to be made, however, the Scottish Ministers may make regulations imposing a requirement to keep and preserve records where no return is required because the transaction is exempt (see **5.6**), or one of the notification exceptions set out in **8.2** applies, with the records maintained being sufficient to demonstrate that the transaction is not notifiable (RSTPA 2014, s 81 – see **8.3**). The Revenue Scotland and Tax Powers Act (Record Keeping) Regulations 2015, SSI 2015/130) provide as follows (reg 4):

- The buyer in a land transaction which is not notifiable must keep such records as may be needed to enable the buyer to demonstrate that the transaction is not notifiable.
- The five year retention period specified in RSTPA 2014, s 74(2) applies with the five year period beginning on the date by which the return would have been required to have been filed, had the transaction been notifiable.
- The records to be preserved include any contract or conveyance and any supporting maps, plans or similar documents.
- The penalties for failure to keep and preserve records apply even though the transaction was not notifiable (see **8.86**).

For most commercial transactions, the requirement to keep records for five years is reasonable. In the case of routine home purchases, where the property may well be re-sold within the five year period, the requirement is not so clearly justified. Many homeowners, unaware of the requirement, may dispose of records in a shorter period.

8.94 Where a person makes a claim (other than in a land transaction return or an amendment to such a return) to Revenue Scotland under RSTPA 2014, s 107 for a repayment of LBTT which they believe to have been overpaid (see **8.54**), that person must retain such records as are required to make a correct and complete claim. The Records must be retained until the later of the following (RSTPA 2014, Sch 3, para 3):

- the end of the three-year period beginning with the date on which the claim was made;
- where an enquiry has been launched into the claim, or an amendment to a claim, the date by which that enquiry is completed; and
- where the claim is amended and no enquiry has been made into that claim, the date by which Revenue Scotland no longer has the power to enquire into the amendment to the claim.

If the person who made the claim fails to keep the required records that person is liable to a penalty of £3,000 (RSTPA 2014, Sch 3, para 5(1)). However, no penalty is payable if Revenue Scotland is satisfied that any facts it requires proved in relation to the claim, that would have been proved by the records, are proved by other documentary evidence provided to them (RSTPA 2014, Sch 3, para 5(2)).

Chapter 9

LBTT Anti-Avoidance Rules

SIGNPOSTS

- Overview of the general anti-avoidance rule (Revenue Scotland and Tax Powers Act 2014, Part 5).
- List of the targeted anti-avoidance rules within the LBTT legislation with references to the paragraphs within this book which cover those rules.
- The Land and Buildings Transaction Tax (Scotland) Act 2013, s 47 provides for a charge to LBTT to be made on certain transfers of interests in Residential Property Holding Companies – the Scottish Ministers have not currently made regulations to bring this provision into effect.

9.1 Prior to the introduction of SDLT in 2003, it was relatively easy to minimise stamp duty costs on many property transactions, as it had proven difficult to introduce effective anti-avoidance rules for this document-based tax. This was a major factor in the decision to replace stamp duty with SDLT, a transaction-based tax not reliant on the manner in which the transaction is documented. The initial SDLT rules were not particularly well drafted and, inevitably, transactions were structured to take advantage of this and minimise tax. Initially, HMRC tackled this by introducing targeted anti-avoidance rules intended to prevent the exploitation of specific reliefs and treatments. Eventually, HMRC concluded that these were having only limited success and, on 6 December 2006, a general anti-avoidance rule for SDLT was introduced in the form of FA 2003, s 75A.

The SDLT general anti-avoidance rule is extremely wide in its scope and whilst its objective is clearly to counter SDLT avoidance, there is no requirement that an SDLT avoidance motive exist to fall within the rule. Consequently, wholly commercial transactions, perhaps structured in an SDLT efficient manner, potentially fall within the provision, leading to uncertainty for taxpayers.

Fortunately, the Scottish Government has decided not to import an equivalent of FA 2003, s 75A into the LBTT legislation. The approach taken by the Scottish Government was to include a number of Targeted Anti-avoidance Rules (TAARs) within the LBTT legislation and to introduce a General Anti-avoidance Rule (GAAR) aimed at counteracting tax advantages obtained by the implementation of tax avoidance schemes that are artificial. Alongside these provisions will sit the principle that the Scottish courts and tribunals will adopt a purposive interpretation of the LBTT legislation (see *Aberdeen Asset Management v HMRC* [2013] CSIH 84).

LBTT is not within the UK system for disclosure of tax avoidance schemes (DOTAS).

9.2 This chapter first looks at the GAAR and then provides a list of the Targeted Anti-avoidance Rules (see **9.14**) – these are dealt with more fully in the relevant chapters examining the transactions or reliefs to which they apply. The chapter also briefly considers the power which Scottish Ministers have to charge LBTT on certain transfers of shares in a company owning residential property (see **9.15**).

GENERAL ANTI-AVOIDANCE RULE

9.3

Focus

- If an 'arrangement' is entered into with **a** main purpose (not necessarily **the** main purpose) of obtaining a reduction in a liability to LBTT (or a payment deferral or an acceleration of a repayment), and that arrangement is 'artificial' (see **9.4**) then Revenue Scotland may seek to counteract the perceived tax advantage by applying the GAAR.

The GAAR provisions are set out in RSTPA 2014, ss 62–72. The rule is designed to apply to a range of taxes in addition to LBTT, in the anticipation of further taxes being devolved to Scotland, and so is couched in fairly general terms. The GAAR is specifically designed to be broader in scope than the UK General Anti-abuse Rule which is found in FA 2013, ss 206–215. In fact the Revenue Scotland guidance (RSTP8001) makes the bold statement that: 'All of the avoidance schemes which have been defeated in the context of SDLT, whether by legislative change or in litigation, would be ineffective under the Scottish GAAR'.

The objective of the GAAR is to counteract 'tax advantages' arising from a 'tax avoidance arrangement' which is 'artificial' (RSTPA 2014, s 62(1)). The Policy Memorandum issued with the Revenue Scotland and Tax Powers Bill 2014 states, at paragraph 59, 'By contrast (to tax evasion), tax avoidance takes place where a taxpayer seeks to reduce, delay or avoid the tax liability by taking action which the taxpayer believes is legal, but which the tax authorities regard as not in keeping with the spirit of or the intention behind the relevant tax legislation.' This definition of tax avoidance puts a lot of power in the hands of Revenue Scotland to determine what is within the spirit of the legislation, and it can be notoriously difficult to determine the intention behind certain legislative provisions. The absence of a role for an Advisory Panel in relation to the GAAR, which acts to provide a safeguard under the UK General Anti-abuse Rule, is regrettable.

9.4 An arrangement is a 'tax avoidance arrangement' if, having regard to all the circumstances, it would be reasonable to conclude that a main purpose (not necessarily the only main purpose) of the arrangement was the obtaining of a 'tax advantage' (RSTPA 2014, s 63(1)). Revenue Scotland make it clear in their guidance that, in their view, the GAAR can still apply to an arrangement even if the obtaining of the 'tax advantage' was secondary to a legitimate commercial (or other) main purpose. Obtaining the 'tax advantage' must however be a main purpose of the arrangement and therefore if obtaining the 'tax advantage' was incidental to, and not a main purpose of, the arrangement, the GAAR should not apply (RSTP8004). See **9.5** for the meaning of the term 'tax advantage'. The term 'arrangement' is widely defined and it is specifically provided that it does not have to be legally enforceable (RSTPA 2014, s 63(2)). Even if there is an arrangement with a main purpose of obtaining a tax advantage the GAAR will only apply if the arrangement is 'artificial'. A tax avoidance arrangement will be 'artificial' if either condition A or B is met, or if both of those conditions are met (RSTPA 2014, s 64(1)).

Condition A is met if entering into the arrangement is not a reasonable course of action in relation to the tax provisions in question (in this case the relevant LBTT legislation), having regard to all of the circumstances including whether the outcome of the arrangement is consistent with: (a) any principles on which the relevant LBTT provisions are based (whether express or implied), and (b) the policy objectives of the LBTT provisions, and whether the arrangement is designed to exploit any shortcomings in the relevant LBTT provisions (RSTPA 2014, s 64(2)). The Revenue Scotland guidance states: 'In identifying the policy objectives of legislation reference may be made to (but is not limited to) any relevant oral or written statements/publications made by or on behalf of the Scottish Ministers, such as statements before the Scottish Parliament and published material accompanying the legislation in question.' (RSTP8005).

Condition B is met if the arrangement lacks 'economic or commercial substance' (RSTPA 2014, s 64(3)). Examples are given of factors which might indicate that a tax avoidance arrangement lacks economic or commercial substance (RSTPA 2014, s 64(4)), and these are as follows:

- The arrangement is carried out in a way which would not normally be used in reasonable business conduct.
- The legal form of the arrangement is inconsistent with the legal substance of the arrangement as a whole.
- The arrangement includes elements which have the effect of offsetting or cancelling each other out.
- The arrangement comprises transactions which are circular in nature.
- The arrangement results in a 'tax advantage' that is not reflected in the business risks undertaken by the taxpayer.

It is specifically provided that this list of indicators is not exhaustive (RSTPA 2014, s 64(6)).

However, it would be an indication that an arrangement may not be 'artificial' if it is in line with established practice and Revenue Scotland had at the time the arrangement was entered into indicated its acceptance of that practice (RSTPA 2014, s 64(5)).

9.5 'Tax advantage' is not comprehensively defined but is stated to include (a) relief or increased relief from tax, (b) repayment or increased repayment of tax, (c) reduction or avoidance of a charge to tax or an assessment to tax, (d) avoidance of a possible assessment to tax or (e) deferral of a tax payment, or advancement of a repayment of tax (RSTPA 2014, s 65(1)). In assessing whether a tax avoidance arrangement has resulted in a tax advantage the legislation specifically provides that regard may be had to the amount of the tax, in this case the amount of the LBTT, which would have been payable had the arrangement not been entered into (RSTPA 2014, s 65(2)).

9.6 Where Revenue Scotland consider that the general anti-avoidance rule may apply, they will seek to make such adjustments as they consider just and reasonable to counter the tax advantage (RSTPA 2014, s 66(1)). Any adjustment to be made under RSTPA 2014, s 66 can be made by (RSTPA 2014, s 66(4)):

- amendment to an LBTT return by either Revenue Scotland or the buyer (RSTPA 2014, ss 83, 87 and 93);
- the correction of an LBTT return by Revenue Scotland (RSTPA 2014, s 84);
- the making of a determination by Revenue Scotland (RSTPA 2014, s 95);
- the buyer filing an LBTT return after Revenue Scotland have made a determination (RSTPA 2014, s 97);
- Revenue Scotland raising an assessment to make good a loss of tax (RSTPA 2014, s 100);
- the entering into of a contract settlement to settle the buyer's liability to make a payment of tax to Revenue Scotland (RSTPA 2014, s 118); or
- any other method considered appropriate by Revenue Scotland (RSTPA 2014, s 66(4)(g)).

9.7 The making of adjustments is governed by the procedural rules in RSTPA 2014, ss 68 and 69. These require Revenue Scotland to notify the taxpayer in writing that a 'designated officer' considers that a tax advantage has arisen to the taxpayer from a tax avoidance arrangement that is artificial, and that it is proposed that the tax advantage be counteracted (RSTPA 2014, s 68(1)). The use of the term 'designated officer' may indicate that any proposal to counteract an arrangement under the GAAR may be restricted to a group of specialists, which may give some comfort that there will not be indiscriminate use of the GAAR every time Revenue Scotland come across a transaction with which they disapprove. The notice issued by Revenue Scotland must include the following (RSTPA 2014, s 68(2)):

- details of the tax avoidance arrangement identified and the tax advantage obtained;
- an explanation as to why the designated officer considers that the tax advantage has arisen from a tax avoidance arrangement which is artificial;
- outline how the designated officer intends to counteract the tax advantage; and
- advise the taxpayer of the period during which he may make representations (see below).

The notice may also set out any steps which the taxpayer could take to avoid the proposed counteraction (RSTPA 2014, s 68(3)).

9.8 The taxpayer has the opportunity to respond and refute the designated officer's view within 45 days from the date upon which the notice was given ((RSTPA 2014, s 68(4)), and the designated officer must then take account of the taxpayer's representations in deciding whether the tax avoidance arrangement is to be counteracted (RSTPA 2014, s 68(6)). The designated officer may, on receipt of a request from the taxpayer (buyer in relation to LBTT) extend the period during which representations may be made beyond the stipulated 45 days (RSTPA 2014, s 68(5)). Once the 45 day period (or any extended period) in which the taxpayer may make representations has expired the designated officer must give the taxpayer written notice as to whether the perceived tax advantage is to be counteracted under the GAAR (RSTPA 2014, s 69(1)). If the tax advantage is to be counteracted the notice must also set out the following (RSTPA 2014, s 69(2)):

- the adjustment(s) to the LBTT payable to give effect to the counteraction; and
- if relevant, any steps which the taxpayer must take to give effect to the counteraction, and the period of time within which these steps must be taken.

9.9 Where a 'designated officer' has given notice under RSTPA 2014, s 69 that the tax advantage is to be counteracted the taxpayer (the buyer in relation to LBTT) must pay any amount of tax chargeable, or penalty or interest imposed, as a result of the adjustments set out in the notice. Payment must be made within the 30 day period beginning with the date on which the notice is issued (RSTPA 2014, s 70(2)).

9.10 A decision under RSTPA 2014, s 66 to make adjustments to counteract a tax advantage can be appealed by the taxpayer to the Tax Tribunals and beyond in the normal way (RSTPA 2014, s 233(1)(a)) or, if no appeal has been made, the taxpayer can request an 'independent review' of the decision, by one or more Revenue Scotland officers not involved in making the decision, under RSTPA 2014, s 234(1) (see **8.89**).

9.11 In any proceedings before a court or a tribunal in relation to the application of the GAAR Revenue Scotland must show both that: (a) there is a tax avoidance arrangement that is artificial, and (b) that the adjustments which they propose to make to counteract the tax advantages arising from the tax avoidance arrangement are just and reasonable (RSTPA 2014, s 67(1)). In coming to any decision in relation to the GAAR a court or tribunal must take into account any guidance published by Revenue Scotland about the GAAR, but fortunately only guidance which has been published at the time the tax avoidance arrangement was entered into (RSTPA 2014, s 67(2)). The court or tribunal may take into account guidance, statements or other material (whether published by Revenue Scotland or anyone else) which was in the public domain when the tax avoidance arrangement was entered into, and may also consider any evidence of established practice at that time (RSTPA 2014, s 67(3)).

9.12 The GAAR applies in relation to any tax avoidance arrangement entered into on or after the date on which the GAAR provisions come into effect (RSTPA 2014, s 72(1)). The GAAR provisions came into effect from 1 April 2015. Where the tax avoidance arrangement forms part of any other arrangements entered into before that date, those other arrangements are to be ignored unless taking account of those other arrangements would mean that the later arrangement would not be artificial (RSTPA 2014, s 72(2) and (3)).

9.13 LBTT differs from other taxes which may eventually be covered by the GAAR in that it is a transaction tax. Consequently, it is perhaps less clear which arrangements have the saving of LBTT as a main objective when, in the absence of the transaction, there would be no LBTT payable.

SPECIFIC ANTI-AVOIDANCE RULES

Introduction

9.14 Many of the conditions surrounding reliefs or treatments could be regarded as anti-avoidance rules. Their purpose is to ensure that the relief or treatment is only available in the circumstances envisaged by the Scottish Parliament. Nonetheless, there are some specific rules which may be recognised as having been included to counter particular arrangements and may be properly regarded as anti-avoidance provisions. These specific rules are described at various points in this book, when dealing with the transactions or circumstances in which they may apply. For convenience, they are also listed below, with references. Some seek to attack specific structures which, under SDLT, were considered to give rise to a tax advantage; others only apply if there is an avoidance motive. The rules apply whether or not the transaction is caught by the GAAR; indeed, by denying a relief or treatment, the specific rules may ensure that the transaction is not within the terms of the GAAR, as the envisaged tax advantage will not be obtained.

Subject	*Description*	*Statute (LBTT(S) A 2013) or other reference*	*Reference in this book*
Sale and lease-back relief	Cannot be combined with group relief	Sch 3, para 3(c)	5.24
Group, reconstruction and acquisition reliefs	Motive test	Sch 10, para 8; Sch 11, para 3(d), 7(e)	5.15
	Arrangements	Sch 10, paras 3–10A, Sch 11, para 7(c)	**5.12** and **5.14** (qualifying condition (3))
	Clawback on leaving group	Sch 10, paras 13–15	5.17
	Clawback on property ceasing to be pledged to lender	Sch 10, para 15A	5.17
	Clawback on change of control	Sch 10, para 28; Sch 11, paras 12–14 and 22–28	**5.19** and **5.20**
Alternative finance reliefs	Not combined with group relief, reconstruction relief or acquisition relief	Sch 7, para 16	5.30
	Arrangements for change of control of financial institution and definition of financial institution	Sch 7, paras 17 and 25	5.30
Charities relief	Change of use from charitable purposes	Sch 13, paras 4–11	5.27
Green freeports relief	Clawback on change of use	Sch 16D, para 8-10	5.39G
Partnerships	Transfer of partnership interest pursuant to earlier arrangements	Sch 17, para 17	6.27
	Withdrawal of value after land transfer	Sch 17, para 18	6.17
Trusts	Grant of lease to bare trustee	Sch 18, para 8	7.5
Leases	Assignment of lease after relief claimed on grant	Sch 19, para 27	4.35
	Loan or deposit in conjunction with the grant of a lease	Sch 19, para 17	4.57
	Grant, assignation or renunciation of a 'qualifying lease' over residential property not exempt	Sch 1, para 3(1)(a)	4.4
Building contracts	Separation of building and land contracts	*Prudential Assurance v CIR* [1992] STC 863	**Example 2.7**

Subject	*Description*	*Statute (LBTT(S) A 2013) or other reference*	*Reference in this book*
Multiple Dwellings Relief	Not combined with group relief, reconstruction relief, acquisition relief or charities relief	Sch 5, para 6(b)	5.25
House Trader Reliefs	Clawback of relief if the property trader: (a) spends more than the permitted amount on refurbishment of the old dwelling, (b) grants a lease or licence of the old dwelling or (c) permits any of its directors, partners or employees to occupy the old dwelling	Sch 4, paras 13–17	5.44

Residential property holding companies

9.15 The LBTT legislation includes a provision (LBTT(S)A 2013, s 47) which, on the making of regulations by the Scottish Ministers, would charge LBTT on a transfer of shares in an unlisted property holding company, investing in residential property (including property situated outside of Scotland), where the transferee of the shares acquires the right to occupy any residential property held by the company. It is assumed that the measure is aimed at preventing the avoidance of LBTT by holding residential property, occupied by the owner of the company, within a company, which would otherwise allow the shares of the company to be transferred free of LBTT. However, based on the wording of the legislation, the provision applies not only where the company's residential property is located in Scotland, but also where the residential property is located outside of Scotland. This point may however be clarified should regulations be made bringing this provision into effect.

9.16 Under LBTT(S)A 2013, s 47 the Scottish Ministers can, by regulation, provide for 'qualifying transfers' of interests in 'residential property holding companies' ('RPHC') to be treated as land transactions which are chargeable to LBTT (LBTT(S)A 2013, s 47(1)). It is assumed that an interest in an RPHC will generally be shares in the company although by using the word 'interest', rather than 'shares', it would seem that the Scottish Government may also be looking to cover other types of ownership interest in corporate bodies which do not have shares, for example, an interest in a company limited by guarantee, membership interests in a US Limited Liability Company etc.

9.17 An RPHC means a company whose sole or main activity is holding or investing in chargeable interests (including interests that would be chargeable interests apart from the fact that they relate to land outside of Scotland (LBTT(S)A 2013, s 47(3))) in residential property, whose assets consist of or include such interests in residential property, and whose shares are not listed on a recognised stock exchange (LBTT(S)A 2013, s 47(2)).

9.18 A 'qualifying transfer' is a transfer of an interest in an RPHC that results in the transferee (ie the buyer) acquiring the right to occupy some or all of the company's residential property (LBTT(S)A 2013, s 47(4)).

9.19 Under LBTT(S)A 2013, s 47(5) the Scottish Minsters can make regulations which set out the following:

- the kinds of interest in an RPHC the transfer of which is a 'qualifying transfer' (see **9.18**);
- the kinds of transfers which are and are not 'qualifying transfers';
- the rights which are rights to occupy a company's residential property for the purposes of a 'qualifying transfer';
- the consideration chargeable to LBTT in the case of a 'qualifying transfer';
- the tax bands and tax rates that are to apply to such transfers;
- the person who is liable to pay any LBTT chargeable in relation to the 'qualifying transfer'; and
- whether any reliefs from LBTT are to apply, or not to apply, to a 'qualifying transfer'.

The regulations may also specify what constitutes 'residential property' for the purposes of the LBTT(S)A 2013, s 47 charging provision (LBTT(S)A 2013, s 47(6)).

At the date of publication, the Scottish Ministers have not made any regulations under LBTT(S)A 2013, s 47, but no doubt they will consider doing so if they come to the conclusion that companies are being used to transfer ownership of property which is to be used as the residence of the purchaser of the interest in the company, or possibly persons connected with the purchaser of the interest in the company.

9.20 Many countries impose a tax on transfers of interests in property-rich companies, although there is no such charge under SDLT, possibly because it would be difficult to enforce such a charge if the owners of the company, potentially based outside of the UK, chose not to pay the tax.

9.21 It seems surprising that the Scottish Ministers consider this provision to be necessary given that ATED (see **2.70** et seq) continued to apply to residential property located in Scotland after 1 April 2015, and imposes an annual tax charge on any residential property held by a company with a value in excess of £500,000 (from 1 April 2016), subject to the availability of certain reliefs (see **2.75**). The revenue from ATED would, of course, go to the UK Government and not the Scottish Government. It may be that the power under LBTT(S)A 2013, s 47 is being held in reserve should ATED cease to apply to residential property situated in Scotland.

Appendix A

Contact details

Contact Revenue Scotland

There is a Revenue Scotland 'Support Desk'. The telephone number for the Support Desk is as follows:

0300 0200 310

The Support Desk is open Monday to Friday 10.00 – 12.00 and 14.00 – 16.00.

Any LBTT queries should be submitted via the Revenue Scotland dedicated mailbox at lbtt@revenue.scot.

Any IT queries/issued should be sent to itsupport@revenue.scot.

Revenue Scotland Opinions

It is possible to ask Revenue Scotland to provide an opinion in writing of their view as to the application of the LBTT legislation to a proposed transaction or to a transaction that has already taken place. Details of the procedure are given at **8.49**. The application for the Opinion should be sent to lbtt@revenue.scot.

Appendix B

Subordinate Legislation

SCOTTISH STATUTORY INSTRUMENTS

2014	No 278	The Revenue Scotland and Tax Powers Act 2014 (Commencement No 1) Order 2014	Brings into force certain provisions of RSTPA 2014 on 7 November 2014 in relation to Ministerial powers to make subordinate legislation and provide for consequential amendments to LBTT(S)A 2013
2014	No 279	The Land and Buildings Transaction Tax (Scotland) Act 2013 (Commencement No 1) Order 2014	Brings into force certain provisions in LBTT(S)A 2013 on 7 November 2014 in relation to Ministerial powers to make subordinate legislation.
2014	No 350	The Land and Buildings Transaction Tax (Prescribed Proportions) (Scotland) Order 2014	Prescribed proportion – multiple dwellings relief – see **5.25** Prescribed proportion – acquisition relief – see **5.14**
2014	No 351	The Land and Buildings Transaction Tax (Qualifying Public or Educational Bodies) (Scotland) Amendment Order 2014	Amendment to LBTT(S)A, Sch 2, para 17(2)(c) – Arrangements involving public or educational bodies – see **5.32** et seq
2014	No 352	The Land and Building Transaction Tax (Definition of Charity) (Relevant Territories) (Scotland) Regulations 2014	Specifies the Republic of Iceland, the Principality of Liechtenstein and the Kingdom of Norway as 'relevant territories' for the purpose of charities relief – see **5.26** et seq
2014	No 355	The Scottish Tax Tribunals (Eligibility for Appointment) Regulations 2014	Eligibility for appointment to the Scottish Tax Tribunals
2014	No 370	The Revenue Scotland and Tax Powers Act 2014 (Commencement No 2) Order 2014	Brings into force certain provisions of RSTPA 2014 on 1 January 2015 establishing Revenue Scotland as a body corporate and providing for the functions it will discharge in the period from its constitution to the date upon which LBTT becomes chargeable

2014	No 375	The Land and Buildings Transaction Tax (Administration) (Scotland) Regulations 2014	Circumstances in which a claim may be made to defer payment of LBTT – see **8.24**
2014	No 376	The Land and Buildings Transaction Tax (Ancillary Provisions) (Scotland) Order 2014	Keeper of Registers of Scotland does need to accept an application for registration in the Books of Council and Session effecting a notifiable land transaction unless the appropriate LBTT obligations have been satisfied – see **8.4**
2014	No 377	The Land and Buildings Transaction Tax (Transitional Provisions) (Scotland) Order 2014	Transitional provisions in respect of the introduction of LBTT – see **2.55** et seq
2015	No 36	The Revenue Scotland and Tax Powers Act (Fees for Payment) Regulations 2015	Provides for a fee of 1.4% to be charged in relation to LBTT paid by credit card
2015	No 38	The Revenue Scotland and Tax Powers Act (Privileged Communications) Regulations 2015	Sets out certain procedures to be followed where there is a dispute between Revenue Scotland and a person to whom an information notice has been given as to whether a document is privileged
2015	No 71	The Land and Buildings Transaction Tax (Transitional Provisions) (Scotland) Amendment Order 2015	Makes an amendment to art 3 of the Land and Buildings Transaction Tax (Transitional Provisions) (Scotland) Order 2014
2015	No 93	The Land and Buildings Transaction Tax (Addition and Modification of Reliefs) (Scotland) Order 2015	Makes amendments to the relief for certain acquisitions by registered social landlords see **5.43** and modifies the means of calculating crofting community right to buy relief – see **5.47** Introduces a number of very specialised reliefs – see **5.50**
2015	No 108	The Land and Buildings Transaction Tax (Scotland) Act 2013 (Commencement No 2) Order 2015	Appointing 1 April 2015 as the day upon which LBTT(S)A 2013 came into force.
2015	No 110	The Revenue Scotland and Tax Powers Act 2014 (Commencement No 4) Order 2015	Brought into force the remaining provisions of RSTPA 2014 including the constitution on 1 April 2015 of the Scottish Tax Tribunals.

2015	No 123	The Land and Buildings Transaction Tax (Sub-sale Development Relief and Multiple Dwellings Relief) (Scotland) Order 2015	Amends the LBTT(S)A 2013 to insert a new Sch 10A providing for a targeted sub-sale development relief: see **5.32** In relation to multiple dwellings relief (see **5.25**) clarifies that the 'minimum prescribed amount' is a percentage of the LBTT which would be payable on the dwellings in the absence of a claim for the relief
2015	No 126	The Land and Buildings Transaction Tax (Tax Rates and Tax Bands) (Scotland) Order 2015	Sets the LBTT rates and bands for residential and non-residential property transactions, and for consideration which consists of rent to apply from 1 April 2015 – see **2.35**
2015	No 128	The Revenue Scotland and Tax Powers Act (Interest on Unpaid Tax and Interest Rates in General) Regulations 2015	Sets the rate of interest payable by the buyer on late payment of LBTT and the rate of interest payable by Revenue Scotland on overpaid LBTT – see **8.36**.
2015	No 129	The Revenue Scotland and Tax Powers Act (Postponement of Tax Pending a Review or Appeal) Regulations 2015	Where a Revenue Scotland review, or an appeal under Part 11 RSTPA 2014, is in progress a buyer may make an application to postpone payment of the LBTT, a penalty or interest. A postponement can be granted if Revenue Scotland considers that there are exceptional circumstances – see **8.89**.
2015	No 130	The Revenue Scotland and Tax Powers Act (Record Keeping) Regulations 2015	Makes provision for the records which must be kept in relation to land transactions which are not notifiable. (see **8.93**)
2015	No 131	The Revenue Scotland and Tax Powers Act (Reimbursement Arrangements) Regulations 2015	Sets out the provisions that must be included in 'reimbursement arrangements' by a person making a claim for repayment of tax under RSTPA 2014, s 107
2015	No 322	The Land and Buildings Transaction Tax (Open-ended Investment Companies) (Scotland) Regulations 2015	Provides for exemptions from LBTT on (a) the conversion of an authorised unit trust to an open-ended investment company, and (b) the amalgamation of an authorised unit trust with an open-ended investment company

2017	No 233	The Land and Buildings Transaction Tax (Additional Amount – Second Homes Main Residence Relief) (Scotland) Order 2017	Provides relief from the Additional Dwellings Supplement (ADS) (see **2.37** et seq) where spouses, civil partners, or cohabitants jointly buy a dwelling as their new sole or main residence but the dwelling disposed of in the 18 months prior to the acquisition, which was previously their sole or main residence, was owned by only one of them. It also allows the ADS to be repaid if, within 18 months of the spouses, civil partners or co-habitants jointly buying a dwelling which is to be their new sole or main residence, one or other of the joint buyers disposes of a dwelling that had been used by both of them as their sole or main residence.
2018	No 221	The Land and Buildings Transaction Tax (First-Time Buyer Relief) (Scotland) Order 2018	Inserts a new Schedule 4A into the Land and Buildings Transaction Tax (Scotland) Act 2013 which provides for a degree of relief from LBTT for first-time buyers.
2018	No 222	The Land and Buildings Transaction Tax (Group Relief Modification) (Scotland) Order 2018	Inserts paras 10A and 15A into Schedule 10 of the Land and Buildings Transaction Tax (Scotland) Act 2013. Para 10A provides for group relief not to be restricted if shares are "pledged" to a lender as security. Para 15A provides withdrawal where these arrangements cease
2018	No 372	The Land and Buildings Transaction Tax (Tax Rates and Tax Bands etc) (Scotland) Amendment Order 2018	Amends the rates of tax and tax bands applicable to non-residential property transactions and increases the rate of the ADS from 3% to 4%
2022	No 375	The Land and Buildings Transaction Tax (additional amount: transactions relating to second homes etc.) (Scotland) Amendment Order 2022	Increases the rate of the ADS from 4% to 6%
2023	No 280	The Land and Buildings Transaction Tax (Green Freeports Relief) (Scotland) Order 2023	Inserts a new schedule 16D into the Land and Buildings Transaction Tax (Scotland) Act 2013 that provides relief for qualifying land transactions within a green freeport tax site, along with provisions for withdrawal of the relief

2024	No 104	The Land and Buildings Transaction Tax (Miscellaneous Amendments) (Scotland) Order 2024	Makes various amendments to the Land and Buildings Transaction Tax (Scotland) Act 2013, with effect from 1 April 2024. These include a new LBTT relief for local authority purchases and significant changes to the way in which the ADS is applied, particularly in the case of joint buyers. The timescale applicable to exemption from or repayment of the ADS is increased from 18 to 36 months.

UK STATUTORY INSTRUMENT

2014	No 3294	The Revenue Scotland and Tax Powers Act 2014 (Consequential Provisions and Modifications) Order 2014	Establishes Revenue Scotland as part of the Scottish Administration and makes provisions about the collection and management of the devolved taxes, including LBTT

Appendix C

Checklist for Revenue Scotland Opinions

Revenue Scotland
Teachd-a-steach Alba

Checklist for Revenue Scotland opinions

It helps us if you follow the order set out in this checklist in your request and use the numbering on any supporting documents.

Requests should be sent to:

Revenue Scotland Opinions, PO Box 24068 GH South, Victoria Quay, Edinburgh EH6 9BR

Users of the Revenue Scotland online portal (SETS) can also submit requests using the portal's secure messaging service.

PLEASE ENSURE THAT YOU ATTACH A COPY OF THE CHECKLIST TO YOUR REQUEST **1. Information about the person making the request:**	
1.1 Your name and address or the name and address of the person carrying on the business (and name of the business if different)	
1.2 Your relevant customer identification number in full, if you have one	
1.3 Please provide a copy of a mandate signed by your client confirming your authority to act on their behalf. Until we have this we will be unable to correspond with you so it is important you provide this. You may wish to use the template available on our website. Where there is more than one buyer, each buyer must sign the form. You do not have to use this template, but the mandate must provide all of this information.	
1.4 A brief indication of the subject matter of the request. Fuller details should be provided under the appropriate headings below	
2. Information about the transaction(s):	
2.1 The details of which tax(es) the application refers to	
2.2 The reasons for undertaking the transaction	
2.3 The relevant facts about the transaction so that we have all the information to provide our response, to include copies of all supporting documents with all relevant parts identified	
2.4 Set out your view of the tax consequences of the transaction and the issues you want us to consider	
2.5 The proposed date of the transaction if it has not yet happened	
2.6 The monetary value of the transaction	

Revenue Scotland
Teachd-a-steach Alba

3. Information about legal points:	
3.1 Outline the specific legislation which you think applies	
3.2 Explain why you believe the application of the legislation is open to different possible interpretations, provide a summary of those different interpretations and explain why the tax consequences are uncertain, including reference to our published guidance and/or to case law	
3.3 Provide copies of any legal advice you have already received which you are content to disclose	
3.4 Provide details of any other relevant advice you are seeking or relevant opinions have previously sought from Revenue Scotland	

Index

[All references are to paragraph number]

www.ingramcontent.com/pod-product-compliance
Ingram Content Group UK Ltd.
Pitfield, Milton Keynes, MK11 3LW, UK
UKHW021036150926
475561UK00003B/135

9 781526 531858